NATIONAL CAPITAL

Containing Notes and Correspondence exchanged between Jefferson, Washington, L'Enfant, Ellicott, Hallett, Thornton, Latrobe, the Commissioners, and others, relating to the founding, surveying, planning, designing, constructing, and administering of the City of Washington

1783-1818

WITH PLANS AND ILLUSTRATIONS

FIRST GREAT SEAL OF THE UNITED STATES
ADOPTED IN 1782

Preface by HAROLD L. ICKES

Edited by SAUL K. PADOVER

UNITED STATES
GOVERNMENT PRINTING OFFICE
WASHINGTON · 1946

UNITED STATES

DEPARTMENT OF THE INTERIOR

HAROLD L. ICKES, *Secretary*

NATIONAL PARK SERVICE

NEWTON B. DRURY, *Director*

SOURCE BOOK SERIES ★ No. 4

⇛⇛THIS BOOK *Relates to The Thomas Jefferson Memorial and the National Capital Parks, Washington, D.C., administered by the National Park Service of the United States Department of the Interior.*

FOR SALE BY THE SUPERINTENDENT OF DOCUMENTS, UNITED STATES GOVERNMENT PRINTING OFFICE, WASHINGTON 25, D.C.

Preface

IT is proper that Thomas Jefferson, the architect of American democracy, should also have been one of the architects and founders of the City of Washington, which is both a symbol and a product of our democratic institutions. It is, furthermore, historically fitting that the National Capital of a republic that is made up of most of the cultural groups and racial strains of the world should have been conceived and built by immigrants.

The man who dreamed and planned the Capital of the world's greatest democracy was Pierre Charles L'Enfant — a French immigrant.

The man who designed the White House was James Hoban — an Irish immigrant.

One of the men who decorated the Capitol was Giovanni Andrei — an Italian immigrant.

These are but a few of the thousands of men who have given their brains, their talents and their genius to America. Others, less conspicuous, millions of them, have given the work of their hands and the devotion of their hearts to make of this country the most flourishing democracy in the world.

Thomas Jefferson, the many-sided genius who, among other things also helped to plan the Capital City of the Nation, as a matter of course encouraged scholars, scientists, and men of letters to settle in this country, with resulting enrichment of our culture.

This rich collection of letters and documents will prove a veritable mine of information and be a source of permanent usefulness to those who are interested not merely in Jefferson but also in city planning and in the early history of our country. I am proud to have my Department publish it.

Harold L. Ickes

Washington, D. C.
June 8, 1944

Table of Contents

1791

XII

1802

1803

1804

1805

List of Illustrations

*The illustrations listed below either face the page
designated or are grouped immediately after it*

Introduction

By CHARLES W. PORTER

☙

D R. Saul K. Padover has been indefatigable in writing the biography of Jefferson and in arranging and editing his writings in single volumes designed to afford a ready intellectual grasp of the political faith and wisdom of Jefferson as the founder of a more vigorous American democracy. A product of this work has been a collection of notes and Jefferson correspondence which portrays the versatile Jefferson as one of our earliest and most successful city planners.

That Jefferson, who viewed city life with marked distrust, should have been a city planner seems contradictory, but such contradictions only indicate the practical statesman that was part and parcel of Jefferson the idealist. For instance, although a strict constructionist of the Federal Constitution, which did not specifically authorize the President to acquire new lands by purchase, Jefferson took the responsibility of purchasing the vast territory of Louisiana which insured the physical greatness of the United States. In almost all things Jefferson took the long-range view which is the distinguishing mark of the statesman; hence, despite his ingrained bias against urban economy, he served with zeal in the locating, planning, and building of our Capital City. He may neither have foreseen nor desired the City of Washington to grow to its present large proportions but he did much to lay the foundations of its greatness and provided, above all, for its enduring beauty.

Many of the papers or notes included in the present work are hitherto unpublished items and some have been taken from printed court records, copies of which are scarce and not generally available to scholars. Others have been found in the standard editions of Jefferson's writings. These last have been checked against available originals for possible inaccuracies. Although Dr. Padover's services with the Armed Forces overseas and his inability to secure certain portions of Jefferson's correspondence now in bomb-proof storage, or otherwise unavailable to historians, have caused the omission of a few Jefferson notes and correspondence which delineate Jefferson's part in the planning and building of the National Capital, the present work, as edited by Dr. Padover, tells an integrated and unified story. The omitted papers, which are in any case not many, would only embroider a pattern which is set forth in the present volume with completeness.

The source materials comprised in the book have been published with a minimum of editorial comment in order that Jefferson may speak for himself. The reader will find that each note or letter tends to explain either those papers which have gone before or which appear later in the Source Book. An appendix dealing with persons and places mentioned in the text has been compiled from notes left by Dr. Padover before he went abroad. The general reader will find this material helpful.

The Editor, if he were here, would wish to thank the Hon. Harold L. Ickes for his ever-inspiring encouragement, and to acknowledge the assistance of Mrs. Joanne Sanborn; the staff of the National Archives, particularly Mr. Herman Kahn of the Interior Archives; Mr. Alexander Bell of the Department of Justice; Mr. H. P. Caemmerer of the Commission of Fine Arts; the staff of the Library of Congress; Mr. William T. Partridge of the National Capital Park and Planning Commission; Mrs. Helen Duprey Bullock; and Mr. H. D. Rouzer, Assistant Architect of the Capitol. On Dr. Padover's behalf I desire to express his sincere gratitude to them.

Those who utilize the Source Book for purposes of research or who read it for its general interest will not fail to perceive how the education and experience of Jefferson ideally equipped him for many phases of city planning work. His aptitude for politics and friendship with Washington enabled him to make the compromise with Hamilton which resulted in the designation of the banks of the Potomac as the site of the Capital City. His knowledge of surveying was of use in the early phases of laying out the boundaries of the District of Columbia. Training as a lawyer qualified him to render legal opinions interpreting the scope of the Executive's authority in planning the Nation's Capital. While traveling abroad he had obtained plans of the European cities of Frankfort, Karlsruhe, Amsterdam, Strasburg, Paris, Orleans, Bordeaux, Lyons, Montpelier, Marseilles, Turin and Milan, valuable comparative data, which he made available to Major L'Enfant, original designer of the Washington City plan. Studies abroad and at home in the fields of architecture, design and the fine arts qualified him to advise with the Commissioners on, or handle directly, the selection of competent architects, designers, and sculptors or to compose differences of opinion among these highly temperamental experts. Experience in the operation and improvement of his Albemarle plantation suggested means of securing types of skilled labor from abroad for the building of the Capital City. A mechanical turn of mind fitted him to speak intelligently about contrivances for the rapid cutting of large quantities of stone for building purposes. Political acumen was a requisite for securing adequate funds or for mollifying the Congress when zealous builders exceeded the limitations of moneys appropriated. The best example of the Renaissance type of man produced in this country, Jefferson with his encyclopedic mind comprehended all interests, from bridges, roads, and the planting of trees to the manner of securing the bars in the city jail. These varied activities he carried on first as a member of the Continental Congress, 1783–1784, then as Secretary of State under Washington, 1789–1794, as Vice President under John Adams, 1797–1801, and finally as President of the United States, 1801–1809.

He was at his best in determining the architectural form of the City of Washington's public buildings. "You know my reverence for the Graecian and Roman style of architecture," he wrote to Benjamin H. Latrobe, Architect of the Capitol, and the Washington buildings still reflect this influence. With Latrobe's principles of what constituted good taste in Grecian architecture, Jefferson's ideas were not always in perfect accord, but their correspondence and friendship, as recorded in this Source Book, reach a high peak of human interest. Of Jefferson, Latrobe wrote:

"It is not flattery to say that you have planted the arts in your country. The works already erected in this city are the monuments of your judgment and of your zeal and of your taste. The first sculpture that adorns an American public building perpetuates your love and your protection of the fine arts."

Well into the evening of life, Jefferson maintained his keen interest in the beauty of the Nation's Capital toward which he had collaborated with Latrobe, Dr. Thornton, and even the temperamental Major L'Enfant, as well as with all others who had participated in this great work. The felicitous phraseology which he used to describe Latrobe's purpose best describes his own, which had been that of:

. . . "embellishing with Athenian taste the course of a nation looking far beyond the range of Athenian destinies."

THOMAS JEFFERSON & THE NATIONAL CAPITAL

JEFFERSON TO THE GOVERNOR
OF VIRGINIA

[BENJAMIN HARRISON]

Philadelphia, Nov. 11, 1783.

Sir,

YOUR EXCELLENCY's letter of the 25th ult. on the determination of Congress as to their future residence has been duly received. You would doubtless soon after have heard of their subsequent determination on the same subject. As all this had taken place before my arrival I can give you an account only from the information of others. Congress, it seems, thought it best to generalize their first determination by putting questions on the several rivers on which it had been proposed that they should fix their residence. Hudson river, the Delaware, & Potomac, were accordingly offered to the vote. The first obtained scarcely any voices; the Delaware obtained seven. This of course put the Potomac out of the way: and the Delaware being once determined on there was scarcely any difference of opinion as to the particular spot. The falls met the approbation of all the states present, except Pennsylvania which was for Germantown, & Delaware which was for Wilmington. As to the latter it appeared that she had been induced to vote for the Delaware on the single idea of getting Congress to Wilmington, and that being disappointed in this they would

I

not wish them on that river at all, but would prefer Georgetown or any other place. This being discovered, the Southern delegates at a subsequent day brought on a reconsideration of the question, and obtained a determination that Congress should set one half of their time at Georgetown and that til accommodations should be provided there, Annapolis should be substituted in its place. This was considered by some as a compromise; by others as only unhinging the first determination and leaving the whole matter open for discussion at some future day. It was in fact a rally, and making a drawn battle of what had at first appeared to be decided against us. What will be its final decision can only be conjectured. I take the following to be the disposition of the several states.

The four Eastern states are for any place in preference to Philadelphia, the more Northern it is however the more agreeable to them.

New York and New Hampshire are for the falls of Delaware.

Pennsylvania is for Germantown first, and next for the falls of Delaware. It is to be noted that Philadelphia had no attention as a permanent seat. Delaware is for Wilmington: but for Georgetown in preference to the falls of Delaware or any other situation which attract the trade of their river. Maryland is for Annapolis, and the smallest hope for this will sacrifice a certainty for Georgetown.

Virginia, every place southward of Potomac being disregarded by the states as every place north of the Delaware, saw it would be useless to consider her interests as to more Southern positions. The falls of Potomac will probably therefore unite the wishes of the whole state, if this fails, Annapolis and the falls of Delaware are then the candidates. Were the convenience of the Delegates alone to be considered, or the general convenience to government in their transaction of business with Congress, Annapolis would be preferred without hesitation. But those who respect commercial advantages more than the convenience of individuals will probably think that every position on the bay of Chesapeak or any of its waters is to be dreaded by Virginia as it may attract the trade of that bay and make us with respect to Maryland what Delaware State is to Pennsylvania. Considering the residence of Congress therefore as it may influence trade, if we cannot obtain it on the Potomac it seems to be our interest to bring it past all the waters of the Chesapeak bay.

The three Southern states are for the most Southern situation. It should be noted that N. Hampshire and Georgia were absent on the decisions of these questions, but considering their interests would be directly opposite, it was thought their joint presence or absence would not change the result. From the preceding state of the views of the several members of our union your Excellency will be enabled to judge what will be the probable determination on any future revision of the present plan: the establishment of new states will be friendly or adverse to Georgetown according to their situation. If a state be first laid off on the lakes it will add a vote to the Northern scale, if on the Ohio it will add one to the Southern. I had the happiness of seeing Gen'l. Washington the other day after a space of seven years. He has more health in his countenance than I ever saw in it before. Among other political conversations he entered earnestly into one respecting the Western section of Virginia, and the late vote of Congress accepting it. He thinks the conditions annexed by Virginia and not acceded to by Congress altogether unimportant, at least much less important than the consequences which would result from the state's adhering to these conditions. He thinks that a friendly and immediate settlement of this matter can alone give us that political happiness and quiet which we must all wish for: and that besides other disagreeable consequences the land will be lost to both as a source of revenue by their settlement of adventurers on it who will never pay any thing. It is now become evident that the nine states North of Potomac have made up their minds on these questions & will act together.

[TH: JEFFERSON]

[Pp. 340–4, Ford, WRITINGS, III.] The key to this and to other similarly abbreviated citations will be found in the Bibliography.

JEFFERSON TO MADISON

Annapolis, Feb. 20, 1784.

TO JAMES MADISON.

Georgetown languishes. The smile is hardly covered now when the federal towns are spoken of. I fear that our chance is at this time desperate. Our object therefore must be if we fail in an effort to remove to Georgetown to endeavor then to get to some place off the waters of the Chesapeak where we may be ensured against Congress considering themselves as fixed. My present expectations are, that as soon as we get a Congress to do business, we shall attend to nothing but the most pressing matters, get through them & adjourn, not to meet again till November, leaving a Commee of the States. That Commee will be obliged to go immediately to Philadelphia to examine the offices & of course they will sit there till the meeting in November. Whether that meeting will be in Philadelphia or Trenton will be the question and will in my opinion depend on the vote of *New York* [?]. Did not you once suppose in conversation with me that Congress had no authority to decide any cases between two differing states, except those of disputed territory? I think you did. If I am not mistaken in this, I should wish to know your good sense of the words which describe those cases which may be submitted to a federal court. They seem to me to comprehend every cause of difference.

[TH: JEFFERSON]

[Pp. 399–400, Ford, WRITINGS, III.]

DRAFT OF RESOLUTIONS FOR THE LEGISLATURES OF
MARYLAND AND VIRGINIA [1]

[*April* 13, 1784]

Resolved that the Governor be desired to propose to the
state of Maryland to concur with this Commonwealth in erecting buildings for the immediate accomodation of the Congress of the United States on the lands on Potowmac offered to be
ceded to them by these two states, & particularly on such parts
of them as they shall have reason to believe will be most agreeable to the Congress, the expence of which buildings with the
purchase of the ground shall not exceed thirty thousand dollars
to be advanced from time to time, as it shall be wanting, by the
said states in equal portions: which advances on the part of this
Commonwealth the Treasurer is hereby authorized & required
to make on warrants from the Auditors according to the established forms of his office.

Resolved that three Commissioners be appointed by joint
balot of both houses of Assembly, to act with Commissioners or
other persons appointed or to be appointed on the part of the
state of Maryland, who shall have powers to purchase sufficient
ground to agree on the buildings necessary to be erected, to
have them erected without delay, to call for & to apply Monies
by way of paiment or of advance for the same, and to tender
the said buildings to Congress for the sole purpose of their general & of their personal accomodation.

Resolved that to prevent any difficulties or delays which
might be produced by doubts in what manner the said Commissioners when assembled shall vote, it be proposed to the
State of Maryland that they shall proceed to business always
with an equal number (not less than two) from each state, that,
so constituted, they shall be considered as forming one Com-

---

[1] Probably drafted while the question of the national capital was under discussion.

mittee, every member whereof shall have one vote and no more
and that if at any time they shall be divided on any question
which may be likely to delay the said work, they shall state the
same in writing to the delegates of the two states, in Congress,
who concurring by a Majority of their respective members
present shall decide the same.

[P. 462, Ford, WRITINGS, III.]

NOTES ON THE PERMANENT SEAT OF CONGRESS [2]

[*April* 13, 1784]

North River — recommended for the permanent seat of Cong.^{s}
chiefly by its security against foreign danger.

Falls of Potomac — By 1. geographical centrality — 2. proximity to Western Country already ceded — 3. inducement
to further cessions from N. C. S. C. & Georgia. 4. remote-
ness from the influence of any overgrown commercial city.

Falls of Delaware — By 1. centrality with regard to number of
inhabitants. 2. centrality as to n.^{o} of States & of Delegates.
3. facility of obtaining intelligence from sea.

TEMPORARY SEAT OF CONGRESS —

Princeton — in favor of it, 1. its neighbourhood to the Permanent seat, 2. inconveniency of a removal. 3. beneficial
effect of a frugal situation of Cong.^{s} on their popularity
throughout the States. 4. the risque in case of removal from
Princeton of returning under the commercial and corrupt
influence of Philad.^{a} — against it — 1. — unfitness for transacting the public business — 2. deficiency of accomodation, exposing ye members attending members to the danger
of indignities & extortions, discouraging perhaps the fittest
men from undertaking the services & amounting to a prohibi-

[2] Probably used during the discussion of this question in Congress, April 13, 1784. *Cf.*
Journals. [P. 458 n, Ford, WRITINGS, III.]

tion of such as had families from which they would not part.

Trenton. arg.^ts in favor & ag.^st it similar to those respecting Princeton. It was particularly remarked that when the option lay ~~between~~ with the President & committee between Trenton & Princeton the latter was preferred as least unfit to receive Cong.^s on their removal from Philad.^a

Philad.^a In favor of it. 1. its ~~infinite~~ unrivaled conveniency for transacting the public business, & accomodating Congress. 2 its being the only place where ~~the~~ all the public offices, particularly that of Finance could be kept under the inspection & controul of, & proper intercourse with Cong.^s 3 its conveniency for F. Ministers, to which, coeteris paribus, some regard would be expected. 4 the circumstances which produced a removal from Philad.^a which rendered a return ~~expedient~~ as soon as the insult had been expiated, expedient for supporting in the eyes of foreign nations the appearance of internal harmony, and preventing an appearance of resentment in Cong.^s ag.^st the state of P.^a or city of Philad.^a an appearance which was very much strengthened by some of their proceedings at Princeton — particularly by an unnecessary & irregular declaration not to return to Phi.^a In addition to these overt reasons, it was concluded by sundry of the members who were most anxious to fix Cong.^s permanently at ~~Georgete~~ the falls of Potowmac that a temporary residence in Philad.^a would be most likely to ~~endeavor~~ prepare a sufficient number of votes ~~in favor of Philadep~~ for that place in preference to the Falls of Delaware ~~for the permanent,~~ and to produce a reconsideration of the vote in favor of the latter — ag.^st Philad.^a were alleged. 1. the difficulty & uncertainty of getting away from it at the time limited. 2 the influence of a large comercial & wealthy city on the public councils. In addition to these objections, the hatred ag.^st Mr. M. and hope of accelerating his final resignation were latent motives with some, as perhaps envy of the prosperity of Philad?. ~~might be~~ and dislike of the support of P?. to obnoxious recommendations of Cong? were with others.

Annapolis. In favor of it, 1.ˢᵗ its capacity for accommodating Cong? and its conveniences for the public business. 2. the soothing tendency of so Southern a position on the temper of the S. States. Ag.ˢᵗ it, 1.ˢᵗ the preposterousness of taking a temporary station so distant from the permanent seat fixed on, especially as better accomodations were to be passed by at Philad? which was ~~not~~ less than 4/5ths of the distance from the Permanent Seat. 2.ᵈ the peculiar force such a step would give to the charge ag.ˢᵗ Cong? of being swayed by improper motives. Besides these considerations it was the opinion of some that ~~way~~ a removal of Cong? to Annapolis would inspire Maryland with hopes that w.ᵈ prevent a co-operation in favor of Georgetown, & favor the commerce of that State at the expence of Virginia.

1. It requires 9 states to appropriate money, and only 7 to adjourn. There cannot therefore be buildings erected at Georgetown without the concurrence of 9 states, a number which I fear we shall never obtain. Yet if the buildings were erected, 7 could adjourn us there, & this number is within hope, but not within certainty.

Obj. It is then but a speculation by which the state may throw away 15000 Dollars.

Answ. True. But this is the extent of their loss. Their possible advantages will be

Common to all the States

1. The firmness & tone which will be given to the federal government by fixing it's administration more nearly central.
2. The placing the federal council within reach of the Western states, & thereby cementing them to it's Eastern part.
3. Securing the seat of federal govmt from sudden enterprize without expensive works or establishments.
4. Adjacence to two states from the one or the other of which a protection may generally be expected.

Common to Suthern States
{
1. Drawing the federal fleets into the bay of Chesapeak.
2. Bringing the federal administration nearer to the Southern States.
3. Rendering an attendance in Congress more convenient to Southern members, and by ~~thus~~ removing obstacles, increase the chances for inducing the best men into the office.
}

Common to Virga & Maryland
{
1. Attracting foreigners, manufacturers and settlers to the two States of Virga & Maryland.
2. Attracting commerce to them.
3. Throwing a very large sum of Money annually into circulation which will be divided between them.
4. Preferment of their citizens ~~to possn of honour profit & Power~~ to the federal administration.
5. The advantages of a favorable biass in the Executive officers.
}

Peculiar to Virginia
{
1. The establishment of Alexandria on a par with Baltimore as a secondary place of commerce.
2. Leaving Norfork in possession of all the advantages of a primary emporium. Add to these that the £100.000 offered by Virginia will never be accepted.
}

	Phila	Trenton	GeorgeTown 146 from P.
N. Hampshire	429	399	575
Massachusetts	365	335	511
Rhode Island	317	287	463
Connecticut	245	215	391
N. York	97	67	243
N. Jersey	30	o $\frac{1303}{2805}$	176
Pennsylva	o $\frac{1483}{2595}$	30	146
Delaware	30	60	116
Maryland	144	174	o $\frac{2621}{1837}$ 784
Virginia	280	310	134
N. Caroli	427	457	281
S. Caroli	797	827	651
Georgia	917	947	771

[Pp. 458–61, Ford, WRITINGS, III.]

RESOLVE ON CONTINENTAL CONGRESS

[*April* 14, 1784?]

6. That the United States should be made capable of acquiring & holding in perpetuum such grounds and buildings in and about the place of their session of Congress as may be necessary for the transaction of business by their own ~~for their~~ body, their committees & officers ~~for the transaction of business and~~ that each state should be made capable of acquiring and holding in perpetuum such grounds and buildings as they may at any time think proper to acquire & erect for the personal accomodation of their delegates: and that ~~all~~ ~~these~~ grounds and buildings before mentioned ~~so long as they shall be~~ so long as Congress or a Commee of the states shall be resident at such place ~~shall~~ should be exempt from taxation.

[Pp. 463-4, Ford, WRITINGS, III.]

JEFFERSON TO MADISON

Annapolis, April 25, 1784.

TO JAMES MADISON.

The place at which Congress should meet in Nov. has been the subject of discussion lately. Alexandria, Philadelphia, & Trenton were proposed. The first was negatived easily. Trenton had the 4 Eastern states, N.Y., N.J., & Penns. We expect Georgia and Delaware shortly, in which case it will become possible that Phila. may be determined on. The question is put off to be considered with the establishment of a com. of the states, which, to my astonishment, would have been negatived when first proposed had not the question been staved off. Some of the states who were against the measure, I believe, because they had never reflected on the consequences of leaving a government without a head, seem to be come over.

[TH: JEFFERSON]

[Pp. 471-2, Ford, WRITINGS, III.]

JEFFERSON NOTE

NOTE ON RESIDENCE BILL

This fiscal maneuvre is well known by the name of the Assumption. Independently of the debts of Congress, the states had, during the war, contracted separate and heavy debts . . . This money, whether wisely or foolishly spent, was pretended to have been spent for general purposes, and ought therefore to be paid from the general purse. But it was objected that nobody knew what these debts were, what their amount, or what their proofs . . . This measure produced the most bitter & angry contests ever known in Congress, before or since the union of the States . . . The great and trying question however was lost in the H. of Representatives. So high were the feuds excited by this subject, that on it's rejection, business was suspended . . . The Eastern members particularly, who . . . were the principal gamblers in these scenes, threatened a secession and dissolution. Hamilton was in despair. As I was going to the President's one day, I met him in the street. He walked me backwards & forwards before the President's door for half an hour. He painted pathetically the temper into which the legislature had been wrought, the disgust of those who were called the Creditor states, the danger of the secession of their members, and the separation of the States. He observed that the members of the administration ought to act in concert, that tho' this question was not of my department, yet a common duty should make it a common concern . . .; and that the question having been lost by a small majority only, it was probable that an appeal from me to the judgment and discretion of some of my friends might effect a change in the vote, and the machine of government, now suspended, might be again set into motion. I told him that I was really a stranger to the whole subject . . .; that undoubtedly if it's rejection endangered a dissolution of our union at this incipient stage, I should deem that the most unfortunate of all consequences, to avert which all partial and temporary evils should be yielded. I proposed to him however to dine with me the next day, and I would invite another friend or two, bring them into conference together, and I thought it impossible that reasonable men, consulting together coolly, could fail, by some mutual sacrifices of opinion, to form a compromise which was to save the union. The discussion took place. I could take no part in it, but an exhortatory one, because I was a stranger to the circumstances which should govern it. But it was finally agreed that . . . it would be better that the vote of rejection should be rescinded, to effect which some members should change their votes. But it was observed that this pill would be peculiarly bitter to the Southern States, and that some concomitant measure should be adopted to sweeten it a little to them. There had before been propositions to fix the seat of government either at Philadelphia, or at Georgetown on the Potomac; and it was thought that by giving it to Philadelphia for ten years, and to Georgetown permanently afterwards, this might, as an anodyne, calm in some degree the ferment which might be excited by the other measure alone. So two of the Potomac members (White & Lee,[3] but White with a revulsion of stomach almost convulsive) agree to change their votes, & Hamilton undertook to carry the other point. In doing this the influence he had established over the Eastern members, with the agency of Robert Morris with those of the middle states, effected his side of the engagement, and so the assumption was passed, and 20 millions of stock divided among favored states, and thrown in as pabulum to the stock-jobbing herd.

[Jefferson, THE ANAS, (ca. May, 1790).]

[3] Alexander White and Richard Bland Lee, both Congressmen from Virginia. Daniel Carroll, of Maryland, also changed his vote. Carroll was appointed a Commissioner of the District [of Columbia] in January, 1791; he was succeeded by Alexander White in 1795.

JEFFERSON TO RANDOLPH

New York, May 30, 1790.

TO THOMAS MANN RANDOLPH.

A motion has been made in the Senate to remove the federal government to Philadelphia. There was a trial of strength on a question for a week's postponement. On that it was found there would be 11 for the removal & 13 against it. The motion was therefore withdrawn & made in the other house where it is still depending, & of very incertain event.

[P. 174, Ford, WRITINGS, V.]

JEFFERSON TO SHORT

New York, June 6, 1790.

TO WILLIAM SHORT.

The question of removal to Philadelphia was carried in the house of representatives by 38. against 22. It is thought the Senate will be equally divided and consequently that the decision will rest on the Vice-president, who will be himself divided between his own decided inclinations to stay here, & the unpopularity of being the sole obstacle to what appears the wish of so great a majority of the people expressed by proportional representation. Rhode island has at length acceded to the Union by a majority of two voices only in their convention. Her Senators will be here in about 10 days or a fortnight. The opposers of removal in the Senate try to draw out time till their arrival. Therefore they have connected the resolution of the lower house with a bill originated with them to fix a permanent residence, & have referred both to the same committee.

[Pp. 178-9, Ford, WRITINGS, V.]

Jefferson to Mason

New York, June 13, 1790.

TO GEORGE MASON.

The House of representatives have voted to remove to Baltimore by a majority of 53. against 6. This was not the effect of
choice, but of the confusion into which they had been brought
by the event of other questions, & their being hampered with
the rules of the house. It is not certain what will be the vote of
the Senate. Some hope an opening will be given to convert it
into a vote of the temporary seat at Philadelphia, & the permanent one at Georgetown. The question of the assumption will
be brought on again, & it's event is doubtful. Perhaps it's op-
ponents would be wiser to be less confident in their success, &
to compromise by agreeing to assume the state debts still due to
individuals, on condition of assuming to the states at the same
time what they have paid to individuals, so as to put the states
in the shoes of those of their creditors whom they have paid off.
Great objections lie to this, but not so great as to an assumption
of the unpaid debts only. My duties preventing me from
mingling in these questions, I do not pretend to be very competent to their decision. In general I think it necessary to give
as well as take in a government like ours.

[Th: Jefferson]

[Pp. 183-4, Ford, writings, V.]

Jefferson to Randolph.

New York, June 20, 1790.

TO THOMAS MANN RANDOLPH.

Congress are much embarrassed by the two questions of
assumption, and residence. All proceedings seem to be ar-
rested till these can be got over, and for the peace & continu-

ance of the union, a mutual sacrifice of opinion & interest is become the duty of everyone: for it is evident that if every one retains inflexibly his present opinion, there will be no bill passed at all for funding the public debts, & if they separate without funding, there is an end of the government, in this situation of things. The only choice is among disagreeable things. The assumption must be admitted, but in so qualified a form as to divest it of it's injustice. This may be done by assuring to the creditors of every state, a sum exactly proportioned to the contribution of the state: so that the state will on the whole neither gain nor lose. There will remain against the measure only the objection that Congress must lay taxes for these debts which might be better laid & collected by the states. On the question of residence, the compromise proposed is to give it to Philadelphia for 15. years, & then permanently to George town by the same act. This is the best arrangement we have now any prospect of, & therefore the one to which all our wishes are at present pointed. If this does not take place, something much worse will; to wit an unqualified assumption & the permanent seat on the Delaware. The Delegations of this state and Pennsylvania have conducted themselves with great honor and wisdom on these questions. They have by a steady (yet not a stipulated) concurrence avoided insidious baits which have been held out to divide them & defeat their object.

[TH: JEFFERSON]

[Pp. 185–6, Ford, WRITINGS, V.]

JEFFERSON TO JAMES MONROE

New York, June 20, 1790.

TO JAMES MONROE.
*   *   *

Congress has been long embarrassed by two of the most irritating questions that ever can be raised among them, 1. the funding the public debt, and 2. the fixing on a more central residence. After exhausting their arguments & patience on these subjects, they have for some time been resting on their oars, unable to get along as to these businesses, and indisposed to attend to anything else till they are settled. And in fine it has become probable that unless they can be reconciled by some plan of compromise, there will be no funding bill agreed to, our credit (raised by late prospects to be the first on the exchange at Amsterdam, where our paper is above par) will burst and vanish, and the states separate to take care every one of itself. This prospect appears probable to some well informed and well-disposed minds. Endeavours are therefore using to bring about a disposition to some mutual sacrifices. The assumption of state debts has appeared as revolting to several states as their non-assumption to others. It is proposed to strip the proposition of the injustice it would have done by leaving the states who have redeemed much of their debts on no better footing than those who have redeemed none; on the contrary it is recommended to assume a fixed sum, allotting a portion of it to every State in proportion to it's census. Consequently every one will receive exactly what they will have to pay, or they will be exonerated so far by the general government's taking their creditors off their hands. There will be no injustice then. But there will be the objection still that Congress must then lay taxes for these debts which would have been much better laid & collected by the state governments. And this is the objection on which the accommodation now hangs with the non-assumptioners, many of whom committed themselves in their advocation of the new constitution by arguments drawn from the improbability that Congress would ever lay taxes where the states could do it separately. These gentlemen feel the reproaches which will be levelled at them personally. I have been, & still am of their opinion that Congress should always prefer letting the States raise money in their own way where it can be done. But in the present instance I see the necessity of yielding for this time to the cries of the creditors in certain parts of the union, for the sake of union, and to save us from the greatest of all calamities, the total extinction of our credit in Europe. On the other subject it is proposed to pass an act fixing the temporary residence of 12. or 15. years at Philadelphia, and that at the end of that time it shall stand *ipso facto* & without further declaration transferred to Georgetown. In this way, there will be something to displease & something to soothe every part of the Union, but New York, which must be contented with what she has had. If this plan of compromise does not take place, I fear one infinitely worse, an unqualified assumption, & the perpetual residence on the Delaware. The Pennsylvania & Virginia delegations have conducted themselves honorably & unexceptionably on the question of residence. Without descending to talk about bargains they have seen that their true interests lay in not listening to insidious propositions made to divide & defect them, and we have seen them at times voting against their respective wishes rather than separate. * * *

[TH: JEFFERSON]

[Pp. 187–9, Ford, WRITINGS, V.]

JEFFERSON TO EPPES

New York July 4. 1790.

TO FRANCIS EPPES.

The Senate has passed the bill for transferring the temporary residence of Congress to Philadelphia for 10. years and the permanent one to George town thenceforward. The other question relative to the assumption of the state debts is still undecided. In the form in which it has been proposed, it will n[ot] can never be admitted. But neither can the proposition be totally rejected without preventing the funding the public debt altogether which would be tantamount to a dissolution of the government. I am in hopes it will be put into a just form, by assuming to the creditors of each state in proportion to the census of each state, so that the state will be exonerated towards it's creditors just as much as it will have to contribute to the assumption, & consequently no injustice done. The only objection then would be that the states could more conveniently levy taxes themselves to pay these debts. I am clearly of this opinion, but I see the necessity of sacrificing our opinions some times to the opinions of others for the sake of harmony.

[P. 194, Ford, WRITINGS, V.]

JEFFERSON TO RUTLEDGE

New York, July 4. 1790.

TO EDWARD RUTLEDGE.

Some questions have lately agitated the mind of Congress more than the friends of union on catholic principles could have wished. The general assumption of state debts has been as warmly demanded by some states, as warmly rejected by others. I hope still that this question may be so divested of the injustice imputed to it as to be compromised. The question of residence you know was always a heating one. A bill has passed the Senate for fixing this at Philadelphia ten years, & then at George town: and it is rather probable it will pass the lower house. That question then will be put to sleep for ten years; & this and the funding business being once out of the way, I hope nothing else may be able to call up local principles.

[P. 197, Ford, WRITINGS, V.]

JEFFERSON TO JAMES MONROE

New York July 11, 1790.

TO JAMES MONROE.

Dear Sir,

I wrote you last on the 20th. of June. The bill for removing the federal government to Philadelphia for 10. years & then to Georgetown has at length passed both houses. The offices are to be removed before the first of December. I presume it will be done during the President's trip to Virginia about the 1st. of September & October. I hope to set out for Virginia about the 1st of September and to pass three or four weeks at Monticello. Congress will now probably proceed in better humour to funding the public debt. This measure will secure to us the credit we now hold at Amsterdam, where our European paper is above par, which is the case of no other nation.

[TH: JEFFERSON]

[P. 198, Ford, WRITINGS, V.]

JEFFERSON TO RANDOLPH

New York July. 11. 1790.

Dear Sir

Your last favor was of May 25. mine was of June 20. having written regularly every third week to you, & the intermediate one to Patsy or Polly. the bill for the removal of the federal government to Philadelphia for 10. years & then to George town has at length past both houses, so that our removal is now certain: and I think it tolerably certain that the President will leave this place on a visit to Mount Vernon about the last of August or first of September. that will fix my visit to Monticello to the same time.

*   *   *   *   *   *   *   *   *   *

[TH: JEFFERSON]

Mr RANDOLPH

[Ms., *Jefferson Papers*, Library of Congress.]

WASHINGTON TO JEFFERSON

Thursday, July 15, 1790.

WASHINGTON TO JEFFERSON.

Dear Sir: Have you formed an opinion on the subject I submitted to you on Tuesday?[4] Have you heard whether the Bill was disputed in both or either House of Congress on the ground of the Constitution, or whether this objection (in its full force) was held in petto for the last move, in the present Stage of the business? If it was debated, as above, whether the arguments adduced by the Author of the Address to the P—— were made use of, and how treated? and what would be the consequence supposing such a case, as he states, should arise? Yours sincerely and Affectionately.

[Pp. 69–70, WRITINGS OF WASHINGTON, Fitzpatrick, Vol. 31.]

JEFFERSON TO WASHINGTON

Th: Jefferson begs pardon of the President for being later in sending the inclosed than he had given him reason to expect. the sole cause has been that the act of copying took him longer than he had calculated. he will have the honor of waiting on the President to answer to any thing which he may have omitted materially in these papers.

July 15. 1790.

[Ms., *Records of the Department of State, Miscellaneous Letters,* June–July 1790, in the National Archives.]

Thursday July 15. 1790.

Sir

I have formed an opinion, quite satisfactory to myself, that the adjournment of Congress may be by law, as well as by resolution, without touching the constitution. I am now copying fair what I had written yesterday on the subject & will have

[4] A marginal note by Jefferson states: "For fixing the seat of the federal govmt"

the honor of laying it before you by ten oclock. — the address
to the President contains a very full digest of all the arguments
urged against the bill on the point of unconstitutionality on the
floor of Congress. it was fully combated on that ground, in the
committee of the whole, & on the third reading. the majority
(a Southern one) overruled the objection, as a majority (a
Northern one) had overruled the same objection the last session
on the Susquehanna residence bill, so that two majorities, in
two different sessions, & from different ends of the Union have
overruled the objection, and may be fairly supposed to have
declared the sense of the whole union. I shall not lose a moment in laying before you my thoughts on the subject. I
have the honor to be with the most respectful esteem

Sir

your most obedient

& most humble serv^t

TH: JEFFERSON

THE PRESIDENT OF THE UNITED STATES

[Ms., *Records of the Department of State, Miscellaneous Letters,* June–July, 1790, in The
National Archives; pp. 204-5, Ford, WRITINGS, V.]

A Bill having passed the two houses of Congress, & being
now before the President, declaring that the seat of the federal
government shall be transferred to the Patowmac in the year
1790, that the session of Congress next ensuing the present shall
be held at Philadelphia, to which place the offices shall be
transferred before the 1st of December next, a writer in a public
paper of July 13. has urged on the consideration of the President that the constitution has given to the two houses of Congress the exclusive right to adjourn themselves, that the will of
the President mixed with theirs in a decision of this kind would
be an inoperative ingredient, repugnant to the constitution,
and that he ought not to permit them to part, in a single instance, with their constitutional rights: consequently that he
ought to negative the bill.

That is now to be considered.

Every man, & every body of men on earth, possesses the right of self-government: they recieve it with their being from the hand of nature. individuals exercise it by their single will: collections of men by that of their majority; for the law of the *majority* is the natural law of every society of men. when a certain description of men are to transact together a particular business, the times & places of their meeting & separating depend on their own will; they make a part of the natural right of self-government. this, like all other natural rights, may be abridged or modified in it's exercise, by their own consent, or by the law of those who depute them, if they meet in the right of others: but — so far as it is not abridged or modified, they retain it as a natural right, & may exercise it in what form they please, either exclusively by themselves, or in association with others, or by others altogether, as they shall agree.

Each house of Congress possesses this natural right of governing itself, & consequently of fixing it's own times & places of meeting, so far as it has not been abridged by the law of those who employ them, that is to say, by the Constitution. this act manifestly considers them as possessing this right of course, & therefore has no where given it to them. in the several different passages where it touches this right, it treats it as an existing thing, not as one called into existence by them. to evince this, every passage of the constitution shall be quoted, where the right of adjournment is touched; & it will be seen that no one of them pretends to give that right; that on the contrary every one is evidently introduced either to enlarge the right where it would be too narrow, to restrain it where, in it's natural & full exercise, it might be too large & lead to inconvenience, to defend it from the latitude of it's own phrases, where these were not meant to comprehend it, or to provide for it's exercise by others where they cannot exercise it themselves.

'A majority of each house shall constitute a quorum to do

business; but a *smaller number* may adjourn from day to day, &
may be authorised to compel the attendance of absent members.' Art. 1, sect. 5. a majority of every collection of men being naturally necessary to constitute it's will, and it being frequently to happen that a majority is not assembled, it was necessary to enlarge the natural right, by giving to 'a *smaller number
than a majority*' a right to compel the attendance of the absent
members, & in the mean time to adjourn from day to day. this
clause then does not pretend to give to a majority a right which
it knew that majority would have of themselves, but to a number *less than a majority* a right which it knew that lesser number
would not have of themselves.

'Neither house, during the session of Congress, shall, without
the consent of the other, adjourn for more than three days, nor
to any other place than that in which the two houses shall be
sitting.' ibid. each house exercising separately it's natural
right to meet when and where it should think best, it might
happen that the two houses would separate either in time or
place, which would be inconvenient. it was necessary therefore to keep them together by restraining their natural right of
deciding on separate times & places, & by requiring a concurrence of will.

But as it might happen that obstinacy, or a difference of object might prevent this concurrence, it goes on to take from
them, in that instance, the right of adjournment altogether, &
to transfer it to another, by declaring Art. 2. sect. 3. that 'in
case of disagreement between the two houses with respect to
the time of adjournment the President may adjourn them to
such time as he shall think proper.'

These clauses then do not import a gift, to the two houses, of
a general right of adjournment, which it was known they
would have without that gift, but to restrain or abrogate the
right it was known they would have, in an instance where, exercised in it's full extent, it might lead to inconvenience, & to

give that right to another who would not naturally have had it. it also gives to the President a right, which he otherwise would not have had, 'to convene both houses, or either of them, on extraordinary occasions.' thus substituting the will of another, where they are not in a situation to exercise their own.

'Every order, resolution, or vote, to which the concurrence of the Senate & house of representatives may be necessary (except on a question of adjournment) shall be presented to the President for his approbation &c.' Art. 1, sect. 7. the latitude of the general words here used would have subjected the natural right of adjournment of the two houses to the will of the President, which was not intended. they therefore expressly 'except questions of adjournment' out of their operation. they do not here give a right of adjournment, which it was known would exist without their gift; but they defend the existing right against the latitude of their own phrases, in a case where there was no good reason to abridge it. the exception admits they will have the right of adjournment, without pointing out the source from which they will derive it.

These are all the passages of the constitution (one only excepted which shall be presently cited) where the right of adjournment is touched: & it is evident that none of these are introduced to give that right; but every one supposes it to be existing, and provides some specific modification for cases where either a defect in the natural right, or a too full use of it would occasion inconvenience.

The right of adjournment then is not given by the constitution; & consequently it may be modified by law, without interfering with that instrument. it is a natural right, &, like all other natural rights, may be abridged or regulated in it's exercise by law; & the concurrence of the third branch in any law regulating it's exercise is so efficient an ingredient in that law, that the right cannot be otherwise exercised, but after a repeal by a new law. The express terms of the constitution itself shew that this right may be modified *by law*, when, in Art. 1. sect. 4. (the only remaining passage on the subject not yet quoted) it sais 'the Congress shall assemble at least once in every year, & such meeting shall be on the 1st Monday in December, unless they shall, *by law*, appoint a different day.' then another day may be appointed, *by law;* & the President's assent is an efficient ingredient in that law. nay further, they cannot adjourn over the 1st Monday of December but by *a law.* this is another constitutional abridgment of their natural right of adjournment; and completing our review of all the clauses in the constitution which touch that right, authorises us to say no part of that instrument gives it; and that the houses hold it, not from the constitution, but from nature.

A consequence of this is that the houses may by a joint resolution remove themselves from place to place; because it is a part of their right of self-government: but that as the right of self-government does not comprehend the government of others, the two houses cannot, by a joint resolution of their majorities only, remove the executive, & judiciary from place to place. these branches possessing also the rights of self-government from nature, cannot be controuled in the exercise of them, but by a law, passed in the forms of the constitution. the clause of the bill in question therefore was necessary to be put into the form of a law, & to be submitted to the President, so far as it proposes to effect the removal of the Executive & Judiciary to Philadelphia. so far as respects the removal of the present houses of legislation thither, it was not necessary to be submitted to the president: but such a submission is not repugnant to the constitution. on the contrary, if he concurs, it will so far fix the next session of Congress at Philadelphia, that it cannot be changed but by a regular law.

The sense of Congress itself is always respectable authority. it has been given very remarkeably on the present subject. the address to the President in the paper of the 13th is a complete

digest of all the arguments urged on the floor of the Representatives against the constitutionality of the bill now before
the President; & they were over-ruled by a majority of that
house, comprehending the delegations of all the states South of
the Hudson, except South Carolina. At the last session of Congress, when the bill for remaining a certain term at New York,
& then removing to Susquehanna or Germantown was objected to on the same ground, the objection was overruled by a
majority, comprehending the delegations of the Northern half
of the union with that of South Carolina. so that the sense of
every state in the union has been expressed, by its delegation,
against this objection, South Carolina excepted, and excepting
also Rhode island which has never yet had had a delegation in
place to vote on the question. In both these instances the
Senate concurred with the majority of the Representatives.
The sense of the two houses is stronger authority in this case, as
it is given against their own supposed privilege.

It would be as tedious, as it is unnecessary, to take up & discuss one by one, the objections proposed in the paper of July
13. every one of them is founded on the supposition that the
two houses hold their right of adjournment from the constitution. this error being corrected, the objections founded on it
fall of themselves.

It would also be a work of mere supererogation to shew that,
granting what this writer takes for granted (that the President's
assent would be an inoperative ingredient, because excluded
by the constitution, as he says) yet the particular views of the
writer would be frustrated. for on every hypothesis of what the
President may do, Congress must go to Philadelphia. 1. if he
assents to the bill, that assent makes good law of the part relative to the Patowmac, and the part for holding the next session
at Philadelphia is good, either as an ordinance, or a vote of the
two houses, containing a compleat declaration of their will, in a
case where it is competent to the object, so that they must go to

Philadelphia in that case. 2. if he dissents from the bill, it annuls the part relative to the Patowmac; but as to the clause for adjourning to Philadelphia, his dissent being as inefficient as his assent, it remains a good ordinance, or vote, of the two houses for going thither, & consequently they must go in this case also. 3. if the President witholds his will out of the bill altogether, by a ten days silence, then the part relative to the Patowmac becomes a good law without his will, & that relative to Philadelphia is good also, either as a law, or an ordinance, or a vote of the two houses, & consequently in this case also they go to Philadelphia.

TH: JEFFERSON

July. 15. 1790.

[Ms., *Records of the Department of State, Miscellaneous Letters*, June–July 1790, in The National Archives; pp. 205–210, Ford, WRITINGS, V.]

JEFFERSON TO SHORT

New York Aug. 25. 1790.

Dear Sir

The President will leave this on the 30th for Mount Vernon and will return to Philadelphia towards the latter part of November. I go hence a day or two after him, for Monticello, and shall return to Philadelphia about the last of October. the other offices will be removed to Philadelphia between the middle of October & of November. I very much wish my letters, written for this purpose may have reached you in time to change the destination of my furniture to Philadelphia directly.

*   *   *   *   *   *   *   *   *   *

[TH: JEFFERSON]

Mr SHORT

[Ms., *Jefferson Papers*, Library of Congress.]

JEFFERSON TO WASHINGTON

Fredericksburg, Sep. 17 1790.

Sir

In the course of the visit we made the day we left Mount
Vernon, we drew our host[5] into conversation on the subject of
the federal seat. he came into it with a shyness not usual in
him. whether this proceeded from his delicacy as having property adjoining Georgetown, or from what other motive I cannot say. he quitted the subject always as soon as he could. he
said enough however to show his decided preference of Georgetown. he mentioned shortly, in it's favor, these circumstances.
1. it's being at the junction of the upper & lower navigation
where the commodities must be transferred into other vessels:
(and here he was confident that no vessel could be contrived
which could pass the upper shoals and live in the wide waters
below his island.) 2. the depth of water which would admit
any vessels that could come to Alexandria. 3. the narrowness
of the river & consequent safeness of the harbour. 4. it's being
clear of ice as earlt at least as the canal & river above would be
clear. 5. it's neighborhood to the Eastern branch, whither any
vessels might conveniently withdraw which should be detained
through the winter. 6. it's defensibility, as derived from the
high & commanding hills around it. 7. it's actual possession
of the commerce & the start it already has.

He spoke of Georgetown always in comparison with Alexandria. When led to mention the Eastern branch he spoke of it
as an admirable position, superior in all respects to Alexandria.

I have committed to writing a Memorandum for mr Carrol
of the kind of conveyance I suggested to him, & which I had
not the opportunity then to put on paper. I inclose it open for
your perusal, and take the liberty of asking you to put a wafer

[5] Gen. John Mason.

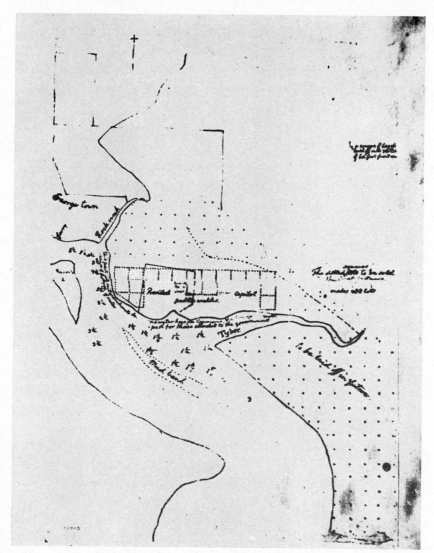

Jefferson's plan for the Federal city, from Jefferson Papers, March 1791, Division of Manuscripts, Library of Congress.

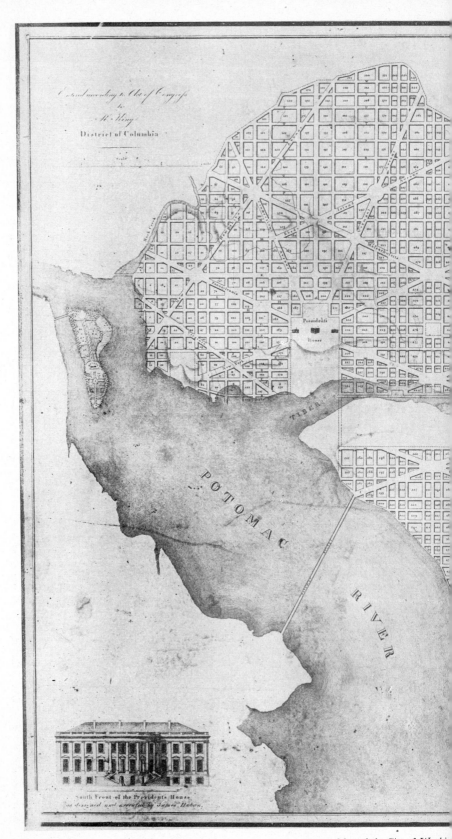

Extend according to Act of Congress
by
R. King
District of Columbia

President's House

TIBER

POTOMAC

RIVER

South Front of the President's House
as designed and executed by James Hoban.

A Map

of the

CITY OF WASHINGTON

in the District of Columbia

established as the permanent Seat of the Government

of the

United States

OF AMERICA

taken from actual Survey, as laid out

on the ground.

by W. King
Surveyor of the City of Washington

Marine Hospital

East Capitol Street

Navy Yard

BRANCH

EASTERN

East Front of the Capitol of the United States
as originally designed by William Thornton, and adopted by General Washington President of the United States.

during Jefferson's administration.

Early Washington, showing the Jefferson poplars on Pennsylvania Avenue.

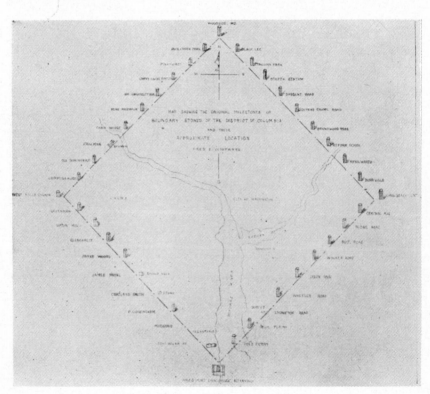

Boundary stones for the Federal district, several of which still stand.   Installed 1791.

into it, when you are done with it, & to forward it to mr Carroll.

I have the honor to be with the greatest respect & attachment, Sir,

Your most obedient & most humble servt.

Th. Jefferson

From THOS. JEFFERSON ESQ and MR. MADISON
    17th Sept. 1790 — Free
The PRESIDENT OF THE UNITED STATES at Mount-Vernon

[P. 131, U.S. *v*. SMITH.]

JEFFERSON TO CHARLES CARROLL

[*September* 17, 1790]

[*Jefferson's memorandum for Mr. Chas. Carroll which he enclosed
with his letter to the President, September 17, 1790*]

The Conveyance to be executed, according to the form of the
laws of Maryland, by the Proprietors of the land designated by
the President for the Federal seat.

The preamble to recite the substance of that part of the
Residence Act which authorizes the President to receive grants
of *lands* or *money* for the use of the United States and to declare
that the object of the conveyance is to furnish both Land and
money for their use. The body of the deed to convey the lands
designated for the city (suppose 1500 acres) to A and B and
their heirs in trust for the following purposes:

1. To reconvey to the commissioners their heirs and successors to be named by the President, such portions of the said
lands as the President shall designate for the site of the public
buildings, public walks, streets, &c., to remain for the use of
the United States.

2. To reconvey the residue of such lands, to such persons,
and on such conditions as the Commissioners shall direct, for

the purpose of raising money, and the money when received to be granted to the President for the use of the United States according to the Residence Act.

The effect of this last clause will be such that the President (without any further legislation from Congress) may proceed to lay out the town immediately into 1, public lots; 2 public walks and gardens; 3 private lots for sale; 4 streets. The 1, 2 and 4th articles to be reconveyed to the Commissioners, and the 3rd to private purchasers as above proposed. It is understood that this conveyance will have been preceded by articles of agreement signed by all the proprietors of the lands in and about those several spots which have such obvious advantages as render it presumable to every one that some one of them will attract the President's notice and choice.

[Pp. 109–10, HISTORY, CITY OF WASHINGTON, Tindall.]

JEFFERSON NOTE
November 29, 1790

Proceedings to be had under the Residence act.

a territory not exceeding 10. miles square (or, I presume, 100 square miles in any form) to be located by metes and bounds.
  3. commissioners to be appointed
     I suppose them not entitled to any salary.

> [if they live near the place they may, in some instances, be influenced by self interest, & partialities: but they will push the work with zeal. if they are from a distance, & Northwardly, they will be more impartial, but may affect delays.]

the Commissioners to purchase or accept 'such quantity of land on the E. side of the river as the President shall deem *proper for the U. S.*' viz. for the federal Capitol, the offices, the President's house & gardens, the town house, Market house, publick walks, hospital. for the President's house, offices & gardens, I should think 2. squares sould be consolidated. for the Capitol

& offices one square. for the Market one square. for the Public walks 9. squares consolidated.

the expression 'such quantity of land as the President shall deem *proper for the U. S.*' is vague. it may therefore be extended to the acceptance or purchase of land enough for the town: and I have no doubt it is the wish, & perhaps expectation. in that case it will be to be laid out in lots & streets. I should propose these to be at right angles as in Philadelphia, & that no street be narrower than 100. feet, with foot-ways of 15. feet. where a street is long & level, it might be 120. feet wide. I should prefer squares of at least 200. yards every way, which will be of about 8. acres each.

The Commissioners should have some taste in architecture, because they may have to decide between different plans.

They will however be subject to the President's direction in every point.

When the President shall have made up his mind as to the spot for the town, would there by any impropriety in his saying to the neighboring landholders, 'I will fix the town here if you will join & purchase & give the lands.' They may well afford it from the increase of value it will give to their own circumjacent lands.

The lots to be sold out in breadth of 50 feet; their depths to extend to the diagonal of the square

I doubt much whether the obligation to build the houses at a given distance from the street, contributes to its beauty, it produces a disgusting monotony, all persons make this complaint against Philadelphia, the contrary practice varies the appearance, & is much more convenient to the inhabitants.

In Paris it is forbidden to build a house beyond a given height, & it is admitted to be a good restriction, it keeps the houses low & convenient, & the streets light and airy, fires are much more managable where houses are low. This however is an object of Legislation.

"The act for establishing the temporary and permanent seat of the Government of the U. States" requires the following steps for carrying the latter into effect.

1. The appointment of three Commissioners of sufficient respectability having good will to the general object without any particular bias of private interest.[6]

[Side note in the original]

[6] Quer. If local situation or interest be an objection outweighing the advantage of proximity and zeal for the object, as the President is to prescribe the place & the commis. only to define the district, and as the subsequent discretion in the Comiss. will give no opportunity of sacrificing their trust to local consid- erations, The essential point seems to be that the Commission's be filled by men who prefer residing (a majority at least) so conveniently to the scene of business as to be able to attend readily & gratis.

any place on the Potowmac to any place elsewhere. On this supposition, it may be easy to find men who would suit.

Should it be advisable after securing a majority near at hand to make an appointment with a view to attach particular parts of the Union to the object. N. England particularly Massa- chusetts, first occurs — and next, S. Carolina & Georgia.

Mr. Ellicott (Mr. *Gorum* Mr. Bull) Mr. Fitzhugh (of Chat- ham) Mr. O. Wolcott Mr. Tucker Mr. Loyd (of Annapolis) Mr. ———— of R. I. Mr. Baldwin Rev'd Mr. Lee Massey.

2. That the President inform himself of the several rival positions; leaving among them inducements to bid against each other in offers of land or money, as the location when com- pleted by the survey will not be mutable by the President, it may be well to have the offers so framed as to become *ipso facto* absolute in favor of the U. S. on the event which they solicit.

3. That the President direct the Survey of the District which he shall ultimately elect. It seems essential that the District should comprehend the water adjoining the establishment, and eligible that it should comprehend the opposite shore. The legality of this seems to be decided by clause confining the pur- chase or acceptance of land for the use of the U. S. "to the East

side of the river within the said district" which imply that the *whole* district was not *necessarily* to be on *that side*. Quer: whether it will not be convenient to accept in the first instance so much less than 10 miles square as will allow places to be afterwards taken in, which may not now be attainable, or it may not be prudent now to accept.

4. The district being defined & the requisite quantity of ground secured, the next step must be to fix the site for the public buildings — and provide for the establishment or enlargement of a town within the district. — as no special authority is given for the latter purpose the consent of proprietors will be necessary: but as they will have a common interest with the public, voluntary arrangements between them and the Commissioners may be readily procured in favor of any plan which the President may patronize. Should any difficulties be apprehended on this point they can be guarded ag'st in the negociations preliminary to the actual location of the district.

5. The plan for the public buildings is to be approved by the President.

The Commissioners will no doubt submit different ones formed by themselves, or obtained from ingenious architects. Should it be thought proper to excite emulation by a premium for the best, the expence is authorized, as an incident to that of the Buildings.

6. The completion of the work will depend on a supyly [sic] of the means. These must consist either of future grants of money by Congress which it would not be prudent to count upon — of State grants — of private grants — or the conversion into money of lands ceded for public use which it is conceived the latitude of the term "use" & the spirit & scope of the Act will justify.

In conversations with Mr. Carrol, Mr. Stoddard and Mr. Dickens they were properly impressed with the idea that if the present occasion of securing the Federal seat on the Potowmack should be lost, it could never more be regained, that it would be dangerous to rely on any aids from Congress, or the assemblies of Virginia or Maryland, & that therefore measures should be adopted to carry the residence bill into execution without recourse to those bodies: and that the requisites were 1st land enough to place the public buildings on; & 2ndly money enough to build them, and to erect moreover about 20 good dwelling houses for such persons belonging to the Government as must have houses to themselves, about as many good lodging houses, and half a dozen taverns.

To obtain this sum, this expedient was suggested to them. To procure a declaration from the proprietors of those spots of land most likely to be fixed for the town, that if the President's location of the town should comprehend their lands, they would give them up for the use of the U. S. on condition they should receive the double of their value, estimated as they would have been had there been no thought of bringing the federal seat into their neighborhood. it was supposed that 1500 Acres would be required in the whole, to wit, about 300 acres for public buildings, walks &c and 1200 Acres to be divided into quarter acre lots, which, due allowance being made for streets, would make about 2000 lots, the vacant lots in Georgetown now sell at £200. those of Alexandria at £600. Suppose those of the new town should bring only £100 clear this would produce 200,000£ a sum adequate to the objects before mentioned. it was further supposed that the Assembly of Maryland would interpose to force the consent of infant or obstinate proprietors for a reasonable compensation.

It was also suggested as a more certain means of ensuring the object, that each proprietor within the whole ten miles square should cede one half his lands to the public, to be sold to raise money; perhaps this would be pushing them too far for the reputation of the new government they were to come under, & further than is necessary when we consider the sum which may be raised by the sale of lots, the donation of 120,000 Dollars by Virginia, & the possible donation of an equal sum by Maryland; at least it might shew a commendable moderation not to push this proposition till experiment should prove the other resources inadequate; great zeal appeared in the gentlemen before mentioned, & they seemed to approve the proposition for the 1500 Acres; that for a moiety of all the lands within the 10 mile square was hazarded only to Mr. Carrol; they will probably proceed immediately to make the best arrangements practicable & to come forward with them to the President.

Queries. 1. Would it not be well if a position below the little falls should be decided on, to begin the 10 miles just above the commencement of the canal; and accept from Maryland, for the present, only from thence down to the Eastern branch, supposed about 7 miles: and to accept from Virginia 10 miles beginning at the lower end of Alexandria, & running up as far as it will extend, which probably will be as far up as the commencement on the Maryland side. this being accepted, & professedly (as to Maryland) in *part* only of their cession, when Congress shall meet they may pass an amendatory bill authorizing the President to compleat his acceptance from Maryland by crossing the Eastern branch and compleating the 10 miles in that direction, which will bring the lower boundary on the Maryland side very nearly opposite to that on the Virginia side — it is understood that the breadth of the territory accepted will be of 5 miles only on each side.

2. In locating the town, will it not be best to give it double the extent on the eastern branch of what it has on the river? the former will be for persons in commerce, the latter for those connected with the Government.

3. Will it not be best to lay out the long streets paralel with the creek, and the other crossing them at right angles, so as to leave no oblique angled lots but the single row which shall be on the river? thus:

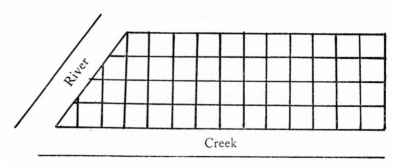

Creek

[Pp. 2155-9, U.S. *v.* MORRIS, Records, Vol. VII.]

WASHINGTON TO JEFFERSON

Sunday, January 2, 1791.

WASHINGTON TO JEFFERSON

Dear Sir: The enclosed Notes[7] are sufficiently descriptive to comprehend the *two* objects fully; but it is necessary to remark, that if the *first* line[8] begins at a point on Hunting Creek, the *fourth* line cannot, in any part *touch* (though it will *include*) the Town of Alexandria; because Huntg. Creek is below the boundaries of the Town. And, if it could be so ordered as for the *first line* to avoid *touching* the town, that is, to allow room for its extending backwards, as well as up and down the River, without throwing too much of the district into Virginia, it would be a desirable measure. Where are the Acts, or Resolutions of the States of Virginia and Maryland (respecting the Cession of the ten miles Square) to be met with? If to be brought from the Archives of these States, much time will be required in obtaining them: but quere, are they not among the deposits of the Genl. Government.? The presumption is, that they were transmitted by the two States above mentioned. Yrs. Affectly.

[Pp. 189, WRITINGS OF WASHINGTON, Fitzpatrick, Vol. 31.]

[7] These notes of the courses and distances are, with this letter, in the *Jefferson Papers* in the Library of Congress.
[8] The southwest boundary line of the District of Columbia.

WASHINGTON TO JEFFERSON

Tuesday [*January* 4,[9] 1791.]

WASHINGTON TO JEFFERSON.

The P. begs to see Mr. Jefferson before he proceeds further in the Proclamation. From a more attentive examination of some Papers, in his possession, he finds that it is in his power to ascertain the course and distance from the Court House in Alexandria to the upper and lower end of the canal at the little Falls with as much accuracy as can be known from *Common* Surveying if not to mathematical truth.

If Mr. Jefferson is not engaged with other matters the President will be at home at nine Oclock.

[P. 191, WRITINGS OF WASHINGTON, Fitzpatrick, Vol. 31.]

JEFFERSON TO COMMISSIONERS

"The President, thinking it would be better that the outline, at least, of the city, and, perhaps Georgetown, should be laid down in the plat of the the territory, I have the honor now to send it and to desire that Major Ellicott may do it as soon as convenient, that it may be returned in time to be laid before Congress."

[*Letter from Jefferson to the Commissioners*, dated Philadelphia, January 15, 1791.[10]]

JEFFERSON TO DANIEL CARROLL

Philadelphia Jan'y 24. 1791.

TO DANIEL CARROLL ESQR.

Dear Sir

The President of the united States desirous of availing him

[9] This date could also be Jan. 24, 1791, *post.*
[10] Records, Columbia Historical Society, vol. 2, p. 170. As Major Ellicott's appointment is dated February 2, 1791, the date of the letter of Mr. Jefferson must be an error.

self of your assistance in preparing the federal seat on the Potomac, is in hopes you will act as one of the Commissioners directed by the law for that purpose. I have the honor now to enclose a joint Commission for yourself and two others, together with a copy of the Proclamation meant to constitute your first direction. The President will from time to time communicate such further directions, as circumstances shall call for. I have the honor to be with great esteem, Dear Sir, &c.

TH: JEFFERSON.

[Ms., p. 198, *American Letters*, Vol. IV, 1788–92, *Letters of the Secretaries of State*, State Department Archives in the National Archives; p. 144, U.S. *v.* SMITH.]

JEFFERSON TO JOHNSON AND STUART

Philadelphia January 24, 1791.

TO THOMAS JOHNSON & DAVID STUART ESQRS.

Dear Sir

The President of the united States desirous of availing himself of your assistance in preparing the federal seat on the Potomac, has appointed you one of the three Commissioners directed by the law for that purpose. a joint Commission is made out and deposited in the hands of the honorable D. Carroll, who is named second therein. I have the honor to enclose you a copy of the Proclamation meant to constitute your first direction. The President will from time to time communicate such further directions as circumstances shall call for. I have the honor to be with great esteem, Dear Sir &c.

TH. JEFFERSON.

[Ms., p. 199, *American Letters*, Vol. IV, 1788–92, State Department Archives in the National Archives; p. 144, U.S. *v.* SMITH.]

JEFFERSON TO JOHNSON AND STUART

Philadelphia January 29. 1791.

TO THOMAS JOHNSON & DAVID STUART ESQRS.

Sir

Mr. Carroll supposing that doubts may arise whether he can act as one of the Commissioners for the federal Seat, while a member of Congress, has declined, and has returned me the commission, which had been deposited with him as one of the members. I have now the honor to enclose it to [you] and to observe that two members suffice for business. I will be some time before a third will be named. The President having thought Major L'Enfant peculiarly qualified to make such a draught of the ground as will enable himself to fix on the spot for the public buildings, he has been written to for that purpose, and will be sent on if he chuses to undertake it. I have the honor to be, Sir &c

TH: JEFFERSON.

NOTE. — In the letter to Mr. Stuart these words were comprised in the Brackets instead of ["you"] viz[t].

["mr. Johnson first named therein"]

[Ms., p. 199, *American Letters*, Vol. IV, 1788–92, State Department Archives in the National Archives; p. 45, U.S. *v.* SMITH.]

WASHINGTON TO JEFFERSON

February 1, 1791

My dear Sir:

Nothing in the enclosed letter superceding the necessity of Mr. Ellicots proceeding to the work in hand I would thank you, for requesting him, to set out on thursday; or as soon after as he can make it convenient: also for preparing such instructions as you may conceive it necessary for me to give him for ascertaining the points we wish to know; *first*, for the *general* view of things, and *next* for the more accurate and final decision.

Yrs. Sincerely and aff^{ly}

[Pp. 206–7, WRITINGS OF WASHINGTON, Fitzpatrick, Vol. 31; p. 56, HISTORY OF WASHINGTON, Tindall.]

JEFFERSON TO ELLICOTT

Philadelphia, February 2, 1791:

TO MAJOR ELLICOTT, —

Sir: You are desired to proceed by the first stage to the Federal territory on the Potomac, for the purpose of making a survey of it. The first object will be to run the two first lines mentioned in the enclosed proclamation to wit: — the S. W. line 160 poles and the S. E. line to Hunting Creek or should it not strike Hunting Creek as has been suggested then to the River. These two lines must run with all the accuracy of which your art is susceptible as they are to fix the beginning either on Hunting Creek or the River, if the second line should strike the River instead of the Creek take and lay down the bearing and distance of the nearest part of the creek and also of any of its waters if any of them should be nearer than the creek itself; so also should either of these two lines cross any water of Hunting Creek let it be noted. The termination of the Second line being accurately fixed, either on the creek or river proceed to run from that at a beginning the four lines of experiment directed in the proclamation, this is intended as the first rough essay to furnish data for the last accurate survey. It is desirable that it be made with all the dispatch possible and with only common exactness, paying regard however to the magnetic variations. In running these lines note the position of the mouth of the Eastern Branch, the point of your first course there will receive the S. W. line from the Cape of the Eastern Branch, — the Canal and particular distance of your crossing it from either end, the position of Georgetown, and mouth of Goose Creek, and send by Post, A plat of the whole on which ultimate directions for the rest of the work shall be sent you, as soon as they can be prepared. Till these shall be received by you, you can be employed in ascertaining a true Meridian, and the latitude of the place, and running the meanderings of the Eastern Branch, and of the River itself, and other waters which will merit an exact place in the map of the Territory. You will herewith receive a draft on the Mayor of Georgetown to cover your expenses.

TH. JEFFERSON.

P.S.—The President writes by Post to Mr. Beall Mayor of Georgetown to furnish you with money for your expenses for which therefore you may apply to him without further order.

[P. 170, COLUMBIA HISTORICAL SOCIETY, *Records*, Vol. 2.]

ELLICOTT TO JEFFERSON

Sir: — I arrived at this town on Monday last, but the cloudy weather prevented any observations being made until Friday which was very fine. On Saturday the two first lines were completed. You will see by the enclosed plat that the second line does not touch any part of Hunting Creek unless the spring drain noted in the plat is to be considered a part of it. It appears to me that in order to make the plan as complete as possible it will be proper to begin the survey of the ten miles square at the Eastern inclination of the upper cape of Hunting Creek, marked on the plat. This plan will include all the Harbor and wharfs of Alexandria, which will not be the Case if the two first lines mentioned in the proclamation are to remain as now. I shall submit to your consideration the following plan for the permanent location which will I believe embrace every object of advantage which can be included within the ten miles square. [Many erasures follow and indistinct writing.] — as marked in plat A. The magnetic variations at this place is somewhat uncertain, arising no doubt from some local cause. It was 20 easterly when the second line struck the river and at the end of the first line, it was nearly as much Westerly. The Latitude of Alexandria, I find to be about 33 48 20 N. This afternoon I intend beginning the rough survey which shall be executed with all possible dispatch, [more erasures]. You will observe by the plan which I have suggested for the Permanent Location a small deviation with respect to the compass from that mentioned in the Proclamation, the reason of which is that the Coup's in the Proclamation, strictly adhered to, would neither produce straight lines, nor contain quite the ten miles square, besides the utmost impropriety of running such lines without tolerable exactness. I am Sir with greatest respect and esteem your o'b'd't Servant.

ANDREW ELLICOTT.

[Letter written either to the President, or to Mr. Jefferson, bears date of Feb. 14th, 1791.]

[Pp. 172–3, COLUMBIA HISTORICAL SOCIETY, *Records*, Vol. 2.]

JEFFERSON TO L'ENFANT

March 1791.

JEFFERSON TO MAJOR L'ENFANT

Sir,

   You are desired to proceed to Georgetown, where you will find Mr. Ellicot employed in making a survey and map of the Federal territory.[11] The special object of asking your aid is to have drawings of the particular grounds most likely to be approved for the site of the federal town and buildings. You will therefore be pleased to begin on the eastern branch, and proceed from thence upwards, laying down the hills, valleys, morasses, and waters between that, the Potomac, the Tyber, and the road leading from Georgetown to the eastern branch, and connecting the whole with certain fixed points of the map Mr. Ellicot is preparing. Some idea of the height of the hills above the base on which they stand, would be desirable. For necessary assistance and expenses, be pleased to apply to the Mayor of Georgetown, who is written to on this subject. I will beg the favor of you to mark to me your progress about twice a week, by letter . . .

[P. 221, WRITINGS OF WASHINGTON, III.]

JEFFERSON TO DANIEL CARROLL

Philadelphia March 4. 1791.

TO DANIEL CARROLL ESQR.

Sir

The President of the united States desiring to avail the public of your services as one of the Commissioners for surveying the district of territory accepted by the act for establishing the temporary and permanent Seat of the Government of the

---

[11] Extracts from Georgetown Weekly Ledger of March 12, 1791.

"Some time last month arrived in this town Maj. Andrew Ellicott, a gentleman of superior astronomical abilities. He was appointed by the President of the United States to lay off a tract of land ten miles square on the Potomac for the use of Congress. He is now engaged in this business and hopes soon to accomplish the object of his mission. He is attended by Benjamin Banniker, an Ethiopian, whose abilities as a Surveyor and Astronomer clearly prove that Mr. Jefferson's concluding that race of men were void of mental endowments was without foundation."

"Wednesday evening arrived in this town Major Longfont, a French gentleman employed by the President of the United States to survey the lands contiguous to Georgetown where the federal city is to be built. His skill in matters of this kind is justly extolled by all disposed to give merit its proper tribute of praise. He is earnest in the business and hopes to be able to lay a plat of that parcel of land before the President upon his arrival in this town."

[P. 2172, U.S. *v.* MORRIS, Records, Vol. VII.]

united States, I have now the honor of enclosing you the Commission, and of expressing to you the sentiments of perfect
esteem with which I am Sir &c.

TH: JEFFERSON.

[Ms., p. 208, *American Letters*, Vol. IV, 1788–92, State Department Archives in the
National Archives; p. 146, U.S. *v.* SMITH.]

WASHINGTON TO JEFFERSON

Sunday, March 6, 1791.

WASHINGTON TO JEFFERSON.

The President would thank Mr. Jefferson for placing all, or
such of the enclosed papers (after he has perused them) in the
hands of the Attorney General as he shall deem necessary for
the purpose of drawing the several documents of the Ceded
Lands or, the form of one. If the former, it is conceived further information than the enclosures contain is wanting. If the
latter, the agreement, and perhaps the plat to which it refers, is
all that is necessary; but the plat referred to, does not apply to
the subsequent purchasers.

[P. 109, HISTORY OF WASHINGTON, Tindall.]

L'ENFANT TO JEFFERSON

Georgetown Mars the 10—1791

L'ENFANT. rec^d Mar. 24.

Sir

On the 17^{ult} the change of the weather at last having permitted me to proceed to the Eastern branch I deed on the after-
nnon of that day set about the survey, but the variety of the
weather has been such since as has much impeded my progress,
I have only been able, to this day, to lay down of that part

which lay between the eastern branch and the tiber so much as includ Jenkins Hill & all the water course from round carroll point up to the ferry landing leaving for a better time some swampy pass which were rendered absolutely impasable by the Eavy rain which overflowing all the low ground determined me to confine myself on the heigh land — I Expected to have before this day attempted to lay down somme part of those laying between the tyber and Rock creek had not a fall of snow and stormy wind which succeeded for these three day past prevented me — I hope to morrow will prove more favorable for me to proceed laying down that part which you prescribe in the letter which I this moment receive from M' Ellicot who brought it himself to me & shall according to your direction join his endeavour to mine in running as much as possible of the wather course as may serve — connect the whole of our different surveys together —

I have the Honor to be with great respect sir your most humble and most obedient servant

P. C. L'ENFANT

THE HON^{ble} TH. JEFFERSON, *Secretary of State.*

[Pp. 150–1, U.S. *v.* SMITH.]

L'ENFANT TO JEFFERSON

Friday March 11—1791.

Sir:

I have the honor of informing you of my arrival at this place where I could not possibly reach before Wednesday last and very late in the evening after having travelled part of the way on foot and part on horse back leaving the broken stage behind.

On arriving I made it my first care immediately to wait on the mayor of the town in conforming with the direction which you gave me — he appeared to be much surprised and he as-

sured me he had received no previous notice of my coming nor
any instruction relating to the business I was sent upon — however next day — yesterday morning — he made me a kind
offer of his assistance in procuring for me three or four men to
attend me in the surveying and this being the only thing I was
in need of every matter has been soon arranged. I am only at
present to regret that an heavy rain and thick mist which has
been incessant ever since my arrival here has put an insuperable obstacle to my wish of proceeding immediately to the survey. Should the weather continue bad as there is every appearance it will I shall be much at a loss how to make a plan of
the ground you have pointed out to me and have it ready for
the President at the time when he is expected at this place. I
see no other way if by Monday next the weather does not
change, but that of making a rough draft as accurat as may be
obtain by viewing the ground in riding over it on horse back,
as I have already done yesterday through the rain to obtain a
knowledge of the whole. I put from the eastern branch towards Georgetown up the heights and down along side of the
bank of the main river and along side of Goose and Rock creeks
as far up as their springs.

As far as I was able to judge through a thick fog I passed on
many spots which appeared to me raly beautiful and which
seem to dispute with each other who command. In the most
extensive prospect of the water the gradual rising of the ground
from Carrollborough toward the Ferry Road, the level and
extensive ground from there to the bank of the Potomack as far
as Goose Creek present a situation most advantageous to run
streets and prolong them on grand and far distant point of
view the water running from spring at some distance into the
creeks, appeared also to me possible to be conducted without
much labour so as to form pounds for watering every part of
that spot. The remainder part of the ground toward Georgetown is more broken — it may afford pleasant seats, but altho'

the bank of the river between the two creeks can command as grand a prospect as any of the other spots it seems to be less commendable for the establishment of a city not only because the level surface it presents is but small but because the heights from behind Georgetown absolutely command the whole.

No proof of the ground between the eastern branch and Georgetown can be say to be of a commanding nature, on the contrary it appear at first sight as being itself surrounded, however in advancing toward the eastern branch these heights seem to sink as the waves of a tempestuous sea and when considering the intended city on that grand scale on which it ought to be planned, it will appear that the only height which would unavoidably.

In it a small town may easily be comprehended in the limit of such a one as is rendered by a proper management in the appropriation of the building that may be thereon erected, a means of protection and of security.

Such the few remarks which I have been able to make in a journey when the badness of the weather much impeded my progress. I therefore hope for your indulgence in hazarding to communicate them to you. I have the honor to be,

 Sir, With very great respect,

P. C. L'ENFANT.

THE HONORABLE THOMAS JEFFERSON,
 Secretary of State.

[P. 150, COLUMBIA HISTORICAL SOCIETY, *Records*, Vol. 2; pp. 149–50, U.S. v. SMITH.]

JEFFERSON OPINION

Opinion relative to locating the Ten Mile Square for the Federal Government, and building the Federal City.

March 11, 1791.

Objects which may merit the attention of the President, at Georgetown.

The commissioners to be called into action.

Deeds of cession to be taken from the land-holders.

Site of the capitol and President's house to be determined on.

Proclamation completing the location of the territory, and fixing the site of the capitol.

Town to be laid off. Squares of reserve are to be decided on for the capitol, President's house, offices of government, town-house, prison, market, and public walks.

Other squares for present sale designated.

Terms of sale to be settled. As there is not as yet a town legislature, and things may be done before there is one to prevent them, which yet it would be desirable to prevent, it would seem justifiable and expedient that the President should form a capitulary of such regulations as he may think necessary to be observed, until there shall be a town legislature to undertake this office; such capitulary to be indented, signed, sealed, and recorded, according to the laws of conveyance in Maryland. And to be referred to in every deed for conveyance of the lots to purchasers, so as to make a part thereof. The same thing might be effected, by inserting special covenants for every regulation in every deed; but the former method is the shortest. I cannot help again suggesting here one regulation formerly suggested, to wit: To provide for the extinguishment of fires, and the openness and convenience of the town, by prohibiting houses of excessive height. And making it unlawful to build on any one's purchase any house with more than two floors between the common level of the earth and the eaves, nor with any other floor in the roof than one at the eaves. To consider in what way the contracts for the public buildings shall be made, and whether as many bricks should not be made this summer as may employ brick-layers in the beginning of the season of 1792, till more can be made in that season.

With respect to the amendment of the location so as to include Bladensburgh, I am of opinion it may be done with the consent of the legislature of Maryland, and that that consent may be so far counted on, as to render it expedient to declare the location at once.

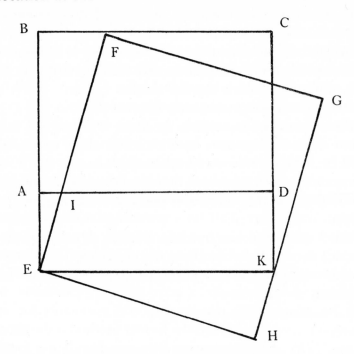

The location A B C D A having been once made, I consider as obligatory and unalterable, but by consent of parties, except so far as was necessary to render it practicable by a correction of the beginning. That correction might be lawfully made either by stopping at the river, or at the spring of Hunting creek, or by lengthening the course from the court-house so that the second course should strike the mouth of Hunting creek. I am of opinion, therefore, that the beginning at the mouth of Hunting creek, is legally justifiable. But I would advise the location E F G H E to be hazarded so as to include Bladensburgh, because it is a better location, and I think will certainly be confirmed by Maryland. That State will necessarily have to pass another act confirming whatever location shall be made, because her former act authorized the delegates *then* in office, to convey the lands. But as they were not located, no conveyance has been made, and those persons are now out of office, and dispersed. Suppose the non-concurrence of Maryland should defeat the location E F G H E, it can only be done on this principle, that the first location A B C D A was valid, and unalterable, but by mutual consent. Then their non-concurrence will re-establish the first location A B C D A, and the second location will be good for the part E I D K E without their concurrence, and this will place us where we should be were we now to complete the location E B C K E. Consequently, the experiment of an amendment proposed can lose nothing, and may gain, and probably will gain, the better location.

When I say it can lose nothing, I count as nothing, the triangle A I E, which would be in neither of the locations. Perhaps this might be taken in afterwards, either with or without the consent of Virginia.

[Pp. 561–3, WRITINGS, Washington ed., VIII.]

WASHINGTON TO JEFFERSON

[*March* 16, 1791.][11a]

WASHINGTON TO JEFFERSON

My dear Sir: Enclosed is the last letter I have received from Messrs. Deakins and Stoddart. What step had I best take to bring matters to a close with Burn's, and by declaring at *once* the Site of the public buildings, prevent some inconvenience which I see may arise from the opinions promulgated by Mr. L'Enfont? as much probably from complaisance as judgment. Yrs.

[P. 244, WRITINGS OF WASHINGTON, Fitzpatrick, Vol. 31.]

[11a] Date received, according to the *Jefferson Papers* in the Library of Congress, Vol. 62, p. 16712.

JEFFERSON TO L'ENFANT

Philadelphia march 17. 1791.

TO MAJOR L'ENFANT

Sir

Your favor of the 11th instant has been duly received: between the date of that and your receipt of the present, it is probable that the most important parts of the ground towards the eastern branch will have been delineated. However, whether they are or not, as the President will go on within two or three days, and would wish to have under his eye, when at Georgetown, a drawing also of the principal lineaments of the ground between Rock Creek and the Tyber, you are desired, immediately on the receipt of this, to commence the survey of that part, beginning at the River, and proceeding towards the parts back of that till his arrival. If the meanders of these two creeks and of the river between them should not have been already laid down either by yourself or mr. Ellicott, it is desired that mr. Ellicott should immediately do this while you shall be employed on the interior ground, in order that the work may be as much advanced as possible on the arrival of the President, and that you will be so good as to notify this to mr. Ellicott. I am with great esteem Sir &c.

TH: JEFFERSON.

P. S. — There are certainly considerable advantages on the Eastern branch: but there are very strong reasons also in favor of the position between Rock creek and Tyber independent of the face of the ground. It is the desire that the public mind should be in equilibrio between these two places till the President arrives, and we shall be obliged to you to endeavor to poise their expectations.

[Ms., p. 216, *American Letters*, Vol. IV, 1788–92, State Department Archives in the National Archives; pp. 148–9, U.S. *v.* SMITH; p. 40, Columbia Historical Society, Records, Vol. 35–6.]

JEFFERSON DRAFT

Mar. 30. 1791.

By the President of the U. S. of A.   *a Proclamation.*

Whereas by a proclamñ bearing date the 24.th day of Jan. of
this present year, & in pursuance of certain acts of the states of
Maryland & Virginia, & of the Congress of the U.S. therein
mentioned, certain lines of experiment were directed to be run
in the neighborhood of Georgetown in Maryland for the purpose of determining the location of a part of the territory of 10.
miles square for the permanent seat of the government of the
U.S. & a certain part was directed to be located within the
said lines of experiment on both sides of the Potomac & above
the limit of the Eastern branch prescribed by the s^d act of Congress:

And Congress by an amendatory act, passed on the 3^d day of
this present month of March, have given further authority to
the President of the U.S. 'to make any part of the territory below the s^d limit & above the mouth of Hunting creek, a part of
the s^d district, so as to include a convenient part of the Eastern
branch, & of the lands lying on the lower side thereof, & also
the town of Alexandria.'

Now therefore, for the purpose of amending & completing
the location of the whole of the s^d territory of ten miles square,
in conformity with the s^d amendatory act of Congress, I do
hereby declare & make known that the whole of the s^d territory
shall be located & included within the four lines following, that
is to say:

Beginning at Jones's point, being the upper cape of Hunting
creek in Virginia, & at an angle, in the outset, of 45 degrees
West of the North; & running in a direct line ten miles for the
first line: then beginning again at the same Jones's point, &
running another direct line, at a right angle with the first,
across the Potomac, ten miles for the second line: then from the

terminations of the s^d first & second lines, running two other direct lines, of ten miles each, the one crossing the Eastern branch afores^d, & the other the Potomac, & meeting each other in a point.

And I do accordingly direct the Commissioners named under the authority of the s^d first mentioned act of Congress to proceed forthwith to have the s^d four lines run, & by proper metes & bounds defined & limited, & thereof to make due report under their hands & seals: and the territory so to be located, defined & limited, shall be the whole territory accepted by the s^d acts of Congress as the district for the permanent seat of the government of the U.S.

~~And WHEREAS the s^d first mentioned act of Congress did further enact that the s^d Commissioners should, under the direction of the President of the U.S. provide suitable buildings for the accomodation of Congress & of the President & for the public offices of the government of the United States; I do hereby further declare & make known that * [the highest summit of lands in the town heretofore called Hamburg, within the s^d territory, with a convenient extent of grounds circumjacent, shall be appropriated for a Capitol for the accommodation of Congress, & such other lands between Georgetown & the stream heretofore called the Tyber, as shall on due examination be found convenient & sufficient, shall be appropriated for the accomodation of the President of the U.S. for the time being, & for the public offices of the government of the U.S.] And I do hereby direct the s^d Commissioners accordingly.~~

In testimony whereof I have caused the seal of the U.S. to be affixed to these presents, & signed the same with my hand. Done at Georgetown aforesaid the 30th day of March in the year of our lord 1791. & of the Independance of the U.S. the fifteenth.

~~* the part within [ ] being conjectural, will be to be rendered conformable to the ground when more accurately examined.~~

[Ms., *Records of the Department of State, Miscellaneous Letters*, January–March 1791, in the National Archives.]

WASHINGTON TO JEFFERSON

Mount Vernon, March 31st, 1791.

TO THOMAS JEFFERSON

Dear Sir,

Having been so fortunate as to reconcile the contending interests of Georgetown and Carrollsburg, and to unite them in such an agreement as permits the public purposes to be carried into effect on an extensive and proper scale, I have the pleasure to transmit to you the enclosed proclamation, which, after annexing your counter signature, and the seal of the United States, you will cause to be published.

The terms agreed on between me, on the part of the United States, and the Landholders of Georgetown and Carrollsburg are That all the land from Rock-creek along the river to the eastern-branch and so upwards to or above the ferry including a breadth of about a mile and a half, the whole containing from three to five thousand acres, is ceded to the public, on condition that, when the whole shall be surveyed and laid off as a city, (which Major L'Enfant is now directed to do) the present Proprietors shall retain every other lot, and for such part of the land as may be taken for public use, for squares, walks, &c they shall be allowed at the rate of Twenty five pounds per acre. The Public having the right to reserve such parts of the wood on the land as may be thought necessary to be preserved for ornament &ca. The Landholders to have the use and profits of all their ground until the city is laid off into lots, and sale is made of those lots which, by the agreement, become public property. No compensation is to be made for the ground that may be occupied as streets or alleys.

To these conditions all the principal Landholders, except the purchaser of Slater's property who did not attend have subscribed, and it is not doubted that the few, who were not present, will readily assent thereto — even the obstinate Mr. Burns has come into the measure.

The enlarged plan of this agreement having done away the necessity, and indeed postponed the propriety, of designating the particular spot, on which the public buildings should be placed, until an accurate survey and subdivision of the whole ground is made, I have left out that paragraph of the proclamation.

It was found, on running the lines, that the comprehension of Bladensburg within the district, must have occasioned the exclusion of more important objects, and of this I am convinced as well by my own observation as Mr. Ellicott's opinion.

With great regard and esteem, I am, dear Sir,
     your most obedient servant,

                                        Go. WASHINGTON.

THOMAS JEFFERSON, ESQUIRE,
     Secretary of State

[Pp. 256–8, WRITINGS OF WASHINGTON, Fitzpatrick, Vol. 31; pp. 155–6, U.S. *v.* SMITH.]

WASHINGTON TO DEAKINS AND STODDERT

WASHINGTON TO WILLIAM DEAKINS, JUNIOR, AND
BENJAMIN STODDERT

                                Mount Vernon, April 1, 1791.

The Mail of Wednesday brought me a letter from Mr. Jefferson dated the 27th.[12] Ulto. in which is the following paragraph.

A bill was yesterday ordered to be brought into the house of representatives here [13] for granting a sum of money for building a federal-hall, house for the President &ca.

This (though I do not wish that it should be expressed as my sentiment) unfolds most evidently the views of P—,[14] at the

[12] *Jefferson's letter* of Mar. 27, 1791 to Washington is in WRITINGS edited by Washington, pp. 230–2, III.
[13] House of Representatives of Pennsylvania.   [14] Pennsylvania.

sametime that it proves in a striking manner the propriety of the measure adopted by the George town and Carrollsburgh proprietors on wednesday last; as also the necessity of their *compleating* the good work they have begun in a speedy, and in an effectual manner that the consequent arrangements may take place without delay. With esteem and regard I am etc.

[Pp. 262–3, WRITINGS OF WASHINGTON, Fitzpatrick, Vol. 31.]

L'ENFANT TO JEFFERSON

jeorgetown april the 4th. 1791

Sir.

I would have reproched myself for not having writen to you as regularly as you had desired I should were it not for circumstances, to which you will I doubt not attribut this seeming neglect in approving of the considerations which made me give the whole of my time to forwards as much as possibly could be the business I had to performe, Great as were my Endeavour to that end it [Steel] remained unfinished at the moment of the President arrival at this place were I could present him no more but a rough drawing in pincel of the several Surveys which I had been able to run — nevertheless the President Indulgent disposition making him account for the difficulties encountered, I had the satisfaction to see the little I had done agreable to his wish — and the confidence with which he has been pleased since to Honor me in ordering the Survey to be continued and the deliniation of a grand plan for the local distribution of the City to be done on principle conformable to the ideas which I took the liberty to hold before him at the proper for the Establishment being to heigly flatering to my Embition to Fail Exacting the best of my hability. it shall be from this moment my Endeavour to Enswer the President Expectation in preparing those plans and having them ready for the time of his return from the Southern tour.

I shall in the mean while, Sir, beg for every information respecting all what may in your jugement appear of most immediate importance to attend to as well as relating to Every desirable Establishment which it will be well to forsee although delaying or perhaps leaving the Execution thereof to a natural succession of time to Effect.

the number and nature of the publick building with the necessary appendix I should be glad to have a statement of as speedily as possible — and I would be very much obliged to you in the meantime if you could procure for me what Ever may fall within your reach — of any of the different grand city now existing such as for example — as London — madry [Madrid] — paris — Amsterdam — naples — venice — genoa — florence together with particular maps of any such sea ports or dock yards and arsenals as you may know to be the most compleat in their Improvement for notwithstanding I would reprobate the Idea of Imitating and that contrary of Having this Intention it is my wish and shall be my Endeavour to delinate on a new and original way the plan the contrivance of which the President has left to me without any restriction soever — yet the contemplation of what exist of well improved situation, iven the parrallel of these, with deffactive ones, may serve to suggest avariety of new Ideas and is necessary to refine and strengthen the Jugement particularly in the present instance when having to unite the usfull with the comodious & agreable viewing these will by offering means for comparing enable me the better to determine with a certainty the propriety of a local which offer an Extansive field for combinations.

I have the Honor to be with great respect
your most humble and most obedient servant

P. C. L'Enfant.

MR JEFFERSON *Secretary of State.*

L'ENFANT rec^d Apr. 9.

[P. 158 U.S. *v.* SMITH; pp. 4–5 n, *Columbia Historical Society*, Records, Vol. 33.]

DANIEL CARROLL TO JEFFERSON

George Town Ap.ˣ 6.ᵗʰ 1791

Sir,

The inclosed for Mˣ Madison is open for yˣ perusal & information.

The prospect before us respecting the great object of the Seat of Govᵗ is pleasing at present here. — I shall have occasion probably at times to comunicate to you what may occur, & shall embrace every occasion of assuring you that I am,

Sˣ with very great regard & esteem,

Yˣ respectful & obᵗ Servᵗ

DANᴸ CARROLL

P. S. — I expect we shall in a few days proceed to take proper deeds.

[Ms., *Jefferson Papers*, Library of Congress.]

JEFFERSON TO L'ENFANT

Philadelphia April 10. 1791.

TO MAJOR L'ENFANT

Sir

I am favored with your letter of the 4 instant, and in complyance with your request I have examined my papers and found the plans of Frankfort on the Mayne, Carlsruhe, Amsterdam, Strasburg, Paris, Orleans, Bordeaux, Lyons, Montpelier, Marseilles, Turin, and Milan, which I send in a roll by this Post. They are on large and accurate scales, having been procured by me while in those respective cities myself. As they are connected with the notes I made in my travels, and often necessary to explain them to myself, I will beg your care of them and to return them when no longer useful to you, leaving you absolutely free to keep them as long as useful. I am happy that the President has left the planning of the Town in such good hands, and have no doubt it will be done to general satisfaction. Considering that the grounds to be reserved for the public, are to be paid for by the acre, I think very liberal reservations should be made for them; and if this be about the Tyber and on the back of the town, it will be of no injury to the commerce of the place, which will undoubtedly establish itself on the deep waters towards the Eastern branch and mouth of Rock Creek; the water about the mouth of the Tyber not being of any depth. Those connected with the Government will prefer fixing themselves near the public grounds, in the center, which will also be convenient to be resorted to as walks from the lower and upper town. Having communicated to the President, before he went away, such general ideas on the subject of the Town, as occurred to me, I make no doubt that, in explaining himself to you on the subject, he has interwoven with his own ideas, such of mine as he approved: for fear of repeating therefore, what he did not approve, and having more confidence in the unbiassed state of his mind, than in my own, I avoid interfering with what he may have expressed to you. Whenever it is proposed to prepare plans for the Capitol, I should prefer the adoption of some one of the models of antiquity, which have had the approbation of thousands of years, and for the President's House I should prefer the celebrated fronts of modern buildings, which have already received the approbation of all good judges. Such are the Galerie du Louvre, the Gardes meubles, and two fronts of the Hotel de Salm. But of this it is yet time enough to consider, in the mean time I am with great esteem Sir &c.

TH: JEFFERSON.

[Pp. 236-7, WRITINGS OF JEFFERSON, Washington, Vol. III; pp. 159-160, U.S. v. SMITH.]

JEFFERSON TO WASHINGTON

Philadelphia Apr. 10. 1791.

Sir

The acquisition of ground at Georgetown is really noble. considering that only £25. an acre is to be paid for any grounds taken for the public, and the streets not to be counted, which will in fact reduce it to about £19. an acre. I think very liberal reserves should be made for the public. your proclamation came to hand the night of the 5th Dunlap's & Bache's papers for the morning of the 6th being already filled, I could only get it into Brown's evening paper of the 6th on the 7th the bill for the federal buildings passed the representatives here by 42. to 10. but it was rejected yesterday by 9. to 6. in the Senate, or to speak more exactly, it was postponed till the next session. in the meantime spirited proceedings at Georgetown will probably, under the continuance of your patronage, prevent the revival of the bill. I received last night from Majr L'Enfant a request to furnish him any plans of towns I could, for his examination. I accordingly send him, by this post, plans of Frankfort on the Mayne, Carlsruhe, Amsterdam, Strasburg, Paris, Orleans, Bordeaux, Lyons, Montpelier, Marseilles, Turin and Milan, on large & accurate scales, which I procured while in those towns respectively. they are none of them however comparable to the old Babylon, revived in Philadelphia, & exemplified. while in Europe I selected about a dozen or two of the handsomest fronts of private buildings of which I have the plates. perhaps it might decide the taste of the new town, were these to be engraved here, and distributed gratis among the inhabitants of Georgetown. the expence would be trifling.

I inclose you extracts from a letter of mr Short's of Jan. 24. one of Jan. 28. has since come to hand, containing nothing but a translation of the letter said to have been written by the emperor to the king of France, but which he suspects to be a forg-

The first Department Building in the National Capital, at 15th Street and Pennsylvania Avenue, comprising 30 rooms with 137 clerks. Occupied 1800. (Old Treasury site, 15th Street at New York Avenue.)

The buildings known for many years as the "Six Buildings," on Pennsylvania Avenue between 21st and 22d Streets NW., approximately as they appeared during Jefferson's administration. A seventh structure had been added by the time this picture was taken.

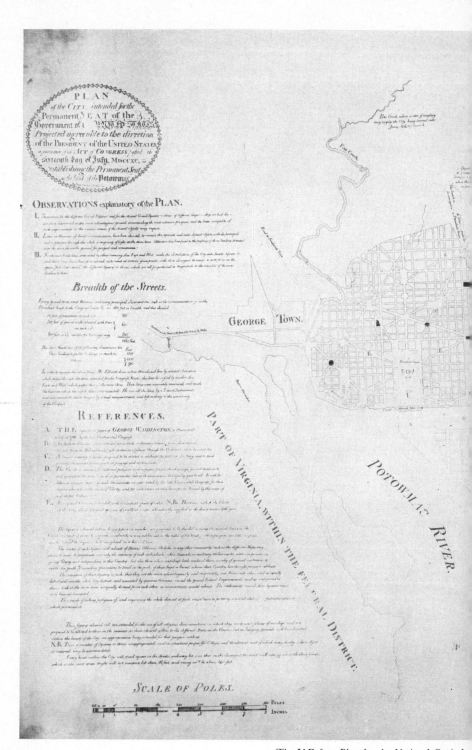

The L'Enfant Plan for the National Capital,

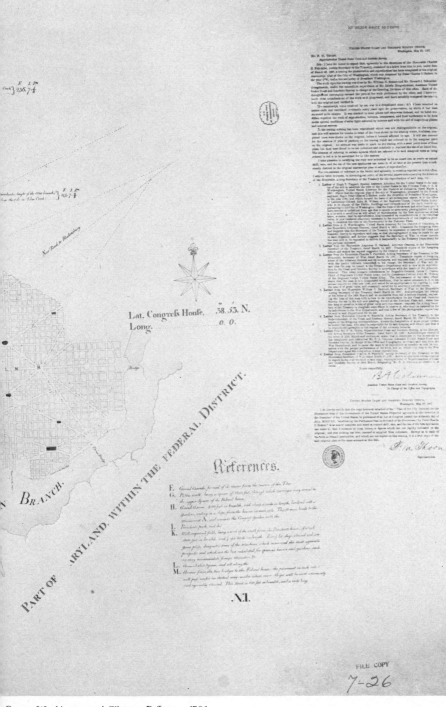

George Washington and Thomas Jefferson, 1791.

The Octagon House.   Built about 1800, at 18th Street and New York Avenue NW.

The "Seven Buildings," at 19th Street and Pennsylvania Avenue NW.   The corner building was used as executive and department offices.   In Jefferson's day—the State Department.

ery, a forged bull of the pope having lately appeared in the same way. he says very serious differences have arisen between the minister of Prussia at Liege, and the Imperial commanding officer there.

I also inclose the debates of the Pennsylvania assembly on the bill for the federal buildings, and the bill itself; and have the honor to be with sentiments of the most perfect respect & attachment

> Sir
>
> > Your most obedient
> > & most humble serv^t
>
> > > > TH: JEFFERSON

THE PRESIDENT OF THE U.S.

[Ms., *Records of the Department of State, Miscellaneous Letters*, April–July 1791 in the National Archives; pp. 237–8, WRITINGS OF JEFFERSON, Washington, III; pp. 160–2, U.S. *v.* SMITH.]

L'ENFANT TO JEFFERSON

> *Georgetown, May the* 10th 1791.

L'ENFANT TO JEFFERSON

Sir:

On the 17th the change of the weather at last having permitted me to proceed to the Eastern branch I did on the afternoon of that day sat about the survey, but the variety of the weather has been such since as has much impeded my progress; I have only been able, to this day, to lay down of that part which lay between eastern branch and the tiber so much as includes Jenkins Hill & all the water course from round Carroll point up to the ferry landing leaving for a better time some swampy parts which were rendered absolutely impassable by the heavy rain which overflowing all the low ground deter-

mined me to confine myself on the heigh land — I expected to
have before this day attempted to lay down some part of those
laying between the tyber and Rock creek had not a fall of snow
and stormy wind which succeeded for these three days past
prevented me — I hope to morrow will prove more favorable
for me to proceed laying down those post which you prescribe
in the letter which I this moment receive from Mr. Ellicott
who brought it himself to me & shall according to your direction join his endeavor to mine in running as much as possible
of the water course as may serve connect the whole of our different surveys together.

    I have the honor to be, with great respect,

        your most humble

            and most obedient servant,

                    P. C. L'ENFANT.

THE HONABLE TH. JEFFERSON,

               Secretary of State.

[P. 2191, U.S. *v.* MORRIS, Records, Vol. VII.]

DANIEL CARROLL TO JEFFERSON

                       George Town July 29th 1791

Dear Sir,

    This will be deliverd by M.r Cabot, a Gentleman of Massa-
chusetts lately setteld in this place. He has expressd a desire of
being acquainted with you. The character he bears, together
with his respectable connections induce me readily to obtain
for him that pleasure. I believe he has been mentioned in
some letters to the President from the East. You will find him
a sensible, intelligent Gentl.n As he has enterd on business
among us, he is desirous of embracing anything which may
suit, with a prospect of advantage, in the transactions respect-

ing the public buildings & federal city. He has been in treaty with the Directors of the Potomack C? ab! supplying a number of his Countrymen for the purpose of makeing the Canal at the Little falls; they did not agree. He intends to Ph.ª with Major L'Enfant; I suppose many matters will be talk'd over respecting the business on hand. Permit me to take the liberty of requesting you, if it should fall in yʳ way, to assist Mʳ Cabot in his views, on those appearing to coincide with the public interest.

It is with pleasure, I take this occasion, of assuring you that I am Dear Sir, with great esteem, & respect,

Yʳ obᵗ & Hᵇˡᵉ Servᵗ

DANL CARROLL

[Ms., *Jefferson Papers*, Library of Congress.]

JEFFERSON TO L'ENFANT

Philadelphia, August 18, 1791.

TO MAJOR L'ENFANT

Sir

The President had understood for some time past that you were coming on to Philadelphia and New York, and therefore has delayed mentioning to you some matters which have occurred to him. Will you be so good as to inform me by return of post whether it is still your purpose to come this way, and when, that the President may thereon decide whether he will communicate his ideas by letter, or await your coming to do it by word? If you are detained by laying out the lots, you had better not await that, as a suggestion has been made here of arranging them in a particular manner, which will probably make them more convenient to the purchasers, and more profitable to the sellers. A person applied to me the other day on the subject of engraving a map of the federal territory. I observed to him that if yourself or Mr. Ellicott chose to have this done, you would have the best right to it — do either of you intend this? If you do I would suggest to you the idea of doing it on a square sheet to hang corner upwards, thus the outlines being N.W. N.E. S.E. & S.W. the meridian will be vertical as they ought to be; the streets of the city will be horizontal and vertical, and near the center, the Potomac and Eastern branch will be nearly so also; there will be no waste in the square sheet of paper. This is suggested merely for your consideration. I am with much esteem Sir &c.

TH: JEFFERSON.

[Ms., p. 278, AMERICAN LETTERS, Vol. IV, 1788–92, State Department Archives in the National Archives; p. 174, U.S. *v.* SMITH.]

JEFFERSON TO HARWOOD

TO Mʳ HARWOOD.   TREASURER OF MARYLAND

Philadelphia August 22. 1791

Sir

The Commissioners for the public buildings at Georgetown inform the President that they are in want of a sum of money for the objects of their appointment, and that they suppose you will accept his draught for the first instalment of the money granted by the State of Maryland. The President being unwilling to make any draught but on a certainty of its acceptance, I am to ask the favor of your information whether, from the circumstances of the funds, you find yourself in a condition to accept his draught for the first instalment or for any, & what, smaller sum. I have the honor to be &c

TH: JEFFERSON

[Ms., p. 279, *American Letters*, Vol. IV, 1788–92, State Department Archives in the National Archives.]

JEFFERSON TO COMMISSIONERS

TO THOMAS JOHNSON, DAVID STUART, & DANIEL CARROLL ESQRS.

Philadelphia August 28. 1791.

Gentlemen

Your joint letter of the 2. instant to the President, as also Mr. Carroll's separate letters of the 5. and 15. have been duly received. Major L'Enfant also having arrived here and laid his plan of the federal city before the President, he was pleased to desire a conference of certain persons, in his presence, on these several subjects. It is the opinion of the President, in consequence thereof, that an immediate meeting of the Commissioners at Georgetown is requisite, that certain measures may be decided on and put into a course of preparation for a commencement of sale on the 17. of October as advertised. As Mr. Madison and myself, who were present at the conferences, propose to pass through Georgetown on our way to Virginia, the President supposes that our attendance at the meeting of the Commissioners might be of service to them, as we could communicate to them the sentiments developed at the conferences here and approved by the President, under whatever point of view they may have occasion to know them. The circumstances of time and distance oblige me to take the liberty of proposing the day of meeting and to say that we will be in Georgetown on the evening of the 7. or morning of the 8. of the next month, in time to attend any meeting of the Commissioners on that day, and in hopes they may be able in the course of it to make all the use of us they make think proper, so that we may pursue our journey the next day. To that meeting therefore the answers to the several letters before mentioned are referred.

The letter is addressed externally to Mr. Carroll only with a requisition to the post master at Georgetown to send it to him by express, under the hope that he will by expresses to the other

Gentlemen take timely measures for the proposed meeting on the 8. I have the honor to be with sentiments of the highest respect and esteem Gentlemen &c.

TH: JEFFERSON

[Ms., p. 281, *American Letters*, Vol. IV, 1788–92, State Department Archives in the National Archives; p. 181, U.S. *v.* SMITH.]

DANIEL CARROLL TO JEFFERSON

rec^d Aug. 29. [1791]

I wrote lately a few lines to Mr Madison directed to him in Ph^a — By which he wrote me from N York I presume he may be there — if not will you be so obligeing as to take Charge of that Letter? I refer you to what I have written him.

Y^r &^{c}

D. C.

Should you pass by George Town on y^r way to N. Y^k permit me to request you if not inconvenient to bring a few of the plans of Chataus you show'd, which shall be returned on y^r way back to Ph^a & Care taken of them.

Y^r D. C.

[Ms., *Jefferson Papers*, Library of Congress.]

WASHINGTON TO JEFFERSON

Monday Morning, August 29, 1791.

Dear Sir: The enclosed for Mr. Young, I pray you to put under cover to Mr. Johnson, the other for Mr. Vaughan may go in like manner, or otherwise, as you may think best; both however by the Packet.

The letter for Mr. Carroll [15] I also return, besides which,

---

[15] Daniel Carroll.

were you to write a line or two to Mr. Johnson, addressed to the care of the Postmaster in Baltimore, *it might be* a mean of giving him earlier notice of the intended meeting. The Plan of Carrollsburgh sent me by D—— Carroll [15] it will be necessary for you to take along with you. To settle something with respect to *that* place and Hambg. which will not interfere with the genl. Plan is difficult, but essential. There are other Papers also which it may be useful for you to have. Mode of improving, regulations, &ca. &ca. will be subjects to occupy your thoughts upon. I am, etc.

[P. 349, WRITINGS OF WASHINGTON, Fitzpatrick, Vol. 31.]

WASHINGTON TO JEFFERSON

WASHINGTON TO JEFFERSON

[*August* 29, 1791]

Will circumstances render a postponement of the Sale of Lots in the Federal City advisable? If not

2. Where ought they to be made.

Will it in that case, or even without it, be necessary or prudent to attempt to borrow money to carry on the difft. works in the City?

Whether ought the building of a bridge over the Eastern branch to be attempted; the Canal set about; and Mr. Peter's proposition with respect to wharves gone into *now*, or postponed until our funds are better ascertained and become productive?

At what time can the several Proprietors claim, with propriety, payment for the public squares wch. is marked upon their respective tracts?

Ought there to be any wood houses in the town?

7. What sort of Brick or Stone Houses should be built; and of wh[a]t height; especially on the principal Streets or Avenues?

When ought the public buildings to be begun, and in what manner had the materials best be provided?

How ought they to be promulgated, so as to draw plans from skilful Architects? and what would be the best mode of carrying on the Work?

Ought not Stoups, and projections of every sort and kind into the Streets, to be prohibited *absolutely?*

11. What compromise can be made with the Lot holders in Hamburgh and Carrollsburgh by which the plan of the Federal City may be preserved?

Ought not the several Land holders to be called upon to ascertain their respective bounderies previous to the Sale of Lots?

13. Would it not be advisable to have the Federal district as laid out (comprehending the plan of the Town) engraved in one piece?

[Pp. 351–2, WRITINGS OF WASHINGTON, Fitzpatrick, Vol. 31.]

JEFFERSON TO WASHINGTON

September 8, 1791.

JEFFERSON TO WASHINGTON

We were detained on the road by the rains so that we did not arrive here till yesterday about ten o'clock; as soon as horses could be got ready we set out and rode till dark, examining chiefly the grounds newly laid open, which we found much superior to what we had imagined, — we have passed this day in consultation with the Commissioners, who having deliberated on every article contained in our paper and preadmonished that they should decide freely on their own view of things, concurred unanimously on, I believe every point with what had been thought best in Philadelphia.

[P. 120, HISTORY OF WASHINGTON, Tindall.]

JEFFERSON NOTE

Sept. 8, 1791 (or *Sept* 9)

[*Jefferson's notes on the meeting between Wm. Deakins, Benjamin Stoddert, Charles Carroll, Mr. Madison and himself at Georgetown on Sept. 8, 1791*]

In conversation with Mr. Carroll, Mr. Stoddert and Mr. Deakins they were properly impressed with the idea that if the present occasion of securing the Federal seat on the Potowmack should be lost, it could never more be regained, that it would dangerous to rely on any aids from Congress, or the Assemblies of Virginia or Maryland, and that therefore measures should be adopted to carry the Residence Bill into execution without recourse to those bodies; and that the requisites were 1st land enough to place the public buildings on; and 2ndly money enough to build them, and to erect moreover about 20 good dwelling houses for such persons belonging to the Government as must have houses to themselves, about as many good lodging houses, and half a dozen taverns.

To obtain this sum, this expedient was suggested to them. To procure a declaration from the proprietors of those spots of land most likely to be fixed for the town, that if the President's location of the town should comprehend their lands, they would give them up for the use of the U.S. on condition they should receive the double of their value, estimated as they would have been had there been no thought of bringing the federal seat into their neighborhood. It was supposed that 1500 acres would be required in the while, to-wit, about 300 acres for public buildings, walks, etc., and 1200 acres to be divided into quarter acre lots, which, due allowance being made for streets, would make about 2000 lots, the vacant lots in Georgetown now sell at £200, those of Alexandria at £600. Suppose those of the new town should bring only £100 clear this would produce £200,000, a sum adequate to the objects before mentioned. It was further supposed that the Assembly of Maryland would interpose to force the consent of infant or obstinate proprietors for a reasonable compensation.

It was also suggested as a more certain means of ensuring the object, that each proprietor within the whole ten miles square should cede one-half his lands to the public, to be sold to raise money; perhaps this would be pushing them too far for the reputation of the new government they were to come under, and further than is necessary when we consider the sum which may be raised by the sale of lots, the donation of 120,000 dollars by Virginia, and the possible donation of an equal sum by Maryland; at least it might show a commendable moderation not to push this proposition until experiment should prove the other resources inadequate; great zeal appeared in the gentlemen before mentioned, and they seemed to approve the proposition for the 1500 acres; that for a moiety of all the lands within the ten miles square was hazarded only to Mr. Carroll; they will probably proceed immediately to make the best arrangements practicable and to come forward with them to the President.

[Pp. 41–2, HISTORY OF WASHINGTON, Tindall.]

NOTES ON COMMISSIONERS' MEETING

Thursday 8th *Sept.* 1791.

At a meeting of the Commissioners at Georgetown on Thursday the eighth day of September, 1791, and continued by adjournment till Friday, the 9th, present Thomas Johnson, David Stuart and Daniel Carroll, Esquires. The Hon. Thomas Jefferson, Secretary of State, and the Hon. James Madison attended the Commissioners in conference, (see Mr. Jefferson's letter of the 28th August last).

The following queres were presented by the Secretary of State to the Commissioners and the answers thereto with the resolutions following were given and adopted:

Will circumstances render a postponement of the sales of lots in
the Federal City advisable? If
not
Where ought they to be made?

Not advisable.

Left to be considered ultimately on
the spot, the general opinion being only that the leading interests be accomodated.

Will it in that case, or even without
it, be necessary or prudent to attempt to borrow money to carry
on the different works in the city?

Doubtful if a loan can be proposed
without previous legislative authority, or filled till a sale shall
have settled something like the
value of the lots which are to secure repayment.

The ready money payments increased to one-fourth.

Whether ought the building of a
bridge over the Eastern Branch
to be attempted — the canal set
about, and Mr. Peter's proposition with respect to wharves gone
into *now* or postponed until our
funds are better ascertained and
become productive?

Must wait for money. The property of reclaimed lands considered of —

At what time can the several proprietors claim with propriety payment for the public squares which
are marked upon their respective
tracts?

Whenever the money shall have
been raised by the sale of their
own lands.

Ought there to be any wood houses
in the town.

No.

What sort of brick or stone should
be built, and of what height, especially on the principal streets
or avenues?

Liberty as to advancing or withdrawing the front, but some limits as to height would be advisable.

"No house wall higher than 35 feet in any part of the town."
"None lower than that on any of the avenues."

When ought the public buildings to
be begun, and in what manner
had the materials best be provided?

The digging the earth for brick this
fall is indispensable, provisions of
other materials to depend on the
funds.

How ought they to be promulgated so as to draw plans from skilful architects, and what would be the best mode of carrying on the work?	By advertisement of a medal or other reward for the best plan — see a sketch or specimen of advertisement.
Ought not stoups and projections of every kind into the streets be prohibited *absolutely?*	No incroachments to be permitted.
What compromise can be made to the lot holders in Hamburgh and Carrollsburgh by which the plan of the Federal City may be preserved?	A liberal compromise will be better than discontents or disputed titles.
Ought not the several land holders be called upon to ascertain their respective boundaries previous to the sale of lots?	Certainly they ought.
Would it not be advisable to have the Federal District as laid out comprehending the plan of the town, engraved in one piece?	It would.
Names of streets, alphabetically one way and numerically the other, the former to be divided into north and south letters, the latter east and west numbers from the Capitol.	To be done but whether by the Commissioners or artist, to be considered of.

Lots with springs on them to be appropriated to the public if practicable, without too much discontent, and the springs not to be sold again.

The public squares to be left blank except that for the Capitol and the other for the executive Department, which are to be considered as appropriated at present, all other particular appropriations of squares to remain till they are respectively wanted.

Soundings of Eastern Branch.
Post road through the City.

Name of the City and Territory — City of Washington & Territory of Columbia.

Meeting of President and Commissioners on afternoon of October 16.

The Geographer General, Mr. Andrew Ellicot presented to the Commissioners the following observations respecting the sale of lots on the 17th Oct. next, viz:

In disposing of lots in the Federal City three things appear necessary to attend to: *first*, those situations which will be considerably increased in value when the public improvements are made. *Secondly*, those situations which have an immediate value from other considerations, and *thirdly*, those situations whose real value must depend upon the increase and population of the City.

With respect to the *first* it is presumed that all the lots about the congress house, the President's House, the public gardens and on the street leading from the Congress House to the President's house will be infinitely more valuable when the public improvements are made, and therefore if reserved until that period must considerably increase the funds.

Secondly, it is not probable that the public improvements will considerably affect either the value of the lots from Georgetown to Funks Town or generally on the Eastern Branch: the proximity of the first to a trading town and good navigation, and the *second* lying on one of the best harbours in the country must have an immediate value; and are therefore the most proper places to confine the first sales to.

Thirdly, would it not be proper to dispose of a part of such situations whose value must depend upon the increase and population of the City, in lots of such magnitude as to answer for meadows, pastures or large gardens?

The following advertisement of the sale of lots, viz:

George Town, Sept. 9th, 1791.

The sales of lots in the Federal City will commence on Mon-

day the Seventeenth day of October next. The Commissioners
finding they may engage materials and workmen for the public
buildings to any desirable extent with a view to draw the funds
into action so as to facilitate the work, instead of a deposit of
eight per cent will require one fourth part of the purchase
money to be paid down, the residue to be on bond with security, payable with interest in three equal yearly payments. The
manner of improvement will be published at the sale.

Signed   T. JOHNSON, DD STUART & DANL CARROLL,
                                                                    Commrs.

[Ms., pp. 21–3, *Proceedings of the Commissioners*, Vol. VI, 1800–2, in the National Archives;
pp. 181–3, U.S. *v.* SMITH.]

COMMISSIONERS TO L'ENFANT

George Town, Sept. 9th 1791.

Sir:

We have agreed that the federal District shall be called "The
Territory of Columbia," and the federal City "The City of
Washington": the title of the map will, therefore, be "A Map
of the City of Washington in the Territory of Columbia."

We have also agreed the streets be named alphabetically one
way, and numerically the other; the former divided into North
and South letters, the latter into East and West numbers from
the Capitol. Maj. Ellicott, with proper assistance, will immediately take and soon furnish you with soundings of the Western
(Eastern) Branch to be inserted in the map. We expect he will
also furnish you with the direction of a proposed post road
which we wish to have noticed in the map.

We request you to inquire for L'Brunt, the brickmaker, of
whom you had a memorandum; and, if he is carrying on his
business, it will be well for you to see his bricks before you converse with him on the subject of his removal next Spring; if you

approve his bricks, to inquire whether we could have him and on what terms.

We are, etc.,

THOS. JOHNSON,
D'D STUART,
DAN'L CARROLL.

P. S.: If you have no contrary directions we wish about 10,000 of the maps to be struck on the best terms, and as soon as possible, leaving what number the President pleases subject to his order; one-half the residue to be left in Phila. subject to our order, and the other half transmitted to us. We shall honor your order for the expences.

[P. 188, U.S. *v.* SMITH; p. 70, Records, Columbia Historical Society, Vol. 35–36.]

JEFFERSON TO WASHINGTON

Nov. 6. 1791.

Sir

I have the honour to inclose you a draught of a letter to Governor Pinkney, & to observe that I suppose it to be proper that there should, on fit occasions, be a direct correspondence between the President of the U.S. and the Governors of the states; and that it will probably be grateful to them to recieve from the President answers to the letters they address to him. the correspondence with them on ordinary business may still be kept up by the Secretary of state in his own name.

I inclose also a letter to Maj^r Pinkney with a blank to be filled up when you shall have made up your mind on it. I have conferred with m^r M. on the idea of the Commissioners of the federal town proceeding to make private sales of the lots & he thinks it adviseable. — I cannot but repeat that if the surveyors will begin on the river, laying off the lots from Rock creek to the Eastern branch, and go on, a-breast, in that way from the river towards the back part of the town, they may pass the avenue from the President's house to the Capitol before the Spring, and as soon as they shall have passed it a public sale may take place without injustice to either the Georgetown or Carrolsburg interest. will not the present afford you a proper occasion of assuring the Commissioners that you leave every thing respecting L'Enfant to them? I have the honor to be with the most sincere respect, Sir, your most obed.t humble serv.t

TH: JEFFERSON

THE PRESIDENT OF THE U.S.

[Ms., *Records of the Department of State, Miscellaneous Letters*, November–December 1791 in the National Archives; pp. 297–8, WRITINGS OF JEFFERSON, Washington, III; p. 206, U.S. *v.* SMITH.]

JEFFERSON TO COMMISSIONERS

TO THOMAS JOHNSON, DAVID STUART & DANIEL CARROLL ESQ'S

Philadelphia Novemr. 21. 1791.

Gentlemen

A Mr. Blodget has a scheme in contemplation for purchasing and *building* a whole street in the new City, and any one of them which you may think best. The magnitude of the proposition occasioned it to be little attended to in the beginning; however, great as it is, it is believed by good judges to be practicable: it may not be amiss, therefore, to be ready for it. The street most desirable to be built up at once, we suppose to be the broad one (the avenue) leading from the President's House to the Capitol. To prepare the squares adjoining to that, on both sides, in the first place, can do no harm; because if Mr. Blodget's scheme does not take effect, still it is part of a work done, which was to be done: if his scheme takes effect, you will be in readiness for him, which would be desirable. The President, therefore, desires me to suggest to you the beginning at once on that avenue, and when all the squares on that shall be laid off, they may go on laying of the rest of the Squares between that and the river, from Georgetown to the Eastern Branch, according to an idea he has suggested to you in a letter not long since. This however is but a suggestion for the good of the undertaking, on which you will decide as you think proper.

I have the honor to be Gentlemen &c.

TH: JEFFERSON

[Ms., *Records of the Department of State, Miscellaneous Letters*, November–December 1791, in the National Archives; pp. 300–01, WRITINGS OF JEFFERSON, Washington, III (incompletely published); p. 207, U.S. *v.* SMITH.]

JEFFERSON TO ELLICOTT

TO MR. ANDREW ELLICOTT

Philadelphia Novem'r 21. 1791.

Dear Sir

It is excessively desirable that an extensive sale of lots in Washington, should take place as soon as possible. It has been recommended to the Commissioners to have all the squares adjacent to the avenue from the President's House to the Capitol, on both sides, and from thence to the river, through the whole breadth of the ground between Rock creek and the Eastern branch, first laid off. The object of the present is to ask your *private* opinion of the earliest time at which this portion of the work can be completed? which I will beg the favor of you to communicate to me by letter. In order that the sale may not be delayed by the engraving, it is hoped that by communicating what is executed from time to time, the engraver may nearly keep pace with you.

I am with great esteem, Dear Sir, &c.

TH: JEFFERSON.

[Ms., pp. 306–7, *American Letters*, Vol. IV, 1788–92, State Department Archives in the National Archives; p. 301, WRITINGS OF JEFFERSON, Washington, III; p. 257 Mem. Ed., VIII; p. 195, U.S. *v.* SMITH.]

Commissioners to Washington

Nov. 25.th 1791

COMM'RS TO THE PRESIDENT

Sir/

We are sorry to be under the dissagreeable necessity of mentioning to you an Occurance which must wound your feelings.
On our meeting here today, we were to our great astonishment
informed that, Maj.^r L'Enfant, without any Authority from us,
& without even having submitted to our consideration, has
proceeded to demolish, Mr Carroll's house. Mr Carroll who
had received some letters, from the Maj.^r on the subject, fearing
the consequences obtained an injunction from the Chancellor,
for him to desist; with a summons to Maj.^r L'Enfant to attend
the Court of Chancery in December, to receive his decision on
the subject, but before his return the houses was in part demolished. Tho' this circumstance is sufficiently unfortunate of itself
it is particularly so with respect to the time at which it has happened. We had just sent up a memorial to the Assembly, on
several subjects which we had deemed of importance to the
Federal City. We therefore fear it may produce unfavourable
impressions in the members respecting the several matters
prayed for. Tho' we have taken every step in our power to prevent it. As soon as we met we issued directions to Maj.^r L'Enfant
and the persons acting under him in his absence, to disist till he
received our instructions which might have obtained, what was
proper in the Case, without any disagreeable consequences. As
he cannot pretend to have Acted from any authority from us,
we have been much hurt at insinuations, that he acted by x. . . .
authority from you. Being fully convinced that these were unfounded, we have not hesitated to declare that they were so.
The Maj.^r is at Dumfries, so that we have had no opportunity,
of communicating, with him on the subject or learning his reasons and justifications. anticipating your feelings on this sub-

ject, and fully apprised of the Maj.^{rs} fitness for the work he is employed in, we cannot forbear expressing a hope that the affair may be still so adjusted that we may not Lose his services. Your letter to Mr Stuart which has been laid before us, has given us the greatest satisfaction. We hope as far as good intentions and diligence on our part, can promote the great work, never to be found deficient in either. We shall give immediate notice to Mr Ellicot to lay out squares agreeable to your directions, so as to be in readyness for as early a sale as possible. We shall also attend to the Ideas suggested by Mr Jefferson in his letter just received. We some time ago contracted with Mr Jendall for the delivery of four thousand perches of foundation stone: And this day compleated a contract with two persons for the two thousand wharf logs to be delivered by the 1st of June so that we hope at the next sale, there will be every proof of our being in earnest. We hope soon to be able to inform you, of a contract for quarries. We are &c.

D.ª STUART
D.^{l} CARROLL

THE PRESIDENT OF THE UNITED STATES.

[LETTERS OF THE COMMISSIONERS OF THE PUBLIC BUILDINGS AND GROUNDS OF THE CITY OF WASHINGTON and DISTRICT OF COLUMBIA, Vol. 1, 1791–1793, (hereafter to be cited as COMMISSIONERS' LETTER BOOK), pp. 40–1, in the National Archives.]

WASHINGTON TO JEFFERSON

TO THOMAS JEFFERSON. ESQRE

Nov. 30th. 1791.

My dear Sir,

Mr. L'Enfant's letter of the 19th. of October to Mr. Lear — Mr. Lear's answer of the 6th. instant (the press copy of which is so dull as to be scarcely legible) — in which I engrafted sentiments of admonition, and with a view also to feel his pulse

under reprehension. — His reply of the 10th. to that letter, together with the papers I put into your hands when here, will
give you a full view of the business; and the Major's conduct;
and will enable you to judge from the complexion of things
how far he may be spoken to in decisive terms without losing
his services; which, in my opinion, would be a serious misfortune. — At the same time *he must know*, there is a line beyond
which he will not be suffered to go. — Whether it is zeal, — an
impetuous temper, or other motives that lead him into such
blameable conduct, I will not take upon me to decide — but
be it what it will, it must be checked; or we shall have no Commissioners. — I am, always

Your obedt. & affecte.

Go. WASHINGTON.

Wednesday, the 30th *Nov.* 1791.

[WASHINGTON'S LETTER BOOK, vol. 11, 158; pp. 197–8, U.S. *v.* SMITH.]

JEFFERSON TO L'ENFANT

Philadelphia Dec. 1. 1791.

Sir

I have recieved with sincere concern the information from
yourself as well as others, that you have proceeded to demolish
the house of m͞r Carrol of Duddington, against his consent, and
without authority from the Commissioners, or any other person. in this you have laid yourself open to the laws, & in a country where they will have their course. to their animadversion
will belong the present case. — in future I must strictly enjoin
you to touch no man's property, without his consent, or the
previous order of the Commissioners. I wished you to be employed in the arrangements of the federal city. I still wish it: but
only on condition that you can conduct yourself in subordina-

tion to the authority of the Commissioners, to the laws of the land, & to the rights of it's citizens.

[TH: JEFFERSON]

MAJOR L'ENFANT

[Ms., *Jefferson Papers*, Library of Congress.]

COMMISSIONERS TO JEFFERSON

FROM COMMISSIONERS TO MR. JEFFERSON

8th *Decr.* 1791

Sir,

Immediately on the receipt of your letter of the 21st ultmo we gave directions to Mr. Ellicot, to lay out squares in the places mentioned — The enclosed letter will inform you of the progress he has made. From the opportunities we have had, of acquiring any knowledge on this subject, we think it will be of importance that some squares on the most eligible situations on Navigation, should be in readyness by the next sale — We are enclined to think from our conversation with Majr. L'Enfant, and Mr. Ellicot, that it will not be advisable to have a sale sooner than the middle of June, Mr. Blodget has not yet arrived — It would certainly be very desirable to form a contract of such magnitude with him — We fear from some Ideas thrown out by a Mr. Welsh who, (we understand) is to be concerned with him in the contract, that he rates the importance of it, to the City so highly, as to expect to get the ground at a low rate — We should be happy in case of an Offer from him, to be favoured with the Presidents, Ideas respecting the terms which might be acceded to — In so great a purchase, as Mr. Blodget contemplates, it would certainly, be wrong to take our late sales as the only guide or standard — But how far short of what they averaged pr Acre would it be proper to stop — The circumstances respecting Mr. Carroll's house we have already laid before the President, and received his late communications

on the subject — As the house was nearly demolished before
the Chancellors injunction arrived, Mr. Carroll did not think
it worth while to have it served, trusting perhaps, that our directions expressly forbidding their further proceedings in it
would have been attended to — We are sorry to mention that
the Majr. who was absent at the time we issued them, paid no
attention to them but completely demolished it on his return,
this instance has given fresh alarm, as the proprietors had flattered themselves, that in any instances in which they might conceive themselves injured, they should be able to obtain redress
from the Commissioners — As we have already more than
once, from our high oppinion of his talents sacrificed our feelings to our Zeal we have done it again — The Majr. has indeed
done us the honour of writing us a letter justifying his conduct
— We have not noticed it, and believe as we are likely to get
every thing happily adjusted between Mr. Carroll and him, it
will be most prudent to drop all explanations — We expect you
will see the Majr. in Philadelphia in a short time — We cannot
conclude, without expressing our Sanguine hopes from the
train in which all matters are now respecting the unhappy
affair, that however reprehensible it may have been, in the
mode of, conducting it, that it will prove Ultimately salutary.

    We are Sir &c—

                      Signed   DA. STEWART
                                      DL. CARROLL

[COMMISSIONERS' LETTER BOOK, Vol. I, 1791–1793, p. 42 in the National Archives; p. 208,
U.S. v. SMITH.]

JEFFERSON'S OPINION ON L'ENFANT LETTER OF DECEMBER 7

*Opinion relative to the demolition of Mr. Carroll's house by Major
L'Enfant, in laying out the Federal City.*

                                        December 11, 1791.

Observations on Major L'Enfant's letter of December 7th,

1791,[16] to the President, justifying his demolition of the house of Mr. Carroll, of Duddington:

He says that "Mr. Carroll erected his house partly on a main street, and altogether on ground to which the public had a more immediate title than himself could claim." When blaming Mr. Carroll, then, he considers this as a street; but when justifying himself, he considers it not yet as a street, for to account for his not having pointed out to Carroll a situation where he might build, he says, "The President had not yet sanctioned the plan for the distribution of the city, not determined if he would approve the situation of the several areas proposed to him in that plan for public use, and that I would have been highly to be blamed to have anticipated his opinion thereon." This latter exculpation is solid; the first is without foundation. The plan of the city has not yet been definitely determined by the President. Sales to individuals, or partition decide the plan as far as these sales or partitions go. A deed with the whole plan annexed, executed by the President, and recorded, will ultimately fix it. But till a sale, or partition, or deed, it is open to alteration. Consequently, there is as yet no such thing as a street, except adjacent to the lots actually sold or divided; the erection of a house in any part of the ground cannot as yet be a nuisance in law. Mr. Carroll is tenant in common of the soil with the public, and the erection of a house by a tenant in common on the common property, is no nuisance. Mr. Carroll has acted imprudently, intemperately, foolishly; but he has not acted illegally. There must be an establishment of the streets, before his house can become a nuisance in the eye of the law. Therefore, till that establishment, neither Major L'Enfant, nor the commissioners, would have had a right to demolish his house, without his consent.

The Major says he had as much right to pull down a house, as to cut down a tree.

[16] Published in Kite, L'ENFANT AND WASHINGTON, pp. 89–91.

This is true, if he has received no authority to do either, but still there will be this difference: To cut down a tree or to demolish a house in the soil of another, is a trespass; but the cutting a tree, in this country, is so slight a trespass, that a man would be thought litigious who should prosecute it; if he prosecuted civilly, a jury would give small damages; if criminally, the judge would not inflict imprisonment, nor impose but a small fine. But the demolition of a house is so gross a trespass, that any man would prosecute it; if civilly, a jury would give great damages; if criminally, the judge would punish heavily by fine and imprisonment. In the present case, if Carroll was to bring a civil action, the jury would probably punish his folly by small damages; but if he were to prosecute criminally, the judge would as probably vindicate the insult on the laws, and the breach of the peace, by heavy fines and imprisonment. So that if Major L'Enfant is right in saying he had as much authority to pull down a house as to cut down a tree, still he would feel a difference in the punishment of the law.

But is he right in saying he had as much authority to pull down a house as to cut down a tree? I do not know what have been the authorities given him expressly or by *implication*, but I can very readily conceive that the authorities which he has received, whether from the President or from the commissioners, whether verbal or written, may have gone to the demolition of trees, and not houses. I am sure he has received no authority, either from the President or commissioners, either expressly or by implication, to pull down houses. An order to him to mark on the ground the lines of the streets and lots, might imply an order to remove trees or *small* obstructions, *where they insuperably prevented his operations;* but a person must know little of geometry who could not, in an open field, designate streets and lots, even where a line passed through a house, without pulling the house down.

In truth, the blame on Major L'Enfant, is for having pulled

down the house, of his own authority, and when he had reason
to believe he was in opposition to the sentiments of the President; and his fault is aggravated by its having been done to
gratify private resentment against Mr. Carroll, and most probably not because it was necessary; and the style in which he
writes the justification of his act, shows that a continuation of
the same resentment renders him still unable to acquiesce under
the authority from which he has been reproved.

He desires a line of demarcation between his office, and that
of the commissioners.

What should be this line? and who is to draw it? If we consider the matter under the *act of Congress* only, the President has
authority only to name the commissioners, and to approve or
disapprove certain proceedings of theirs. They have the whole
executive power, and stand between the President and the subordinate agents. In this view, they may employ or dismiss,
order and countermand, take on themselves such parts of the
execution as they please, and assign other parts to subordinate
agents. Consequently, under the *act of Congress*, their will is the
line of demarcation between subordinate agents, while no such
line can exist between themselves and their agents. Under the
deed from the proprietors to the President, his powers are much
more ample. I do not accurately recollect the tenor of the deed;
but I am pretty sure it was such as to put much more ample
power into the hands of the President, and to commit to him
the whole execution of whatever is to be done under the deed;
and this goes particularly to the laying out the town: so that as
to this, the President is certainly authorized to draw the line of
demarcation between L'Enfant and the commissioners. But I
believe there is no necessity for it, as far as I have been able to
judge, from conversations and consultations with the commissioners. I think they are disposed to follow implicitly the will of
the President, whenever they can find it out; but L'Enfant's
letters do not breathe the same moderation or acquiescence;

and I think it would be much safer to say to him, "the orders of the commissioners are your line of demarcation," than by attempting to define his powers, to give him a line where he may meet with the commissioners foot to foot, and chicane and raise opposition to their orders whenever he thinks they pass his line. I confess, that on a view of L'Enfant's proceedings and letters latterly, I am thoroughly persuaded that, to render him useful, his temper must be subdued; and that the only means of preventing his giving constant trouble to the President, is to submit him to the unlimited control of the commissioners; we known the discretion and forbearance with which they will exercise it.

[Pp. 564–7, WRITINGS OF JEFFERSON, Washington, VII.]

WASHINGTON TO JEFFERSON

WASHINGTON TO JEFFERSON

Philadelphia, December 14, 1791.

Dear Sir:

   I am very glad to find that matters, after all that has happened, stand so well between the Comrs. and Majr. L'Enfant. I am sorry, however, to hear that the work is not in a more progressive State.

   Yesterday afternoon I wrote a letter, of which the enclosed is the copy to Majr. L'Enfant. and receivg. his of the 10th. added the Postscript thereto. I hope the two will have a good effect. I am etc.

[P. 445, WRITINGS OF WASHINGTON, Fitzpatrick, Vol. 31.]

WASHINGTON TO JEFFERSON

WASHINGTON TO JEFFERSON

December 25, 1791.

My dear Sir:

   You will find by the enclosed that our troubles in the Federal

City are not yet at an end. I pray you to give the letters a consideration and inform me of the result, tomorrow, or next day.[17] Yours, etc.

[P. 449, WRITINGS OF WASHINGTON, Fitzpatrick, Vol. 31.]

WASHINGTON TO JEFFERSON AND MADISON

WASHINGTON TO JEFFERSON AND MADISON

[*January* 14, 1792.] [18]

The P. begs that Mr. J——— and Mr. Ma——— would give the enclosed letters from the Commrs.[19] an attentive perusal, and the whole of that business a serious consideration before nine oclock tomorrow morning, at which hour the P——— would be glad to converse with them on the subject.

Friday Morning.

[*Jefferson Papers* in the Library of Congress; p. 458, WRITINGS OF WASHINGTON, Fitzpatrick, Vol. 31.]

WASHINGTON TO JEFFERSON

WASHINGTON TO JEFFERSON

Sunday Morng. [*January* 15, 1792] [20]

The enclosed came to my hands yesterday afternoon. The documents respecting the dispute between Majr. L'Enfant and Dan Carroll of D. have been sent for the Attorney Genl. to form his opinion upon the case. The whole are sent for Mr. J.s

---

[17] No further record of this matter has been discovered in either the *Washington Papers* or *Jefferson Papers.*

[18] Date received, according to the *Jefferson Papers* in the Library of Congress, Vol. 69, p. 12068.

[19] "Copies of the letters from the Commissioners of the District of Columbia of January 7 and 9 are filed in *District of Columbia Letters and Papers* in the Library of Congress." [P. 458 n, WRITINGS OF WASHINGTON, Fitzpatrick, Vol. 31.]

[20] Date received, according to the *Jefferson Papers* in the Library of Congress, Vol. 69, p. 12075.

perusal previous to the conversation he proposed to have with
Majr. L E. The President has not read the Papers, nor is he in
any hurry to do it.

[P. 459, WRITINGS OF WASHINGTON, Fitzpatrick, Vol. 31.]

JEFFERSON TO WASHINGTON

Th: Jefferson has the honor to return to the President the
letters of the Commissioners on their discharge of the workmen
Etc. in the Federal city. the copy of the Extracts from them for
Maj^r L'Enfant was not finished till last night, & therefore
could not be sent to him till to-day. consequently the conference with him is put off to tomorrow. Th: J. incloses a copy of
his letter to Maj^r Lenfant covering them.

The letter & papers on the subject of Duddington Carrol's
house are likewise returned. they are worthy the perusal of the
President.

M^r. Peters has desired that his commission may be held back
a few days to give time to the Senate to make up their minds
about his successor.

Jan. 15. 1792.

[Ms., *Jefferson Papers*, Library of Congress.]

WASHINGTON TO JEFFERSON

WASHINGTON TO JEFFERSON
                                    Wednesday, January 18, 1792.
Dear Sir:

The conduct of Majr. L'Enfant and those employed under
him, astonishes me beyond measure! and something more than
even appears, must be meant by them! When you are at leisure
I should be glad to have a further conversation with you on
this subject. Yrs. etc.

[Pp. 462–3, WRITINGS OF WASHINGTON, Fitzpatrick, Vol. 31.]

JEFFERSON TO DANIEL CARROLL

THOMAS JEFFERSON TO DANIEL CARROLL

January [27], 1792

Be pleased to consider this letter as from one private individual to another. The conduct of the agents who ought to be subordinate is properly viewed here . . . In the mean time the President apprehends that accident or malice may throw down the stakes by which the lots are marked on the ground and thus a whole summer's work be lost. He thinks the attention of one ¹person might be savingly employed in a daily visit to these stakes; and fastening such as may be getting loose or replacing those which may be withdrawn. I have thought it not improper to suggest this to you and am with great esteem,

Dear Sir —.

[Elizabeth S. Kite, L'ENFANT AND WASHINGTON, 1791–1792. HISTORICAL DOCUMENTS, INSTITUT FRANÇAIS DE WASHINGTON, CAHIER III (The Johns Hopkins Press, Baltimore, Md., 1929) pp. 134–5. Reprinted through the courtesy of the Johns Hopkins Press.]

DANIEL CARROLL TO JEFFERSON

George Town. Feby. 3ᵈ 1792

Dear Sir,

Yʳ favor of the 27ᵗʰ Ulᵒ came to hand yesterday — when the Comˢʳˢ were compelled to discharge Mʳ Roberdeau, they employ'd a carefull person with instructions "to pay attention in a very particular manner to the posts and Marks in the federal City, as their being distroyed or misplac'd may occasion a repetition of heavy expences besides delay equally injurious."

In addition to what the Comˢʳˢ did, I have thought it prudent to send for a Mʳ Orm who was employd by Mr. Ellicot, as an assistant in surveying & fixing the Stakes to go over the ground occasionally with Mʳ Williams, the person we have employed — & I will myself pay all the attention in my power to this important object. Mr. Orme may not possess all the knowledge wishd for on this occasion, but it is the best now to be done. M.ʳ Williams will make his dayly visits to see that the Stakes are kept secure in their proper positions.

I have reason to believe Mʳ Johnson will be with you before this gets to yʳ hands. I beg leave to refer to him for many matters, & to subscribe myself Dear S.ʳ with great esteem,

Y.ʳ respectfull & Obᵗ Servᵗ

DAN! CARROLL

Ms., *Jefferson Papers*, Library of Congress.]

WASHINGTON TO JEFFERSON

WASHINGTON TO JEFFERSON

[February 7, 1792.]

The enclosed came to my hand yesterday evening. I have heard nothing more of Mr. Johnson. I wish the business to which these letters relate,[21] was brought to an issue, an agreeable one is not, I perceive to be expected.

[P. 476, WRITINGS OF WASHINGTON, Fitzpatrick, Vol. 31.]

WASHINGTON TO JEFFERSON

WASHINGTON TO JEFFERSON

Thursday Morng. [*February* 9, 1792.] [22]

The P——— requests that Mr. J——— would give the enclosed letter and papers a reading between this and dinner; and come an hour before it, that he may have an opportunity of conversing with him on the subject of them.

Mr. Walker of George Town is in this City; from him, if Mr.

[21] The business was the difficulty with L'Enfant.
[22] Date received, according to the *Jefferson Papers* in the Library of Congress, Vol. 70, p. 12231.

J—— could contrive to get him to his house, he might learn the sentiments of the people of that place. Carrolsburg &ca., with respect to the dispute between the Comrs. and Majr. L', and generally of the State of the business.

[Pp. 477–8, WRITINGS OF WASHINGTON, Fitzpatrick, Vol. 31.]

WASHINGTON TO JEFFERSON

WASHINGTON TO JEFFERSON

Saturday, February 11, 1792.

Dear Sir:

If you and Mr. Madison could make it convenient to take a family dinner with me today; or, if engagements prevent this, wd. come, at any hour in the afternoon most convenient to yourselves we would converse fully, and try to fix on some plan for carrying the affairs of the Federal district into execution.

Under present appearances it is difficult, but it is nevertheless necessary to resolve on something. Yrs. etc.

[P. 479, WRITINGS OF WASHINGTON, Fitzpatrick, Vol. 31.]

WASHINGTON TO JEFFERSON

WASHINGTON TO JEFFERSON

Wednesday, February 15, 1792.

Dear Sir:

Before I give any decided opinion upon the letter you have written to Majr. L'Enfant,[23] or on the alterations proposed for the engraved plan, I wish to converse with you on several matters which relates to this business. This may be, if nothing on your part renders it inconvenient, immediately after 8 Oclock

[23] Probably the letter from Jefferson to L'Enfant, Feb. 22, 1792, which is in the Digges-Morgan-L'Enfant Papers in the Library of Congress.

tomorrow; at wch. hour I breakfast, and at which if agreeable to yourself I should be glad to see you.

In the meanwhile, I send for your perusal an address from Mr. Welsh, which, (though dated yesterday) is but just received. You will recollect the communications of Mr. Walker on Saturday afternoon. From these, those of Sunday differed but little. But as he said Major L'Enfant had declin'd committing, or suffering to be committed to writing any ideas of his, forasmuch as he had given them to me *before* in a letter, I have looked these over, and send the only one I can find in which he has attempted to draw a line of demarkation between the Commissioners and himself. I also send you the *general* ideas of another person, principally on the subject of a loan, that you may, if leisure and inclination will permit give the whole a perusal before I see you. Yours etc.

P.S. If Mr. Madison can make it convent. to come with you I should be glad to see him also. In that case, it might be well to give him a previous perusal of the enclosed papers.

[Pp. 480-1, WRITINGS OF WASHINGTON, Fitzpatrick, Vol. 31.]

WASHINGTON TO JEFFERSON

WASHINGTON TO JEFFERSON

Wednesday, 7 Oclock AM [February 22, 1792.] [24]

Dear Sir:

The enclosed meets *my* approbation. Did Walker accord willingly, or reluctantly?

The Plan I think, ought to appear as the Work of L'Enfant. The one prepared for engraving not doing so, is, I presume, one cause of his dissatisfaction. If he consents to act upon the conditions proposed, and can point out any radical defects, or others

[24] Date received, according to the *Jefferson Papers* in the Library of Congress, Vol. 71, p. 12270.

to amend which will be a gratification to him, not improper in themselves, or productive of unnecessary, or too much delay, had he not better be gratified in the alterations? This, yourself and Mr. Walker can think of. The Plans of the buildings ought to come forward immediately for consideration. I think Mr. Walker said yesterday he (L'Enfant) had been shewing the different views of them to Mr. Trumbul. Yrs.

[Pp. 482–3, WRITINGS OF WASHINGTON, Fitzpatrick, Vol. 31.]

JEFFERSON TO L'ENFANT

Philadelphia, Feb. 22, 1792.

Sir:

The advance of the season begins to require that the plans for the buildings and other public works at the Federal city, should be in readiness, & the persons engaged who are to carry them into execution, the circumstances which have lately happened have produced an uncertainty whether you may be disposed to continue your services there. I am charged by the President to say that your continuance would be desirable to him; & at the same time to add that the law requires it should be in subordination to the Commissioners. They will of course receive your propositions, decide on the plans to be pursued from time to time, & submit them to the President to be approved or disapproved, & when returned with his approbation, the Commissioners will put into your hands the execution of such parts as shall be arranged with you, & will doubtless see from time to time that these objects, & no others, are pursued. It is not pretended to *stipulate* here however the mode in which they shall carry on the execution. They alone can do that, & their discretion, good sense & zeal are a sufficient security that those whom they employ will have as little cause to be dissatisfied with the manner as the matter of their orders. To this, it would be injustice to them not to add, as a motive the more in this particular instance, the desire they have ever manifested to conform to the judgment & wishes of the President. The same disposition will ensure an oblivion of whatever disagreeable may have arisen heretofore on a perfect understanding being established as to the relation to subsist in future between themselves & those they employ, in the conduct of the works. I must beg the favor of your answer whether you will continue your services on the footing expressed in this letter; and am with esteem, Sir,

> Your most obedt. humble servt.,
>
> THOS. JEFFERSON.

MAJOR L'ENFANT.

NOTE:

"In the letter to the President the 14th of January, it will show I was not behind in measure to determine a speedy renewal of the work." L'ENFANT.

[Pp. 148-49, COLUMBIA HISTORICAL SOCIETY, *Records*, Vol. 2.]

L'ENFANT TO JEFFERSON

MAJOR L'ENFANT TO THOMAS JEFFERSON

> *Philadelphia, February* 26, 1792

Sir;

I received your favor of the 22nd instant; the sentiments therein expressed I have attentively considered, nor can I discover any idea calculated to accomodate those dissentions which so unfortunately have invaded the interests of the Federal city. I am well aware that the season for preparing for the operations of the ensuing summer, if any are intended, has far advanced. Indeed the time in which I conceived they ought to have been in readiness, past. You well know my wishes for arrangements tended in great measure to that object, consequently fault cannot be mine, as my every exertion to accomplish it was impeded by the Commissioners; The circumstances attending these inconvencies [*sic*] have afforded me much anxiety, solicitous as I have always been for the interest of that city; at the same time I acknowledge that I am not a little surprised to find that a doubt has arisen in the mind of your self or the President of the uncertainty of my wishes to continue my services there; the motives by which I have been actuated during the time I have been engaged in it; the continual exertions I have made in its promotion, the arrangement for this purpose which I lately handed to the President, indeed every step I have taken, cannot but evince most strongly how solicitously concerned I am in the success of it, and with what regret I should relinquish it —.

My desire to conform to the judgment and wishes of the President have really been ardent. and I trust my actions always have manifested those desires most uncontrovertably; nor am I conscious in a single instance to have had any other motive than an implicit conformity to his will. Under this impression at the most early period of the work, no attention nor politeness as a gentleman has been wanting in me to attain the confidence and secure the friendship of the Commissioners — I coveted it, I sincerely wished it, knowing that without a perfect good understanding between them and myself, whatever exertions I should make, would prove fruitless; and embracing in my mind the immensity of the business to be undertaken, evinced to me the necessity that I should be disengaged from every concern, and be devoted wholly to forming and carrying into execution a plan in which I promised myself every support from them, trusting they felt a similar interest in the prosperity and success of the undertaking, and that therefore they would freely have relied upon me in all matters relating to my professional character, and requested from me all the information and assistance in my power to aid them in the performance of their share of the business, which in men so little versed in the

minutiae of such operations would have been judicious and
might in propriety have been done, without descending from
that pride of office which, I am mortified to be obliged to say it,
has been their chief object . . . and has afforded me much concern, knowing that the President had always entertained a
different opinion of their dispositions, and delicately situated as
I was, put it out of my power to assure him that his expectations of these gentlemen adhering to their protestations to him
. . . were erroneous; as on the contrary, though apparently
acknowledging themselves obliged to me for affording necessary information, on receiving it have uniformly acted in opposition thereto . . . and appear rather to have endeavored to
obtain that knowledge from me the more effectually to defeat
my intentions . . . The inquietude I feel must continue to the
end to impede the business, which will oblige me to renounce
the pursuit of that fame, which the success of the undertaking
must procure, rather than to engage to conduct it under a system which would . . . not only crush its growth but make me
appear the principal cause of the destruction of it . . . seeing
there is much stress laid upon the propriety of their conduct
and the motives by which . . . [it] is inspired lays me under the
necessity, in justification of my own feelings, to enumerate
some instances that occurred in the course of the work, in which
in my opinion, they have been rather deficient, and such as the
President himself will recollect — In the first instance then, you
must remember what difficulties were encountered to obtain
ground proportional to the plan then under consideration of
the President, and how greatly these difficulties were aug-
mented by the non-concurrence of the Commissioners in any
steps I had taken to that effect. — Also the unwearied efforts
made by them to cause some alterations in the plan since approved by him, all which evinces in them a greater concern to
favor individual interests, than attention to secure the public
good. — This disposition has been particularly manifested in

the business of the Boundary line . . . before the President himself had determined . . . [its] extent . . . directing Mr. Ellicott to proceed according to their own ideas. The consequence of this . . . was a general opposition to deed the land granted the public, every individual justly conceiving they had as much right to partiality as Mr. Notley Young, whose interest it seemed to be the sole object of the Commissioners thereby to benefit. The difference with Mr. Stoddert originated from this source alone, by leaving out of that line his spring, which it was intended to exclude and which became a forciable argument to that gentleman to obtain his wish — to the evident disfiguration of the plan. Afterwards . . . when I actually prevailed upon Mr. Robert Peters . . . to . . . wharf that part of the harbor belonging to him on terms advantageous to the public; this idea the Commissioners rejected . . . conceiving that this improvement would be injurious to the Carrollsburg interest, which in fact it would have . . . promoted . . . The object of the canal . . . they prevented from being begun . . . disregarding the benefit . . . to the city in an easy transportation to the various parts . . . under the influence . . . [of] the Georgetown opposition . . . as injurious to the rapid development of that place . . .

Constantly mislead by the allurement of parties . . . with a temperament little addicted to business . . . involving themselves in contention and disputes . . . [they] have created dissentions with the principles concerned in the execution and encouraged mutiny among the people.

Admitting however their confined ideas . . . to be a kind of apology for the injudicious manner in which the business . . . has been conducted, . . . yet . . . how wonderfully deficient they have been in the prosecution . . . of contracts of supplies of provisions etc . . . their inattention to a regular and economical method to obtain necessary supplies and the uncertain mode of procuring money . . . are facts so evident as to need no comment.

The only purchase of any magnitude was that of the stone quarry. For full information of the manner in which this business was conducted I refer you to the enclosed letter that I wrote to Mr. Brent upon particular application from his brother, a copy of which has been forwarded by me to Georgetown . . .

It is also necessary to enter upon the subject . . . of those proceedings for which every dispassionate, impartial observer must . . . condemn them — the imprisonment of Mr. Roberdeau acting under my orders and without even a suspicion of their design, was highly injurious and rash seeing . . . I shall be obliged publically to expose these transactions in my own justification, to their dishonor and to the evident disadvantage of the public cause . . .

I rest satisfied that the President will consider . . . that erecting houses for the accomodation of Government, is not the only object, nay, not so important an one, as the encouragement to prepare buildings at those principal points, on the speedy settlement of which depends the rapid increase of the city . . . while the prosperity of the undertaking depends upon that spirit of enterprise by which all improvements must be made and that prudent manner by which the sale of lots and all establishments both public and private shall be conducted.

. . . nor must it be expected that anything short of what I propose will answer that purpose . . . to change a wilderness into a city, to erect and beautify buildings etc. to that degree of perfection necessary to receive the seat of Government of a vast empire the short period of time that remains to effect these objects is an undertaking vast as it is novel — and reflecting that all this is to be done under the many disadvantages of opposing interests . . . the only expedient is to conciliate and interest the minds of all ranks of people . . . by holding out forcible inducements . . .

I hope it will be . . . too well evidenced that all my opposition to them [the Commissioners] and the determination I have taken no longer to act in subjection to their will and caprice, is influenced by the purest principles and warmest good wishes to the full attainment of the main object . . .

If therefore the law absolutely requires without any equivocation that my continuance shall depend upon an appointment from the Commissioners — I cannot nor would I upon any consideration submit myself to it . . .

D - 3814

I have the honor to be — etc. etc.

[Elizabeth S. Kite, L'ENFANT AND WASHINGTON, pp. 145–50. The dots in the text are here reproduced as printed by Miss Kite. Reprinted through the courtesy of the Johns Hopkins Press, Baltimore, Md.]

WASHINGTON TO JEFFERSON

WASHINGTON TO JEFFERSON

4 *Oclock, February* 26, 1792.

Sir:

I have perused the enclosed answer [25] to your letter, to Majr. L'Enfant. Both are returned. A final decision thereupon must be had.[26] I wish it to be taken upon the best ground, and with the best advice. Send it, I pray you, to Mr. Madison who is better acquainted with the *whole* of this matter than any other. I wish also that the Attorney General may see, and become acquainted with the circumstances (I can think of no other, at this moment to call in), and wish that all th[mutilated] of you would be with me at half after Eight o'clock tomorrow, if convenient, [if not,] [27] at a later hour to be named, that I may be at home and disengaged. Yours, etc.

[Pp. 486–7, WRITINGS OF WASHINGTON, Fitzpatrick, Vol. 31.]

[25] L'Enfant's letter of February 26. . . .
[26] This final decision resulted in Jefferson's letter to L'Enfant, Feb. 27, 1792. . . .
[27] Words in brackets supplied for mutilated space.

JEFFERSON TO L'ENFANT

TO MAJOR L'ENFANT

Philadelphia Feby. 27. 1792.

Sir

From your letter received yesterday in answer to my last, &
your declarations in conversation with Mr. Lear, it is understood that you absolutely decline acting under the authority of
the present Commissioners. If this understanding of your meaning be right I am instructed by the President to inform you that
notwithstanding the desire he has entertained to preserve your
agency in the business the condition upon which it is to be done
is inadmissible, & your services must be at an end.

I have the honor to be Sir &c.

TH: JEFFERSON.

[P. 212. U.S. *v.* SMITH; Ms. p. 354, American Letters, IV, 1788–92, State Department
Archives in the National Archives; pp. 151–2, L'ENFANT AND WASHINGTON, Kite.]

JEFFERSON TO JOHNSON

In a Letter [28] I received from him (Daniel Carroll of Duddington) Yesterday, he sent me the Copies I now inclose from
Mr. Brent, Major L'Enfant and Mr. Young — waiving the
rudeness of Mr. Walker's and Major L'Enfant's Letters, it is
apparent that they both hold the Commrs in sovereign Con-
tempt and that the Major would have them act a very subordinate part or not at all — Major L'Enfant in his Conversation
with Mr. Fenwick and Mr. Walker in his Letter refers to the
filling up of a Hole as if countenanced by the president when

[28] Unable to locate this letter. — S.K.P.

the Major must remember very different Things past at the
time —

THOMAS JEFFERSON

to

THOMAS JOHNSON,

29 Feby. 1792.

[P. 249, COLUMBIA HISTORICAL SOCIETY, *Records*, Vol. 2.]

JEFFERSON TO WALKER

THOMAS JEFFERSON TO GEORGE WALKER

Philadelphia, March 1, 1792

Sir

I was sorry that, being from home at the time you were so
good as to call upon me I missed seeing you. The president being engaged also, was equally unlucky. As you left no letter for
me I took for granted that your negotiations with Mjr Lenfant
had proved fruitless. After your departure the President sent
Mr. Lear to Majr. Lenfant to see what could be made of him.
He declared unequivocally that he would act on no condition
but the dismission of the Commissioners or his being made independent of them. — the latter being impossible under the
law and the former too arrogant to be answered he was notified
that his services were at an end. I think you have seen enough
of his temper to satisfy yourself that he never could have acted
under any control, not even that of the President himself: and
on the whole I am persuaded the enterprise will advance more
surely under a more temperate direction; under one that shall
proceed as fast and no faster than it can pay. Measures will be
take to procure plans for the public buildings, in which business five months have been lost in a dependance on Majr. Lenfant, who has made no preparations of that kind. I wish yourself and the inhabitants of Georgetown to be assured that every

exertion will be made to advance and secure this enterprise.

I have the honor to be etc.

TH: JEFFERSON.

[Elizabeth S. Kite, L'ENFANT AND WASHINGTON, pp. 156–57. Reprinted through the courtesy of the Johns Hopkins Press, Baltimore, Md.]

JEFFERSON TO DANIEL CARROLL

Philadelphia Mar. 1. 1792.

Dear Sir

Much time has been spent in endeavoring to induce Major Lenfant to continue in the business he was engaged in, in proper subordination to the Commissioners. he has however entirely refused, so that he has been notified that we consider his services as at an end. the plan is put into the hands of an engraver, and will be engraved within three or four weeks. about the same time mr̄ Ellicot will return to finish laying out the ground. as to every thing else it will rest on your board to plan & to have executed. the President desires you will call a meeting at the earliest day you can after the 11th instant. by that time you will receive from hence such general ideas & recommendations as may occur. you will then have to advertise for plans of the buildings. — it is taken for granted the design of the Commissioners in the action commenced against Roberdeau was merely to suspend his operations, and produce in him a proper conviction of his error. under this idea they will probably feel no difficulty in consenting to let him off as easily as they can. you will receive formal letters on the general business, shortly; in the mean time I am with great & sincere esteem Dear Sir

Your friend & serv^t

TH: JEFFERSON

D. CARROL. ESQ.

[Ms., *Jefferson Papers*, Library of Congress.]

WASHINGTON TO JEFFERSON

WASHINGTON TO JEFFERSON.

11 *Oclock, A. M., March* 4, 1792.

The enclosed came by the Post yesterday. I send it for your perusal.

Have you had any conversation with Mr. Ellicot respecting the completion of the Survey, and lots of the Federal City? If so, what was the result? He ought, if he undertakes it, to proceed to that place immediately, so as to be there at the proposed meeting of the Commissioners.

The Engravers say *eight weeks* is the *shortest* time in which the Plan can be engraved; (probably they may keep it eight months). Is not this misteriously strange! Ellicot talked of getting you to walk with him to these People. The current in *this* City sets so strongly against the Federal City, that I believe nothing that *can* be avoided will ever be accomplished in it.

Are there any good Engravers in Boston? If so, would it not be well to obtain a copy (under some other pretext) and send it there, or even to London, with out any one (even Ellicot's) being appris'd of it? Yrs. etc.

[P. 495, WRITINGS OF WASHINGTON, Fitzpatrick, Vol. 31.]

JEFFERSON TO COMMISSIONERS

JEFFERSON TO MESSRS. JOHNSON, CARROL, AND STEWART

Philadelphia, March 6, 1792.

Gentlemen:

It having been found impracticable to employ Major L'Enfant about the federal city, in that degree of subordination which was lawful and proper, he has been notified that his services are at an end. It is now proper that he should receive the

reward of his past services; and the wish that he should have no
just cause of discontent, suggests that it should be liberal. The
President thinks of two thousand five hundred, or three thousand dollars; but leaves the determination to you. Ellicot is to
go on, the week after the next, to finish laying off the plan on
the ground, and surveying and platting the district.[29] I have
remonstrated with him on the excess of five dollars a day and
his expenses, and he has proposed striking off the latter; but
this also is left to you, and to make the allowance retrospective.
He is fully apprised that he is entirely under your orders, and
there will be no person employed but under your orders. The
enemies of this enterprise will take advantage of the retirement
of L'Enfant, to trumpet an abortion of the whole. This will require double exertions, to be counteracted. I enclose you the
project of a loan which is agreed on, if you approve it. Your
answer will be immediately expected, and is kept entirely secret, till the subscriptions are actually opened. With this money,
in aid of your other funds, the works may be pushed with such
spirit as to evince to the world that they will not be relaxed.

The immediate employment of a superintendent, of activity
and intelligence equal to the nature of his functions and the
public expectations, becomes important. You will, doubtless,
also consider it as necessary to advertise immediately for plans
of the Capitol and President's house. The sketch of an advertisement for the plan of a Capitol, which Mr. Johnson had sent
to the President, is now returned with some alterations, and
one also for a President's house. Both of them are subject to
your pleasure, and when accommodated to that, if you will

[29] On Feb. 17, 1792, L'Enfant wrote to Tobias Lear: "I daily attended the progress of the
business in all its stages until Mr. Andrew Ellicott gave me to understand that he was
ordered by Mr. Jefferson to attend himself to that business in consequence of which he
had already agreed with an engraver, this determined me to concern myself no more
about it being confident that the meaning of Mr. Jefferson's order to Mr. Ellicott could
not be to publish the plan without my knowledge or concurrence, and convinced that it
would not be completely finished without recourse to the large map in my possession."

[P. 145, RECORDS, COLUMBIA HISTORICAL SOCIETY, Vol. 2.]

return them, they shall be advertised here and elsewhere. The President thinks it of primary importance to press the providing as great quantities of brick, stone, lime, plank, timber, &c., this year as possible. It will occur to you that the stone should be got by a skilful hand. Knowing what will be your funds, you will be able to decide which of the following works had better be undertaken for the present year.

The cellars of both houses.

The foundations of one, or both.

Bridge over Rock Creek, and the post road brought over it.

Canal.

Wharves.

The affair of Mr. Carrol, of Duddington's house, seems to call for settlement. The President thinks the most just course would be, to rebuild the house in the same degree, using the same materials as far as they will go, and supplying what are destroyed or rendered unfit; so that the effect will be in fact, only the removal of the house within his lot, and in a position square with the streets. Do you not think it would be expedient to take measures for importing a number of Germans and Highlanders? This need not be to such an extent as to prevent the employment of eastern laborers, which is eligible for particular reasons. If you approve of the importation of Germans and have a good channel for it, you will use it, of course. If you have no channel, I can help you to one. Though Roberdeau's conduct has been really blamable, yet we suppose the principal object of the arrest was to remove him off the ground. As the prosecution of him to judgment might give room to misrepresentation of the motives, perhaps you may think it not amiss to discontinue the proceedings. You will receive herewith a packet of papers, among which are several projects and estimates which have been given in by different persons, and which are handed on to you, not as by any means carrying with them any degree of approbation, but merely, that if you find anything good in them, you may convert it to some account. Some of these contain the views of L'Enfant.

I have the honor to be, with the most perfect esteem and respect, gentlemen, your most obedient, and most humble servant.

[Pp. 336–8, WRITINGS OF JEFFERSON, Washington, Vol. III.]

13.th March   Received a Letter from the Secretary of State, advising of Maj.r L'Enfant's
1792   dismissal — inclosing the project of a Loan, a copy of an Advertizement for
              the plan of a Capitol and presidents house — proposing particular objects
              of attention, &c.

[P. 80, Proceedings of the Commissioners, Vol. I, 1791–5, in the National
Archives.]

A PREMIUM

of 500 dollars, or a Medal of that value, at the option of the party, will be given by the Commissioners of the federal buildings to the person who before the —— day of —— next shall produce to them the most approved plan for a President's house to be erected in the city of Washington & territory of Columbia. The site of the building, if the artist will attend to it, will of course influence the aspect & outline of his plan, & its destination of the building will point out to the artist him the number, size & distribution of the apartments. it will be a recommendation of any plan that if the central part of it may be detached & erected for the present, with the appearance of a complete whole, and the other parts added be capable of admitting the additional parts in future if they shall be wanting.

[March 6, 1792: enclosed in Jefferson's letter to the Commissioners on that date.]

[Ms., *Jefferson Papers*, Library of Congress.]

Pencilled note by President Washington at the bottom of Jefferson's draft: "I see nothing wanting but to fill the blanks, and that I presume the Comrs. will do, unless, after the words 'destination of the buidling' is added 'and situation of the ground' for I think particular situation wd. require parlr. kind or shaped buildings." [P. 500, WRITINGS OF WASHINGTON, Fitzpatrick, Vol. 31.]

DECLARATION TO BE MADE BY WASHINGTON

Philadelphia Mar. 6. 1792.

A Declaration to be made by the President.

That the sales of Lots of public property in the town of Washington shall never be extended so far, but that there shall remain & be reserved so many of the said lots unsold as shall at the rate of 100. Dollars per lot be sufficient to secure the proportion of this loan not yet reimbursed, of which lots, two fifths shall be South of an East & West line drawn through the President's house, & three fifths North of that line, which said reserved lots shall be a security for the said principal not yet reimbursed & all arrears of interest.

On the above security it is proposed
to borrow half a million of dollars

10,000 dollars to be deposited by the Contractor at the time of receiving the warrants, & to be forfeited if the first instalment be not compleated according to contract.

40,000 dollars to be paid on the ——— day of May next

50,000 dollars on the same day of November following and so [30] 50.000 more every six months till the whole shall have been paid.

the interest to be paid half yearly at the rate of 6. per cent per annum, to run

on each payment from the time it is made, & to be reserveable out of each instalment, while there are instalments to be paid.

The whole sum is to be divided into 1000. shares of 500 dollars each.

[30] This was a mistake for 100,000. at the time of writing the paper & will be corrected the first time Th:J. can see mr̄ Blodget. it was meant that 40. per cent should be paid every year till all should be paid. [*Footnote in the original.*]

No reimbursement shall be made till the ——— day of May
1800. after which time they may be made at such times
as the borrower shall think proper; provided that no
smaller sum shall be reimbursed at any one time than
25,000 dollars.

All payments by either party to be made at the bank of the
United States or such branch thereof as the Commissioners of the federal buildings shall use.

This sketch is to be obligatory on mr̄ Blodget, who contracts
to take the whole loan, but not on the President or Commissioners till the said Commissioners shall consent.

(signed)   SAM. BLODGET

Witness TH: JEFFERSON

[Ms., *Jefferson Papers*, Library of Congress; enclosed in Jefferson's letter of March 6, 1792
to the Commissioners.]

DANIEL CARROLL TO JEFFERSON

George Town March 6th, 1792.

Dear Sir

This is principally to acknowledge the receipt of your favour
of the 1st Instant — previous to the receipt of it I had rec^d a line
from Doct^r Stuart informing me that he shou'd see me on the
11th Inst. we shall then take measures to have a communication with Mr. Johnson according to circumstances — I have
written to that Gent^n inclosing a Copy of yours.

It gives me much pleasure to find we shall have the Engraved
plan in circulation soon, which is not only essintial against the
Next Sales but to the Object in general.

I am, Dear Sir, with great esteem & regard
Yr Most Obt & respectful Hble Servt

DAN^L CARROLL

[TO MR JEFFERSON]

[P. 232, U.S. *v.* SMITH.]

WASHINGTON TO JEFFERSON

WASHINGTON TO JEFFERSON

[*March* 7, 1792.]

Dear Sir:

I do not recollect whether any notice has been taken in your letter to the Commrs. of Mr. Johnsons suggestion of bringing the Canal navigation to the City. The ascertainment of the practicability ought by all means to be encouraged. Yours.

G. W.

Thursday ⎫
Morning ⎭

[Ms., *Jefferson Papers*, Library of Congress.]

JEFFERSON TO THOMAS JOHNSON

Philadelphia Mar. 8. 1792.

Dear Sir

I received your favor of Feb. 29 [31] — the day after I had written a public letter to the Commissioners, which touched on some of the subjects of yours. I may say in this private letter what could not be so well said in a public one, that there never was a moment's doubt about parting with Major Lenfant rather than with a single commissioner. I must correct an error in my public letter. I said there that the engraving would be done in three or four weeks: this idea had been given, but on further enquiry I find we cannot have it these two months. you formerly hinted the expediency of bringing the navigable canal from the little falls down to Washington. the President thinks the practicability of this should be properly examined into, as it would undoubtedly be useful.

In my public letter, I sent you the outlines of a proposed

---

[31] Unable to locate this letter. — S.K.P.

Dates of instalments	Amount of each install-ment	Aggregate sum of the inter-est of which is to be de-ducted from each payment	Amount of the interest to be de-ducted from each in-stalment	Sum actu-ally re-ceived by the bor-rowers	Sums of interest to be paid by sales or otherwise
	Dollars				
1792. May 15.......	50,000	....	....	50,000	
Nov. 15.......	50,000	50,000	1,500	48,500	
1793. May 15.......	100,000	100,000	3,000	97,000	
Nov. 15.......	100,000	200,000	6,000	94,000	
1794. May 15.......	100,000	300,000	9,000	91,000	
Nov. 15.......	100,000	400,000	12,000	88,000	
1795. May 15......	....	....	....	....	15,000
Nov. 15......	....	....	....	....	15,000
1796. May 15......		....	....	....	15,000
Nov. 15......	....	....	....	....	15,000
1797. May 15......	....	....	....	....	15,000
Nov. 15......	....	....	....	....	15,000
1798. May 15......	....	....	....	....	15,000
Nov. 15......	....	....	....	....	15,000
1799. May 15......	....	....	....	....	15,000
Nov. 15......	....	....	....	....	15,000
1800. May 15......	....	....	....	....	15,000
	500,000			468,500 +	165,000 = 665,000 [sic]

It appears from the above that the commissioners will receive 468,500 dollars, & have to pay after 4 considerable intervals 665,000. dollars. Now 468,000 : 665,000 : : 100 : 142. that is for every 100.D. they receive, they will have to pay in the long run 142.D. but we may certainly hope that the effect of the 468,000 dollars, if judiciously employed, will be to raise the value of the lots more than 42 per cent.

Suppose the interest, after 1794, is kept down by the sale of lots to raise it.

D.

100 lots a year at 300.D. each will pay the annual interest of 30,000   say 550. lots.
1666. do ——— at 300.D.   will pay the principal........500,000   1666
The whole loan then will absorb from beginning to end (@ 300.D.).......2216 lots.

[Ms., *Jefferson Papers*, Library of Congress.]

loan. I now inclose you a calculation, somewhat on the plan of yours. I think there is no doubt but that the lots will sell better after the employment of the money than before it. consequently that it is better to raise money by a loan, and to sell for repayment after that money shall have been employed to raise the value of what is to be sold: the mortgage on this plan is put on the best footing possible. no doubt it will be well to be making sales for repayment as fast as they may be advantageously made, even before the lapse of the' eight years. We have questioned mr̄ Ellicot very particularly whether the plan now in hand is exact. he says the original one mixed conjecture with fact: but that the conjectural parts are since ascertained by exact survey and that this plan is corrected from the survey, and may be relied on to the utmost minuteness. we see in fact that some whole squares of lots in the original plan are occupied by the channel of the creek in the corrected one. I fear your other apprehension is better founded; to wit, that the avenues are made to converge to the ends of a building of supposed extent, that the building may very probably be of less extent, & consequently not reach the points of view created for it's use. I believe the only remedy is acquiescence for the present, & hope for the future that our building may extend with the fortunes of our government. the angular buildings at the commencement of the avenues, may probably be offensive to the eye, if not well managed. I have seen this deformity obviated by terminating the house at that end with a bow-window, or with a semicircular portico, & with other fancies. should not rows of trees in the avenues & streets be an object of early attention? Majr̄ Lenfant had no plans prepared for the Capitol or government house. he said he had them in his head. I do not believe he will produce them for concurrence. on speaking with the President on mr̄ Stewart of Baltimore's idea of facing the buildings with stone of different colours, he seemed rather to question whether from the water-table, perhaps from the ground upwards, brick facings with stone ornaments would not have a better effect but he does not decide this. the remains of antiquity in Europe prove brick more durable than stone. the Roman brick appears in these remains to have been 22 inches long, 11 I. wide & 2 I. or 2½ I. thick. the grain is as fine as that of our best earthen ware. before I conclude, I will mention that in bringing the canal from the little falls into the city, it is worth while to consider whether it should not be delivered into the canal of the Tyber, to ensure the due cleansing of that by it's current. I am with great & sincere esteem Dear Sir

Your friend & serv^t

Th: Jefferson

P. S. you seem to suppose the Commissioners liable in their private fortunes on the plan of the loan you had seen. ours is certainly clear of that, in it's plan. nothing could make the commissioners liable but fraud, or such gross negligence as is as impossible as fraud; and then I presume it could only be each for his own individual act.

MR JOHNSON

WASHINGTON TO STUART

WASHINGTON TO DAVID STUART

Philadelphia, March 8, 1792.

Dear Sir:

. . .

The idea of importing Germans and Highlanders, as Artizans and labourers, has been touched upon in the letter from Mr. Jefferson to the Commissioners. It is, in my opinion worthy of serious consideration in an œconomical point of view, and because it will contribute to the population of the place.

[Pp. 507–8, WRITINGS OF WASHINGTON, Fitzpatrick, Vol. 31.]

WALKER TO JEFFERSON

[TO THOMAS JEFFERSON]

Georgetown March 9th 1792

Sir

Your favour of the first instant I had the honour to receive and was certainly sorry that I missed seeing you the evening before I left Philad[a] although I then had been able to obtain no reply from Major L'Enfant to the letter I had the honour to hand him from you: therefore did not think it necessary to write.

This dismission of Major L'Enfant has given great alarm to the Proprietors, and all those interested in the City of Washington; although I have fully explained to them, the difficulties the President had to surmount in treating with him.

I this day received the enclosed letter, which they wish should be laid before the President when convenient. — I am sorry to discover such a want of confidence in the ability of the Commissioners, and am afraid the affairs of the City will come into public investigation if means cannot be adopted by which Major L'Enfant may be yet continued.

I have the honour to be with reverence and respect

Sir Your Mo. obt. St.—

GEORGE WALKER

[Elizabeth S. Kite, L'ENFANT AND WASHINGTON, pp. 167–68. Reprinted through the courtesy of the Johns Hopkins Press, Baltimore, Md.]

PROPRIETORS TO WALKER

PROPRIETORS TO GEORGE WALKER

Georgetown, March 9, 1792.

Sir: We are obliged by your communication of the letter from the Secretary of State.

We cannot but lament extremely that the misunderstanding between the Commissioners and Major L'Enfant, has ended in the dismission of the latter — for, having from our own knowledge of his Conduct, formed the highest opinion of his Talents, his unwearied zeal, his firmness, (though sometimes perhaps improperly exerted, in general highly useful), his impartiality to this or to that end of the City; or to the views of those proprietors, with whom he has been in Friendship or otherwise — and from his total disregard for all pecuniary considerations, we greatly doubt whether a successor can be found in this country, or indeed in any country, qualified to be so eminently useful to the object in which we are all so Interested, — and certainly none can be found possessing in a higher degree, the public confidence, a circumstance which we cannot help thinking of very great importance in the business where as much depends on public opinion. Thus thinking, we anxiously hope that some mode will yet be devised by the friends of this place at Philadelphia, to secure to the City, the benefit of Major L'Enfant's future services.

The Commissioners we presume, would do everything they could do, consistently with their duty, to accommodate to his views, and however he may have been misled by the warmth of his Temper, we are persuaded from his well known attachment to the object, which has employed so much of his time and study, that he will on cooler reflexion and on knowing the highest confidence placed in him by the Bulk of the proprietors, stand less on Punctilio than he has hitherto done; especially if he could have assurances, that in things really in his province (and in which from his Scientific knowledge and approved Taste, He would be most competent to Decide) he would be left without controul.

As you are in correspondence with the Secretary of State, and as it is but justice to Major L'Enfant that the Opinion the proprietors entertain of his merit, from their own observation, should be known to those to whom he owed his appointment, we request you will enclose this letter with your own. We are, Sir,

Your most obed servts,

ROBERT PETERS,	BEN STODDERT,
JOHN DAVIDSON,	URIAH FORREST,
SAM DAVIDSON,	WM. PROUT,
JAS. M. LINGAN,	OVERTON CARR,
ABRAHAM YOUNG,	DAVID BURNES,
WM. KING,	ELIPHAZ DOUGLAS.

[Pp. 140–1, HISTORY OF WASHINGTON, Tindall.]

JEFFERSON TO COMMISSIONERS

Philadelphia Mar. 11. 1792.

Gentlemen

I inclose you two letters, the one from a m͞r Leslie of this place, offering to make a clock for some one of the public buildings at Washington, the other from m͞r R. B. Lee proposing that m͞r Ciracchi a statuary now at this place should be employed to erect at Washington a monument he has proposed. with respect to Leslie, he is certainly one of the most ingenious artists in America; and as to m͞r Ciracchi he has given unquestionable proofs here of very superior talents in his line, & of great worth. the letters are meant merely to be lodged with you, to be taken up when you think that your works are advanced to a proper stage for them.

I have the honour to be with the most perfect esteem Gentlemen

Your most obed^t & humble serv^t

TH: JEFFERSON

[TO THE COMMISSIONERS]

[Ms., *Jefferson Papers*, Library of Congress.]

COMMISSIONERS' NOTE

13.th March   Wrote a Letter to the Secretary of State, acknowl-
1792   edging the receipt of his of the 6th Inst. informing
              of the compensation they have made M^r L'En-
              fant requesting him to form a contract with Maj^r
              Ellicot for his services this year and observing on
              the intended operations the ensuing season.

[P. 83, PROCEEDINGS OF THE COMMISSIONERS, Vol. I, 1791–5, in the National Archives.]

COMMISSIONERS TO JEFFERSON

COMMISSIONERS TO JEFFERSON

George Town 14th *March* 1792

Sir/

Your favour of the 6th Instant is now before us. We doubt not but every advantage will be taken of the dismission of Maj^r L'Enfant. It is to be regretted that his Temper made it a necessary measure. As far as our exertions can Counteract any ill effects expected from it they may be relied on. With respect to his compensation we have adopted the Presidents Ideas, in a letter to Mr Stewart. As he has already received £225 from us besides having his expences of living here paid we flatter ourselves he will have no Cause to Complain of having met with an inadequate reward. Enclosed is a Copy of our letter to the Maj^r. Tho' Mr Ellicott from his conversation with you, has appeared disposed to make some abatement in his own wages, so far at least as respects his expences in living, he has informed us that his Brothers, expects [sic] if they return to have three Dollars a Day. He mentions that they were offered this Sum last Year by the Jerssie Company, which is now increased to a Dollar more. Their wages last year were two Dollars a day and their expences paid. If they will bear their own expences, it will be more satisfactory to us to give them three Dollars than to

have them on the former terms. We have accordingly informed
M.ʳ Ellicott, that we would give them this Sum, provided, they
paid their own expences. As it would be particularly unfortunate at this time, to meet with a second dissappointment in
those who have been in our employment, we beg you will settle
the matter with him. Whatever you do will be confirmed by us.
We shall have no difficulty in dismissing the Action against M.ʳ
Roberdeau. As we consider him as a misled young man, we are
even disposed to employ him again, if he chuses it. The President on his return from Charlestown, last Summer, mentioned
to us an Architect who had been highly recommended to him
by some of the first Characters in the place. If he still approves
of him and we can be informed of his name we will endeavor to
engage him. Or will it be best to advertise for a Superintendant. If you think the latter the most eligible, as there is no time
for delay, we request when you Advertise for Plans, you will
advertise for Superintendants also. If you think it necessary to
mention his Salary, as it must depend much on the talents and
abilities we shall leave it to be settled by you and the President.
The advertisements for Plans of the buildings, having our approbation, are returned for insertion.   From our conversation
with M.ʳ Ellicott in December last, respecting the time at which
a second sale might take place, he was of oppinion it could not
be sooner, than the End of June. from the unexpected disapointment we have met with about the engraved plans, perhaps it
would be most eligible now, to defer it till the last of July, to
give as much time as possible for their dispersion and circulation. It appears to us to be important to have the Plans of the
buildings at that time for general inspection. If approved they
will no doubt contribute much to generous bids. For these reasons we think the blanks may be filled up with the 20.ᵗʰ July.
But as you have the opportunity of conversing M.ʳ Ellicott on
the subject we beg you will fill them up as you may think
proper. It would certainly be desirable to have the Plans as

much sooner as possible, but we apprehend this cannot be expected. We have the satisfaction of informing you, that we have got a very large Quantity of Earth thrown up at the Presidents house, and that we shall soon set in to making Bricks. The erection of a bridge over rock-Creek and turning the Post Road over it has always appeared to us, as a measure which demanded our earliest attention. As we shall be in immediate want of a Wharf, for the landing of materials, we shall set about it as soon as the Logs we have contracted for arrive. Our time at present will not permit us to give our Ideas more at large on the several subjects you have suggested. We shall take the earliest opportunity of adjusting the affair respecting M.ʳ Carroll's house. Your Ideas concerning the importation of Germans & Highlanders meet with our approbation, and we shall be glad to receive from you any Plans you may have formed on the subject, or calculation of the terms on which they can be had. We hope the great objects which so immediately press on us, at present will be so far forewarded by an other Spring, as to give us an opportunity of extending our Ideas to many other matters than what at present offer themselves to our contemplation. We are &c.

D.ᵈ STUART
DAN.ˡ CARROLL

HON.º THO. JEFFERSON
Secretary of State, Philadelphia.

N.B. Your favour of the 9.ᵗʰ just received.

[Pp. 66–8, COMMISSIONERS' LETTERBOOK Vol. I, 1791–1793, in the National Archives; pp. 233–4, U.S. *v.* SMITH.]

COMMISSIONERS TO JEFFERSON

George-Town 14ᵗʰ *March* 1792

COMMISSIONERS TO JEFFERSON

Sir

The plan of the Loan from M.ʳ Blodget which you enclosed

us, appears to us to be very eligible. It has therefore our warmest approbation. Tho' we have not the smallest apprehension from the best attention we have been able to bestow on it that we can in any measure be liable in our private capacities, yet we think it prudent, to express our desire, that this may be well understood by M.ʳ Blodget. We are &c.

D.ᵈ STUART
DAN.ˡ CARROLL

TO M.ᴿ JEFFERSON

[P. 65, COMMISSIONERS' LETTERBOOK Vol. I, 1791–1793, in the National Archives.]

DRAFT OF COMPETITION FOR PLAN OF A CAPITOL

PROGRAM OF COMPETITION FOR THE
UNITED STATES CAPITOL [32]

Washington, in the Territory of Columbia
A Premium

of a lot in the city, to be designated by impartial judges, and $500, or a medal of that value, at the option of the party, will be given by the Commissioners of Federal Buildings to persons who, before the 15th day of July, 1792, shall produce them the most approved plan, if adopted by them for a Capitol to be erected in the city, and $250 or a medal for the plan deemed next in merit to the one they shall adopt; the building to be of brick and to contain the following compartments, to wit:

A conference room   Sufficient to accommodate ⎫
A room for Representatives   300 persons each ⎪ These rooms to
A lobby or antechamber to the latter   ⎬ be of full
A Senate room of 1,200 square feet of area   ⎪ elevation.
An antechamber and lobby to the latter   ⎭

Twelve rooms of 600 square feet area each for committee rooms and clerks, to be of half the elevation of the former.

[32] This draft was prepared and approved by Thomas Jefferson.

Drawings will be expected of the ground plats, elevations of each front, and sections through the building in such directions as may be necessary to explain the material, structure, and an estimate of the cubic feet of the brick work composing the whole mass of the walls.

THOS. JOHNSON,
DD. STUART,
DANL. CARROLL, *Commissioners*

March 14, 1792

[P. 15, DOCUMENTARY HISTORY OF . . . THE CAPITOL . . .; GAZETTE OF THE UNITED STATES, Philadelphia, March 24, 1792.]

JEFFERSON TO WALKER

THOMAS JEFFERSON TO GEORGE WALKER

March 14, 1792

Your favor of March 9 came to hand yesterday with the letter of several of the proprietors of Georgetown, desiring the reemployment of Mj. Lenfant and were duly laid before the President. He would be happy to satisfy the wishes of those gentlemen wherever propriety and practicability admitted. The retirement of Majr. Lenfant has been his own act. Nobody knows better than yourself the patience and condescensions the President used in order to induce him to continue. You know also how these were received on his part. When the President sent his Secretary to take Major Lenfant's ultimate conditions, they were, as I informed you in my former letter a dismission of the Commissioners or his independence of them. Such conditions could produce one idea only; that his reemployment was never more to be thought of. That it was believed he might have been useful, the efforts to continue him have fully proved, but that the success of the enterprise depended on his employment is impossible to believe.

[Elizabeth S. Kite, L'ENFANT AND WASHINGTON, p. 173. Reprinted through the courtesy of the Johns Hopkins Press, Baltimore, Md.]

WASHINGTON TO JEFFERSON

GEORGE WASHINGTON TO THOMAS JEFFERSON

Wednesday, March 14, 1792

At the time Mr. Jeffersons letter to the President was put into his hands he was so much engaged as hardly to find time to read it. The general purport of it, however, he well recollects was agreeable to him but whether the following ideas if they are not already substantially expressed, might not with propriety be conveyed, Mr. Jefferson will judge of, and act accordingly.

That no farther movement on the part of Government, can ever be made towards Majr. L'Enfant without prostration, *which will not be done*. That the P——— thinks himself insulted in the answer given to his Secretary, who was sent to him for the *express* purpose of removing some of his *unfounded* suspicions, viz "that he had already heard enough of this matter."

No farther overtures will *ever* be made to this Gentn. by the Government; in truth it would be useless, for in proportion as attempts have been made to accommodate what *appeared* to be his wishes, he has receded from his own ground. If therefore his conduct should change and a reinstatement of him is desired, the *only* way to effect it is by a direct application to the Commissioners.

[Pp. 3–4, WRITINGS OF WASHINGTON, Fitzpatrick, Vol. 32.]

COMMISSIONERS' NOTE

15 March Received a Letter from Mr Jefferson respecting proposals of Mr Leslie to
1792   erect a Clock in the City, and of Mr Ceracchi to erect a Monument in memory of American Liberty and inclosing a Letter from Ra B Lee.

[P. 83, PROCEEDINGS OF THE COMMISSIONERS, Vol. I, 1791–5, in the National Archives.]

WALKER TO JEFFERSON

GEORGE WALKER TO THOMAS JEFFERSON

March 21, 1792

Sir,

   Your favor of the 14th Inst I had the honour to receive and have communicated the contents to the Proprietors of this City. In consequence of which I this day received the enclosed letter which they wish may be laid before the President of the United States. As I may some time after take an oppt. of conveying to you my Sentiments on this business I shall not add at present but that I am with great esteem and respect

> Sir

> > Your mo. obt. Servant

> > > GEORGE WALKER.

[Elizabeth S. Kite, L'ENFANT AND WASHINGTON, p. 175. Reprinted through the courtesy of the Johns Hopkins Press, Baltimore, Md.]

PROPRIETORS TO WALKER

THE PROPRIETORS TO GEORGE WALKER

Georgetown, March 21, 1792

Sir

   In answer to your communication of Mr. Jefferson's letter to you of the 14th Inst., permit us to request the favor of you to inform Mr. Jefferson, as a piece of justice which seems requisite to ourselves, that we are very far from being so unreasonable as to expect that Maj. L'Enfant would be or to think that he ought to be employed on either of the conditions mentioned in his [Jefferson's] first letter to you & repeated in the second. If M. L'Enfant persists in not returning on any other, we know that all ideas on the subject must be abandoned. — but if on the contrary he should now be willing to accept such conditions as can with propriety be given we should hope that the simple circumstance of his once asking more, would not be deemed sufficient to deprive forever the City of the services of a man of acknowledged Capacity and Merit, who has already been found highly useful.

The Commissioners are respectable men and our own interest as well as a Public Duty would prompt us to give all the little aid in our power to their efforts, which we have no doubt will be directed at least, by good intentions and zeal towards the growth of the City — But we must still lament as a very great misfortune to the object, the loss of a man deservedly (at least in point of talents, zeal, industry & total disinterestedness) possessing in a high degree the public confidence.

The sentiments contained in this, & our former letter, are those of individuals deeply interested in the progress of the city, who do not pretend to set up a claim that additional weight should be given them from the circumstance of their coming from proprietors. A distinction we wish to be made.

We are sir Your Most Obt. Serts.

Jas. M. Lingan	Robert Peters
John Davidson	David Burnes
Sam. Davidson	Abraham Young
Overton Carr	Wm. King
	W. Prout
	U. Forrest
	Ben Stoddert

[Elizabeth S. Kite, L'ENFANT AND WASHINGTON, pp. 175–6. Reprinted through the courtesy of the Johns Hopkins Press, Baltimore, Md.]

WASHINGTON TO JEFFERSON

GEORGE WASHINGTON TO THOMAS JEFFERSON

[Received, March 21, 1792.]

. . . . .

I hope Mr. Blodget does not begin to hesitate concerning the loan? And I hope the Commissioners, when they are about it, will build a Stone bridge and a complete one, over Rock Creek, it will be the cheapest in the end. Yrs. etc.

Wednesday⎱
Afternoon ⎰

GEORGE WASHINGTON

[Ms., *Jefferson Papers*, Library of Congress.]

JEFFERSON TO COMMISSIONERS

JEFFERSON TO THE COMMISSIONERS

Philadelphia March 21st 1792

Gentlemen

Your favors of March 14th have been duely received, as also Mr Carrol's seperate letter of March 15th I now enclose you copies of the two advertisements inserted in Freneau's, Fenno's, and Dunlaps', papers of this place. You will probably think it proper to have them inserted in papers of other parts of the Union, following herein, your own choice. It is rather desired too that you adopt such method as you think best for obtaining a Superintendant of proper qualifications, whether by advertising, or by private enquiry. the President is not able to give you any satisfactory information as to the Charlestown architect. Mr. Ellicott being of oppinion he cannot be in readyness for a Sale before the last of July, the blanks for the day of producing the plans are filled up with 15th of that month, so as to allow time for decision between them, before the sale. Mr Ellicott sets off the day after tomorrow, he says it was his intention that his brothers, receiving 3 Dollars a day should bear his own expences. I have advised him to reconsider with you his own demand of 5 Dollars, and abate from it what reason my require, so that he considers, that allowance as still open. there is at Amsterdam a Mr Hermen-Hend Damen a merchant-broker (conected with the Van Stephorsts) who is from the Palatinate.

One of the boundary stones at the north point of the
District of Columbia.

Tripoli Column, erected in the Navy Yard, 1808, the first monument
on public grounds in the National Capital.

The Capitol as it stood in the administration of Thomas Jefferson (Statuary Hall, the old House of Representatives, at right; the Senate at left; and connecting covered way, 100 feet long, where is now the Rotunda. (Courtesy of National Commission of Fine Arts.)

The old Capitol Building, completed by Charles Bulfinch in 1827.

Robert Brent's first commission as mayor of the City of Washington, reproduced in Volume 2, Records of the Columbia Historical Society.

he informed me that the Palatines who emigrate to America, come down the Rhine to embark at Amsterdam. he undertook to procure any number I should desire, and to deliver them at Richmond, clear of all expence, for 10. Guineas a man, paid at Amsterdam, or 11 Guineas at Richmond. they were to be indentured to serve me one year for their passage, and to remain 7 years tenants on my lands on half-stocks, you would have to propose wages instead of this and a shorter contract; and very moderate wages would probably do. if you have no preferable channel of your own, and will be good enough to do what is necessary on your part, I will forward your letters, and accompany them with my own to M.ͬ x x x Damer. & to the Vanstapherhsts so as to have your purpose answered with zeal and fidelity. the temporary check on the price of public paper, occasioned by M.ͬ Duer's failure, induces M.ͬ Blodget to think it will be better to pospone for a few days the opening of the Loan proposed, as he thinks it important that the present panic should be so far over, as to enable him to get it through at once, when proposed. I have the honour to be with the most perfect esteem and respect   Gentlemen — Yours &c.

TH: JEFFERSON

P.S. The President thinks the bridge over
Rock-creek should be of stone, and that it will be the cheapest in the end.

[Pp. 84–5, COMMISSIONERS' LETTERBOOK, Vol. I, 1791–1793, in the National Archives.]

WASHINGTON TO JEFFERSON

GEORGE WASHINGTON TO THOMAS JEFFERSON

[*March* 24, 1792.]

The Letters from Mr. de Mirbeck [33] and Mr. Vall-travers [34]

[33] "Not now found in the *Washington Papers*." [Fitzpatrick, Vol. 32 p. 11 n. 27.]
[34] "Rodolph Vall-travers wrote half a dozen letters from Rotterdam. . . . Some of these . . . are in the *Washington Papers*." [Fitzpatrick, Vol. 32 p. 11 n. 28.]

to the P—— and from the Proprietors of the Federal City [35] to Mr. Walker, he wishes Mr. Jefferson to read and consider, that answers to, or proper notice of them, may result from it.

[P. 11, WRITINGS OF WASHINGTON, Fitzpatrick, Vol. 32.]

JEFFERSON TO WALKER

Philadelphia Mar. 26, 1792.

Sir

I have duly received your favor of the 21st with the letter from sundry inhabitants of George town which it inclosed, and have laid them before the President. you have before understood, Sir, that Maj^{r} L'Enfant was originally called into the service by m$\bar{r}$ Carrol, who doubting, before Maj^{r} L'Enfant's arrival here, whether he could with propriety act as a Commissioner while he remained a member of the legislature, it fell on the President to point out to the Maj^{r} the objects of his attention & to send him on to the other Commissioners under whose employment & direction he was explicitly informed that he was to act. this accident alone gave an appearance of an original interference by the President, which it neither was, nor is his intention to practise. whoever wishes for employment, whether it be Maj^{r} Lenfant or any other, must apply to the Commissioners directly, the President being decided not to meddle with those details. he would certainly wish to do what would gratify the inhabitants, in any instance where it could be consistent with propriety. in the present he can do no more than leave the Commissioners free to follow their own judgment.

I am with great esteem, Sir

[35] "This letter is in *District of Columbia Letters and Papers* and is signed by Robert Peter, John Davidson, Samuel Davidson, James M. Lingan, Abraham Young, William King, Ben Stoddert, Uriah Forrest, Wm. Prout, Overton Carr, David Burnes, and Elephaz Douglas." [Fitzpatrick, Vol. 32 p. 11 n. 29.]

Your most obed^t serv^t

Th: Jefferson

MR GEORGE WALKER.

[Ms., *Jefferson Papers*, Library of Congress; p. 180, Kite, L'ENFANT AND WASHINGTON.]

COMMISSIONERS TO JEFFERSON

COMMIS^{RS}. TO M^R. JEFFERSON, SECRETARY OF STATE

Georgetown 30th *March* 1792

Sir/

Having felt much anxiety at our last meeting, to see business of some sort, commenced here, we determined on the immediate erection of a Bridge over Rock-Creek, and advertised for models to be exhibited to us by the 26th. Mr. Herbaugh, from Baltimore, an artist with whose ingenuity, you must be acquainted from his patents, exhibited to us the enclosed one, which has our approbation, as well as that of all here —

We had some doubts at first whether one Arch might be sufficient for the discharge, of the water in times of great floods, but have been fully satisfied on that head by those, who are best acquainted with it — A conditional agreement was immediately made with him, of which you have enclosed a Copy, together with his estimate of the expences — The proprietors of the ground from the Creek to George-Town, made a cession last fall of half their interest, in it, for the purposes of a bridge and Causeway which was deposited with Maj^r. L'Enfant, who has it still — This made it necessary for us to apply to them, for a renewall of it, which we have obtained, and send you a Copy of — You will observe we are bound to complete both the bridge and causeway, before we can be entitled to the benefits of the Cession — As the River at present occupies almost, the whole of the Street, leading from G. Town over the Bridge, this would be perfectly useless without the Causeway: As the latter however is not included within the limits of the City, we do not think ourselves authorised to destine any part of the funds entrusted to us, to any purpose not so encluded, tho' immediately conected with it, and have thought it proper to submit the matter to the Presidents consideration — Allowing the property ceded to the Public, to sell only at one half the price which such property commands at present in Baltimore and Alexandria, the Public will be more than reimbursed the expences of the Bridge, and Causeway provided no sale is made till these are completed — So that the Money advanced for effecting these objects, may be considered only as a loan, and for a very short time — Upon the whole, then, we doubt not but the President will approve of our making an absolute contract for them — To enable you to judge better of the value of the property, we enclose you a Survey we caused to be made of the ground, with a sketch of the lots to be devided between the Public and the individuals — Mr. Harbugh gives us reason to think he will undertake the Causeway likewise — He returns to Baltimore, tomorrow, to prepare for the undertaking he has entered into conditionally, if it receives the Presidents assent, of which we promised him, to request you to drop him immediate notice, at Baltimore that there may be no delay — Such indeed is the important point of view in which we consider this matter, that sooner than have incurred, this we should notwithstanding, the doubt respecting our authority, have agreed absolutely with him — It was our intention founded on the expectation of meeting Mr. Ellicott here to have employed hands on the Post-road — A Skillfull hand is engaged to superintend the work at the Quarries, which will commence next week — We are in dayly expectation of a person from Baltimore, who has been highly recommended to us, to superintend the making of Bricks — Many offers of lime from the Eastward have been made us, but so exorbitent, that they have been declined; and we think ourselves fortunate in having done so, as we now have infinitely better, made us, from the upper parts of the Potomac — Indeed our pursuits from this Quarter are very flattering both with respect to Plank and lime — If lime can at present be supplied on cheaper terms from thence, then the Eastward, what may not be expected Summer twelve month, when we have the strongest assurance of the Navigation being completed, and when we shall have the greatest demand for it — With respect to its quality our information from those who have had experience of each is, that the Potomack line is one fifth superior — Advertisements of the Plans have been sent to Boston, Baltimore Charlestown & Richmond — As soon as we are informed of the success of the event you mention, our Views will of course be extended to every possible object — From our short acquaintance with Mr. Herbaugh, we are impressed with the most favourable, opinion of him, and besides flattering ourselves that he will be found generaly usefull, think he will be the most proper person we can engage, when it shall be necessary to undertake the Canal and the contraction of Goose-Creek — We have received a letter from Majr. L'Enfant refusing our offer to him and requesting we would recall our draft in his favour — This place is becoming an object of much consequence, as to the atracting the notice of artists and laborers from all Quarters — This being the Case we will defer our answer to your offer respecting Germans, till Mr. Johnsons arrival whom we expect in the Course of a few days — We have conversed with Mr. Carroll on the subject of his house, who readly accedes to the proposition, of having it rebuilt to the same State as when it was destroyed — We shall therefore employ persons immediately, upon it — We are &c

(Signed)   DD STUART
DANL CARROLL

TO MR. JEFFERSON

[P. 71, COMMISSIONERS' LETTERBOOK Vol. I, 1791–1793, in the National Archives; pp. 234–6, U.S. v. MORRIS.]

WASHINGTON TO JEFFERSON

GEORGE WASHINGTON TO THOMAS JEFFERSON

[*March* 30, 1792.]

The enclosed Instrumt. does not accord with my recollection of Mr. Blodgets proposed Loan, and I confess I had much rather see a clear expression of the intention than to meet an explanation of it afterwards by one of the parties, to the contract.

The *number* of Lots to be Mortgaged I do not positively recollect; but sure I am one half were to be North of an East and West line from the Presidents House. I do not remember that the words *"valuable Lots"* were inserted in the proposition of Mr. Blodget and think the Mortgaged Lots were releasable by the substitn. of others. If therefore the subsequent instrument should not place these matters in a very precise point of view, a foundation will be laid for much discontent, and probably disputes.

Did you see Mr. White [36] yesterday? and in that case what was his opinion respecting M—n's [37] acceptance in the manner suggested?

[Pp. 13–14, WRITINGS OF WASHINGTON, Fitzpatrick, Vol. 32.]

ELLICOTT TO JEFFERSON

Geo. Town April 3 1792

Sir/

I arrived at this place on friday evening last, after the Commissioners had sent their Letters for you, to the Post Office; which will account for their not mentioning my arrival in their

[36] "Alexander White. He was a Member of Congress from Virginia, who became a Commissioner of the District in 1795." [Fitzpatrick, Vol. 32 p. 14 n. 35.]
[37] "Daniel Morgan." [Fitzpatrick, Vol. 32 p. 14 n. 36.]

despatches. I understand that Mr George Walker, has been
sent on to Philadelphia by the Proprietors of the Lands in the
City of Washington, to prevail upon the President, to restore
M^r L'Enfant to his former employment in the City. This measure, I am informed was taken, in consequence of a Letter from
Mr Cabot, to Mr Davidson, which Letter in my opinion is
highly exceptionable and if the Commissioners should be able
to procure a copy of it, they will no doubt send it to you. I sus-
pect that some of the Proprietors are now sorry, that they appeared in the above business. Several of them, have acknowledged to me, that their desire for the restoration of Major
L'Enfant, arose from a wish to dispose of their lands the ensuing
season: and expected, that his extravagant plans, added to his
great confidence, and mad zeal, would be highly favourable to
them; but confessed at the same time, that on account of his
ungovernable temper, his dismission must unavoidably take
place at no very distant period. After the next meeting of the
Commissioners, which will be on the 9th of this month, I shall
be able to write to you more particularly. in the mean time,

> I am Sir
>> Your H^{le} Servt

AND^W ELLICOTT

HON^{BLE} THOMAS JEFFERSON ESQ^R

[Ms., *Jefferson Papers*, Library of Congress.]

JEFFERSON TO HARBAUGH

TO MR HERBAUGH

Philadelphia April 5. 1792

Sir

The President of the United States has approved the Contract of the Commissioners of the federal building with you, for

erecting a bridge over Rock Creek, of which I notify you according to their desire. I am Sir &c.

TH: JEFFERSON

[Ms., p. 371, *American Letters*, Vol. IV, 1788–92, State Department Archives in the National Archives.]

JEFFERSON TO THE COMMISSIONERS

JEFFERSON TO THE COMMISSIONERS

Philadelphia, April 5th 1792

Gentlemen

I now send you 500 obligations for your Signature. should Mr Johnson not be with you it will be proper to send them to him by express, as soon they have received all your signatures if you will be so good as to return them to me, the business shall be finally compleated. I received yesterday yours of March 30 & laid it immediately before the President. tho' he thinks the estimate of the Bridge very high, yet not doubting you have satisfied yourself, by proper enquiry, he approves of the Contract. Indeed he thinks and wishes that having once consulted him, on the works to be undertaken, you would make your contracts, and proceed in the execution, without farther reference to him; as he has perfect confidence in the endeavours you will use, to do every thing in the best way possible, and he has hardly time to attend to any details, he thinks that if you were to reduce the foot ways, of the bridge to 6 feet each, and make the Carriage way 26 feet, it might be better.

I have the honor to be with great esteem and respect Gentlemen

Your m.^o &c

TH: JEFFERSON

P.S. — I notify Mr Herbaugh by this Post.

[Pp. 85–6, COMMISSIONERS' LETTERBOOK Vol. I, 1791–1793, in the National Archives.]

Jefferson to the Commissioners

JEFFERSON TO THE COMMISSIONERS

Philadelphia April 9.th 1792

Gentlemen

In a former letter I enclosed you an Idea of Mr Lee's for an immediate appropriation of a number of Lots, to raise a sum of Money for erecting a national monument in the City of Washington. it was scarcely to be doubted but that you would avoid appropriations for matters of ornament till a sufficient Sum should be secured out of the proceeds of your sales to accomplish the Public buildings, bridges & other such objects as are essential. Mr Ceracchi, the artist, who had proposed to execute the monument, has had hopes that a subscription set on foot for that purpose, would have sufficed to effect it. that hope is now over, and he is about to return to Europe. he is unquestionably an artist of the first Class. he has had the advantage of taking the model of the President's person in plaster, equal to every wish in resemblance and Spirit, it is pretty certain, that the Equestrian Statue of the President can never be executed by an equal workman, who has had equal advantages, and the Question is, whether a prudent caution will permit you to enter into any engagement, now taking time enough before the term of payment, to have accomplished the more material objects of the public buildings &c. He says that to execute the Equestrian Statue with the cost of the materials in marble, will be worth 20,000 Guineas. That he could begin it on his return, if four or five years hence you can engage to pay him 20,000 Dollars, and the same sum annually afterwards till the whole is paid, before which time the Statue shall be ready. It is rather probable that within some time Congress would take it off our hands, in compliance with an antient Vote of that body. The Question for your consideration are whether, supposing no difficulty as to the means, you think such a work might be undertaken by you? whether you can have so much confidence in the productiveness of your funds, as to engage for a residuum of this amount, all more necessary objects being first secured, & that this may be within the times, before proposed? And in fine which will preponderate in your minds, the hazard of undertaking this now, or that of losing the aid of this Artist. The nature of this proposition will satisfy you, that it has not been communicated to the President, and of course would not be unless a previous acceptance on your part should render it necessary to obtain his sanction. Your answer is necessary for the satisfaction of M.ʳ Ceracchi, at whose instance I submit the proposal to you, & who I believe will only wait here the return of that answer. I have the honour to be with the most perfect esteem,

> Gentlemen, yours &c.

TH: JEFFERSON

[Pp. 86–7, COMMISSIONERS' LETTERBOOK Vol. I, 1791–1793, in the National Archives; p 322, Mem. Ed., VIII.]

COMMISSIONERS TO JEFFERSON

COMMISSIONERS TO SECRETARY OF STATE

George-Town 11.ᵗʰ *April* 1792

Sir/

We now send you the Warrants executed on our part: by our counting there are 519 which you'll be pleased to notice. By the rigour of this Loan the whole number of lots remains in Mortg.ᵃ till the intire pay.ᵗˢ. it is desireable if it can, as we suppose, be changed without inconvenience so far as that on Payment of every 200 Dollars one Lot should be released from the Incumbrance. by this the Sale may go on with Safety to Purchasers, as soon as the time of Payment comes, and may much accomadate the public. However, if there's the least Difficulty we do not wish it to be insisted on. We have left the Numbers blank. The situation of things here is very different from what we expected, or you perhaps have any Idea of. People are on tip Toe to come from all parts, we might probably have 2000 mechanics and labourers here on very short notice. we think therefore, there is no occasion to import People from abroad unless Stone-cutters of whom there are but few and their wages high of them indeed 20, or 30 from Scotland are desirable & we wish them introduced. We are of Oppinion that in the application of the Funds, we ought to class our work, into Necessary, Usefull, and Ornamental, preferring them in that order. Without going into the Question of right to apply the money to defray the expence of Mʳ. Cerachie's Design or the propriety of the design itself, we decline going into that business. You may be assured Sir that our Coolness does not proceed from any Disinclination to concur in monumental Acknowledgments of the Favour of Heaven and the Virtues of the Heroe but it certainly ought to be a National Act. We cannot but be unesy at the situation. . . chosen for the Capitol we have had a free conversation with Majʳ Ellicott on it and on View of the ground, taking in the value of Mʳ Youngs improvements which must be paid for on the present plans taking place, and which may be left clear by a small alteration, we reckon the difference of expence must be at least 15,000£ but that still is not the worst, within three Hundred Yards the inviting Situation will always reproach the Choice presuming that the delay and Expences influenced we should be glad this business was reconsidered. Ellicott says in his letter which we enclose, it will not take above 3, or 4 weeks to correct what will be necessary. this may be shortened, we have no doubt by introducing a few accurate measures, and the difference of expence much in favour of it. we have told Majʳ Ellicott that we wish an opportunity, to make him a present at the Close of the work for his Expedition in doing it. He says and the Fact is that the Deviation for the

Plate will be imperceptable but on measuring, and that the Plate will convey an Idea of the work sufficiently exact to any man living. We would avoid Importunity but the President will bear a little with our anxiety and let us know his Resolution soon which will be chearfully executed though it should be contrary to our wish. We are Sir &c.

THO. JOHNSON
DR STUART
DAN^L CARROLL

[Pp. 78–80, COMMISSIONERS' LETTERBOOK Vol. I, 1791–1793, in the National Archives.]

COMMISSIONERS TO JEFFERSON

COMMISSIONERS TO JEFFERSON

George-Town 14th April 1792

Sir/

We are just closing our Business this Evening so that we may seperate in the morning. Nothing very particular has happened in the Course of this meeting. Your Letter of the 9th Instant has again brought under our Consideration the Business of Mr Cirecchi and on every view of it, we cannot bring ourselves to depart from the Sentiments communicated in our last. We have hitherto been anxious to get things in order for a Public Sale of Lots in the Summer, if the Loan is filled up we think it will be well to depart from that Idea advertising that the State of our Funds makes a Public sale unnecessary, though to promote Improvement the Commissioners will treat the first day of every Month if not on a Sunday, or if it happens on a Sunday, the next day with Purchasers under Condition of Improvement. It is with Reluctance, we at any time, trouble the President: the reason for our submitting the Bridge Contract to him and making it Conditional was because the Expenditure tho' highly necessary will be without the limits of the City. And be-

cause the Time of suspension would not at all delay the Operation. We shall wait for the Plans with Impatience, before they
are approved we do not wish to be too deeply officered. Perhaps
the draftsman of one, or both, may be desirous of conducting
the execution and if proper in other respects we should wish to
engage him. Our delicacy on this head when Maj.ʳ L'Enfant
was expected to be superintendant, has led to the Embarrassment and delay we now suffer, we have had many applications
for more Employments without work than we had ever thought
of. At present we have a Cap.ᵗ Williams who has given us much
Satisfaction by his Activity and Attention in the little we have
to do and M.ʳ Harbaugh who is a modest well tempered Man.
Seems equally disposed and able to be very usefull to us. Perhaps when the Plans are agreed on we may be able to get both
Foundations as well and Soon done with very little additional
assistance, as with all that may be necessary in a more advanced
State of the Work. By Accident a Prospect has opened of getting a sufficient Number of Stone-Cutters from N. York. We
are Sir, &c.

THO. JOHNSON
D.ᴿ STUART
DAN.ᴸ CARROLL

[Pp. 82–3, COMMISSIONERS' LETTERBOOK Vol. I, 1791–1793, in the National Archives.]

JEFFERSON TO COMMISSIONERS

JEFFERSON TO
COMMISSIONERS

Philadelphia April 20.ᵗʰ 1792

Gentlemen

Your favour of the 11.ᵗʰ has been duly received and laid before the President. He thinks it best to decline making any
alterations in the plan of the City. The consideration which

weigh with him are the expediency of fixing the public opinion on the thing as stable & unalterable, the loss of the work done if altered, the changing all the Avenues which point to the Capitol, removing the two houses to a still greater distance, change in the engraving, and that it will not be necessary to dig away the hill to the Eastward, since were it to be dug away, private buildings would as effectually exclude prospect from the Capitol, except merely along the avenues. He thinks that the obstruction given by M.ʳ Youngs house need not bring on any question for years to come.

The warants are received, and your desire shall be attended to for releasing the lots mortgaged [there is a space left here in the book] with redemption, but I do not know that, that can now be effected. You have certainly heard of the extraordinary crush which has taken place, here at N York and Boston, of persons dealing in paper, & of good merchants and others who had dealings with paper-men. it has produced a general stagnation of money contracts, which will continue till it is known who stands and who falls, during this crisis, M.ʳ Blodget thinks it prudent to suspend proposing our loan, & indeed we think so too. this will oblige you to keep back, some of your operations. Perhaps proper offers to workmen, and labourers, without being addressed to any place in particular, might at this moment draw great numbers from New-York, Boston and this place. The procuring workmen from Scotland is an object of importance: and it may be doubted whether the importation of some Germans might not be a good experiment as well in economy, as to have a certain dependance. They are distinguished for their industry & sobriety, and might do good as an example & model to be refered to. I have the honor to be with the utmost respect and esteem   Gentlemen &c.

TH: JEFFERSON

[Pp. 87-8, COMMISSIONERS' LETTERBOOK Vol. I, 1791-1793, in the National Archives; U.S. v. MORRIS, pp. 2213-14, Vol. 7.]

BLODGET TO JEFFERSON

[TO THOMAS JEFFERSON]

New York 20th *April* 1792.

Sir

In reply to my letter respecting the Plan of the City of Washington my friend has written vizt "Mr Hill fears it will take 2 months to compleat the engraving & estimates the expense at about 160 Doll'rs, no time shall be Lost to have it compleated in his best maner."

—— This City wears a very gloomy aspect owing to the late failures, fraudulent conveyances are much talked of, & one (suposed from Mr. McComb to his Brother in Canada, for upwards of £70 000 in Real Estate,) it is said might be rendered null provided the Bankrupt Law now Pending in Committe is passed this Session of Congress. excuse the Liberty I have taken to mention this, of which I am at present unable to form an opinion, and believe me to be with the most perfect respect your ever devoted humble servant,

S BLODGET JUN'R

I return in a few days to Philadelphia & hope the honor of paying you Immediately my respects on Business.

[P. 219, U.S. *v.* SMITH.]

BLODGET TO JEFFERSON

New York 3d *May* 1792

Sir

By last nights post I have recd information that Mr Hill contracted to engrave the Plan of the City of Washington for 150 Dollars, he has promised to touch nothing in the line of his proffesion till this work is compleated which he hopes may be

in all June at furthest. I expect to wait on you the seventh Instant at Phila & am with great respect

       your most obedt servant

                           S BLODGET JUNR

    This City has remained very quiet since my last. a Ship ar-
rived this day from London but without later Intelligence than
we have had. it is said that Clinton will be re elected but this is
mere conjecture at present. I mention these circumstances
merely to shew my desire to give you news of which there is
scarce any at Present

    BLODGET S. 3 *May* 1792 *recd. May* 5.

[P. 220, U.S. *v.* SMITH.]

JEFFERSON TO COMMISSIONERS

JEFFERSON TO COMMISSIONERS

                       Philadelphia May 11.th 1792

Gentlemen

    I am to acknowledge the receipt of your joint favour of April
14th and Mr. Carrol's separate one of April 16th. I had informed
you in a former Letter that the Catastrophe among the paper
dealers would retard the Completion of the Loan. I now enclose you a Letter from Mr Blodget, by which you will perceive
its effect to be greater than he had at first supposed. He thinks
that the payment of June, which if the Loan had been filled up,
would have been of 50,000 Dollars must now be thrown back
and consolidated, with that of November, except as to 10,000
Dollars which he undertakes to pay on the 15th June for 180
Shares he takes himself, and 20 he has disposed of. After consultation with the President, we concluded nothing better was
to be done than still to leave the matter in Blodget's hands. I
therefore yesterday delivered him 500 warrants for which I
enclose his receipt, & I return you the 19 Supernumerary

which he wishes you to preserve, lest accident might destroy or deface some of those he has. He is Sanguine in his expectations that he can dispose of the whole in the Summer and for so much as he can he will obtain earlier payments than November of the first hundred Dollars a Share. You will of course however not enter into engagements faster than the actual sales. I have the honour to be, with the most perfect esteem & respect, Gentlemen, &c.

TH: JEFFERSON

[Pp. 94–5, COMMISSIONERS' LETTERBOOK, Vol. I, 1791–1793, in the National Archives.]

ELLICOTT TO JEFFERSON

Geo. Town May 13th 1792

Sir/

The Commissioners for the City of Washington, have had two meetings since my last, and in my opinion have conducted their business with judgment, and firmness; they nevertheless continue to meet with a decided opposition from several Gentlemen in this place; who are doubtless actuated more from private animosity, and disappointment, than a desire to serve the business. This opposition appeared to be on the decline, when Mr Cabot returned; but since that period, has not only revived, but made its appearance in the public papers printed in this Town. I am in hopes that no reply will be made, because silence in such cases, generally produces the best effects by witholding the fuel, which supplies envy, and disappointment with fire.

I have taken a level of the ground between Tyber, and St James's Creek; and find the averaged elevation above the common high-water almost six feet, and the distance three hundred and sixty eight poles in the direction of the proposed Canal. My opinion is now, as it always has been, that joining those Creeks, ought to be delayed to some future period, as the execution of that part of the business, is almost unconnected with the accommodation of Congress; which ought to be the point kept constantly in view, and to which all the present exertion should be directed. When this object is fully accomplished, others of less magnitude will of course receive that attention, which they severally merit.

> I am Sir with much
> esteem and respect
> Your H.^{bl} Servt

 AND.^W ELLICOTT.

HON.^{BLE} THO.^S JEFFERSON *Esqr*
Secretary of State.

[Ms., *Jefferson Papers*, Library of Congress.]

COMMISSIONERS TO JEFFERSON

COMMISS.^{RS} TO MR JEFFERSON

George-Town 2^d *June* 1792

Sir/

The State of our Funds is such that we can with Convenience agree to the Indulgence Mr Blodget desires. We have fixed on the 8.th of October for a Public Sale of Lots, agreeable to the enclosed Advertisement. The Introduction of Mechanicks, and Labourers from Europe being thought by the friends of the City so advisable a measure, we have again taken up that subject it may indeed, eventually be usefull, perhaps almost necessary, and considering this a favourable Time, to hold out additional Motives, for Emigration we shall endeavour to concert a Plan with some of the Scots Merchants to bring over some Stone-cutters and others, from that Country. We request you also to fall on Measures to procure about 100 Germans single men and as many of them Stone-cutters Masons, & Brick-layers, as can be readily had we will make any Arrangements you may think proper to pay the common passage Money to Alexandria or George-Town. The Tradesmen to work 16, the Labourers 20 months for their Passage. This number may not be a sufficient Inducement to send a Ship in purpose to this River, but we have no doubt but that any number of Passengers may be immediately disposed of here on the common Terms, we hold it essential the Ship should come here, as this may begin to be known a proper place for the Destination of Emigrants.

We are Sir, &c

THO. JOHNSON

D?. STUART

DAN!. CARROLL

[Pp. 90–1, COMMISSIONERS' LETTERBOOK, Vol. I, 1791–1793, in the National Archives; p. 16, . . . DOCUMENTARY HISTORY . . . OF THE CAPITOL, incomplete text.]

COMMISSIONERS TO JEFFERSON

THE COMMISSIONERS TO JEFFERSON

George Town, 6.th *June*, 1792.

Sir, We had through Maj.^r Ellicott for the Presidents View a Draft for the Capitol by William Hart of Toney Town and an imperfect Essay of Mr. Law, these are all we have yet received. Nothing has happened in the Course of this Meeting worth Communicating.

We are, Sir &.^c

TH. JOHNSON

DD. STUART

DAN!. CARROLL

TO MR. JEFFERSON

[P. 94, COMMISSIONERS' LETTERBOOK, Vol. I, 1791–1793, in the National Archives; incomplete text in DOCUMENTARY HISTORY . . . OF THE CAPITOL . . ., p. 16.]

Jefferson to Commissioners

Philadelphia June 9. 1792.

Gentlemen

I have been duly honoured with your favor of the 2^d inst. and have thought that I could not do better, with respect to the German emigrants, than to address the inclosed letter to the Messieurs Van Staphorsts & Hubbard of Amsterdam, leaving it to yourselves to point out the number & description of persons you want, and the conditions, and to opening a correspondence with them yourselves directly on the subject, as it is probably this may not be the only occasion in which you may want similar supplies. if mr̄ Damon is living, I think you may count on his executing your wishes; if any accident should have happened to him, the Messrs Van Staphorsts & Hubard will be able to put your commission into other trusty hands. — mr̄ Blodget is gone, I believe, to Boston. I shall hope to hear from him in the course of the ensuing week as to the 10,000 Dollars which ought to be paid on the 15th inst. I have the honor to be Gentlemen

          Your most obed^t
               & most humble serv^t

                                        Th: Jefferson

Mess.^{RS} Johnson, Stuart, & Carrol

[Ms., *Jefferson Papers*, Library of Congress; p. 16, documentary history . . . of the capitol . . ., incomplete text, under date of June 3, 1792.]

Jefferson to Van Staphorst & Hubbard

Philadelphia June 9. 1792

Gentlemen

When I was at Amsterdam you were so good as to make me acquainted with a Mr Herman Hend Damen, a merchant broker, connected with you, who, being from the Palatinate informed me he could at any time procure any number of emigrants from the country to come over on certain conditions then mentioned between us, or others equivalent, and that he would undertake to send me any number whenever I should be in readiness on paying him 10. guineas each at Amsterdam or 11. guineas at the port of delivery, in lieu of all charges of procuring & transporting them. being not yet in a situation to avail myself of this proposal, it is not for myself that I mention it to you, but for the Commissioners of the New City of Washington on the Potowmac which is to be our future Seat of government. these gentlemen having occasion for a number of labouring people, tradesmen & others, I informed them that I thought by addressing themselves to Mr Damen himself, or to him through you they could probably be furnished. they therefore propose to do it and will specify the kind of people they want, the number and the conditions; and the object being interesting to our government, I take the liberty of adding to their sollicitations for your attention and aid herein those of, gentlemen, your most obedient humble Serv!

[TH: JEFFERSON]

MESS.RS VAN STAPHORST & HUBARD

[Ms., *Jefferson Papers*, Library of Congress.]

JEFFERSON TO COMMISSIONERS

JEFFERSON TO THE COMMISSIONERS

Philadelphia June 11th. 1792

Gentlemen

I have the honor to enclose you the Presidents order on the Treasurer of Maryland for 24,000. Dollars according to the desire expressed in your letter of the 6th Instant, and of adding assurances of the esteem and respect with which I am, Gentlemen &c.

TH: JEFFERSON

[Ms., p. 389, *American Letters*, IV, 1788–92, State Department Archives in the National Archives; p. 96, COMMISSIONERS' LETTER BOOK, Vol. I, 1791–1793, in the National Archives.]

JEFFERSON TO BLODGET

Philadelphia June 22. 1792.

Sir

The 15th inst. being past when a deposit of 10,000 dollars was expected by the Commissioners of the Federal city, & not having heard from you, I take the liberty of asking a line from you, on account of the Commissioners who wish to know what they may be permitted to count on. I am Sir

Your most obed^t humble serv^t

TH: JEFFERSON

MR BLODGET

[Ms., *Jefferson Papers*, Library of Congress; Ms. p. 393, *American Letters*, IV, 1786–92, State Department Archives in the National Archives.]

BLODGET TO JEFFERSON

Boston June 25th 1792

Sir

Mr H, Otis, the Bearer of this will deliver you four first Impressions of the City of Washington, from the plate executed by your order, for Mr Hill, who wishes to make some slight additions before he sends it forward to you. I hope by return of Post to receive your permission to take off a few for my friends provided you may deem that the circulating them as presents may be conducive to the general good of the object I have so much at heart

I have found everyone much disposed to favour the Plan of the City, & believe we shall obtain many good Citizens from this Place, where I have disposed of as many of my lots as I thought were sufficient to make it of general notoriety; but this I have done at a low price — however I doubt not, by the next season, that the laying the foundation for the principle Buildings will give due encouragement to settlers, many of whom are only waiting to see the principle objects rising at their approach to the seat of our future greatness; ———— (merely owing to a want of Cash of all the persons who promised to assist in the Loan not one have paid in their first Instalment except myself, & this I have done at some disadvantage however the circulating money will increase by means of the late establishment of a new Bank in which this state are concerned one third, under the title of the *Union Bank* this has been effected on a plan of mine with the assistance of Mr S Adams, Dr Jarvis Mr Austin, & the "*Old Whigs* in order *some* say to counteract *in part* the too great Influence of the U. S. Bank & its Branches in tending fast *toward ye Consolidation* of the State Governments &c. &c. I must beg pardon for diviating in part from my orders by paying one half of the money only to Vizt 5000 dollars into the Branch Bank which remains subject to the order of the Commissioners, by any Bill at Sight that may be signed by them for the amount. The other 5000, dollars rests with the agents for the Union Bank & an draft Order for that amount on me or on Benj'a Green their treasurer, will be as duly honored as the former Mr Bulfinch, through modesty, has declined presenting his Plan & this has frightned me out of my Intention. however I doubt not but that there will be enough to make a choice from, — The Plate I will keep till I hear from you & am till then and ever after with much respect your devoted servant

S BLODGET JUNR

BLODGET SAML.   1792. 25 *June recd. July* 11.

T. Jefferson Esqr
    Secy of State & for foreign affairs
                    Philadelphia
hand by Mr Otis
forwarded by Sir yr most obedt hum.

                                 H. G. Otis

[P. 220–21, U.S. v. SMITH.]

Jefferson to Ellicot

                       Philadelphia July 3. 1792.

Dear Sir

    I inclose a letter [38] for D.ʳ Stewart, open to you, because I think, besides taking care that he receives it, you will have the goodness to make the same inquiries which I press on him, and that this will double my chance of finding out a level road which I am justly sure exists, and would be an immense convenience to me. be so kind as to stick a wafer in the D.ʳ's letter. I am with great esteem D.ʳ. Sir

       Your most obed.ᵗ humble serv.ᵗ

                            Th: Jefferson

M.ᴿ ANDREW ELLICOT.

Commissioners' Note

3.ᵈ July 1792   Received a Letter from the Secretary of State of the 11.ᵗʰ June inclosing the following order on the Treasurer of the Western Shore of Maryland, to wit

                            "Philadelphia June 11.ᵗʰ 1792

     Sir

        Be pleased to pay to Thomas Johnson David

[38] Unable to locate this letter . . . S.K.P.

[Ms., *Jefferson Papers*, Library of Congress.]

Stuart & Daniel Carroll Esq. Commissioners of the Federal Buildings, or to their order or to the order of any two of them, twenty-four thousand in part of the sum given by the Assembly of Maryland towards defraying the expence of the public buildings within the said District.

G? WASHINGTON

THOMAS HARWOOD ESQUIRE,
Treasurer of the Western Shore of Maryland."

[P. 118, PROCEEDINGS OF THE COMMISSIONERS, Vol. I, 1791–5, in the National Archives.]

COMMISSIONERS TO VAN STAPHORST AND HUBBARD

COMMISSIONERS TO MESS.^RS VAN STAPHORTS & HUBBARD

City of Washington 4th July 1792

Gentlemen

The enclosed letter from Mr Jefferson,[38a] will explain the Occasion of this Address to you, with the addition mentioned in his letter to us that he has not lately had any Intercourse with Mr Damen, nor knows if he is now in the way of complying with our wishes. We request you Gentlemen if Mr Damen is living, that you will put the enclosed letter, from us, into his hands, or if he is dead or from any Circumstances declining to gratify us, that you will transfer it to some other proper Hand. Your Instances in favour of our Views will be forwarding our public Measures, and giving us the very pleasing opportunity of returning the personal thanks of

    Gentlemen, &c

TH. JOHNSON
D? STUART
DAN.^L CARROLL

[P. 97, COMMISSIONERS' LETTERBOOK, Vol. I, 1791–1793, in the National Archives.]
^{38a} See Jefferson's letter to the Commissioners, June 9, 1792.

COMMISSIONERS TO DAMEN

COMMISSIONERS TO MR. HERMAN HEND DAMEN

Sir   *City of Washington* 4 *July* 1792

To facilitate the erection of the public buildings in the new City which committed to our care, we have thought it advisable to introduce a number of Mechanicks, and Labourers from abroad and wish about one hundred Germans, Single men and as many of them, Stone masons, Ston Cutters, and Brick Layers as may be, of the Number. M.ʳ Jefferson from the Acquaintance he obtained with you, has advised us to apply to you, for your Assistance, we understand the Terms on which you would furnish M.ʳ Jefferson, were the Payment of 10 Guinias at Amsterdam, or 11 Guineas at the Port of delivery in Lieu of all Charges, of procuring and transporting them. We expect the best men may be inclined to come to us. they will be employed in public work only, and their living found as free men. we desire the Mechanicks to work only, Sixteen Months, and the Labourers two Years, from their arrival at this Port. We will pay down the Eleven Guineas for each on their Arrival. The Small number proposed may not perhaps, open Field enough alone, but we have no difficulty in Assuring you there is no Port in America, where German passengers may be disposed of more readily, than here, to the Profit of the importer, and if you chuse to add to the Number on your own Account, to the address of any Merchant here, none more proper than William Deakins, Junior, we will make it our pleasure to see that the Emigrants, are placed with those who will use them well, and can pass our Honour, that your Interest will be attended to. If this Essay proves satisfactory, it is probable a like Importation, may be requested annually for several Years. We are Sir

&c   THO. JOHNSON
                                                D.ᴰ STUART
TO M.ᴿ HERMEN HEND DAMEN   DAN.ᴸ CARROLL

Merchant Amsterdam

[Pp. 97–8, COMMISSIONERS' LETTERBOOK, Vol. I, 1791–1793, in the National Archives.]

BLODGET TO JEFFERSON

Boston July 5, 1792.

Sir,

I Informed you pr Post & pr Mr. Henry Otis of my having paid 5000 Dollars into the Branch Bank U. S. (of Boston) the other 5000 remains, part in my hands, & part in the Union Bank lately established here — as this diviation was intended to favour a plan of mine & cannot operate to the Injury of the Commissioners for the City I hope for their & your pardon

some unforseen circumstances have prevented my obtaining any aid to the Loan except for my own private account *notwithstand every exertion* to circulate the warrants, yet I hope for a favourable turn as soon as the Public Buildings are begun

The Plate from which Mr. Otis carried you 4 impressions will go by water pr first Vessell

The Commissioners may draw on the two Banks as soon as they Please & their money will be paid at sight; yet I shall be much Indebted if they will give me a letter of advice whenever they draw on the Union Bank *of which I* am one of the trustees & stand Bound for the sum not having taken the rect of the treasurer to be written on the Warrants lest such trust might be disapproved where I had not authority sufficient from the Commissioners or from you for what might *then* be thought *a meterial diviation* if not a breach of trust in me which I conceive nothing at present could justify

I am respectfully your Obliged & humble sert

S BLODGET JUN

THOS JEFFERSON ESQ
    Secy. of State

[P. 110, Letters Received by Commissioners of Public Buildings and Grounds, Washington, D.C., Vol. II, June, 1792–Jan., 1793, in the National Archives; pp. 221 U.S. *v.* SMITH.]

COMMISSIONERS TO JEFFERSON

THE COMMISSIONERS TO JEFFERSON

Washington July 5.th 1792

Sir, We have received several plans for the Public Buildings which we had prepared to send forward and expect several more will be presented, but as we have just heard from the President's Steward that he may be expected here by the 15th Instant, we shall to save the Trouble of carrying and returning, retain them for his Inspection and Choice here.

Mr Hoben applies himself closely to a Draft of the Presidents House. He has made very favourable Impressions on us.

Our Affairs in general are in rather a Pleasing Train and we hope that as soon as plans are approved we shall be able to proceed with Vigour. We are &.^c

> TH. JOHNSON
> DD. STUART
> DANL. CARROLL

TO MR JEFFERSON

[P. 99, COMMISSIONERS' LETTERBOOK, Vol. I, 1791–1793, in the National Archives; p. 17, . . . DOCUMENTARY HISTORY . . . OF THE CAPITOL . . . incomplete text.]

JEFFERSON TO COMMISSIONERS

MR. JEFFERSON TO COMMISSIONERS.

Philadelphia 11th *July Rec* 16th *July* 1792

Gentlemen,

I am honored with yours of the 5th Instant. The President has left this place, this afternoon — being encumbered with lame and Sick horses he was uncertain when he should reach George-Town — perhaps on Monday morning — I forward to you by Post this morning two Plans you had formerly sent to the President, and a plan of a Capitol and another of a President's House by a Mr. Hallet, I now send a proof sheet of the plan of the Town engraving at Boston. I observe the Soundings of the Creek and River are not in it. It would be well to know of Mr. Ellicott whether they were in the original sent to Boston — If not you will probably think it adviseable to insert them in this proof Sheet, and send it to Boston, addressed to Mr. Blodget, under whose care the ingraving is going on — I enclose you a letter [39] received from him this day, informing you that the deposite of 10,000 D. is made in the two Boston Banks and will be paid to your orders — I enclose you an account and voucher of my Office against you, no appropriation which would cover this purpose having been made by Congress, we should not be able to pass these articles in the Accounts of the Office — I have the honor to be with great esteem, Gentlemen, &c.

TH JEFFERSON

TO THE COMMISSIONERS OF THE FEDERAL BUILDINGS

[P. 101, COMMISSIONERS' LETTERBOOK, Vol. I, 1791–1793, in the National Archives; p. 17, DOCUMENTARY HISTORY . . . OF THE CAPITOL . . ., incomplete text; p. 222, U.S. *v*. SMITH.]

JEFFERSON TO BLODGET

Philadelphia July 12. 1792.

Sir

I have duly rec^d your favor of June 25. & forwarded the letter it inclosed for the Commissioners. I am setting out tomorrow for Virginia, & therefore in the midst of hurry have only time to say that I suppose it will be well to retain a few copies of the plan of the town, disposing of them where they will be most seen. I observe the soundings are not in the sheets you send me. I have written to the Commissioners recommend^g to desire mr Ellicot, if they were not in the original, to insert them in one of these proof sheets & forward it to you that they may be put into

[39] Blodget to Jefferson, July 5, 1792.

the plate. some good plans of buildings have been proposed.

I am Sir

Your most obed^t humble serv^t

TH: JEFFERSON

MR. BLODGET

[Ms., *Jefferson Papers*, Library of Congress.]

JEFFERSON TO COMMISSIONERS

MR. JEFFERSON TO COMMISS^{RS}

Rec^d. 27th *August* 1792
Monticello July 29th 1792

Gentlemen/

I enclose you a letter and receipt for the engraved plate of the City, just comed to hand, from M^r. Blodget — as the plate will probably be delivered, in my absence to Mr. Taylor chief clerk of my Office. I write to him by this post to hold it subject to your orders, and to execute anything you may choose to have done with it —

I have the honor to be with the greatest respect, Gentlemen, etc.

TH. JEFFERSON

MESS^{RS}. JOHNSON, STUART, AND CARROLL

[P. 107, COMMISSIONERS' LETTERBOOK, Vol. I, 1791–1793, in the National Archives; p. 222, U.S. *v*. SMITH.]

JEFFERSON TO WASHINGTON

Monticello July 30. 1792.

Dear Sir

I inclose a letter just received from Col? Humphreys; as also one for the Commissioners of the federal territory from myself, covering one from m^r Blodget. — the inhabitants of Culpepper are intent on opening a short and good road to the new city.

they have had a survey of experiment made along the road I have so much enquired after, by Slate run church, Champs' racepath, & Songster's tavern to George town, and they have reason to believe they may make it shorter by 20. miles and better than any of the present roads. this once done, the counties from Culpepper Southwardly will take it up probably and extend it successively towards Carolina. I have the honor to be with the most perfect respect & attachment D.ʳ Sir

Your most obed.ᵗ & most humble serv.ᵗ

Tн: Jefferson

THE PRESIDENT OF THE U.S.

[Ms., *Records of the Department of State, Miscellaneous Letters*, July–September 1792, in The National Archives.]

DANIEL CARROLL TO JEFFERSON

George Town Oct.ʳ 13.ᵗʰ 1792

Dear Sir,

It may be some satisfaction to you to know that the letter you drop.ᵈ from M.ʳ Madison came to hand the next day by post. I conclude from thence that you have likewise got the packet.

We have been in anxious expectation of receiving some of the Ph.ᵃ plans of the City of Washington with the Soundings on them.

The Sales average ab.ᵗ £80 p Lott some were sold by Squares. The average of those sold by Single Lotts ab.ᵗ £91. p Lott. The sales not considerable. We have a good prospect of doing well in the private Sales. Several of the late purchasers will become improvers & settlers immidiately.

I am, Dear Sir, with great esteem
& respect
Y.ʳ most Ob.ᵗ Serv.ᵗ

Dan.ᴸ Carroll

[Ms., *Jefferson Papers*, Library of Congress.]

DANIEL CARROLL TO JEFFERSON

Baltimore Oct. 25.th 1792

Dear Sir,

Y^r favor respecting Mr Hallet [40] came to my hands just as I was leaving home. I presumed you received by him the letter which Doc^r Stuart & myself wrote to you. I hope what we did for him was sufficient for his purposes, & that I shall meet him at George-Town the 1st of Next week.

On my reaching this place I found a letter from George Town giving me information that Mr Blodgett had in consequence of what had passed between him and the Commissioners disposed of 12 Lotts (£100 each) to persons residing to the Northwards who came down after the public Sale. The Commissioners have said something in their letter to you as well as the President respecting this Gentleman. I cannot forbear adding that he appears to me to be very much in earnest for the prosperity of the City of Washington, & I believe may have it in his power to render it great Service.

I am, My dear Sir, with great esteem
Y^r most respectful hble Servt

DAN^L CARROLL

P.S. I should be glad to hear
something of the plans of the
City with the Soundings.

[Ms., *Jefferson Papers*, Library of Congress.]

COMMISSIONERS TO JEFFERSON

COMMISSRS TO MR. JEFFERSON SECRETARY OF STATE

GeorgeTown 5th *Novr* 1792.

Sir,

We have to beg you will lay before the President of the United States, our request that he would favour us with a

[40] Unable to locate this letter. — S.K.P.

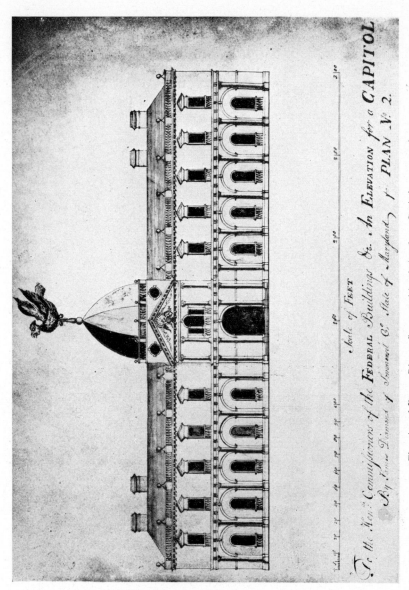

To the Honble Commissioners of the Federal Buildings &c. An Elevation for a CAPITOL
By James Diamond of Somerset Co. State of Maryland. PLAN Nº 2.

Scale of FEET

Elevation of James Diamond's competitive design for a Capitol, unaccepted.

Elevation of Stephen Hallet's design for a Capitol, unaccepted.

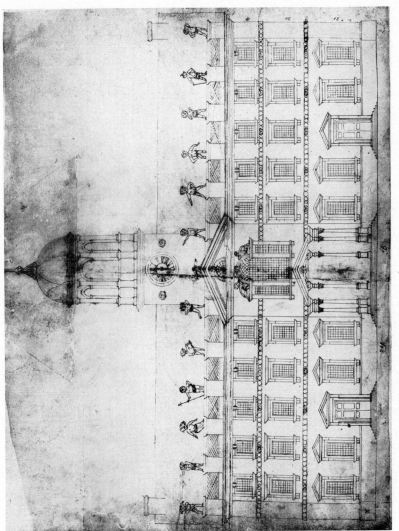

Front elevation of Philip Hart's competitive design for a Capitol, unaccepted.

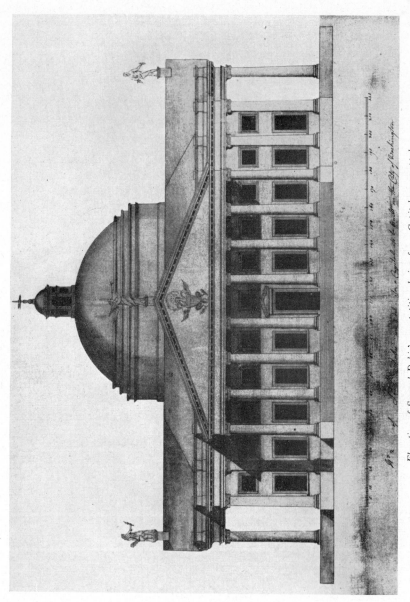

Elevation of Samuel Dobie's competitive design for a Capitol, unaccepted.

Draft on the Governor of Virginia, for such a part of the Donation of that State as is due for the Second year — Besides other Circumstances which require a replenishment of our funds, some of the proprietors have called on us for a payment of the appropriations which have been made of their property, to which they are entitled by the Terms of their alienation — We have the pleasure to inform you that since the Public Sales we have sold by private bargain, fifteen Lots, at one hundred Pounds each — Enclosed is a list of the lots sold and the Purchasers — As they are all men of Large Property, and from the Eastward, we consider it as the most Valuable Sale yet made — We must at the same time confess our obligations to Mr. Blodget, for his instrumentality in effecting it — Applications are made to us by the Merchants here, for the Plans now executing in Philadelphia, as most correct to send to their Correspondents in Europe — If finished we must beg you will cause them to be forwarded on to us — We have observed in a late Philadelphia paper, a description of a Machine for cutting and polishing Stone, which if it answers the description must be very Valuable — We are sensible your time at present must be much engrossed; but when your leasure, will permit it we shall thank you to make some enquiry respecting it — We are Sir &c.

Signed   DD. STUART

DANL CARROLL

P.S. Just as the letter was sending to the Office we received a letter from Mr. Taylor which will be answered by the next post D.S.

[P. 117, COMMISSIONERS' LETTERBOOK, Vol. I, 1791–1793, in the National Archives; pp. 226–7, U.S. v. SMITH.]

JEFFERSON TO COMMISSIONERS

MR. JEFFERSON TO COMMISSRS. *Recd. 3 Dec.* 1792.

Gentlemen/   *Philadelphia, Nov.* 13th. 1792

Your letter of the 5th Instant came duly to hand, and you

will receive by tomorrows Stage, 500 Copies of the City of
Washington with the Soundings — It has been proposed here
to sell them at ¾ of a Dollar, and the Boston plans at ⅜. on
this you will be pleased to decide — I have the honor to enclose
you the Presidents, order on the Treasurer of Virginia for the
second Instalment of the Money given by that State, and the
letter of advice to the Treasurer, (also enclosed) will explain to
you why the Draft is in that form — The merits of the Machine
for cutting and polishing Stone, shall be enquired into and
communicated to you — In the mean time permit me to add,
that in the French Encyclopedie, you will find the drawings of
mills for this purpose — The Idea which has been suggested, of
our employing a superintendant, to execute all the *details* of
your institution under your *general orders*, if finally approved by
yourselves, would meet the approbation of the President, but
whether it should be Mr. Blodget, of whom you appear to think
well, or what other person, the President would leave entirely
to yourselves — I have the honor to be with great esteem Gentlemen &c

TH JEFFERSON.

TO THE COMMISSIONERS OF THE FEDERAL BUILDINGS

[Ms., p. 149, *American Letters*, IV, 1788–92, State Department Archives; p. 123, COMMIS-
SIONERS' LETTERBOOK, Vol. I, 1791–1793, in the National Archives; p. 238, U.S. *v.* SMITH.]

JEFFERSON TO TREASURER OF VIRGINIA

To the Treasurer of Virginia
Philadelphia Novem! 13. 1792

Sir

The Commissioners of the federal buildings having desired
the President to draw on you, for the monies unpaid and payable on the part of the State of Virginia, towards those buildings, the President has this day drawn on you in their favor for

the second instalment of those monies. He has been obliged so to express it, without specifying the sum, because it happens that no copy of the Act granting the money is possessed here; if you could favor me with a copy of the Act, it would enable the President to conform his draughts more satisfactorily to the tenor of it. I have the honor to be with great & sincere esteem Sir &.^c

TH: JEFFERSON

[P. 430, *American Letters*, IV, 1788–92, State Department Archives in the National Archives.]

JEFFERSON TO WASHINGTON

Th: Jefferson has the honor to inform the President that the papers from Monsr Cointeraux of Paris contain some general ideas on his method of building houses of mud. he adds that he has a method of making incombustible roofs and cielings, that his process for building is auxiliary to agriculture, that France owes him 66,000 livres, for so much expended in experiments & models of his art, but that the city of Paris is unable to pay him 600. livres decreed to him as a premium, that he is 51. years old has a family of seven persons, and asks of Congress the expences of their passage & a shop to work in.

Th: Jefferson saw M. Cointeraux at Paris, went often to examine some specimens of mud walls which he erected there, and which appeared to be of the same kind generally built in the neighborhood of Lyons, which have stood perhaps for a century. instead of moulding bricks, the whole wall is moulded at once, & suffered to dry in the sun, when it becomes like unburnt brick. this is the most serious of his papers. he proceeds further to propose to build all our villages incombustible that the enemy may not be able to burn them, to fortify them all with his kind of walls impenetrable to their cannon, to erect a like wall across our whole frontier to keep off the Indians, observing it will cost us nothing but the building, &c &c &c.

The paper is not in the form of a petition, tho evidently intended for Congress, & making a proposition to them. it does not however merit a departure from the President's rule of not becoming the channel of petitions to that body, nor does it seem entitled to any particular answer.

TH: JEFFERSON

Nov. 18. 1792.

[Ms., *Records of the Department of State, Miscellaneous Letters*, October — December 1792, in The National Archives; p. 135, Ford, WRITINGS, Vol. VI.]

ELLICOTT TO JEFFERSON

City of Washington Nov.^br 26th 1792

Sir

I have taken the liberty of sending you an Almanac for the year 1793, which I calculated, and compiled during my sickness last september. The Astronomical part is adapted to the meridian, and latitude of the City of Washington.

   I am Sir
    Your Hb! Serv!

AND.^W ELLICOTT

HON.^BLE THO.^S JEFFERSON ESQ.^R

[Ms., *Jefferson Papers*, Library of Congress.]

COMMISSIONERS' NOTE

3^d *December*   Received sundry Letters, and among them one
1792   from the Secretary of State inclosing the following order

"Philadelphia Novr 13th 1792

   Sir

   Be pleased to pay to Messrs Johnson, Stuart &

Carroll, Commissioners of the Federal buildings on the Patowmac or to their order, or to the order of any two of them, the second instalment of the monies granted by the State of Virginia towards the said buildings.

G° WASHINGTON

THE TREASURER OF VIRGINIA"

[Pp. 150-1, Proceedings of the Commissioners, Vol. I, 1791-5, in the National Archives.]

COMMISSIONERS TO JEFFERSON

COMMISSRS. TO MR. JEFFERSON

George-Town 5th *Decr.* 1792.

Sir/

We have now to acknowledge the receipt of your Letter, enclosing to us the Presidents order on the Treasurer of Virginia for the second Instalment due from that State — The Plans are also received, & we shall have them distributed for sale immediately at the price you have rated them — We beg you to inform the President, that we shall take into mature consideration at our next meeting, the several matters, mentioned by him, particularly that respecting an Agent for conducting the sale of lots in the different States as soon as Mr. Blodget shall have submitted to us, his plan — Our conversation with him on this subject was but short, but approving of the Idea, we mentioned it to the President at his request to give him an opportunity of explaining himself more fully — From this conversation we were led to expect he would have submitted to the Presidents consideration some digested plan on the subject — We are sorry to inform you that there has not only been a great want of punctuality among those who purchased at the first sale, in their second payments, but even among those who were purchasers at the last, of their first advance — They have all been written to pressingly — We have received a letter from Mr. Mullikin, offering to set up a mill for cutting stone — We shall postpone answering it, till we are informed of the result of your enquiries respecting it — We have not an opportunity of consulting the Encyeclopdie Methodique but think it probable that Mr. Hallet's design of that kind, which he has shewed us is derived from that source — We have equal discouragement to our attempts to procure Mechanics from Scotland, with what Mr. Van Staphorts letter presents us & have consequently, just reasons to ferar a poor progress next Spring — A Mr. Thornton of Philadelphia informs us he has a plan of a Capitol to send us, as we expect by our next meeting Mr. Hallet's plan will be ready to send on to the President we have desired him to lay his before you, for the President's Inspection, in the first place, that he may have an opportunity, of judging of their comparative merits — We are happy to inform you that the outlines of the territory are nearly compleated, and that Mr. Ellicott, informs us we shall have it in our power next month of sending in our report, to the President on this subject — We are &c

Signed)   D<small>D</small> S<small>TUART</small>
D<small>ANL</small> C<small>ARROLL</small>

[P. 127, COMMISSIONERS' LETTERBOOK, Vol. I, 1791–1793, in the National Archives; pp. 239–40, U. S. *v.* SMITH.]

JEFFERSON TO COMMISSIONERS

JEFFERSON TO THE COMMISSIONERS

Philadelphia 13th *Dec.* 1792

Gentlemen/

I have according to the desire expressed in your letter of the 5th Instant examined the model of Mr Millikin's mill for polishing and sawing Stone, lodged in my Office. it is always an objection that a thing is new and untried. His method of giving motion backwards and forwards to a sawframe by a spiral plane is ingenious: but I confess it does not appear promising to me. it is certainly inferior to that used in Europe of which there is a drawing in the Encyclopedie Methodique. I have made a rough drawing of the latter merely to explain to you the principle. You will find that the sawframe is moved by a Crank, as that in a saw mill for wood, except that the sawframe lies horizontal instead of perpendicular. it is more simple than the mill for sawing wood, because the part is omitted which brings the Stock up to the saw. your workmen seeing the principle will easily contrive all the details. I shewed this plan also Millikin's model to the President, & he prefers the former. Doctor Thornton has not yet presented any Plan of a Capitol. I have the honor to be with perfect respect and esteem, Gentlemen &c

TH: JEFFERSON

MESS.^{RS} STUART, & CARROLL

[Pp. 128-9, COMMISSIONERS' LETTERBOOK, Vol. I, 1791-1793, in the National Archives.]

JEFFERSON TO COMMISSIONERS

JEFFERSON TO COMMISSIONERS

Philadelphia 17.th *Dec.* 1792

Gentlemen

Knowing that there was a Major here (Traquair) who was in the practice of importing workmen in his own line from Edinburgh, I took occasion to enquire of him whether it might not be possible for you to have some imported thro the means of his correspondent, whom he represented as having both address & zeal to forward his countrymen to this country, to which he means after some time to come himself. he is of opinion that this person, can, and will forward numbers to you if

desired, and that he will be contented with the customary premium of a Guinea a head for all sent, which he supposes will
cover the little expences he may be at. their passage will be, to
be paid, and he expects the wages of good plain workmen will
be about thirty guineas a year & their board. the best workmen,
that is, such as can carve a Capital, will be higher, he thinks he
can send common labourers also, if you think proper to try this
chance M.ʳ Traquair will become the channel of inducing his
friend to engage in it. A thought strikes me here which I will
venture. Traquair is a Capitel stonecutter here. if you are in
want of such a one, possibly inviting him to Washington, under
pretext of consulting about the importation of workmen, he
might on sight of the place, be induced to move all his hands
there. the experiment would cost you his expences there and
perhaps daily pay. I have the honor to be with great esteem

Gentlemen, &c

TH: JEFFERSON

[Pp. 129–130, COMMISSIONERS' LETTERBOOK, Vol. I, 1791–1793, in the National Archives.]

JEFFERSON TO COMMISSIONERS

JEFFERSON TO THE COMMISSIONERS

Philadelphia 23.ᵈ *December* 1792

Gentlemen, Thinking it best that you should received all possible information on the subject of procuring workmen, in order
that you may avail yourselves of such parts of it as circumstances render eligible, I have the honor to mention to you, that
in a conversation with M.ʳ Pierpoint Edwards and Colonel
Wadsworth of Connecticut, they inform me that any number
of house Carpenters may be got in that State, as far perhaps as
500, or 1000, their wages ⅔ of a Dollar and to be fed. They
have but few Masons, however some may be had, they combine
their, [sic] the cutting and laying stone, and laying brick. they

mention one Trowbridge as one of their best workmen. however I could not find that he had ever done anything higher than stonesteps. he never had even cut a column. his wages a Dollar a day and fed. they think also that common labourers may be got there, they observe that Connecticut is a better place to apply to than Boston where there being a greater deman for workmen, they are dearer and more difficult to draw from their own Country. I have the honor to be with great esteem, Gentlemen, &c.

TH: JEFFERSON

[Pp. 130–131, COMMISSIONERS' LETTERBOOK, Vol. I, 1791–1793, in the National Archives; pp. 20–21, . . . DOCUMENTARY HISTORY . . . OF THE CAPITOL. . . .]

COMMISSIONERS TO JEFFERSON

COMMISSIONERS TO JEFFERSON

Washington 5.th *Jan.* 1793

Sir/

We have your two favours of the 13.th and that of the 17.th of last m.° before us. It appears to us more, and more desirable to expedite the Stone-cutting by Machinery, not more on account of the expences, which the State of our Funds require to be attended to, then to ensure the Quantity wanted in Time, for we have as yet only about ⅙ done of what will be wanted, on the large scale of the Presidents House, to the Water Table of it. Mr Harbaugh who is very ingenious, and cheerfully renders us every assistance in his power, after seeing the sketch enclosed by you a Draft by Mr Hallet, and having as it seems to us a perfect Idea of Mr Millikins plan has made and shewn us a Model, of a stone saw mill to be worked with Horses, or Oxen, on the principle of giving motion to the Saws by a Spiral Line, the simplicity and cheapness of it and our hope of its effecual [sic] operation have induced us to desire him to set up one instantly which he has undertaken. We do not however rely on the success of this effect. we have agreed on the most generous Terms, for the Introduction of Foreigners and enclose you a Copy of them, as well as our Letter open to M.ʳ Traquair, if the whole number which we do not expect should be engaged we should be rather overburthened for the too probable State of our Finances, otherwise we could wish to have the cutt-stone so forward that a sufficient number might be early spared to assist private Buildings, which would tend to Beautyfy the City. Mess.ʳˢ Mason and Fenwick will have the Charge of this Business in France, assisted by a Letter from M.ʳ Hallet. — M.ʳ Delier's House — Brewine for Germany and M.ʳ Hoben has fallen on measures for some from Dublin, as M.ʳ Williamson has for some from Scotland, and we hope M.ʳ Traquair may succeed at least in part. As it is not expected to get Higher next year than the water Table. J. E. 13 feet elevation there are Carpenters enough who may be had on the spot. And we shall want but a few additional masons next Season, for some in each line have already purchased and agreed to sink the price, by their work, so that we think it can be no object to introduce others from connecticut. Yet we are almost certain that there will be Employment for a great many Mechanicks in the City, and George: Town next Season, on private buildings on Connecticut wages which are rather lower than here. the provisioning of workmen draws after it so many Expences, and so much waste that we have hitherto left them to provide for themselves, we are under a necessity, of doing otherwise as to the labourers, a part of whom we can easily make up of Negroes and find it proper to do so. Those we have employed this Sumer have proved a very useful check & kept our Affairs Cool. We have agreed with M.ʳ Blodget for his Services, and hope that his Assistance will be very usefull, he has great Confidence in a Lottery, we find ourselves at liberty and agree to it our Communications with him go into some particulars which we suppose need not be repeated here. M.ʳ Walker we understand will go soon for Scotland, any thing he could do there, for us we imagine may be done at least as well by M.ʳ Traquair through his Correspondent and we must be excused from giving Signs of Approbation and confidence that we do not feel. M.ʳ Hallet looses nothing of our Estimate of him, he has not been able to finish his Plan so soon as he hoped, but says it shall be ready in about three weeks. The Survey seems to us very tedious and we know it is very Expensive. we have had some explanations with Maj.ʳ Ellicott, but do not yet know how they may End, indeed in the other parts of our Business we have necessarily, not precisely entered into Engagements to a great Amount with Officers, which will be thought extravagant unless our funds hold out to fill up with actual Labour. Much depends on the next Sale, on weighing every thing within. one Sale on the 17th September gives the best Chance. We are Sir &c

> TH: JOHNSON
> D.ᴰ STUART
> DAN.ᴸ CARROLL

[Pp. 139–41, COMMISSIONERS' LETTERBOOK, Vol. I, 1791–1793, in the National Archives.]

ELLICOTT TO JEFFERSON

Geo. Town Jan.ʸ 9ᵗʰ 1793

Sir/

From a conversation which I had with you some time ago, I remember you was desirous of discovering the Indian name of the Eastern Branch of the Potomak: by some old surveys it appears to be *Annakostia*.

The reasons of my disagreement with the Commissioners, and ultimate determination to quit the business of the City of Washington, on the first day of May next, shall be published

immediately after that date: And I have no doubt, but that
from a clear investigation of facts, my conduct, and exertions,
will be approved of by the candid and discerning.

I am with much esteem
Your Real Friend

ANDREW ELLICOTT

HON^{BLE} THOMAS JEFFERSON ESQ.

[Ms., *Jefferson Papers*, Library of Congress.]

MEMORANDUM

MEMORANDUM [41] TO PLANS SENT FROM PHILA.
TO THE COMMISSIONERS 3 DIFFT TIMES, 500 EACH TIME

1792		*Small*	*Large*
		500	1,000
Octr. 13	To Major Wm. Brown, master of the Coffee House Savanna in Georgia...............	300	
22	To Robert Hodge, booksel'r New York.......	500	
Nov. 24	To Peter Gilman Mercht, Boston...........		200
Decr. 22	To Markland & McIver Printers & Booksellers Chaston So Carr.......................	500	300
26	To Mr. Jefferson to send abroad............		72
	To the President of the U. States...........		2
		1,800	1,574
Jany. 3	To Mr. Jefferson to send abroad.............		6
		1,800	1,580

[P. 242, U. S. *v.* SMITH.]

[41] Attached to a letter from George Taylor, Jr., to the Commissioners.
January 10, 1793: "In mine of 28 October I mentioned the number of small plans then
distributed, and by advice of Mr. Jefferson omitted sending off any more until there
should be some of the large ones to accompany them. The printer has not been able to
finish, having broken his press twice, which consumed much time in repairing, but supposes as it is now in order that he can accomplish the whole in a few days."

ELLICOTT TO JEFFERSON

TO MR. JEFFERSON

City of Washington, January 12th., 1793.

Sir: —

From a conversation which I had with you some time ago I remember you was desirous of discovering the Indian name of the Eastern Branch of the Potamack. By some old surveys it appears to be "Anna Kastia." The reasons of my disagreement with the Commissioners and ultimate determination to quit the business of the City of Washington on the first day of May next shall be published immediately after that date and I have no doubt but that from a clear investigation of facts my conduct and exertions will be approved of by the candid and deserving.

I am Sir with esteem your real friend,

ANDREW ELLICOTT.

[Pp. 182–83, *Records*, Columbia Historical Society, Vol. 2.]

JEFFERSON TO ELLICOTT

Philadelphia Jan. 15. 1793.

Dear Sir

I have duly recieved your favor of the 9.th the President thinking it would be better that the outlines at least of the city, and perhaps of George town should be laid down in the plat of the territory, I have sent it back to the Commissioners from whom it came, that you may do this. suppose you were to consult them on the propriety of adding to *the Eastern branch*, the words '*or Annakostia.*' This would probably revive the antient Indian name instead of the modern one. I am extremely sorry to learn that there has arisen any dissatisfaction between the Commissioners & yourself. I am sure it is without a fault on either side, such is my confidence in both parties. the work you are employed in must be slow from it's nature: and it is not wonderful if the Commissioners should think it too much so. however I hope you will change your mind about bringing it before the public. this cannot be done without injuring the expectations built on the city, nor can it be necessary in a case unknown beyond the circle of George town. within that circle, verbal explanations will certainly answer equally well as a justification to you. indeed I hope nothing will take place to render your future services there unobtaineable with the Commissioners, and that you will suspend any resolution you may have taken on the subject. —

*   *   *

I am with great esteem   Dear Sir
Your very humble serv^t

TH: JEFFERSON

MR ANDREW ELLIC^T.

[Ms., *Jefferson Papers*, Library of Congress; also printed under date of January 15, *1794*, pp. 188–89, *Records*, Columbia Historical Society, Vol. 2.]

JEFFERSON TO COMMISSIONERS

Philadelphia Jan. 15. 1793

Gentlemen

The President, thinking it would be better that the outlines at least of the city and perhaps of Georgetown should be laid down in the plat of the Territory, I have the honor now to send it, and to desire that mr Ellicot may do it as soon as convenient that it may be returned in time to be laid before Congress. I have the honor to be with perfect esteem, Gentlemen,

Your most obed^{nt}
& most humble serv^t

TH: JEFFERSON

MESS^{RS} JOHNSON, STEWART & CARROLL

[Ms., *Jefferson Papers*, Library of Congress.]

JEFFERSON TO DANIEL CARROLL

Philadelphia, February 1, 1793.

JEFFERSON TO MR. CARROLL

Dear Sir:

Doctor Thornton's plan of a capitol [42] has been produced, and has so captivated the eyes and judgment of all as to leave no doubt you will prefer it when it shall be exhibited to you; as no doubt exists here of its preference over all which have been produced, and among its admirers no one is more decided than him whose decision is most important. It is simple, noble, beautiful, excellently distributed, and moderate in size. The purpose of this letter is to apprize you of this sentiment. A just respect for the right of approbation in the commissioners will prevent any formal decision in the President till the plan shall be laid before you and be approved by you. The Doctor will go with it to your meeting in the beginning of March. In the meantime, the interval of *apparent* doubt may be improved for settling the mind of poor Hallet, whose merit and distresses interest every one for his tranquillity and pecuniary relief. I have taken the liberty of making these private estimates, thinking you would wish to know the true state of the sentiments here on this subject, and am with sincere respect and esteem for your colleagues and yourself, dear Sir, your most obedient humble servant.

[P. 508, WRITINGS OF JEFFERSON, Washington, III.]

[42] The prize-winner, Dr. William Thornton, was a self-taught architect. He recalled in a letter written on October 12, 1802: "The president and secretary of state published a premium of a gold medal of $500 and a lot for a house in the city of Washington for the best plan and elevation of a capitol of the United States. I lamented not having studied architecture, and resolved to attempt the grand undertaking and study at the same time. I studied some months and worked almost night and day, but I found I was opposed by regular architects from France and various other countries." *Records of the Columbia Historical Society*, Washington, D.C., XVIII, 176. Reprinted through the courtesy of the Columbia Historical Society, Washington, D.C.

COMMISSIONERS' NOTE

4ᵗʰ February   At a meeting of the Commissioners at George
1793   Town on the fourth Day of February 1793 and
to 8ᵗʰ Febʸ   continued to the 8ᵗʰ of the same month.

          The map of the Territory, was returned by
the Secretary of State in order to have the additions, mentioned in his letter, made to it.

[P. 165, *Proceedings of the Commissioners*, Vol. I, 1791–5, in the National Archives.]

COMMISSIONERS TO JEFFERSON

Washington 7ᵗʰ *Febʸ* 1793.

COMMISSIONERS TO JEFFERSON

Sir

The Plat of the Territory was sent by Mᵣ Carroll, as soon as
it arrived to Mᵣ Ellicott, who has informed us, that he will have
the additions required by the President compleated by Sunday,
so as to be in readyness to be sent by the Post upon Tuesday.
We are sorry to mention Mᵣ Ellicott still continues in a very ill
humor with us, and has refused to give us any information relative to his department until May when he means to dismiss
himself. If he persists in this Temper, we shall certainly not
wait till that period: should this happen we have no doubt but
his place will be well supplied by Mᵣ Briggs. From some indisposition in his family we have not the pleasure of Mᵣ Johnson's
company at this meeting. We expect him next week when we
shall come to some final decision on the Subject. It is our wish
to wait his own time if it be possible. We have as yet received
only the ten thousand Dollars on the Presidents second Draft
on Virginia. We have to day written to the Executive of Virginia, requesting a payment of the ballance. Governor Lee who
is in Philadelphia can probably inform you of the Success to be

expected from thence. As a disapointment will be very embar-
rassing to us and prevent us from commencing our operations
the approaching season with the Spirit we could wish, we think
it advisable, the President should send us his Draft on the
Treasurer of Maryland, for the third Installment. We have information that part of the money is ready. We shall send you by
the first opportunity to be met with, some of the Samples of
Marble from the Potomac which we have had polished. Tho'
we are much pleased that we shall at length be furnished with
the Plan of a Capitol so highly satisfactory to the President, and
all who have seen it, we feel sensibly for poor Hallet, and shall
do every thing in our power to sooth him, we hope he may be
usefully employed notwithstanding. Not to discourage M.ʳ
Traquair from corresponding with us, by the expence of post-
age, we take the liberty of sending the enclosed letter for him to
your address. It being on business relating to the Public. We are
Sir &c.

D.ᴰ STUART
DAN.ᴸ CARROLL

P.S.   We are this moment informed by a
gentleman who had it from M.ʳ Ellicott himself that
he was appointed Superintendant of the inland
Navigation of Pensylvania.

[Pp. 155–6, COMMISSIONERS' LETTERBOOK, Vol. I, 1791–1793, in the National Archives;
p. 23, . . . DOCUMENTARY HISTORY . . . OF THE CAPITOL . . ., incomplete text.]

COMMISSIONERS TO JEFFERSON

COMMISSIONERS TO JEFFERSON

City of Washington 11.ᵗʰ Feb.ʸ 1793

Sir/

We have the pleasure to send you by Mʳ Ellicott the plat of
the Territory executed according to the Presidents request. We
are happy to inform you that we have had some explanations

with him, which render us better satisfied with him than we were at the time of our last.   We are Sir &c

D? STUART

DAN? CARROLL

[P. 161, COMMISSIONERS' LETTERBOOK, Vol. I, 1791–1793, in the National Archives.]

COMMISSIONERS TO JEFFERSON

George Town 12.th *Feb*^y 1793

COMMISSIONERS TO JEFFERSON

Sir /

From the short notice we had of Mr Ellicots intention to go to Philadelphia we omitted sending the Ac.^t of the expences incurred in running the outlines of the Territory. We now send it, that if it is thought proper, we may be reimbursed. The original from whence the present Acc.^t is taken was signed by Mr Ellicott, who, if it be necessary will no doubt sign this. The specimens of Marble alludded to in a former letter, were sent by Mr Ellicott. We are with great respect your &c.

D? STUART

DAN? CARROLL.

[P. 161, COMMISSIONERS' LETTERBOOK, Vol. I, 1791–1793, in the National Archives.]

COMMISSIONERS NOTE

11.th & 12.th   Wrote to the Secretary of State two letters, the
Febr^y 1793   first dated the 11.th Ins^t accompanying the Map of
the Territory, the second respecting the expences
of the Surveyor's Department, with an account
inclosed, of the amount of expences incurred in
running the permanent Lines — 2986 Dollars &
25 Cents.

[Pp. 166–7, Proceedings of the Commissioners, Vol. I, 1791–5, in the
National Archives.]

JEFFERSON TO WASHINGTON

Philadelphia ~~January~~ *Febr.* 18th. 1793

Sir,

The Commissioners of the Territory of the United States on the Potomac having, according to law, had the said Territory surveyed and defined by proper metes and bounds, and transmitted their report with a plat of the boundary, I have now the honor to lay them before you. As this work has been executed under the authority of the Legislature, I presume it would be proper to communicate the report to them, and to submit the Plat also to their inspection, that they may be duly informed of the progress of the work.

I have to add that these papers, being original, are again to be deposited with the Records in the Office of the Department of State.

I have the honor to be, with Sentiments of the most perfect esteem and attachment,

   Sir,

     Your most obedient and

      Most humble Servant,

          TH: JEFFERSON

THE PRESIDENT OF THE UNITED STATES

[Ms., *Jefferson Papers*, Library of Congress.]

JEFFERSON TO WASHINGTON

TH: JEFFERSON presents his respectful compliments to the President. apprehensive that there has been some misconception of his correspondence with mr̄ Ellicot, he incloses to the President full copies of the only letters he has written to mr̄ Ellicot in the course of the years 1792 & 1793. the last of them

was written with no other view than to prevent public alterca-
tion between m͞r Ellicot and the Commissioners, and after having received the President's opinion that it was desireable to
prevent it. Th: J. will thank the President to make any use of
the letters which may remove any suspicions excited by an in-
exact idea of them.

March 4, 1793

[Ms., *Jefferson Papers*, Library of Congress.]

WASHINGTON TO JEFFERSON

GEORGE WASHINGTON TO THOMAS JEFFERSON

March 9, 1793

Dear Sir: The enclosed from Messrs. Johnson and Carroll
have this instant come to hand. Along with them you will receive the letter (this day read) from Doctr. Stuart, that the
sentiments of all three of the Commrs. may appear in one
view.

I pray you, before Mr. Madison leaves town, to lay all three
before him and the Attorney Genl.; and give me a written
Memo. of the measures which you, and they, shall think most
advisable for me to pursue, provisionally, or otherwise, in this
business.

You will all recollect the points that were touched upon to
day; I shall not, therefore, repeat them.

I am always Yours etc.

[Endorsed by Jefferson]: recd. Mar. 9 93. what sacrifice to
retain Johnson? sum in gross and what? if he goes, any sacrifice
to retain other Commrs in town? Commrs. in town, sum in
gross?

[P. 379, WRITINGS OF WASHINGTON, Fitzpatrick, Vol. 32.]

JEFFERSON MEMORANDUM

MEMORANDUM RELATIVE TO COMMISSIONERS FOR LAYING OFF THE
FEDERAL CITY

March 11th, 1793.

Question 1st. — What sacrifice may be made to retain Mr.
Johnson in the office of commissioner for the federal territory?

Answer. — For such an object, it is worth while to give up
the plan of an allowance per diem; to give, instead of that, a
sum in gross, and to extend that sum to five hundred dollars
per annum, and expenses; the latter to be rendered in account.

If Mr. Johnson persists in resigning, as it is evident Dr.
Stewart will not continue even for the above allowance, and
Mr. Carroll does not appear to make any conditions, the President will be free as to Mr. Carroll and two new associates, to
adhere to the allowance per diem already proposed, or to substitute a sum in gross.

Question 2d. — May new commissioners be chosen in the
town?

Answer. — It is strongly desirable that the commissioners
should not be of the town, nor interested in it; and this objection is thought a counterpoise for a sensible difference in talents; but if persons of adequate talents and qualifications cannot be found in the country, it will be better to take them from
the town, than to appoint men of inadequate talents from the
country.

Question 3d. — How compensate them?

Answer. — If they come from the country, the per diem allowance is thought best; if from the town, a sum in gross will be
best, and this might be as far as three hundred dollars a year,
and no allowance for expenses. If partly from the town, and
partly from the country, then three hundred dollars a year to
the former, and the same, with allowance of expenses, to the
latter.

Mr. Madison, Mr. Randolph and Thomas Jefferson having consulted together on the preceding questions, with some shades of difference of opinion in the beginning, concurred ultimately and unanimously in the above answers.

[P. 437, WRITINGS OF JEFFERSON, Washington, VII.]

JEFFERSON TO MORRIS

JEFFERSON TO GOUVERNEUR MORRIS

Philadelphia, March 12, 1793.

I sent you, by the way of London, a dozen plans of the city of Washington in the federal territory, hoping you would have them displayed to public view where they would be most seen by those descriptions of men worthy and likely to be attracted to it. Paris, Lyons, Rouen, and the sea port towns of Havre, Nantes, Bordeaux and Marseilles, would be proper places to send some of them. I trust to Mr. Taylor to forward you the newspapers by every direct occasion to France.

[P. 523, WRITINGS OF JEFFERSON, Washington, III.]

JEFFERSON TO ELLICOTT

Philadelphia, March 22, 1793.

Sir: — Your letter of the 16th to the President has been duly received wherein you require an examination into the execution of the general plan of the city by men of known profesional abilities, if this be addressed to the President under an expectation that he should order such an examination, I have to observe to you that it would be out of the line of his interference to originate orders relative to those employed under the Commissioners, their plans come to him for approbaton or disapprobation, but everything concerning the execution is left to themselves; and particularly the President declines all interference with those employed by them, or under them. The President is sincerely concerned at the difference which has taken place, but does not suppose it to be a case for any interposition on his part. To these expressions of his sentiments on the subject of your letter I have only to add those of regard and esteem from Sir

Your most obed't humble serv't,

TH. JEFFERSON.

MR. ANDREW ELLICOTT

[P. 190, Columbia Historical Society, *Records*, Vol. 2.]

ELLICOTT TO JEFFERSON

Rec.ᵈ March 28

Geo. Town March 26ᵗʰ 1793

Sir/

I have been most injuriously treated by the commissioners: Accused, and dismissed on a charge of errors where there were none, and my character degraded so far, as they could degrade it. In this situation I thought the most respectful mode of obtaining redress, was by an appeal to the President: but by your letter of the 22ᵈ I am cruelly disappointed. Has a man in public service, tho' under the direction of the commissioners, no resource for vindication from calumny, and oppression, but in an appeal to the candid public? If the President will have the patience to inform himself fully of the truth of the charges made against me by the commissioners, I would chearfully submit to his decision. I am the more sanguine in the hope of this indulgence, from having seen a letter from the commissioners to a gentleman in this place dated the 14ᵗʰ saying, "Having taken our resolution with respect to Major Ellicott, and on a very different state of facts than he has communicated to you, we have laid them before the President, and with candour, and an

effectual decision on our conduct, can come only from him."
This is the very decision I wish for. I am Sir with

much regard and
esteem Your Hb.ᵉ Serv.ᵗ
AND.ᵂ ELLICOTT

HON.ᴮᴸᴱ THO.ˢ JEFFERSON ESQ.ᴿ

[Ms., *Jefferson Papers*, Library of Congress.]

JEFFERSON TO WASHINGTON

Th: Jefferson with his respects to the President, incloses a
description of a new plan of a Capitol in which m.ʳ Hallet is
engaged, who has expressed very earnest wishes that the ultimate decision may not be pronounced till he can bring it forward.

Mar. 26. 93.

[Ms., *Records of the Department of State, Miscellaneous Letters*, March–April, 1793 in The
National Archives.]

SUCCINCT DESCRIPTION OF A NEW PLAN OF A CAPITOL
BY M.ᴿ HALLET

The principal front is in a streit line of 320. feet in length,
having in the middle a circular projection of 105. feet diameter,
very nearly of the proportions of the Pantheon, and crowned in
the same taste. the same Cornish surmounted by a balustrade,
crowns the whole edifice which is proposed to be covered in
terrasses. the sub-basement will raise the first floor to some
steps above the level of the highest ground, & will afford a
great number of offices & lodgings for doorkeepers & other
conveniences. in the circular mass, a large open vestibule of
nine arches, 10 feet wide, gives room to enter in carriages, from
whence is a communication by a circular staircase to the cen-

tral vestibule on the first floor, which has an entry on the same level to the East, giving passage to the antichambers, stair-cases & other interior communications. the Representatives room is in the same stile & placed in the same manner as in my preceding plan. the Senate is at the other end & disposed so that all the effects of the light are symmetrical as if it occupied the whole mass. the Conference room is in the middle in the circular projection on the second floor. it's inside is an exact sphere in imitation of the Pantheon. all the rooms, without exception, are lighted and aired directed [sic], because they have all windows in outer walls.

[Ms., *Records of the Department of State, Miscellaneous Letters*, March–April 1793, in The National Archives.]

COMMISSIONERS TO JEFFERSON

COMMRS TO MR JEFFERSON

George Town 25. *June* 1793

Sir //

Maj.^r Ellicott has returned to us at this meeting a new map of the Territory of Columbia which as well as the old one we have committed to Mr Sears care for you.

We are Sir
Your Most Obd.^t Serv.^{ts}

TH. JOHNSON
D.^D STUART
DAN.^L CARROLL

[P. 183, COMMISSIONERS' LETTERBOOK, Vol. I, 1791–1793, in the National Archives.]

WASHINGTON TO JEFFERSON

GEORGE WASHINGTON TO THOMAS JEFFERSON

Mount Vernon, June 30, 1793

Dear Sir: You will find by the enclosed letter from the Commissioners that Mr. Hallet reports unfavorably of Doctr. Thornton's Plan "on the great points of practicability, time and expence." And that I am referred "to Mr. Blodget, Hoben and Hallet whose verbal information will be better than any we can give you" on which to form ultimate Instructions.

Mr. Blodget I met at Baltimore in the moment I was about to leave it; consequently I had little conversation with him on the subject referred; but Mr. Hallet is of opinion that the execution of Doctor Thornton's Plan (independent of the cost, which would far exceed our means; and the time allowed for the accomplishment of the buildings) is impracticable; or if practicable, would not in some parts answer the ends proposed. Mr. Hoben seemed to concur in this opinion; and Mr. Blodget, as far as I could come at his sentiments in the short time, I was with him approved the alterations in it which have been proposed by Mr. Hallet.

It is unlucky that this investigation of Doctor Thornton's plan, and estimate of the cost had not preceeded the adoption of it: but knowing the impatience of the Carrollsburg interest and the anxiety of the Public to see both buildings progressing; and supposing the plan to be correct, it was adjudged best to avoid delay. It is better, however, to correct the error, though late, than to proceed in a ruinous measure, in the adoption of which I do not hesitate to confess I was governed by the beauty of the exterior and the distribution of the appartments, declaring then, as I do now, that I had no knowledge in the rules or principles of Architecture, and was equally unable to count the cost. But, if there be such material defects as are represented, and such immense time and cost to complete the buildings, it would be folly in the extreme to proceed on the Plan which has been adopted. It has appeared to me proper, however, that before it is laid aside, Justice, and respect to Doctor Thornton, requires, that the objections should be made known to him and an opportunity afforded to explain and obviate them, if he can.

For this reason, and because Mr. Blodget is in Philadelphia and it might not be convenient for Doctr. Thornton to leave it; I have requested Mr. Hallet and Mr. Hoben to repair without delay to Philadelphia, with all the plans and documents which are necessary to elucidate this subject, and do pray you to get all the parties herein named together, and after hearing the objections and explanations report your opinion on the case and the plan which ought to be executed. Nothing can be done to the foundation until a final decision is had, and this decision ought not to be delayed one moment that can be avoided; because time is wasting fast; because the public expectation is alive, and because the daeman Jealousy may be at work in the lower Town when one building is seen to progress rapidly, and a plan for the other not yet decided on. Whether it be practicable (even at an expence) to call in the aid of any other scientific Character in Philadelphia to assist in deciding this point; or whether there be any thence, is more than I can tell. Your own knowledge of this, and judgment, will decide. The case is important. a Plan must be adopted; and good, or bad, it must be entered upon. I am etc.

[Pp. 510–12, WRITINGS OF WASHINGTON, Fitzpatrick, Vol. 32.]

COMMISSIONERS TO JEFFERSON

COMMISSIONERS TO JEFFERSON

July 7, 1793.

Though we are much pleased that we shall at length be furnished with a plan of a Capitol so highly satisfactory to the President, and all who have seen it, we feel sensibly for poor Hallett, and shall do everything in our power to sooth him. We hope he may be usefully employed notwithstanding.

[P. 176, HISTORY OF WASHINGTON, Tindall.]

JEFFERSON TO WASHINGTON

Philadelphia July 17. 1793.

Sir

According to the desire expressed in your letter of June 30. I
called together Doct.̅ Thornton, M.̅ Hallet, M.̅ Hoben, and a
judicious undertaker of this place, M.̅ Carstairs, chosen by D.̅
Thornton as a competent judge of the objections made to his
plan of the Capitol for the City of Washington. These objections were proposed and discussed on a view of the plans: the
most material were the following.

1. The intercolonnations of the western and central peri-
styles are too wide for the support of their architraves of Stone:
so are those of the doors in the wings.

2. The colonnade passing through the middle of the Conference room has an ill effect to the eye, and will obstruct the
view of the members: and if taken away, the cieling is too wide
to support itself.

3. The floor of the central peristyle is too wide to support
itself.

4. The stairways on each side of the Conference room want
head room.

5. The windows are in some important instances masked by
the galleries.

6. Many parts of the building want light and air in a degree
which renders them unfit for their purposes. this is remarkably
the case with some of the most important apartments, to wit,
the chambers of the Executive and the Senate, the anti-cham-
bers of the Senate and Representatives, the Stair-ways &.̅
Other objections were made which were surmountable, but
those preceding were thought not so, without an alteration of
the plan.

This alteration has in fact been made by m.̅ Hallet in the
plan drawn by him, wherein he has preserved the most valua-

ble ideas of the original and rendered them susceptible of execution; so that it is considered as D.ʳ Thornton's plan reduced into practicable form. The persons consulted agreed that in this reformed plan the objections before stated were entirely remedied; and that it is on the whole a work of great merit. But they were unanimously of opinion that in removing one of the objections, that is to say, the want of light and air to the Executive and Senate chambers, a very capital beauty in the original plan, to wit, the Portico of the Eastern front, was suppressed, and ought to be restored; as the recess proposed in the middle of that front instead of the Portico projecting from it, would probably have an extreme ill effect. They supposed that by advancing the Executive chamber, with the two rooms on it's flanks, into a line with the Eastern front, or a little projecting or receding from it, the Portico might be reestablished, and a valuable passage be gained in the center of the edifice, lighted from above, and serving as a common disengagement to the four capital apartments, and that nothing would be sacrificed by this but an unimportant proportion of light and air to the Senate and Representatives rooms, otherwise abundantly lighted and aired.

The arrangement of the windows in front on different levels was disapproved, and a reformation of that circumstance was thought desirable though not essential.

It was further their opinion that the reformed plan would not cost more than half what the original one would.

I need not repeat to you the opinions of Col.ᵒ Williams an undertaker also produced by D.ʳ Thornton, who on seeing the plans and hearing the objections proposed, thought some of them removeable, others not so, and on the whole that the reformed plan was the best. This part in your presence, and with a declaration at the same time from Col. Williams that he wished no stress to be laid on opinions so suddenly given. but he called on me the day after, told me he had considered and conferred with D.ʳ Thornton on the objections, and thought all of them could be removed but the want of light and air in some cases. he gave me general ideas of the ways in which he would remove the other objections, but his method of spanning the intercolonnations with secret arches of brick, and supporting the floors by an interlocked framing appeared to me totally inadequate; that of unmasking the windows by lowering the Galleries was only substituting one deformity for another, and a conjectural expression how head-room might be gained in the Stair-ways shewed he had not studied them.

I have employed m.ʳ Carstairs to calculate the cost of the whole masonry of the building, according to the Philadelphia prices, because the cost of the walls of a building furnishes always a tolerable conjecture of the cost of the whole, and because I thought that a statement in detail of the Philadelphia prices of materials and work might be of some value to the Commissioners.

I have the honor to be with the most perfect esteem and respect, Sir

> Your most obedient &
> most humble Servant.

TH: JEFFERSON

THE PRESIDENT OF THE UNITED STATES

[Ms., *Records of the Department of State, Miscellaneous Letters,* July–August 1793, in The National Archives; pp. 26–27, . . . DOCUMENTARY HISTORY . . . OF THE CAPITOL . . .]

JEFFERSON TO COMMISSIONERS

JEFFERSON TO THE COMMISSIONERS

Philadelphia Aug.ᵗ 15.ᵗʰ 1793

Gentlemen, By this day's post I have the honour to return the drawings of the Capitol, which had been left here in order to have an estimate made; I send also that estimate together

with the rates of the different work, as made by a skilful workman here, the sum total it is supposed will enable you to form
some idea of the whole cost of your building, as there is a tolerably well known proportion between the cost of the Walls of a
building and its whole cost; and the rates will serve as information perhaps in contracts which you may have to make hereafter.

I have the honor to be with great respect, Gentlemen, Your
most Obt. & most Hum. Servt.

TH: JEFFERSON

[P. 28, DOCUMENTARY HISTORY OF . . . THE CAPITOL . . .]

JEFFERSON TO WASHINGTON

TO G. WASHINGTON

Monticello, October 17, 1793.

Dear Sir:

I have carefully considered the question whether the President may call Congress to any other place than that to which
they have adjourned themselves, and think he cannot have such
a right unless it has been given him by the Constitution, or the
laws, and that neither of these has given it. The only circumstance which he can alter as to their meeting, is that of *time* by
calling them at an *earlier day* than that to which they stand adjourned, but no power to change the place is given. Mr. Madison happened to come here yesterday, after the receipt of your
letter. I proposed the question to him, and he thinks there was
particular caution intended and used in the direction of the
Constitution, to avoid giving the President any power over the
place of meeting; lest he should exercise it with local partiali-
ties. With respect to the Executive, the Residence law has fixed
our office at Philadelphia till the year 1800, and therefore it
seems necessary that we should get as near them as we may

with safety. As to the place of meeting for the Legislature, were we authorized to decide that question, I should think it right to have it in some place in Pennsylvania, in consideration of the principles of the Residence bill, and we might furnish no pretext to that state to infringe them hereafter. I am quite unacquainted with Reading and its means of accommodation. Its situation is perhaps as little objectionable as that of Lancaster, and less so than Trenton or perhaps Wilmington. However, I think we have nothing to do with the question, and that Congress must meet in Philadelphia, even if it be in the open fields, to adjourn themselves to some other place. I am extremely afraid something has happened to Mr. Bankson, on whom I relied for continuance at my office. For two posts past I have not received any letter from him, nor dispatches of any kind. This involves new fears for the duplicates of those to Mr. Morris. I have the honor to be, with sentiments of the most perfect esteem and attachment, dear Sir, your most obedient, and most humble servant.

TH: JEFFERSON

[Pp. 72–3, WRITINGS OF JEFFERSON, Washington, IV.]

TAYLOR TO JEFFERSON

Rec.^{d} Nov. 11
New York Nov. 8. 1793.
½ past 11 AM.

Dear Sir,

Your favor of the 3.rd instant [43] I have had the honor to receive a few moments ago. Ever willing to fulfil my duty to the utmost of my power I shall take immediate steps for complying with your desire to take arrangements for resuming the Business of the office. To this end I shall set off with my little family in the first days of the next week.

[43] Unable to locate this letter. — S.K.P.

From the present state of the weather and of the disorder in Philadelphia, communicated thro' the medium of the public prints, it would seem rather imprudent to risk a residence in that City. I should therefore give a preference to Germantown for the present, tho' the expense should be greater than my circumstances will afford; being convinced that on this occasion Congress will readily allow any extraordinary expenses necessarily incurred in prosecuting the public Business.

I shall immediately forward a copy of your letter to Mr Blackwell, who I am informed is on Long Island. As to the other Gentlemen, I am totally ignorant of their places of Residence. I have not rec.^d a line from Mr Bankson since the 7. of Octr last tho' I have written three letters to him since that date.

Apprehensive that I may miss this days post I must close.

With every Sentiment of Respect and sincere Regard, I have the honor to be

Dr Sir,

Your mo. ob. &

Mo. humble Servt

GE.^o TAYLOR J.^R

MR JEFFERSON

[Ms., *Jefferson Papers*, Library of Congress.]

WASHINGTON TO JEFFERSON

TO THOMAS JEFFERSON

PHILADA,

15th *March*, 1795.

Dear Sir,

I received your letter of the 23d ultimo; but not at so early a period as might have been expected from the date of it.

My mind has always been more disposed to apply the shares in the inland navigation of Potomac and James Rivers, (which were left to my disposal by the legislature of Virginia) towards the endowment of an University in the United States, than to any other object it had contemplated. In pursuance of this idea, and understanding that other means are in embryo for establishing so useful a seminary in the Federal City, I did, on the 28th of January last, announce to the Commissioners thereof my intention of vesting in perpetuity, the fifty shares I hold under that act, in the navigation of Potomac, as an additional mean of carrying the plan into effect, provided it should be adopted upon a scale so liberal as to extend to and embrace a *complete* system of education.

I had little hesitation in giving the Federal City a preference of all the places for the institution, for the following reasons. 1st On account of its being the permanent seat of the Government of this Union, and where the laws and policy of it must be better understood than in any local part thereof. 2d, because of its centrality. 3d, because one half (or near it) of the District of Columbia is within the Commonwealth of Virginia, and the whole of the State not inconvenient thereto. 4th, because, as *part* of the endowment, it would be useful, but *alone* would be inadequate to the end. 5th, because many advantages, I conceive, would result from the jurisdiction, which the general Government will have over it, which no other spot would possess. And, lastly, as this seminary is contemplated for the *completion* of education and study of the sciences, (not for boys in their rudiments,) it will afford the students an opportunity of attending the debates in Congress, and thereby becoming more liberally and better acquainted with the principles of law and government.

My judgment and my wishes point equally strong to the application of the James River shares to the same object at the same place; but, considering the source from whence they were derived, I have, in a letter I am writing to the Executive of Virginia on this subject, left the application of them to a seminary *within the State*, to be located by the Legislature.

Hence you will perceive, that I have in a degree anticipated your proposition. I was restrained from going the whole length of the suggestion by the following considerations. 1st, I did not know to what extent, or when any plan would be so matured for the establishment of an University, as would enable any assurances to be given to the application of M. D'Ivernois. 2d, the propriety of transplanting the professors *in a body* might be questioned for several reasons; among others, because they might not all be good characters, nor all sufficiently acquainted with our language: and again, having been at variance with the levelling party of their own country, the measure might be considered as an aristocratical movement by more than those, who, without any just cause that I can discover, are continually sounding the bell of aristocracy. And, 3d, because it might preclude some of the first professors in other countries from a participation, among whom some of the most celebrated characters in Scotland, in this line, might be obtained.

Something, but of what nature I am unable to inform you, has been written by Mr. Adams to M. D'Ivernois. Never having viewed my intended donation as more than a part of the means, that were to set this establishment afloat, I did not incline to go too far in the encouragement of professors, before the plan should assume a more formal shape, much less to induce an entire college to migrate. The enclosed is the answer I have received from the commissioners; from which, and the ideas I have here expressed, you will be enabled to decide on the best communication to be made to M. D'Ivernois.

My letter to the commissioners has bound me to the fulfilment of what is therein engaged; and if the Legislature of Virginia, in considering the subject, should view it in the same light I do, the James River shares will be added thereto; for I think one good institution of this sort is to be preferred to two imperfect ones, which, without other aid than the shares in *both* navigations, is more likely to fall through, than to succeed

upon the plan I contemplate; which, in a few words, is to supersede the necessity of sending the youth of this country abroad
for the purpose of education, (where too often principles and
habits unfriendly to republican government are imbibed, and
not easily discarded,) by instituting such an one of our own, as
will answer the end, and associating them in the same seminary, will contribute to wear off those prejudices and unreasonable jealousies, which prevent or weaken friendships and im-
pair the harmony of the Union. With very great esteem, I am
&c.

[Pp. 118–120, *Records of the Columbia Historical Society*, Vol. 17. Reprinted through the
courtesy of the Columbia Historical Society, Washington, D.C.]

JEFFERSON TO WHITE

TO ALEXANDER WHITE, ESQ.

Monticello, September 10, 1797.

Dear Sir:

So many persons have of late found an interest or a passion
gratified by imputing to me sayings and writings which I never
said or wrote, or by endeavoring to draw me into newspapers
to harass me personally, that I have found it necessary for my
quiet and my other pursuits to leave them in full possession of
the field, and not to take the trouble of contradicting them even
in private conversation. If I do it now, it is out of respect to
your application, made by private letter and not through the
newspapers, and under the perfect assurance that what I write
to you will not be permitted to get in a newspaper, while you
are at full liberty to assert it in conversation under my authority.

I never gave an opinion that the Government would not remove to the federal city. I never entertained that opinion; but
on the contrary, whenever asked the question, I have expressed
my full confidence that they would remove there. Having had

frequent occasion to declare this sentiment, I have endeavored to conjecture on what a contrary one could have been ascribed to me. I remember that in Georgetown, where I passed a day in February in conversation with several gentlemen on the preparations there for receiving the government, an opinion was expressed by some, and not privately, that there would be few or no private buildings erected in Washington this summer, and that the prospect of there being a sufficient number in time, was not flattering. This they grounded on the fact that the persons holding lots, from a view to increase their means of building, had converted their money at low prices, into Morris and Nicholson's notes, then possessing a good degree of credit, and that having lost these by the failure of these gentlemen, they were much less able to build than they would have been. I then observed, and I did it with a view to excite exertion, that if there should not be private houses in readiness sufficient for the accommodation of Congress and the persons annexed to the Government, it could not be expected that men should come there to lodge, like cattle, in the fields, and that it highly behoved those interested in the removal to use every exertion to provide accommodations. In this opinion, I presume I shall be joined by yourself and every other. But delivered, as it was, only on the hypothesis of a fact stated by others, it could not authorize the assertion of an absolute opinion, separated from the statement of facts on which it was hypothetically grounded. I have seen no reason to believe that Congress have changed their purpose with respect to the removal. Every public indication from them, and every sentiment I have heard privately expressed by the members, convinces me they are steady in the purpose. Being on this subject, I will suggest to you, what I did privately at Georgetown to a particular person, in confidence that it should be suggested to the managers, if in event it should happen that there should not be a sufficiency of private buildings erected within the proper time, would it not be better for the commissioners to apply for a suspension of the removal for one year, than to leave it to the hazard which a contrary interest might otherwise bring on it? Of this however you have yet two summers to consider, and you have the best knowledge of the circumstances on which a judgment may be formed whether private accommodations will be provided. As to the public buildings, every one seems to agree that they will be in readiness.

I have for five or six years been encouraging the opening a direct road from the southern part of this State, leading through this county to Georgetown. The route proposed is from Georgetown by Colonel Alexander's, Elk-run Church, Norman's Ford Stevensburg, the Racoon Ford, the Marquis's Road, Martin Key's Ford on the Rivanna, the mouth of Slate River, the high bridge on Appomattox, Prince Edward Courthouse, Charlotte Courthouse, Cole's ferry on Stanton, Dix's ferry on Dan, Guilford Courthouse, Salisbury, Crosswell's ferry on Saluda, Ninety-six, Augusta. It is believed this road will shorten the distance along the continent one hundred miles. It will be to open anew only from Georgetown to Prince Edward Courthouse. An actual survey has been made from Stevensburg to Georgetown, by which that much of the road will be shortened twenty miles, and be all a dead level. The difficulty is to get it first through Fairfax and Prince William. The counties after that will very readily carry it on. We consider it as opening to us a direct road to the market of the federal city, for all the beef and mutton we could raise, for which we have no market at present. I am in possession of the survey, and had thought of getting the Bridge company at Georgetown to undertake to get the road carried through Fairfax and Prince William, either by those counties or by themselves. But I have some apprehension that by pointing our road to the bridge, it might get out of the level country, and be carried over the hills, which will be but a little above it. This would be inadmissible. Perhaps you could suggest some means of our getting over the obstacle of those two counties. I shall be very happy to concur in any measure which can effect all our purposes. I am with esteem, dear Sir, your most obedient servant.

TH: JEFFERSON

[Pp. 201–3, WRITINGS OF JEFFERSON, Washington, IV; Mem. Ed., IX, 424–28.]

JEFFERSON TO MADISON

JEFFERSON TO MADISON

Philadelphia, April 5, 1798

The bill for the federal buildings labors hard in Senate, tho', to lessen opposition, the Maryland Senator himself proposed to reduce the 200.000 D to one third of that sum. . . . I conjecture that the votes will be either 13 for & 15 against it, or 14 & 14. Every member declares he means to go there. . . .

[P. 231, WRITINGS OF JEFFERSON, Washington, IV.]

WHITE TO JEFFERSON

Commissioners Office

5th Decr 1800

Dear Sir

I have examined my correspondence with Col: Little and Mr Strade respecting the proposed road; I find Colonel Little only engaged to join with Mr Strade in tracing the ground, in which he said three other gentlemen one a surveyor and all good Woods men, would assist; but I never heard of any thing being done; and unless Mr Strade was on the ground (and of this he would probably have informed) there certainly has not. I am with sentiments of great respect

Dear Sir
Your Most Ob^t Servt
ALEX^R WHITE

[Ms., *Jefferson Papers*, Library of Congress.]

COMMISSIONERS TO JEFFERSON

Commissioners Office, 4th *March* 1801

Sir,

The enclosed writing sufficiently explains it's object, and we presume, the utility of the Measure proposed must be apparent, especially to those who have seen the number of wooden stoups lately erected by the Description of people whose accommodation is more immediately contemplated. We however respectfully submit the Subject to your consideration, and if the Measure be approved, we request the writing may be returned with your Signature, that those inclined to erect wooden Houses in the City, may have early notice of the suspension of the prohibitory articles. We are, with sentiments of the highest Respect, &c.

W. THORNTON
A. WHITE

THE PRESIDENT OF THE UNITED STATES

[Pp. 59–60, COMMISSIONERS' LETTERBOOK, Vol. 6, 1800–02, in the National Archives.]

DECLARATION SUSPENDING BUILDING REGULATIONS

By the President of the United States [44]

Whereas by the first article of the Terms and conditions declared by the President of the United States on the 17.th day of October 1791, for regulating the Materials and manner of Buildings and Improvements on the Lots in the City of Washington it is provided, "that the outer and party walls of all

[44] March 11.th The President of the United States this Day signed & delivered to the Board a Proclamation, authorizing a further suspension of the first & third articles for regulating the materials & manner of buildings & improvements on the Lots in the City of Washington which the Board direct may be printed in the National Intelligencer & the Museum, twice a Week for six Weeks. He also delivered to the Board an Estimate made by James Hoban, relative to the Presid.$^{t's}$ House.

[P. 123, PROCEEDINGS OF THE COMMISSIONERS, Vol. VI, 1800–02, in the National Archives.]

Houses in the said City, shall be built of Brick or Stone," and by the third article of the same Terms and Conditions, it is declared, "that the wall of no House shall be higher than forty feet to the Roof, in any part of the City, nor shall any be lower than thirty five feet on any of the Avenues" and whereas the above recited articles were found to impede the settlement in the City of Mechanics and others whose Circumstances did not admit of erecting Houses authorized by the said Regulations for which cause the President of the United States, by a writing under his Hand, bearing Date the twenty fifth Day of June 1796 suspended the operation of the said Articles until the first Monday of December 1800, and the beneficial effects arising from such Suspension having been experienced, it is deemed proper to revive the same. Wherefore, I Thomas Jefferson, president of the United States do declare, that the operation of the first and third Articles above recited shall be, and the same is hereby suspended until the first Day of January 1802, and that all the Houses which shall be erected in the said City of Washington previous to the said first day of January 1802 conformable in other respects to the regulations aforesaid shall be considered as lawfully Erected except that no Wooden House shall be erected within twenty four feet of any brick or Stone House.

Given under my Hand this 11.th Day of March 1801.

TH: JEFFERSON

[Letters of the Presidents of the U.S. to the Commissioners of Public Buildings and Grounds, original in Manuscripts Division, Library of Congress; photostat in National Archives.]

COMMISSIONERS NOTE

March 13.th 1801   Ordered that James Hoban be desired to have the work executed according to the Directions given by the President of the United States.

[P. 124, Proceedings of the Commissioners, Vol. VI, 1800–02, in the National Archives.]

JEFFERSON TO ELLICOTT

TH: JEFFERSON having referred m . Ellicott's letter to the Secretary of the Treasury (m͞r Dexter) received from him the inclosed note. he leaves this place on the 21ˢᵗ inst. to be absent one month, when m Madison will also enter on his office. in the mean time m͞r Lincoln will have charge of the Secretary of State's office & will recieve any application from m͞r Ellicott, & do justice on it. he presents him his friendly salutations.

Mar. 13. 1801

[Ms., *Jefferson Papers*, Library of Congress.]

JEFFERSON PROCLAMATION

THOMAS JEFFERSON,

President of the United States of America.

To Thomas Sim Lee, Daniel Reintzell, Thomas Corcoran, Daniel Carroll, Cornelius Cunningham, Thomas Peter, Robert Brent, Thomas Addison, Abraham Boyd, Benjamin Moore, John Mason, William Thornton, Benjamin Stoddert, William Hammond Dorsey, Joseph Sprigg Belt, Esquires, Greeting:

KNOW YE, That reposing special Trust and Confidence in your Integrity, Ability, diligence and discretion, I have appointed you, jointly and severally and every one of you Justices of the Peace in the County of Washington in the District of Columbia, and to keep and cause to be kept all laws for the good of the peace, and for the preservation of the same, and for the quiet rule and government of the people, made in all and singular their Articles in the said County, according to the force, form and effect of the same, and further to do and perform every act and thing within the said County, which by law, you or either of you may do and perform as Justices of the Peace; with all the Powers, Privileges and Emoluments to the same office of Justice of the Peace of right appertaining. This commission to continue in force until the end of the next Session of the Senate of the United States and no longer.

IN TESTIMONY WHEREOF, I have caused these Letters to be made Patent and the Seal of the United States to be hereunto affixed.

GIVEN under my hand at the City of Washington the Sixteenth day of March, in the year of our Lord one thousand eight hundred and one, and of the Independence of the United States of America the twenty-fifth.

TH: JEFFERSON.

By the President:
    LEVI LINCOLN,
        Acting as Secretary of State.

[P. 266, *Records of the Columbia Historical Society*, Vol. 5.   Reprinted through the courtesy of the Columbia Historical Society, Washington, D.C.]

COMMISSIONERS NOTE

March 16.th   Ordered that the Proclamation of the President
1801   of the United States of the 15.th Inst: be directed
                   to be published in the American Daily Advertiesr
                   & the Aurora of Philad.^a & in the Telegraph of
                   Baltimore, twice a Week for six Weeks.

          [P. 125, PROCEEDINGS OF THE COMMISSIONERS, Vol. VI, 1800–02, in the
          National Archives.]

JEFFERSON TO DANIEL BRENT

Mar. 18 1801

Sir

I am to appoint a Marshall for the District of Columbia. it has been imparted to me by a mutual friend that you might perhaps be willing to accept of that office. on this suggestion I take the liberty of proposing it to you. as a court is to be held here on Monday next, it becomes necessary for me to ask the favor of an answer by the bearer, [illegible] [illegible] [illegible]

[illegible] for this purpose, because should you decline it, I shall still have to make an appointment before Monday. my anxiety to place in the offices men who will give weight to them & command the public confidence inspires an earnest desire that this may be acceptable to you.

Your most obed! serv!

TH: JEFFERSON

DANIEL CARROL BRENT ESQ.

[Ms., *Jefferson Papers*, Library of Congress.]

HADFIELD TO JEFFERSON

Sir

Be pleased to allow me to lay before you, the case of an artist, who chearfully quitted his occupations and prospects in London, to accept through Colonel John Trumbull; the invitations of the Commissioners of Washington to visit this country, for the purpose of superintending the building of the Capitol. —

After having continued in that Office, for three years, and superintended the execution of the most difficult part of that building; I was abruptly dismissed to the great injury of my professional reputation.

Sensible, that such treatment could not fail to cause me to experience very serious consequences, if left unnoticed: I hastened to lay my situation before the late President of the United States, but after considerable delay and anxiety, I found that I had no hope of redress, in consequence of which I have had the painful mortification, not only of seeing my work remain for the praise and reputation of those, who have meditated and effected my ruin: but also, of having my productions for Public buildings surreptitiously taken from me, and executed, without my receiving any compensation for them.

I hope that I shall not be thought too presumptuous if I am desirous to shew, that the great increase of expence in consequence of the unnecessary alterations made in the Capitol;

after I had left it, as well as the present leakiness and other defects of that building: arise from an entire ignorance of the plans
& mode intended by me, and of course lost in consequence of
my dismission.

And I will further venture to say, that had I been permitted
to superintend my work & designs in the building of the Executive Offices, that the late unfortunate fire in one of them, would
not have happened from the causes, by many supposed & al-
ledged; and it appears, that those buildings, from the manner
of their execution, will always be subject to similar accidents, if
suffered to remain in their present state.

I shall not, Sir, at present trouble you, with a tedious detail
of particulars, but should you think my case, worthy of your
notice, I trust that I shall be able to substantiate my assertions,
supported by some of the most respectable characters in this
City.

I shall only say for the present that I suffer considerably
through the oppressive treatment which I have received from
the Commissioners of the City: but encouraged as I am, by
letters lately received from Col. Trumbull in Europe, and by
other friends here, and presuming that the advantages I have
had during the pursuit of my studies might be of further utility
in the present state of the City, I have taken the liberty thus to
lay my case before you, with no other view, Sir, than to endeavour to make myself useful, and thereby obtain a subsistence
in a country which I have chosen to spend the remainder of my
life in. —

I have the honor to be

with most profound respect,

Sir,

Your very obedient

humble servant

Washington. March 27th 1801   GEORGE HADFIELD
THE PRESIDENT OF THE UNITED STATES

[Ms., *Jefferson Papers*, Library of Congress.]

Commissioners to Jefferson

Commissioners Office, 28th *March* 1801

Sir,

Deeply impressed with the necessity of bringing the Business of the Commission as near as possible to a close previous to the Meeting of the next Congress and of promoting the Interest of the City in the mean Time, we have had under consideration the Means of accomplishing those objects; but the Difficulties which occur are so great as to prevent an unanimous Opinion of the Board with regard to the Measures to be pursued. We therefore find ourselves under the necessity of stating the Subject of disagreement to the President for his Direction.

We have already advertised for Sale on the 12th of May next all the Property purchased by Morris and Greenleaf which we consider as liable to be resold for non-payment of the purchase-money, except such as has been already sold for the same cause, but there remains other Property liable to be resold, either purchased at private Sales, or at public Sales of Property resold for non-payment of the original purchase money — of the last description, the Sum of $33,802 97/100 exclusive of Interest, is due on four notes drawn by Uriah Forrest, one for $16,407 04/100 endorsed by Benjamin Stoddert — one for Doll^{s} 6,269 92/100 endorsed by Gustavus Scott, and two endorsed by John Templeman & Benjamin Stoddert, one for $6,641 & the other for $4485 — and the Sum of 1675 68/100 drawn by William Thornton and endorsed by Mr Blodget. It is to be observed that the said Gustavus Scott, William Thornton and Uriah Forrest, together with James M. Lingan, are sureties for the sum of fifty thousand Dollars United-States six per cent: Stock borrowed of the State of Maryland under the Circumstances stated to the President in a Representation of the Commissioners dated 28th Jany last on the affairs of the City of Washington, an Extract from which is enclosed (A) and it is urged that they might not to pay these Sums until the Money becomes due to the State of Maryland, they paying into the Hands of the Commissioners, a Sum equal to the Interest in the Mean Time which we admit they have exceeded, and have had Property equivalent conveyed to them which consequently cannot be resold. It is admitted that a payment to the State of Maryland, or an exoneration of the Public for so much, would be considered a payment for the Property purchased, and in giving their Notes, these Gentlemen reserved to themselves Time to negotiate that Business with the Legislature of Maryland, but we do not find that it was accomplished.

The points on which we wish the decision of the President are, whether we shall immediately pursue the most efficacious measures for the recovery of Debts generally — whether there shall be an exception of those above-mentioned — and if not whether it will be most eligible to bring Suits on the Notes, or to sell the Property agreeably to the Summary-Mode authorised by the Act of the Assembly of Maryland, and if the latter, whether the Sale shall be for ready money or on credit, and finally, whether it would be better to post-pone the Sale now advertised, and unite the whole Property in one Advertisement, or to suffer the Sale to take place on the 12.th of May on the Terms published, and to advertise a Sale Money of the remainder of the Property which is liable to be resold at as early a Day as circumstances will admit and here we would observe, that we think if payment of the Debts due from the Gentlemen who stand sureties to the State of Maryland is enforced, provision ought to be made for meeting the Demands of that State, which may, with more certainty be done by Sales on credit, than for cash. We are &c.

W. THORNTON
A. WHITE
T. DALTON

PRESIDENT OF THE UNITED STATES.

(P.S.) Since writing the above, General Forrest has written a Letter to the Board, a copy of which we think proper to transmit to the President for his consideration.

W. T.

A. W.

T. D.

[Pp. 63–5, COMMISSIONERS' LETTERBOOK, Vol. 6, 1800–02, in the National Archives.]

JEFFERSON TO COMMISSIONERS

Th: Jefferson will take the liberty of calling on the board of commissioners at their hour of meeting this morning, to confer on the subject of their paper lately sent him. as some questions of law are involved, he has asked the favor of the Attorney general to accompany him. he tenders to the board his high consideration & respect.

Monday Mar. 30. 1801.

[Letters of the Presidents of the U.S. to the Commissioners of Public Buildings and Grounds, original in Manuscripts Division, Library of Congress; photostat in National Archives.]

WHITE TO JEFFERSON

Washington, 6.th *April* 1801 [45]

Sir,

Agreeably to a Resolution of the Board of Commissioners of the 30.th Ult.^o I went to Annapolis on thursday last. The Governor was in Virginia and not expected to return soon. M.^r.

[45] April 6.th A Letter written to the President of the U.S. by Alex.^r White, stating the result of the application made to the Governor and Council of Maryland agreeably to the resolution of the Board of the 30.th Ul.^o and enclosing a copy of the Commissioners letter on the subject of that application, also a copy of a Note presented by the said A. White to the Governour & Council on the 11.th [?] Ins.^t. [P. 131, PROCEEDINGS OF THE COMMISSIONERS, Vol. 6, 1800–02, in the National Archives.

Shoaff, one of the Council was likewise absent, but expected on ·friday Evening. I waited on the other Member of the Council and procured a meeting on Saturday, when all the Members in the City attended, but M.ʳ Shoaff had not arrived. I presented to them the Commissioners' letter (of which a copy is enclosed) and conversed fully on the subject of my Mission in presence of the Agent and Auditor of the State, who had been notified to attend. It appeared that the State had found it necessary to borrow thirty thousand Dollars to answer the current Expenses of the last Year, and that without the Interest on the Money lent to the City, their funds were inadequate to the Expenses of the present Year, even though they should not pay any part of the Money borrowed. Under the circumstances, the Council were against granting any Indulgence with respect to the payment of that Interest.

I also presented a note (of which a copy is enclosed) the Council wished not to act on the subject of that Note till M.ʳ Shoaff should be present, as some legal Difficulties were suggested. I did not think it necessary to attend their Deliberation, having said all that appeared proper for me to say. The result I expect to receive by post tomorrow. I am, &c.

A. WHITE

PRESIDENT OF THE UNITED STATES.

[Pp. 67–8, COMMISSIONERS' LETTERBOOK, Vol. 6, 1800–02, in the National Archives.]

COMMISSIONERS TO JEFFERSON

Commissioner's Office 7.ᵗʰ *May* 1801.

Sir

Several applications have lately been made to us to sanction the establishing of a market in the public reservation "beginning at the intersection of the north side of Canal Street, & the east side of Ninth Street west, thence North, to the south side of an Avenue drawn in Front of Square No. 382, thence north-easterly with the South side of said Avenue until it intersects the South side of Pennsylvania Avenue, thence with the South side of said Avenue until it intersects the West side of Seventh Street west, thence with the West side of said Street until it intersects Canal Street, thence West with the north side of Canal Street to the beginning." —

The above was reserved, and originally intended for a market, but not having been called for till lately, no appropriation was made. It is thought to embrace so many advantages, and is so central, that were a market established there, it would be a great accommodation to the City in general, & we therefore consider it as a Duty to submit to your Determination the propriety of appropriating it to a market, subject to such Regulations as the proper Authorities may hereafter establish. —

We have the honor to be

May 8. 1801.

The appropriation of the ground herein described for a market, as proposed by the Commissioners, is approved.

TH: JEFFERSON

PRESIDENT OF THE UNITED STATES}

Sir,

with Sentiments of the highest respect & Consideration

WILLIAM THORNTON
TRISTRAM DALTON

[P. 76, COMMISSIONERS' LETTERBOOK, Vol. 6, 1800–02, in the National Archives.]

KING TO JEFFERSON

28th *May* 1801

THE PRESIDENT, OF THE U.S.

Sir,

A premium having been offered for the best design for Barracks, agreeably to the dimensions of one of the Squares designated for building Lots; that design having been given, and

approved; and the contract for erecting the buildings adver-
tized; It might be well before the foundation is dug, to examine
the title of the U.S. to the ground designated as the scite; to see
how far it agrees with the Plans of the City, with the sales to
individuals, with public faith, and with the Deeds of Trust,
under which the President and Commissioners are authorized
to proceed.

On the first appearance of the affair, all respect for the Deeds
of Trust seems to be lost, and, it appears one of these Strange
and venturious steps which none but the City Commissioners
would take, and which had already placed us on the verge of
desolation. My Ideas, on the propriety of this measure may be
crude and erroneous, & I may be now exposing my own vanity. Yet, it is better than an individual should be pitied for his
opinions or his weakness, than injury should be done to the
purchasers of Lots, to the City or the public.

The following doubts have occurred to me as necessary to be
examined, before a decision on the Propriety of fixing the Barracks on the intended Capitol Square can be made.

By the Deeds of Trust from the original proprietors, the
President is authorized to locate such squares for public uses as
he considered necessary; the remaining Squares and Lots to be
equally divided into two parts; *one of which reverts to the original
proprietor, the other part is to be sold and the monies arising therefrom
given to the President, as a Donation for the purpose of erecting the
buildings necessary to the accomodation of Congress*, agreeably to the
Act in that case provided. — One half of the Square in question, was assigned to Mr Prout the original proprietor, — the
other half to the public, *for sale*, as stipulated in the Deed of
Trust. Can the Commissioners under this Deed, give the Property away, and thereby lessen the Funds of the City for public
purposes? They not only give the half assigned to the public for
Sale, but exchange Lots with Mr Prout so as to give his half
also.

If this Square is to be considered as a public appropriation for the use of the United States and made by the President under the Deeds, Mr P. ought to be paid therefor at the rate of 25 £, the acre; — and not as is proposed, by other Lots to twenty times that amount. It has never been shewn as such appropriation on any of the plans; and to consider it so now, would be a breach of faith, and deception to those who have bought and selected public property in its vicinity.

Let it once be admitted that the Commissioners can divert the Lots directed to be sold, to other purposes than contemplated in the plans and Deeds which direct such sale, and what Security is left that those Lots which now remain unsold, will contribute to the City funds.

Whether Barracks in the Commercial part of the City (as that eventually must be) are desireable, or not, I cannot say: they certainly were never calculated upon by those who have purchased in that part of the City, and erecting them in the Situation proposed, will be a real injury to those who dislike to reside in such a neighbourhood.

While there are such extensive appropriations for public Uses, in situations equally eligible; it may afford room for censure to divert to this purpose Lots which were expressly reserved for private buildings.

I can make no other Apology for this intrusion than my wish to benefit the City, and prevent any premature decision on the part of the Commissioners as their obtaining the assent of the Executive until the inconveniences were adverted to, and the right ascertained.

I am Sir,

With the greatest respect

Yours

Nich^s King

[Ms., *Jefferson Papers*, Library of Congress.]

Commissioners to Jefferson

Commissioner's Office 1ˢᵗ June 1801.

Sir,

We have taken into consideration the prospect of an increased Representation in Congress, and have concluded that the present House will not, after the next apportionment of Members be Sufficient for their accommodation. We in consequence requested M.ʳ Hoban to sketch plans or Estimates of a Building which may temporarily answer that purpose; — he has made out Estimates on three different plans, and will wait on you to give any explanations that may be required to enable you to form an opinion of the propriety of adopting any of them if means cannot be obtained to finish the South Wing. We are, &c.

W. Thornton
A. White
T. Dalton

PRESIDENT OF THE
UNITED STATES.

[P. 84, COMMISSIONERS' LETTERBOOK, Vol. 6, 1800–02, in the National Archives.]

Commissioners to Jefferson

Commissioners Office 1st June 1801.

Sir,

By a Regulation of the Commissioners of this City approved by the President July 15ᵗʰ 1794, Areas were permitted in front of dwelling Houses to the extent of five feet in breadth, but from experience these have been found too confined, and this has been frequently represented to us as a Subject worthy of consideration. We are convinced they are too confined and think it our duty to submit to your decision the propriety of

extending the permission to seven feet, which is deemed a sufficient extent for an Area in any situation. We are, with Sentiments of the greatest respect,

>Sir,

>>Your mo. Ob^t Serv^{ts}.

June 1. 1801.

>Approved

WILLIAM THORNTON —

ALEX^R WHITE

TH: JEFFERSON.

President of the United-States.

TRISTRAM DALTON

[Letters of the Presidents of the U.S. to the Commissioners of Public Buildings and Grounds, original in the Manuscripts Division, Library of Congress; photostat in National Archives.]

JEFFERSON TO COMMISSIONERS

On consideration of the three plans presented by Capt Hobens for providing an apartment for the H. of Representatives
of the US. that appears to me most to be approved which proposes to raise, to the height of one story only, the elliptical wall
or arcade in the Southern wing destined ultimately for their
occupation; without carrying up at present the external square
wall which is to include it.

It seems preferable to that which proposes a temporary room
of scantling in the center, to cost between 4. & 5000. D. the
whole of which would be to be taken away in future, & nothing
saved but what the scantling might then be worth. Whereas, of
the elliptical room thought preferable, & which he supposes
will cost 5600. D. he thinks not more than 1000. D. will be lost
when the wing shall be compleated in future: and it seems desireable that, whatever money is expended should go as much
as possible to the execution of the permanent building.

The plan of raising the elliptical building only one story
seems preferable to that for raising it two stories. 1st because it
will cost but half as much [illegible] circumstance desireable to

the present state of the City funds & to their immediate prospects. 2. Mr. Hobens observes there will be considerable inconveniencies in carrying up the elliptical wall now without
the square one, & the square one in future without the elliptical
wall, and that these difficulties increase as the walls get higher.
This obstacle then is lessened more than one half by raising the
south elliptical wall only to one half of it's height only.

Another advantage in adopting the elliptic building is that,
if before it is raised one story the prospects of money should
brighten & the difficulties of proceeding with it separately from
the square wall should be found less than has been apprehended, we can then proceed to raise it's second story.

TH: JEFFERSON

June 2.ᵈ 1801.

THE COMMISSIONERS

OF THE CITY OF WASHINGTON.

[Copied from a photostat in the National Archives of the original in the Library of Congress; published in Documentary History . . . of the Capitol, 96–7.]

WILLIAMSON TO JEFFERSON

City of Washington Jun 11ᵗʰ 1801

Honourable Sir

Pleas remember that soon after your being apointed to the
high office of presedente, I called upon you at your lodging and
hade a short Intercouse, one the subjet of the commissioners
how they hade behaved Towards me, and others that was in
there employe and that I have got a Judgment for the contents
of my contract, they pleaded to refer the execution to the nixt
court that if they hade any defence to make to bring it forward,
and me to prove my Servicess acordingly I attended the court
with my prooffes but the commissioners nor any witness from
them did not apear the trouth is they hade non that could be
acartaind as a witness except Hoben hade been admited who

has led them into all the mischef that has been Don in the city, as they did not attende I have got a dispensation from the court, to exemen the witness here, it is a small mater for the commissioners to be throwing away the publice money as they have don in defence of a Just caus, I was looked upon by all the Information that the first commissioners could find to be the only man fitest for the task, and it is sirtaint hade I been alowed to conduct the work in ginerel as my contract expreses, it would have been good for the publice as well as for me, but then how could the thives have hade liberty to steale and take the public matereals as they have don to a great extinte I was early instructed in arcticetry altho I only was employed heer as master mason, and in different stages of the work was under the necessity of giving instructions to him who was apointed to instruct me I built the first story of the presedents House and brought all the capatol above ground; before my dismission from the publice emplye and it is to be seen what hand was made of it after wards, as I still supose my self in the publice employe at least untill the laws of the land shall discharge me, I thought it my deuty to Inform your excelency which I expect will atone for troubling you I should be verry hapy I hade somthing to do in the way of my business, while I expect to be paid I expect it will not apear to your excellency a small mater that I was Indulzed to come from New york where I hade the best of employe and be treated as I have been.

Honoure Sir I am with great Respect your most obedent Houmble Serv^{nt}

COLLEN WILLIAMSON

[Ms., *Jefferson Papers*, Library of Congress.]

COMMISSIONERS TO JEFFERSON

Commissioner's Office, 12th *June* 1801

Sir,

On the 13th Feby last, the claim of George Walker respecting

two spaces of Ground in the City of Washington, which he con-
ceives ought to be paid for and appropriated to public use, was
laid before the late President, and all the Information, which
the Board thought necessary for his Information, transmitted.
We take the liberty of requesting your attention to this Business, as the payment of a Debt due from M.ʳ Walker depends on
the President's decision, and we have agreed to wait till that
decision shall be known. We are, with sentiments of the greatest
respect, &c.

W. THORNTON
A. WHITE
T. DALTON

PRESIDENT OF THE UNITED STATES.

[P. 87, COMMISSIONERS' LETTERBOOK, Vol. 6, 1800–02, in the National Archives.]

JEFFERSON TO COMMISSIONERS

JOHN ADAMS, PRESIDENT OF THE UNITED STATES
TO THOMAS BEALL OF GEORGE & JOHN M. GANTT.

You are hereby requested to convey a certain Square, parcel
or lot of Ground in the City of Washington, bounded as follows
— Beginning in the line of the east side of eleventh Street east,
at the distance of ninety feet south of the south-west corner of
Square numbered nine hundred and eighty eight — thence
east eight hundred and twenty six feet, six Inches — thence
South four hundred and forty feet — thence west, eight hundred and twenty six feet, six Inches — thence north, four hundred and forty feet, to the Beginning, to William Thornton,
Alexander White and William Cranch, Commissioners appointed under the Act of Congress, entitled "an Act for establishing the temporary and permanent seat of the Government
of the United-States." To have and to hold to the said William

Thornton, Alexander White and William Cranch, and their Heirs to the use of the United-States forever.

Given under my Hand and the Seal of the United-States, this day of February in the Year of our Lord one thousand eight hundred and one.

On considering the case between the Commissioners and m$\bar{r}$ George Walker relative to the Semicircular area at the intersection of K. and 17th streets & the Pensylv$\bar{a}$ & Kentucky avenues, there appear but two ways in which that Area can be disposed of agreeably to law & practice

1. We may continue the s^{d} streets & avenues to the Water street. There would then be no reasonable cause for laying out a circular street; consequently there would be considerable triangles or points, which would be to be divided between the public and the proprietors, as building lots.

2. We may assume there a public area. in this case it is proper there should be a circular street round it, and a water street, to give to the town it's necessary communications: assuming the area within these for public use. This appears to me most advantageous to the city, and is accordingly preferred. consequently this area exclusive of the streets is to be paid for according to the original contract. forming this opinion on such views of the subject as occur to myself, and as yet not sufficiently intimate with the affairs of the city, to be satisfied that I am apprised of all the circumstances which may bear on the question, if there are any such unknown to me, which would be strongly against the opinion here given, I should wish to be informed of them, and to suspend the opinion in the meantime

Th: Jefferson
June 14. 1801.

[*Letters of the Presidents of the U. S. to the Commissioners of Public Buildings and Grounds*, original in Manuscripts Division, Library of Congress, photostat in National Archives.]

COMMISSIONERS TO JEFFERSON

Commissioner's Office 17.th *June* 1801

Sir,

We transmit the form of an Act to appropriate the two parcels of Ground which have been under your consideration; the last mentioned being described agreeably to the Ideas expressed in your communication of the 14.th Instant, except that no reservation of a Water Street is made. This we did under an impression, that the Government may lay out a Water Street more convenient than the one now described.

We are, &c.

W. THORNTON
A. WHITE
T. DALTON

PRESIDENT OF THE UNITED-
STATES.

[P. 88, COMMISSIONERS' LETTERBOOK, Vol. 6, 1800–02 in the National Archives.]

JEFFERSON TO BEALL AND GANTT

THOMAS JEFFERSON, PRESIDENT OF THE UNITED STATES,
TO THOMAS BEALL OF GEORGE & JOHN MACKALL GANTT

You are hereby requested to convey two squares, parcels or Lots of ground in the City of Washington, one bounded as follows — Beginning in the line of the East side of eleventh street East, at the distance of ninety feet south of the south west corner of square numbered nine hundred and eighty eight; thence east, eight hundred & twenty six feet six inches; thence south, four hundred and forty feet; thence west, eight hundred and twenty six feet six inches; thence north, four hundred and forty feet, to the beginning — The other bounded by part of a circle, beginning at the shore of the Eastern branch from the south point of square numbered eleven hundred and six, and at the distance of ninety feet, from the curve front of the said square going in a paralel and concentric circle to the curve designated by the curve of fronts of squares numbered eleven hundred and six square south of square numbered one thousand and twenty nine, square numbered One thousand and seventy seven, square numbered one thousand and seventy eight, square numbered One thousand and seventy nine, and square south of square numbered one thousand and seventy nine, until it falls in with the shore of the Eastern branch thence along the said branch to the beginning — to William Thornton Alexander White and Tristram Dalton Commissioners appointed under the Act of Congress entitled "An Act for establishing the temporary and permanent seat of the Government of the United States." To Have and to hold to the said William Thornton, Alexander White and Tristram Dalton and their heirs to the use of the United States forever.

GIVEN under my hand & the seal of the United States this seventeenth day of June in the year of our Lord One thousand eight hundred and one

TH: JEFFERSON

[*Letters of the Presidents of the U.S. to the Commissioners of Public Buildings and Grounds*, original in Manuscripts Division, Library of Congress, photostat in National Archives.]

ALEXANDER WHITE TO JEFFERSON

Washington 8.th *August* 1801

rec.d *Aug.* 13.

Sir

To enable me to comply with your request respecting Samuel Davidsons claim, I have re-examined all the papers in the Commissioners Office relative to that case, and find that his claim rests solely on a supposition that L'Enfants Plan is the proper plan of the City; that it received its confirmation by the transmission thereof to Congress; In respect to which President Washington, in his letter dated 20th February 1797 in answer to the Commissioners letter enclosing Mr Davidsons Memorial says "That many alterations have been made from Major L'Enfants Plan by Major Ellicott (with the approbation of the Executive) is not denied, that some were deemed essential, is avowed." Again "Mr Davidson is mistaken if he supposes that the transmission of Major L'Enfant's Plan of the City to Congress was the completion thereof; so far from it, it will appear by the message which accompanied the same, that it was given as matter of information to show what state the business was in, and the return of it requested; that neither House of Congress passed any Act consequent thereupon; that it remained, as before, under the controul of the Executive; that after wards several errors were discovered and corrected, many alterations made, and the appropriations (except as to the Capitol and Presidents house) struck out, before it went to the Engraver, including that work and the promulgation thereof were to give it the final and regulating stamp." Although the words "Presidents House" were retained in the engraved Plan, the Square was laid down differently from that of L'Enfant, and the President in his Act appropriating the same, has described it as delineated on the engraved Plan, on the same principle Mr Davidson has been paid for his Land within the Square. These circumstances appear to me conclusive; the Land thus described, is vested in the U. States; and the President cannot restore it, or any part of it to the original Proprietor, I therefore deem it unnecessary to detail the desultory matter which Mr Davidson has introduced in his various applications; but I would observe, that if M.^r L'Enfants Plan is to be admitted, as a matter of right, in one instance, it must be so in the whole; that this would set the City property afloat; the Streets, public appropriations, and building lots being laid out without any reference to that plan; but generally corresponding with the engraved plan, as nearly as the same could be adapted by actual survey, to the surface of the earth. This letter, I expect, will be considered as a private communication only. The Board if called upon will answer Mr Davidsons complaint

I am with sentiments of the highest respect

Sir

Your most Obed^t

Servant

ALEX^R WHITE

PRESIDENT OF THE U. STATES

[Ms., *Jefferson Papers*, Library of Congress.]

COMMISSIONERS TO JEFFERSON

Washington, 17th *August* 1801

Sir,

On taking a view of the Business entrusted to us, we are of opinion that with the Money now in hand and the Sums which we may depend on receiving, we shall be able to compleat the several Works recommended to us and to pay the current Expenses of the Year, provided no more than four thousand Dollars shall be expended on the Streets, and no more laid out on the temporary House of Representatives than the Contract calls for. But without further payments, there will be an arrear of Interest due to the State of Maryland on the first of October next to the amount of $10,500. We cannot rely on voluntary payments to answer this Sum. We therefore submit to the President of the United-States whether we shall proceed to enforce further Payments particularly from those who are bound to the State of Maryland for the re-payment of fifty thousand Dollars United States six per cent Stock, (Resolution of the Assembly of that State (A) and whose Debts to the City Funds originated in purchases of Property resold for default in payment at public Sales in the Years 1799 & 1800 on the Terms enclosed (B) and for which, the following Notes have since been given, payable 4th Feb'y 1801 — vizt —

One Note drawn by Uriah Forrest and endorsed by Gustavus
  Scott — for $6,269.92
Ditto — endorsed by Benjamin Stoddert for   16,407.04
Ditto — endorsed by John Templeman &⎱
  Ben: Stoddert for   ⎰   6,641.00
Ditto — endorsed by the same for   4,485.00
Ditto — drawn by William Thornton &⎱
  endorsed by S. Blodget   ⎰   1,675.68
                                             Doll^s   35,418.64

We understand that the right of the Commissioners to enforce the payment of these Sums will be disputed, should a Sale be proposed, and we think it improper to risk involving the Affairs of the City in a dispute without acquainting the President with the Grounds thereof, and receiving his Sanction to the Measures to be pursued. The facts of the case are, that on the application of Gustavus Scott and William Thornton two of the Commissioners, the Legislature of Maryland authorised the Loan of fifty thousand Dollars six per cent Stock, on the Terms mentioned in the aforesaid Resolution — that the said Gustavus Scott and William Thornton with Uriah Forrest and James M. Lingan as their Sureties, entered into Bond to the State of Maryland, and Uriah Forrest executed a mortgage on 420 acres of Land, for securing the payment of the said fifty thousand Dollars Stock on the first of November 1802, with Interest quarter-yearly, agreeably to the Terms of the Said Resolution. The said Gustavus Scott & William Thornton having engaged by Letter, to hold all the City property (except that pledged by Act of Congress to secure the Payment of three hundred thousand Dollars) as a security for the re-payment of

the said Stock, and to sell the said Property, or such part thereof
as might be necessary, on notice from the said Forrest and
Lingan; and to pay over the Notes or money arising therefrom
to the State in discharge of that Debt. The correspondence on
this subject is enclosed (C) Gustavus Scott has since deceased,
and it is supposed that he was interested in this property, and
that it has descended to his infant children. The Questions arising from these facts are, — 1st Whether the Commissioners had
a right to pledge the public property in the manner stipulated
by the aforesaid Correspondence, and what effect will it have
on the right of enforcing the payment of Debts either from the
Sureties or others, although the Debts from the Sureties were
not due, and although it appeared evident that the Commissioners were incapable of obtaining by legal process or otherwise, the Money then due to the City; therefore without this
Loan, the public Buildings could not be so far compleated as to
accommodate the several Departments of Government. Note —
we must add, that the Monies received as well from the
Sureties to the State of Maryland, as from others, have been
indiscriminately applied to the general Expenditures on the
Seat of Government, except that a preference has been given in
the Payment of one Quarter's Interest of the said Loan of
50,000 Dollars.

2^{d} Whether Infants are entitled to any privileges in Proceedings under the Act of Assembly, an Extract of which is enclosed
(D) — and third, whether property once sold under that Act
can be resold for default of Payment by the second Purchaser.

It may be proper to observe that between seven and eight
thousand Dollars have been paid by General Forrest and the
Endorsers of the Notes drawn by him; and that Mr Stoddert
purchased Property at the public Sale in May last to the
amount of upwards of ten thousand Dollars, for which by the
Articles of Sale, he was entitled to a credit of nine Months; but
he has paid the Money in expectation of Indulgence for the

same time in the Payment of an equal Sum on the Note endorsed by him. We would likewise submit to the President's consideration whether it is necessary to enforce Payments beyond the Interest to the State of Maryland, having as we suppose already the Means of accomplishing the other objects contemplated for the present Year. The Debts being well secured, and bearing an Interest, can be called in as the exigencies of the City may require. We are, &c.

W. THORNTON
A. WHITE
T. DALTON

PRESIDENT OF THE UNITED-
STATES — MONTICELLO.

P.S. Doctor Thornton has always observed that he will give no opposition to any measures which the President may think proper to direct respecting the Debts due from him.

A. W.
T. D.

[Pp. 93-6, COMMISSIONERS' LETTERBOOK, Vol. 6, 1800–02, in the National Archives.]

STODDERT TO JEFFERSON

Geo Town 18 *August* 1801.

Sir

Knowing that the Com^{rs} of Washington were about addressing you on a subject in which I have an Interest, I sent to them a letter, the copy of which I take the liberty to lay before you; as I find they had made up their dispatches before the rest of the letter.

Mr White, the Com^r alluded to as not Joining in the engagement to the State of Maryland, informs me, that I have misstated his motive for the refusal — that it was not the apprehension of pecuniary loss, but a doubt of the powers of the Com^{rs}

to pledge the lots to the State, which with-held him. — Be it so
— my object was to prove some little merit, & no crime in
those who notwithstanding such doubts would risk themselves
to obtain money for the City, at a time when it could be got by
no other means, and when it was known the necessary accomodations for the Gov^t could not be prepared without it. I have
the honor to be with great respect Sir
       Y^r most obed Servt

                                              BEN STODDERT

[Ms., *Jefferson Papers*, Library of Congress.]

COMMISSIONERS TO JEFFERSON

Washington 24.th *August* 1801.

Sir,

We should think an apology necessary for intruding on your
retirement, were we not convinced that your solicitude for the
advancement of the City authorizes this liberty.

In reviewing the objects you were pleased to recommend to
our attention, and calculating what has been done and what is
yet to accomplish, we find our means will be inadequate to fulfil the whole of your intentions respecting the Roads within the
Estimate. We therefore thought it proper to state what has
been executed, and the Expenditures —

For Work executed.

	Doll. Cent.
The former Expenses on Pennsylvania Avenue and the Capitol Hill, since the Month of June inclusive	2,130.00
The Work on the President's Square & on 15.th Street West, gravelled principally, has cost	693.00
The Work on New Jersey Avenue, including a good Road up the Hill & a free-stone Bridge has cost	872.99
Doll^s	3,695.99

For Work to be executed of necessity

The Road between the upper end of Pennsylvania
Avenue & the upper Bridge on Rock-Creek has
been calculated, and the Work by mensuration, to
make an easy Passage, will cost $800. The people   700.00
of George Town have taken & will require as much
Sand &c as will lessen the Expense $100.

Work Contemplated

The circular Road on the West side of the Capitol
continued into A Street North & A Street South,
also 1st Street east on the Capitol Square, between
the two above mentioned Streets, but particularly   . . . .
A Street North, now commenced, and 1st Street
east in front of Mr Carrolls Buildings

To round Pennsylvania Avenue from the President's
Square to 26th Street west, ready to receive the   . . . .
Gravel.

To continue from the new Bridge down New Jersey
Avenue, rounding it so as to receive the Gravel.   . . . .

These last objects are unprovided for, and as we cannot execute the whole, we solicit your determination respecting the
choice, should we be able to expend a few hundred Dollars
more than the Sum calculated.

We have the satisfaction of informing you that the Brick
Work of the Chamber of Representatives advanced with such
rapidity that the whole will be finished ready for the Roof by
the end of next week, and the Roof is in forwardness. Previous
to the departure of our Colleauge Mr White, for Winchester
some Days ago, he joined in our opinion respecting the propriety of making this Statement as soon as the proper Returns
were collected. We have the honor &c.

W. THORNTON
T. DALTON

PRESIDENT OF THE UNITED-STATES.

[Pp. 97–9, COMMISSIONERS' LETTERBOOK, Vol. 6, 1800–02, in the National Archives.]

JEFFERSON TO COMMISSIONERS

Monticello Aug. 24. 1801.

Gentlemen

Your favor of the 17.th came to hand on the 20.th but as it's contents required greater consideration than and time than the stay of the post and pressure of other business permitted I have been obliged to take another post for it's answer. the questions indeed which it proposes are so much blended with law that I should have been glad to have had the opinion of the Attorney general for my government: but his distance & the urgency of the case rendering this impracticable, I must venture to form opinions myself; which I shall do the more readily as such of the questions as it is now necessary to determine do not present great difficulties. you state that for the works contemplated now to be done, & the current expences of the year you have a prospect of money sufficient; but that without further paiments there will be a deficiency in the paiment of interest to the state of Maryland on the 1.st of Oct. next to the amount of 10,500. D. & that you cannot rely on voluntary paiments for that sum. when we consider that by the terms of the loan a failure in the paiment of interest gives the state a right to recover the whole principal *immediately,* and the ruinous distress on the funds of the city which this would induce, duty leaves us but one alternative, to *enforce paiments.* but as you observe, at the close of the letter, that you have the means of accomplishing the other objects contemplated for the present year, and it is desireable to produce no unnecessary distress, we should limit ourselves to enforce paiment only *to the extent of the interest* due to Maryland. that a contribution towards this should be required from the sureties to the state of Maryland as well as others, seems both just and lawful. the case as to the principal of these is shortly this. General Forrest being indebted to the city about 33,800 D. paiable at short days, becomes security for the city for 50,000.

D. payable at a long day. this is no legal payment of his 33,800. D. the contracts have no connection. it is possible that if by *subsequent events* the affairs of the city were verging to evident bankruptcy, the Chancery might stay his paiment till counter security should be given. but that is not our case. and were he to propose it to the Chancery, we would save them the question by saying, pay the money into the treasury of Maryland & all purposes will be answered, ours of the payment of interest, & his of lessening his responsibility by exactly as much as should be paid. I have heard it suggested that he might object to payment till he is countersecured as to the amount of securityship beyond his debt. but I think no lawyer will say this. — the advance of 10,000. D. by m͞r. Stoddart 9 months before it was due seems justly to entitle him to an equal delay of an equal portion of the note endorsed by him & Genl. Forrest.

To the question whether property sold under the act of Maryland of Dec. 28. 1793. can be resold on default of payment? I should say that act in all cases of sale *on credit*, authorises a re-sale. it is true that it allows the resale to be for *ready money*, but if it be *on credit*, then a 3^d sale for default of paiment is within the very words as well as the purview of the act. and I should extremely doubt whether the purview as well as the letter of this act will not be understood to have, as far as it extends, repealed, in these cases, the general principle which saves the rights of infants till they come of age. but will not all these questions be saved by a voluntary assesment by the debtors themselves, in proportion to their debts respectively, to the amount of the sum we want? less than 5/ in the pound would probably make it up. but if they consent to this, it should be in such a way as to render disappointment impossible.

My idea of the functions of the Board of commissioners is that they are to form resolutions, on which the President has an affirmative or negative. had I been at Washington I would have asked of them to resolve first on what they themselves should think right, & have reserved my own opinion for a simple approval or disapproval. it is at their request only, & to avoid the delay which a reference back to them might occasion, that I have presumed to originate propositions, which I do however on the express condition that they shall be deemed of no effect until approved by a vote of the commissioners. as such of them as shall be so approved will then include their opinion as well as that of the President, it will be of less importance which opinion was first given.

I pray you to accept assurances of my high consideration & respect.

Th: Jefferson

THE COMMISSIONERS OF WASHINGTON

[*Letters of the Presidents of the United States to the Commissioners of Public Buildings and Grounds*, original in Manuscripts Division, Library of Congress, photostat in National Archives.]

JEFFERSON TO THE COMMISSIONERS

Monticello Aug. 29. 1801.

Gentlemen

Your favor of the 24.th is duly recieved. I consider the erection of the Representatives chamber and the making a good gravel road from the new bridge on Rock creek along the Pensylvā & Jersey avenues to the Eastern branch as the most important objects for ensuring the destinies of the city which can be undertaken. all others appear to me entirely subordinate and to rest on considerations quite distinct from these. for the first of these works the ordinary funds of the city are understood to be competent; but not for the second. tho' according to rigorous law, the price of the site of the Marine barracks (pledged to Congress) should only have been credited by them to the city, I ventured to have 4000. D. part of it advanced from the treasury to be applied to the sole purpose of making the road above mentioned. I supposed that Congress in consideration of the utility of the object & the ampleness of the [rest] of the grounds pledged to them as a security would relax the rigor of their rights and approve what has been done. 4000. D. for 4 miles of road were then estimated to be sufficient. but from your statement 3695.99 D. have been expended, and half the distance (tho not half the work) remains to be finished. in this situation I should think it adviseable to postpone the circular street round the Capitol, because we have already a very practicable road ascending the Capitol hill at the North [end] of the building: then to apply what remains of the 4000. D. and any funds the city can spare to rounding the ~~road from~~ Pensylvā avenue from the President's square to Rock creek & on to the upper bridge; & then to round the Jersey avenue from the work already done to the Eastern branch. I write by this post to the Secretary of the Navy to know whether any more & how much can be spared from the 20,000.D. appropriated by Congress for the Marine barracks beyond the 4000.D. already paid the Commissioners. I fear it will be little. but if any thing remain of that fund, I will venture to direct a further portion of the price of the Site to be paid you for compleating this road, on the same principles & presumption on which the 4000.D. were advanced from the treasury. in the mean time will you have the goodness to forward to me by post as just a statement as possible of what it will cost to accomplish these portions of the road I have designated, over and above the remains of the 4000.D. & the city funds which can be spared for this object? I shall at the same time recieve an answer from the Secretary of the navy, & on a view of the whole decide on the further aid which can be given. Accept assurances of my high consideration & respect.

TH: JEFFERSON

THE COMM^RS. OF WASHINGTON

[*Letters of the Presidents of the U.S. to the Commissioners of Public Buildings and Grounds*, original in Manuscripts Division, Library of Congress, photostat in National Archives.]

Sep. 1st 1801. Two Letters received from the President of the United States, one of the
24th Ult.^o & the other of the 29th.

> [P. 201, Proceedings of the Commissioners, VI, 1800–02, in the National
> Archives.]

JEFFERSON TO THE COMMISSIONERS

Monticello Sep. 3. 1801.

Gentlemen

I take the liberty of referring to you the inclosed application
from Bishop Carrol & others for respecting the purchase of a site
for a church. it is not for me to interpose in the price of the lots
for sale. at the same time none can better than yourselves estimate the considerations of propriety & even of advantage
which would urge a just attention to the application, nor better
judge of the degree of favor to it which your duties would admit. with yourselves therefore I leave the subject, with assurances of my high consideration & respect.

TH: JEFFERSON

[Letters of the Presidents of the U. S. to the Commissioners of Public Buildings and Grounds,
original in Manuscripts Division, Library of Congress, photostat in the National Archives.]

COMMISSIONERS TO JEFFERSON

Washington 4.th *Sept^r* 1801.

Sir,

We have had the honor of your Letter of the 24th and 29th
Ult^o which we take the earliest opportunity of answering.

We presume the impression you were under respecting our
Subjection to the payment of the whole Debt of 250,000 Dollars
to the State of Maryland, might have weight in your decision
relative to the part we were to pursue in enforcing payment
from the Debtors and we percieve that we have been deficient

in our Information on that Subject. The State of Maryland have the power of subjecting us to the payment of only the last Loan on default of Payment of the Interest, but the debt of $200,000 not being subject to the same procedure raises a doubt regarding your Instructions to us.

We have not only conceived the law of Maryland authorised us to resell the property in default of Payment, but to repeat the Sales, and we have thus uniformly proceeded: it therefore gives us great satisfaction to find that we have the indirect approbation of such high authority. The Titles being still in us as Trustees and agents for the public we imagine would diminish the doubt of our power to sell the property to whomsoever it belonged, otherwise the spirit of the Act for the accommodation of Government might be defeated by common process.

We are in hopes that nothing will be left undone by the Debtors to raise such a Sum as will be necessary, and when we can have their assurances of what they expect and intend to do, we shall not fail to communicate them to you, with our opinions, which we acknowledge with sensibility ought rather to have been submitted than required, to meet your decision.

To the objects stated in your Letter of the 29.th, we have paid particular attention and shall expedite them as much as possible.

The Returns that have lately been made are less favourable to our progress than we had supposed — the very dry and hot Weather that we have so long experienced, diminished much the progress of our Labourers, and we have now changed entirely our mode of operating by which we can execute as much in One day as we have done in two. We have got strong ploughes, and two thousand Dollars will finish we hope the Roads you have recommended to our attention, in such a manner as will make them convenient and good. Half this Sum will finish rounding the Road to Rock Creek Bridge from the President's House, including the cut through the Hill. The other thousand will round the Road in New Jersey Avenue & first Street east on the Capitol Square. The Road is compleated to the seven Buildings in Sq. 118 and A Street north on the Capitol Hill. The whole Expense incurred on the Roads till the 1st Instant amounts to four thousand & eighteen Dollars. Our present Expenses on Pennsylvania & New Jersey Avenues amount to fifty Dollars per Day; but on a review of our Funds, we cannot proceed much further on the Roads unless we obtain Resources upon which we cannot at present calculate or presume on a favorable answer from the Secretary of the Navy.

We have the honor to be &c.

W. THORNTON
T. DALTON

PRESIDENT OF THE UNITED-
STATES,
    Monticello.

[Pp. 100–01, COMMISSIONERS' LETTERBOOK, Vol. 6, 1800–02, in the National Archives.]

ALEXANDER WHITE TO JEFFERSON

Washington 14.th *September* 1801

Sir

I returned on the 6.th instant a good deal indisposed. Although my dicease (a diarrhoea) is in some measure checked, yet my health is not so far restored as to enable me to take an active part in business.

My Colleagues having answered your letters of the 24.th and 29.th Ul.^o before my arrival I have nothing to say on the subjects of them, except to observe, that it has been the practice of this Office when a legal difficulty occurred to state the case to the President; not for his individual opinion, but for the opinion of his Law Officer; which opinion when transmitted to the Board has been considered as the instruction of the Executive. I expected the present business would have taken the same course, and altho' I had myself no doubt on any of the points stated, yet I thought the sanction of the Government absolutely necessary to enable us to carry into effect any coercive measures with respect to the Parties concerned. I am with sentiments of the highest respect

Sir
Your most Ob^{t} Servant
ALEX^{R} WHITE

PRESIDENT OF THE U. STATES

[Ms., *Jefferson Papers*, Library of Congress.]

COMMISSIONERS TO JEFFERSON

Commissioners' Office, 3^{d} *Oct^{o}* 1801.

Sir,

We enclose an Estimate of the Sums which we consider as necessary to carry on the operations of the Season, and to pay the Interest to the State of Maryland to the end of the Year. This Estimate we do not consider as perfectly accurate but think it may be so far relied on as to enable the President to determine whether the Sum stated as necessary to complete the Streets, or what other Sum shall be expended thereon. This work which has been recommended by the President, we are very desirous of accomplishing, but wish to have his sanction for the necessary Expenditures.

We are &c

W. THORNTON
A. WHITE
T. DALTON

PRESIDENT OF THE UNITED-STATES.

[P. 110, COMMISSIONERS' LETTERBOOK, Vol. 6, 1800–02, in the National Archives.]

COMMISSIONERS' NOTE

Oct. 13th   Yesterday the President of the United States having
1801   communicated personally with the Board at their
           office on the Affairs of the City, directed that the
           Streets from the President's Square to the Upper
           Bridge over Rock Creek; and New Jersey Avenue
           from the Bridge to the Capitol shall be compleated,
           Pennsylvania Avenue first done — the footways in,
           & adjacent to, the Capitol Square repair'd; & a
           footway made to the South side of the President's
           Enclosure. N.B. It is not to be understood that the
           Gravelled Streets are made with any other view
           than a temporary accommodation, & that the
           Graduation is not to be ultimately affected by the
           present operations.

[P. 221, Proceedings of the Commissioners, VI, 1800–02, in the National Archives.]

COMMISSIONERS TO JEFFERSON

Commissioners' Office, 15th *Oct^o* 1801

Sir

An application was this day made to us to grant lots at a cash price and permit the value to be laid out in improving F Street N. from the President's Square to 11th Street west then down to Pennsylvania Avenue and again from 11th Street west along E Street north to 8th Street west, and to Pennsylvania Avenue.

We are of opinion, that the Improvement of F Street north, as far as 11th Street west, and to the Avenue, would be highly advantageous; but, while we contemplate and acknowledge the utility of the undertaking by the mode proposed, we however cannot forbear alluding to the specific purposes to which the funds arising from the Property vested in the public by the

original proprietors were destined and though in many Instances the strict Letter of the original intention has been devi-
ated from, these deviations have comprehended many general
advantages to the Public; and being peculiar in themselves they
could not lead as examples to general consequences, yet, if the
present application be admitted we fear the danger of similar
applications to an extent that would create immediate inconveniences, by taking out of the public funds, the most saleable
lots.

To the President, however, we submit the decision with the
greatest deference. We are, with sentiments &c.

W. THORNTON
A. WHITE
T. DALTON

TO THE PRESIDENT OF THE UNITED-STATES.

[P. 113, COMMISSIONERS' LETTERBOOK, Vol. 6, 1800–02, in the National Archives.]

L'ENFANT TO JEFFERSON

City of Washington November 3^d 1801

Sir,

The peculiarity of my position and the embarrassement
ansuing from the conduct of the Board of the Commissionaires
of the City of Washington in regard to requests and communications made to them rendering the freedome of a direct address to you unavoidable — I hope the necessity will plead my
excuse, and seeing the time near approaches when it is presumable you will wish to call Congress attention to the State of
things relative to this new Seat of Government; I now with
great dependance on your goodness beg your consideration of
the circumstance with me.

Noticing that my object with the Board of Commissionaires
was to have obtained through their mediation a Compensation

for Services and for Injuries experienced at the hands of the
Jealousers of the reputation and of the fortune which the plan-
ing and Executing of the City of Washington promised to me?
it would be usless for me to relate how I became charged of the
entreprise and to what extant my agency was Serviciable to it
— my plans orriginally met your approval and the zeal the
Integrity and impartiallity of my management being generally
acknowledged especially of those whose property the opperations affected, assures me the Service still must be fresh to memory and be remembered as deserving —. therefore passing over
my Endeavours to promote the public object, the difficulties
subdued, the contrarieties met and all the reasons for the resignation of my agency: the treatment experienced being likewise
reminded of by letter to the Board of Commissionaires [August
1800] and by two subsequent memorial to Congress [december
same year and february 1801 Inst.] the latter together with
papers accompaying it remaining with other business of the
Committee of claim not reported upon I believe I may spare
the recital of any the contents! — but attributing the repulse of
my prayer, by the first petition, to misconception of the manner
of my engagement and connexion of agency with the Commissionaires, finding they have deceived the dependance I placed
in them for Explanation of matters to the Committee of claim,
and — unable to account way that Board elluded answering
the request and communication to them, and on what principle
having themselves advised, and offered their aide to, the petition to Congress, they can have deneyed to the Committee my
having any cause for the call on Government I presume the Inclosed paper (A) may with propriety be here offered in explanation of certain transaction, the Injuries from which answering,
gave me some right to the expectation but the Board of Com-
miss^{rs} would have proved more earnest to help an obtainment
of the redress and Compensation prayed for.

Deeming it to be here manifest that the conduct of the Board

forbided the possibility of further call on them about the pending business exciting at the same time a mistruest of the end,
and, making my difficulties the greater by thus discouraging
what assistance it has been my unhappy lot for many years past
to have had to recur to for Sustainance, I forbear more to ani-
madvert upon the proceeding wishing but by this plain expos-
ure of to shew the necessity of the appeal to your and to the
Equity of Government.

Ensuring thus the exact state of thing will be known to you
which it seem were kept from former administrations to an
hindrance of the hearing of my call on different deportments —
what ever be those Interests the Jealousies and machinations,
of which I have been dupe and victime they will not be feared
where your power is extant. — and allowing the private ani-
mosities, as of late years were fostered by parties politique, may
yet stimule opposition to affording me a Compensation commensurate to the greatness of objects of national import in
which I had a principal — primary and essential agency . . .
possible as it is too for some minds not to feel the obligation to
repay voluntary Sacrifices or Compensate the deprivation of
great promises and of employements of great Expectancy — I
nevertheless trust but upon the whole the propriety will be
generally acknowleged, of an honorable return being due to
honorable acts and for the liberal use I have made of my talents
and fortune particularly in the business of the City of Washington as also in other Services constantly volunteered to this
Country for these twenty five years past both in a military and
Civil employement to which I might add the merite of wounds
of painfull captivity and of exertions, in a mission abroad too,
at the close of the revolution war the success of which obtained
at a great personal cost to me first of all embarrassed my affairs
and never has been redeemed.

About these military matters: I have, in Jun last given in a
statement to the Secretary at war *Gen^{al} Dearborn* claiming par-

ticular dues and respecting the manner of eventual cessation of my Services as the abituate [sic] Engineer to the United States; of which having beged the representation to be made to you, I only remind here to bring together to your view every circumstances which Joined to the absolut destruction of family fortune in Europe concured at almost the same Instant to reduce me here from a state of ease and of content, to one the most distressed and helpless? and the only raisonable hope I can maintain of relief from — being in the Justice and liberality with which Government may reward my long Services I will own deed urged me to more minute enumeration of performance, to my own praise and with more reflection perhaps upon the treatment experienced than is congenial to my habit and disposition to have done. and, having thus out of necessity explained upon transactions the most Injurious to the reputation dear to all artists and also upon the most hurtfull to my fortune.

Now, Ser, permit me to observe as before expressed by the petitions above reffered to — that none of the related by me flowed from wish of disgracing any one, not even those who acted the most unfriendly to me, being with much reluctancy that I related particular proceedings and yelded to the Suggestion by the Board of Commissionaires of the propriety of the petition, to the late Congress. — and although the Sum stated by those petitions as the loss by me sustained be an exact nay moderate Compute of the value of the maps taken from me and of other benefits expected and of Right for a first year of the opperation of my plan. — observing that I mean not to dictate what should the Compensation be for all that. but mearly by the enumeration of what my expectancy and right were, to invite the Consideration of the hardship of the reverse of my fortune: to render that reverse more sensible I gave the Contrast of the richess I would have now necessarily been accumulating and how these were werested from me by those Speculations and Jealousies which having left nothing possible to have pursued but with dishonor, it is well known made me resign all the Concern.

Believing that honesty and greatness of the Sacrifices I have made of Enticing prospects universally acknowledged, as that also my care to have ensured first the public advantage in all the bargain and Scheme by me brought within power of effecting carried me to a disregard of myself. — an impossibility then being that in the hurry of so extansive business, whilst Endeavouring my best in all thing I could have watched the usage made of my plans & &ᶜ — or have thought of procuring Surety to the promises to me so as to be able as in ordinary business to have produced those and made up accounts for Settlement. — I cannot imagine possible that any thing the like be demanded nor expected from me. and — to speak openly — were this in my power to do, I would not think of offering other Support to the claim profered than what I have offered — a Comprehensive view, and general Sum up, of the Interest in the business in which I was employed — Conceiving best consistant with the liberality of unconditional Services and with the Confidence I place in the propriety of my System of plans and of opperation altogether to wait from the Public Sense of the merite of performance the Government award of the Compensation due for all the Injuries of the end.

Agreable to these Impressions and Sentiments I confine, Ser, to Sollicite your kind consideration of the misfortune depriving me of the necessary to existance. — the small remain of hope, till very lately Indulged in, of regaining at least in part, some stocks of Bank, my only having in the country being now vanished away — by reason of Rᵗ Morris taking the benefit of the bankrupt act and the property on which he made me believe to have been secured being found absorbed by treble previous mortgage for Sum each far excedant the worth of that property. — thus for a generous friendly assistance afforded him (on request for only three or four days) — for these seven years

past, both Capital and Interest, were inhumanly retained and I
necessitated all the while to live upon Borrowed bread the obligations for which at this time to repay Comming with Imperi-
ous call and the addition of exorbitant charges for the advance,
I must be excused for bringing to notice in this address being
indeed what has been determining me to the desagreable dis-
closure of my situation and Confidently to request your permission now absolutly to leave the adjustment of the matters of the
Subject of this address, to your Benevollance and Justice. —

Doing this I will no more than express — that I after many
heavy pecuniary Sacrifices occasioned by variety of Situations
during the revolution war — I since the peace of 1783 was also
differently Encouraged and Invited by many Commissions to
the free spending of my own, dependant upon promises of regular reappointment with promotion all which ended to my loss
and absolut ruin. — that on the particular Instance of my
agency to the Entreprise of the City of Washington I have received no renumeration what ever, that — no kind of precon-
vention were for the Service no price agreed upon for plans, nor
the Copy right conceded to the Commissionaires nor to any
ones else, and that — extanded as was my Concerns and agency
beyond the usual to Architects; although by the grand Combination of new Schems I contributed eminently to the ensur-
ance of the city establishment by which numbers of Individuals
and the Country to an immense distance desire a increasing of
their wealth I deed by no one opperations nor transactions
worked to my own profit.

Acquainted Ser as you necessarily must have became with
managements of the City affairs in which my free exertions
were not the least usefull to the promotion of the national object — the merite, and that of orriginating of the plan you,
doubtless, will readily allow to me and certain I am that — for
all what I suffered, the only reproach to which I may be liable
(in this and business of military description) is my having been

more faithfull to principle than ambitions — too zealous in my pursuits — and too hazardous on a dependance on mouth friends — admitting I would deserve reproach if I had imagined every man actuated by liberal honorable views — I nevertheless believe my Conduct in all Instance stand well applauded and Justified by all who knew the Spirite of the oppositions I met and the personages in whom I Confided and — Since Seeing you, Ser, occupying the same heigh Station as the chief under whose order I acted as a Military and at whose Invitation my Services were engaged and by whose Instructions I Conducted in the affairs of the City now become the Seat of Government. — esteeming your dispositions equally as I esteemed his, to be to redress Injuries and to recompense active honest Services — knowing your power is all commensurate to — I for all the reasons I have to lament the decease of that chief, feel reassured that the loss of his good testimonial and promised support shall not opperate my way detrimentally to my present expectancy and that in all respect your Justice will grant me the prayer made.

with great respect

I have the honor to be

Ser

your Most humble and
obedient Servant
P. CHARLES L'ENFANT

TO THOMAS JEFFERSON
President of the United States

[Ms., *Jefferson Papers*, Library of Congress.]

COMMISSIONERS TO JEFFERSON

Commissioners Office 4 December 1801

Sir

We have the honour of addressing to you a memorial stating

such facts as appear to us requisite for your information in addition to those stated in a representation made to your Predecessor during the late session of Congress; which representation with the documents accompanying it, being on the files of Congress, and in the hands of the President and members of the legislature, we supposed a general reference thereto sufficient. We are &c

W. Thornton
A. White
T. Dalton

PRESIDENT OF THE UNITED STATES.

[P. 1294, Annals of Congress, 7–2.]

COMMISSIONERS TO JEFFERSON

THE COMMISSIONERS TO THE PRESIDENT

December 4, 1801

The memorial of the Commissioners appointed by virtue of an act of Congress, entitled "An Act for establishing the temporary and permanent Seat of Government of the United States," respectfully sheweth:

That on the 28th of January last, the Commissioners, addressed to the late President of the United States, a representation, stating such facts respecting the Business committed to their charge, as appeared necessary for the Information of the Government; which Representation was by him transmitted to Congress, and by their order referred to a committee; but no measures having taken place in consequence thereof, either by the Executive or Legislature, your memorialists deem it expedient to recapitulate the most important facts then stated, and to add such other facts and observations as may tend to enable the President to judge of the measures proper to be pursued by him, and to aid the Legislature in their deliberation, should the subject be submitted to their consideration.

The act of Congress authorizing the President to locate a District for the permanent Seat of the Government of the United States; the actual location of that District; the grant of lands for a federal city; the power given by the President to the Commissioners to sell that part of the Land so granted, which was placed at his disposal; the sale of six thousand lots to Morris and Greenleaf, by agreement dated 23^d December, 1793; the modification of that agreement by another, entered into in April, 1794; the failure of those gentlemen to fulfil their contracts, and the various measures pursued to obtain money to carry on the public Buildings, are recited in the above-mentioned Representation; and copies of the Legislative acts, Deeds, and other writings therein referred to, are annexed, and the whole printed for the use of the Members of Congress. The property belonging to the public is therein stated to consist of 24,655,735 Square feet of ground in the City of Washington, equal to 4,682 lots, of 5,265 Square feet each, exclusive of lots which bind on navigable waters — these form fronts to the extent of 2043 feet, and on them are four wharves in an useful state. Of the first mentioned lots, 3,178 lie N.E. of Massachusetts avenue, the remainder being fifteen hundred and four are situated S.º W. of that Avenue; also, an Island, containing free Stone, in Aquia Creek in the State of Virginia. The above property your memorialists consider as worthy of public attention; its' value may be estimated by the prices at which lots have been heretofore sold, the cost of the wharves and the price of the Island.

Lots on the S.º W. Side of Massachusetts avenue sold by the Commissioners since passing the guarantee Bill in 1796, average 343 Dollars per lot. Those on the N.E. Side of that Avenue sold by the Commissioners and proprietors average 105 Dollars p[er] lot. Lots binding on navigable waters, sold within the same period, average $12 71/100 the foot front. The Island cost 6000 Dollars, and the Wharves $3,221 88/100, the whole amounting, at the rate lots have heretofore been sold, with the original cost of the Island, and wharves to $884,819 88/100. The lots sold by the Commissioners since the date of the above-mentioned Representation, exclusive of a Square sold to the United States, for the site of Marine Barracks, average $470 71/100 p[er] lot. To elucidate more fully the real value of City Property, they have endeavored to ascertain the prices at which Proprietors have sold lots within the last eighteen Months, and so far as they have obtained Information, their Sales average $579 15/100 for cash and on short credit. $921 37/100 on a credit of 4, 5 & 6 Years, per lot, and their ground Rents are from one to three Dollars per foot front.

Your Memorialists readily admit that the public property remaining for sale, is not on an average, equal in value to that which has been sold; yet, a great abatement was, in many Instances, made in the price of lots, in consideration of Building Contracts, and as inducements to purchase in the City have much increased; they conceive those on hand may, in the course of a few years be disposed of, at least to as great advantage as those already sold; but if the Law authorising a Loan for the use of the City of Washington, should be carried strictly into effect, your Memorialists are apprehensive, that this property must be, in a great degree sacrificed. It is known that 200,000 Dollars have been borrowed of the State of Maryland under the Sanction of that Law, and that the City Property above-mentioned is to be sold under the direction of the President of the United States, for the re-payment of that sum: an arrear of Interest to the amount of nine thousand Dollars is now due thereon; the accruing Interest of $12,000 per annum, payable quarter-yearly, and the principal which is payable by annual Instalements of $40,000 after the year 1803, are Sums which your Memorialists conceive, cannot be raised without frequent

Sales for ready money, a measure which they consider as highly injurious, if carried to the extent necessary to answer those objects, and which they have in no Instance attempted, although the difficulties they have experienced in collecting Debts convince them that Sales on credit cannot be relied on for the punctual payment of the abovementioned Interest and Instalments; they therefore with great deference suggest the propriety of the Governments' paying the Money borrowed, and reserving the Property pledged for it's repayment, to be sold as advantageous offers may occur — a policy which dictated the guarantee in 1796, and which has been fully justified by the Sales, made since that period. By pursuing a contrary policy, the property pledged will be greatly diminished by the payment of Interest only, while much larger Sums than are necessary to discharge both principal and Interest will probably lie dead in the Treasury.

Your memorialists also beg leave to state, that the Sum of fifty thousand Dollars in United States six per cent. stock, has been borrowed from the State of Maryland, to be repaid on the 1st of Nov.ʳ 1802, secured by the Bond of the Commissioners, and real and personal security given by private persons. The only fund applicable to the payment of this Sum at the disposal of the President or the Commissioners is, the Debts contracted for city lots purchased previous to passing the guarantee Law; this fund is indeed much more than sufficient, could those Debts be called in, to accomplish which, your memorialists have never ceased their exertions. They are now pursuing a measure not before attempted; a ready money Sale, in which, if they fail to sell the Property for as much as is due thereon to the public, the same policy would dictate to the Government to pay this sum of fifty thousand Dollars likewise, the last-mentioned Debts to a much greater amount, being ultimately secure.

The Commissioners have only received Doll.ˢ 53,281 81/100

from the sales of property pledged by virtue of the guarantee law. They have paid in conformity to that law, the Sum of $29,687 92/100 to the original proprietors for property appropriated to public use, and 42,000 Dollars Interest which has accrued on money borrowed under the sanction of the same Law. This, the sum of $18,406 11/100 derived from the funds applicable to the payment of Debts contracted on the personal security of the Commissioners, has been applied to the purposes of the guarantee, and thereby the necessity of selling at depreciated rates the Property pledged to Congress, has been avoided.

Your memorialists would also observe, that the Debts due and to become due, to the City Fund, and which were considered as good, were stated in the last Representation to the President at $144,120 80/100. Since which, $46,081 99/100 of those Debts have been received; but it may be observed, that the Sum of $80,000, which by the agreement of April 1794, was to rest on the Bond of Morris, Greenleaf, & Nicholson, is not included in that description, although your Memorialists are advised by their Counsel that certain Squares in the City of Washington containing 1,000 lots are liable to the payment of that Sum; the same being designated by an agreement of 9.th July 1794 as the lots, the payment for which was to rest on the said Bond; and this point is now depending for decision in the Court of Chancery of the State of Maryland.

To shew the progress and the present state of Buildings in the City, your Memorialists have had the number of dwelling Houses taken, and find, by an accurate Report, that on the 15.th of May 1800, there were 109 of brick & 263 of wood — and on the 15.th of the last month there was an addition of 98 of brick & 151 of wood, besides 79 of brick, and thirty-five of wood, in an unfinished state; total amount, 735. Their particular situations will appear from the Schedule which accompanies this Memorial.

The above statement of facts and observations, are, with sentiments of the highest respect, submitted to the consideration of the President of the United-States.

WILLIAM THORNTON
ALEXANDER WHITE
TRISTRAM DALTON

Comm.^rs Office 4.th Dec. 1801.

[Pp. 239–44, PROCEEDINGS OF THE COMMISSIONERS, Vol. VI, 1800–02, in the National Archives; an inaccurate and abbreviated copy is printed in DOCUMENTARY HISTORY OF . . . THE CAPITAL, 97–8; Annals of Congress, p. 1294, 7–2.]

COMMISSIONERS TO JEFFERSON

An enumeration of the houses in the City of Washington, made November, 1801

Squares.	Houses in a habitable state on the 15th May, 1800.		Houses finished since 15th May, 1800.		Houses proposed to be finished before the 15th of November, 1801.		Houses unfinished.	
	Brick.	Wood.	Brick.	Wood.	Brick.	Wood.	Brick.	Wood.
1	1	5	. . .	. . .	. . .	. . .	. . .	. . .
W. of 4	. . .	. . .	2	1	1	. . .	. . .	. . .
4	1	. . .	. . .	. . .	. . .	. . .	. . .	. . .
5	3	2	. . .	. . .	. . .	. . .	. . .	. . .
8	. . .	1	. . .	. . .	. . .	. . .	. . .	. . .
9	1	1 [1]	. . .	. . .	. . .	. . .	. . .	. . .
16	2	5	. . .	. . .	. . .	. . .	. . .	. . .
22	. . .	2	. . .	. . .	. . .	. . .	. . .	. . .

[1] A large stone warehouse.

Squares.	Houses in a habitable state on the 15th May, 1800.		Houses finished since 15th May, 1800.		Houses proposed to be finished before the 15th of November, 1801.		Houses unfinished.	
	Brick.	Wood.	Brick.	Wood.	Brick.	Wood.	Brick.	Wood.
32	......	......	......	1	......	......	......	......
33	......	2	......	......	......	......	......	......
38	1	......	......	1	1	......	4	1
74	6	......	......	......	......	2	......	1
75	......	......	......	3	1	......	......	......
77	......	......	3	......	4	......	......	......
80	......	1	......	......	......	......	......	......
78	4	3	1	3	1	......	......	......
86	......	6	......	3	......	......	......	......
101	1	1	......	1	......	......	......	......
106	1	1	......	1	1	......	......	......
113	......	......	......	1	......	......	......	......
126	......	3	......	......	......	......	......	......
127	......	2	1	......	......	......	......	......
105	......	......	......	1	......	......	......	......
118	......	......	7	3	4	1	......	......
119	......	1	3	......	......	......	......	......
121	......	......	1	1	......	......	......	......
141	......	1	......	4	......	......	1	......
142	......	1	1	2	......	1	2	......
143	2	......	......	......	......	......	......	......
168	......	......	5	3	......	......	2	......
169	......	1	2	......	......	......	1	......
170	......	......	3	3	......	......	......	......
171	......	......	......	1	......	......	......	......
S. of 173	......	1	......	......	......	......	......	......
104	1	4	1	1	......	......	1	1

Squares.	Houses in a habitable state on the 15th May, 1800.		Houses finished since 15th May, 1800.		Houses proposed to be finished before the 15th of November, 1801.		Houses unfinished.	
	Brick.	Wood.	Brick.	Wood.	Brick.	Wood.	Brick.	Wood.
122	......	......	......	I	......	......	......	......
84	......	7	......	2	......	......	......	I
87	......	I	......	......	......	......	......	......
E. of 88	......	I	......	......	......	......	......	......
88	......	I	......	......	......	......	......	......
62	......	I	......	I	......	......	......	......
63	......	......	......	I	......	......	......	......
200	2	2	......	......	......	......	......	......
222	......	I	......	......	......	......	......	......
284	......	I	......	......	......	......	......	......
370	......	I	......	......	......	......	......	......
375	......	I	......	......	......	......	......	......
224	6	5	3	......	......	......	......	......
225	......	3	2	3	......	......	2	......
253	2	3	6	3	......	......	......	......
254	I	7	I	6	......	......	2	......
252	......	......	......	2	......	......	......	I
288	......	......	......	2	......	......	......	......
289	......	4	2	3	......	......	I	......
290	......	2	......	5	......	......	......	I
320	......	2	I	2	......	......	......	I
321	......	0	I	2	......	......	......	......
346	......	3[1]	......	......	......	......	......	......
347	......	2	......	2	......	......	2	......
376	......	I[2]	......	......	......	......	......	......
377	I	3	......	3	......	......	3	I

[1] church.
[2] A Church.

Squares.	Houses in a habitable state on the 15th May, 1800.		Houses finished since 15th May, 1800.		Houses proposed to be finished before the 15th of November, 1801.		Houses unfinished.	
	Brick.	Wood.	Brick.	Wood.	Brick.	Wood.	Brick.	Wood.
256	.....	.....	.....	.....	.....	.....	.....	2
291	.....	I	4	.....	.....	.....	I	.....
292	.....	.....	.....	I	.....	.....	.....	.....
258	.....	.....	.....	I	.....	.....	.....	I
322	2	.....	.....	.....	.....	.....	I	.....
323	.....	.....	.....	.....	.....	.....	.....	2
348	.....	.....	.....	2	.....	.....	.....	2
380	.....	I	.....	.....	.....	.....	.....	2
378	.....	.....	.....	3	.....	.....	2	.....
379	.....	I	.....	.....	.....	.....	.....	.....
406	.....	4	.....	I	.....	.....	I	.....
430	.....	.....	.....	.....	.....	.....	I	.....
431	.....	.....	I	2	.....	.....	.....	2
432	.....	I	.....	2	.....	.....	.....	.....
456	.....	3	.....	.....	.....	.....	.....	.....
457	2	.....	.....	.....	.....	.....	.....	.....
407	.....	5	.....	.....	.....	.....	.....	.....
460	3	.....	.....	.....	.....	.....	.....	2
461	.....	.....	2	I	.....	.....	3	.....
489	.....	I	.....	.....	.....	.....	.....	.....
490	I	2	I	.....	.....	.....	.....	.....
523	.....	I	.....	.....	.....	.....	.....	.....
532	I	.....	.....	.....	.....	.....	.....	.....
491	.....	.....	.....	.....	.....	.....	.....	I
533	.....	.....	2	.....	.....	.....	.....	.....
554	.....	I	.....	.....	.....	.....	.....	.....
575	.....	.....	I	.....	.....	.....	.....	I
634	2	.....	.....	.....	.....	.....	.....	.....

Squares.	Houses in a habitable state on the 15th May, 1800.		Houses finished since 15th May, 1800.		Houses proposed to be finished before the 15th of November, 1801.		Houses unfinished.	
	Brick.	Wood.	Brick.	Wood.	Brick.	Wood.	Brick.	Wood.
685	......	2	......	......	......	......	......	......
686	......	......	2	......	3	......	1	......
E. of 725	2	2	1	1	......	......	......	......
758	......	1	......	2	......	......	......	1
724	......	......	......	1	......	......	......	......
784	......	1	......	......	......	......	......	......
785	......	......	......	2	......	......	......	......
728	5	4	......	1	......	......	......	......
759	1	2	......	......	......	......	......	......
729	2	......	4	9	......	......	......	1
688	......	1	......	......	......	......	......	1
690	5	4	1	5	......	......	2	3
689	4	......	......	......	......	......	......	......
762	......	......	......	1	......	......	......	......
693	......	1	7	1	......	......	3	......
736	1	......	......	......	......	......	......	......
695	1	3	1	4	......	......	......	1
696	......	......	1	1	......	......	......	......
738	......	7	......	......	......	......	......	......
739	1	......	......	1	......	......	......	......
737	......	1	......	......	......	......	......	......
140	2	......	......	......	......	......	......	......
741	3	4	......	......	......	......	......	......
742	3	1	......	......	......	......	......	......
N. of 743	2	4	......	......	......	......	......	......
743	......	8	......	......	......	......	......	......
787	......	......	......	4	......	......	......	......
701	1	......	......	......	......	......	......	......

	Houses in a habitable state on the 15th May, 1800.		Houses finished since 15th May, 1800.		Houses proposed to be finished before the 15th of November, 1801.		Houses unfinished.	
Squares.	Brick.	Wood.	Brick.	Wood.	Brick.	Wood.	Brick.	Wood.
744	1	2	......	......	......	......	......	1
770	1	3	......	......	......	......	......	......
771	2	......	......	......	......	......	......	......
802	......	6	......	......	......	1	......	......
799	......	......	......	1	......	......	......	......
825	......	3	......	......	......	1	......	1
S. of 825	......	......	1	......	......	......	......	......
798	......	1	......	......	......	......	......	......
796	......	......	2	1	......	......	......	......
882	......	1	......	3	......	......	......	......
881	......	1	2	1	......	......	......	......
907	......	1	......	3	......	......	1	......
906	......	2	1	2	......	......	2	1
929	......	......	......	1	......	......	......	......
762	......	......	......	......	......	......	......	1
732	......	......	1	......	......	......	......	......
764	......	......	......	......	......	......	1	......
875	1	1	......	......	......	......	......	......
882	......	......	......	......	......	......	1	......
925	1	......	......	......	......	......	......	......
926	......	3	......	......	......	......	......	......
948	......	2	......	......	......	......	......	......
993	......	1	......	......	......	......	......	......
949	......	5	......	......	......	......	......	......
973	......	1	......	......	......	......	......	......
927	......	1[3]	......	......	......	......	......	......
905	......	2	......	3	......	......	......	......

[3] And barracks.

Squares.	Houses in a habitable state on the 15th May, 1800.		Houses finished since 15th May, 1800.		Houses proposed to be finished before the 15th of November, 1801.		Houses unfinished.	
	Brick.	Wood.	Brick.	Wood.	Brick.	Wood.	Brick.	Wood.
928	......	1	......	......	......	......	......	......
974	......	......	......	1	......	......	......	......
975	......	......	......	1	......	......	......	......
951	......	4	......	......	......	......	......	......
953	......	3	......	......	......	......	......	......
977	......	......	......	1	......	......	......	......
1,001	......	......	......	2	......	......	......	......
1,000	......	......	......	2	......	......	......	......
E. 1,025	......	1	......	1	......	......	......	......
1,024	......	1	......	......	......	......	......	......
1,067	......	1	......	......	......	......	......	......
1,044	......	2	......	......	......	......	......	......
1,106	......	1	......	......	......	......	......	......
1,114	1	......	......	......	......	......	......	......
651	6	3	......	......	......	......	24	......
700	......	1	......	......	......	......	......	1
701	1	......	......	......	......	......	......	......
703	......	3	......	......	......	......	......	......
705	......	2	......	......	......	......	......	......
704	......	1	......	......	......	......	......	......
708	......	1	......	......	......	......	......	......
662	......	......	......	1	......	......	......	......
E. of 662	......	......	......	1	......	......	......	......
664	......	1	......	......	......	......	......	......
E. of 613	......	1	......	......	......	......	......	......
546	......	3	......	......	......	......	4	......
503	8	15	......	......	......	......	8	......
504	2	2	......	......	......	......	2	......

Squares	Houses in a habitable state on the 15th May, 1800.		Houses finished since 15th May, 1800.		Houses proposed to be finished before the 15th of November, 1801.		Houses unfinished.	
	Brick.	Wood.	Brick.	Wood.	Brick.	Wood.	Brick.	Wood.
502	3	11	. . . . .	. . . . .	. . . . .	. . . . .	. . . . .	. . . . .
501	1	3	. . . . .	. . . . .	. . . . .	. . . . .	. . . . .	. . . . .
500	. . . . .	1	. . . . .	. . . . .	. . . . .	. . . . .	. . . . .	. . . . .
300	. . . . .	2	1	. . . . .	. . . . .	. . . . .	. . . . .	. . . . .
462	. . . . .	. . . . .	. . . . .	2	. . . . .	. . . . .	. . . . .	. . . . .
390	1	. . . . .	. . . . .	. . . . .	. . . . .	. . . . .	. . . . .	. . . . .
	109	263	82	145	16	6	79	35

Houses on public appropriations, &c. viz.

	Stone	Brick	Wood
President's square,.	1	6	15
Capitol square,.	1	—	6
Navy yard,.	—	—	2
National church square,.	—	—	2
Judiciary square,.	—	—	6
Marine hospital square.	—	—	3
Canal street, between M and N streets,	—	—	4
	2	6	38

Copy of the original filed in the Commissioners' office.

THOMAS MUNROE, *Clerk to Commissioners.*

[Pp. 256–7, AMERICAN STATE PAPERS, MISCELLANEOUS, Vol. I.]
[This enumeration accompanied the Commissioners' memorial to the President, Dec. 4, 1801.]

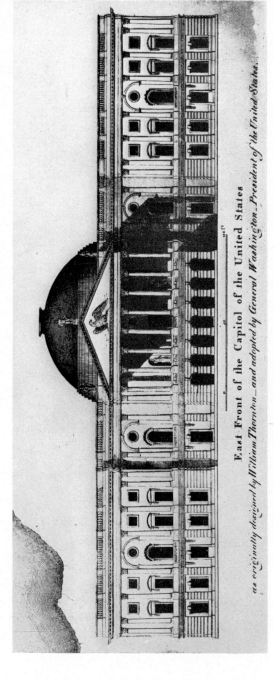

East Front of the Capitol of the United States as originally designed by William Thornton, 1793.

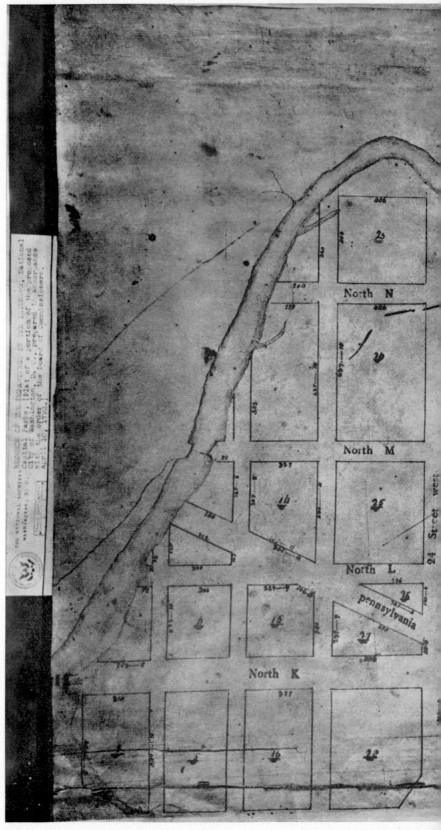

Plat of proposed City of Washington, D. C., prepared in accordance wit

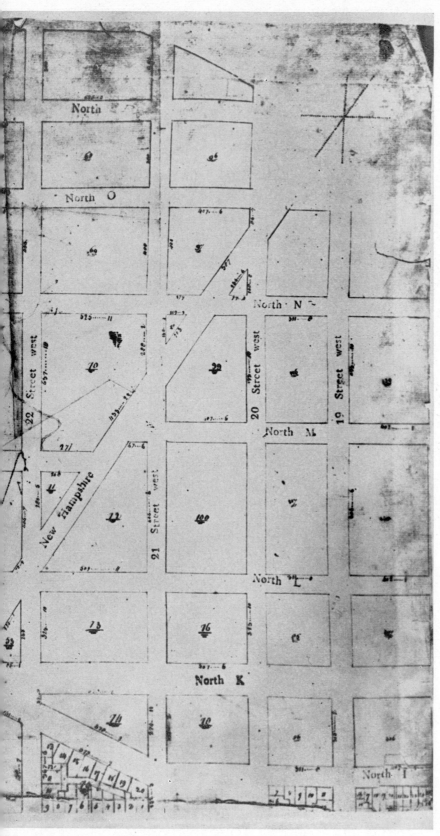

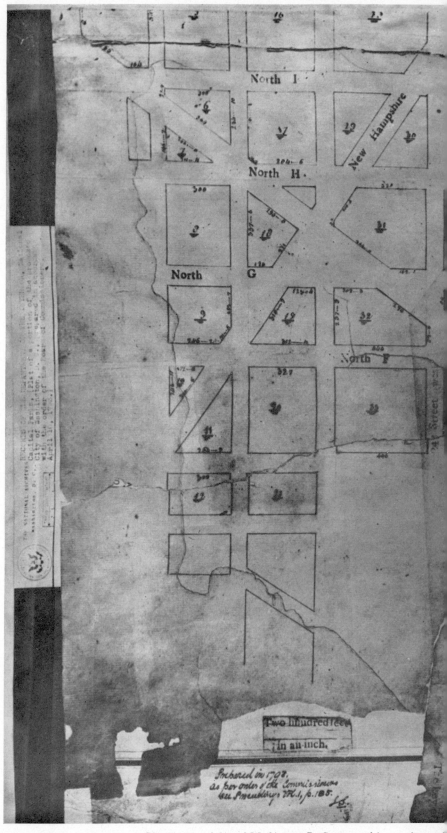

Plat of proposed City of Washington, D. C., prepared in accordance wi

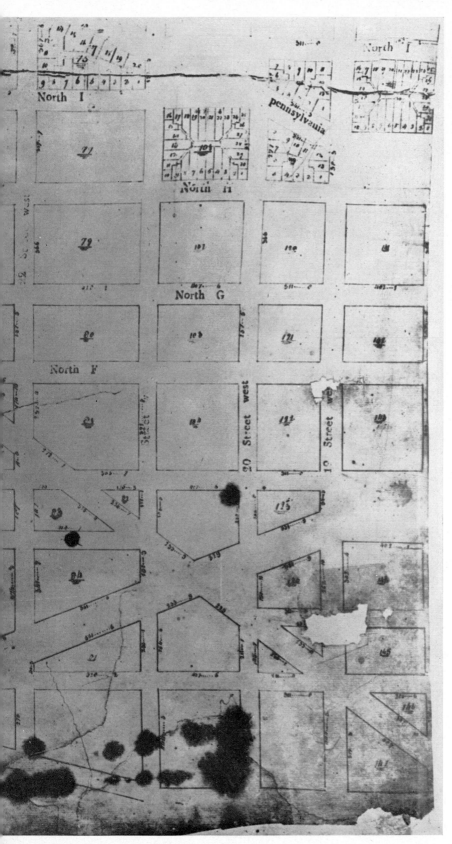

Commissioners, April 10, 1793. The National Archives. (Part two.)

Ellicott's map of Washington, 1792—

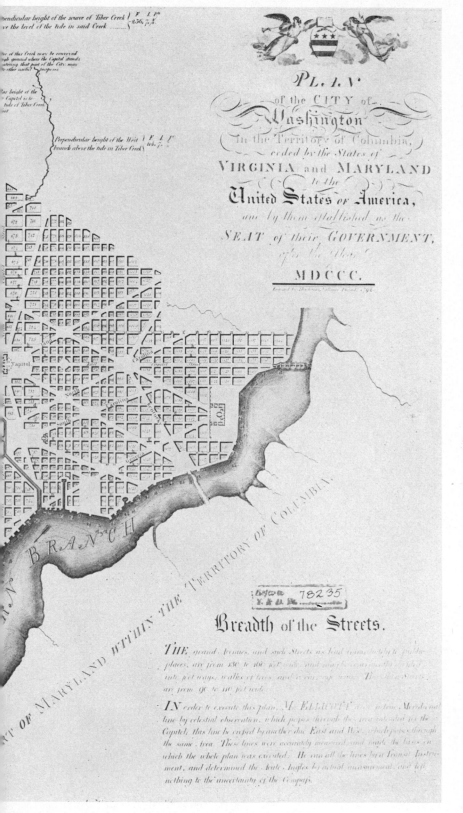

PLAN

of the CITY of

Washington

(in the Territory of Columbia,)

ceded by the States of

VIRGINIA and MARYLAND

to the

United States of America,

and by them established as the

SEAT of their GOVERNMENT,

after the Year

MDCCC.

78235

Breadth of the Streets.

THE grand Avenues, and such Streets as lead immediately to public places, are from 130 to 160 feet wide, and may be conveniently divided into foot ways, walks of trees and carriage ways. The other Streets are from 90 to 110 feet wide.

IN order to execute this plan, Mr. Ellicott drew a true Meridional line by celestial observation, which passes through the area intended for the Capitol; this line he crossed by another due East and West, which passes through the same area. These lines were accurately measured, and made the bases on which the whole plan was executed. He ran all the lines by a Transit Instrument, and determined the acute angles by actual measurement, and left nothing to the uncertainty of the Compass.

(Engraved by Thackara & Vallance of Philadelphia).

The Ellicott Topographic Map of the District of Columbia.

COMMISSIONERS TO JEFFERSON

Commissioners Office 10.th *December* 1801.

Sir

Since we had the honor of addressing to you our memorial relative to the affairs of the City, we wrote to M.^r L'Enfant, and received his answer, copies of which we take the liberty of enclosing to you, with the memorial to which his letter refers. We send the Original, not knowing whether M.^r L'Enfant has before transmitted a Duplicate to the President, and we request this may be returned after perusal, a copy of which we shall send if not already received, or if desired. We are &c

> WM. THORNTON
> A. WHITE

PRESIDENT OF THE UNITED STATES.

[P. 119, COMMISSIONERS' LETTERBOOK, Vol. 6, 1800–02, in the National Archives.]

COMMISSIONERS TO JEFFERSON

Commissioners' Office, December 19, 1801.

Sir:

Agreeably to the information given in our memorial of the 4th instant, we have held a sale of lots for ready money, which we kept open ten days. It has produced, by actual sales, 4,234 dollars, and by payments made by debtors, to prevent their property from being sold, 7,613 dollars, making, together, 11,847 dollars; yet our expenditures have been such as to leave at this time no more than 5,880 dollars in our hands. During the sale, we pursued our general policy of not selling any property for less than the sum due on it to the public; thinking it improper to change that system until it should be known what measures Government will take with respect to it, although (besides the interest due to the State of Maryland) the commissioners' note for 5,000 dollars discounted at the Bank of Columbia, will become due 22d (25th) January next, and we estimate the sums due for operations on the roads and buildings, expenses of the commissioners' office, and other contingencies to the end of the year, at 1,870 dollars, demands to which our present means are very inadequate.

We are, with sentiments of the highest respect, sir, your obedient servants.

WILLIAM THORNTON,
ALEXANDER WHITE,
TRISTRAM DALTON.

THE PRESIDENT OF THE UNITED STATES.

[P. 256, AMERICAN STATE PAPERS, MISCELLANEOUS, Vol. I.]

JEFFERSON MESSAGE TO THE SENATE

January 6, 1802

Gentlemen of the Senate:

During the late recess of the Senate, I have issued commissions for the following persons and offices, which commissions will expire at the end of this present session of the Senate. I therefore nominate the same persons to the same offices, for re-appointment, to wit:

.   .   .   .

William Kilty, of Columbia, Chief Judge of the Circuit Court of the District of Columbia, vice Thomas Johnson, declined.

John Oakly, of Columbia, Collector and Inspector of the Revenue, for the District of Georgetown, vice Matthew Lingan, resigned.

.   .   .   .

Walter Jones, Jun. of Columbia, Attorney for the District of Potomac.

William Baker, of Columbia, Marshal for the District of Potomac.

.   .   .   .

John Thompson Mason, of Columbia, Attorney for the District of Columbia, vice Thomas Swan, nominated February 28, but not appointed.

Daniel Carroll Brent, of Columbia, Marshal for the District of Columbia, vice Jas. L. Lingan, nominated February 28, but not appointed.

George Gilpin, of Columbia, Judge of the Orphans' Court for Alexandria county, Columbia, vice John Herbert, nominated March 2, but not appointed.

John Hewitt, of Columbia, Register of Wills for Washington county, Columbia, vice John Peter, nominated March 2, but not appointed.

.   .   .   .

The nominations which took place on the 2d of March, of Justices of the Peace, for the District of Columbia, having been thought too numerous, a commission issued to fourteen of those then nominated for Washington county, to wit: Thomas Sim Lee, Daniel Reintzell, Daniel Carroll, Cornelius Cuningham, Thomas Peter, Robert Brent, Thomas Addison, Abraham Boyd, John Laird, John Mason, William Thornton, Benjamin Stoddert, William Hammond Dorsey, and Joseph Sprigg Belt, and to one other, to wit: Thos. Corcoran, to be Justices of the Peace for Washington county; and another commission issue to eleven of those then nominated for Alexandria county, to wit: George Gilpin, William Fitzhugh, Francis Peyton, Richard Conway, Charles Alexander, George Taylor, Josiah Thompson, Abraham Faw, John Herbert, Cuthbert Powell, and Jacob Houghman, and to four others, to wit: Elisha Cullen Dick, Alexander Smith, Peter Wise, Jun. and Thomas Darne, to be

Justices of the Peace for Alexandria county; all of whom are now nominated for re-appointment to the same offices.

[JOURNAL OF THE EXECUTIVE PROCEEDINGS OF THE SENATE, I, 400–04.]

COMMISSIONERS TO JEFFERSON

Commissioners Office 6.th *January* 1802.

Sir

William Rhodes having raised a frame for the purpose of a Stable within 8 feet of the building in which this office is kept, but little more than 12 from the Office of the Clerk of the County of Washington, and still nearer than either to another brick building; the Commissioners on the 10th Ultimo wrote him a letter (A) Whereupon Mr Rhodes agreed with a Gentleman for liberty to place the frame on an adjacent lot, and declared his intention to remove it thither, as soon as it should be in a state to remove with ease and safety; we however observed that he was preparing to underpin the Frame where it now stands, and in consequence wrote him another letter (B) since which we understand legal advice has been sought, and an opinion obtained that no power exists in us to remedy this evil in a summary way. A principle which leads to important consequences, and which we presume may as well be determined in the present as in any future case; but altho we are of opinion that such avowed infractions of established rules should be checked and that this building in particular should be removed or demolished yet we do not think it prudent to engage in a measure which may probably end in litigation, without the direction of the President, or the opinion of his Council, as to the power of the Commissioners to enforce a compliance with the rules and regulations established by the President respecting the materials and manner of building in the City, and the mode of carrying that power into effect. That such an opinion may be obtained we inclose an Extract from the Deeds of

Trust (C) and a Copy of the rules & regulations established by President Washington in pursuance thereof (D). It may be proper to observe that the Operation of the 1st and 3rd Articles of those rules has been suspended till the first day of the present month, with this exception that no wooden building should be placed within 24 feet of a brick or Stone building, this frame being within that distance we presume must be subject to the rules first established. We are &c.

Wᴹ Thornton
A. White
T. Dalton

[P. 123, COMMISSIONERS' LETTERBOOK, Vol. 6, 1800–02, in the National Archives.]

Jefferson to the Commissioners

Washington Jan. 7. 1802

Gentlemen

I have recieved and duly considered your letter of yesterday on the subject of the frame house erected contrary to rule by mr̄ Rhodes, and approve of your opinion that measures should be taken for it's removal. I suppose it will be best for you to apply to mr̄ Mason the Attorney for the district. Accept my respect & best wishes.

Tʜ: Jefferson

THE COMMISSIONERS OF WASHINGTON

[Ms., *Jefferson Papers*, Library of Congress.]

Jefferson Message to Congress

THE PRESIDENT TO THE SENATE AND HOUSE OF REPRESENTATIVES

January 11, 1802

I now communicate to you a memorial of the Commissioners of the City of Washington, together with a letter of later date,

which, with the memorial of January 28, 1801, will possess the
Legislature fully of the state of the public interests and of those
of the City of Washington confided to them. The moneys now
due, and soon to become due, to the State of Maryland, on the
loan guaranteed by the United States, call for an early attention. The lots in the city which are chargeable with the payment of these moneys are deemed not only equal to the in-
demnification of the public, but to insure a considerable sur-
plus to the city, to be employed for its improvement; provided
they are offered for sale only in sufficient numbers to meet the
existing demand. But the act of 1796 requires that they shall be
positively sold in such numbers as shall be necessary for the
punctual payment of the loans. Nine thousand dollars of interest are lately become due; three thousand dollars quarter-
yearly will continue to become due; and fifty thousand dollars,
an additional loan, are reimbursable on the first day of November next. These sums would require sales so far beyond the
actual demand of the market, that it is apprehended that the
whole property may be thereby sacrificed, the public security
destroyed, and the residuary interest of the city entirely lost.
Under these circumstances I have thought it my duty, before I
proceed to direct a rigorous execution of the law, to submit the
subject to the consideration of the Legislature. Whether the
public interest will be better secured in the end, and that of the
city saved, by offering sales commensurate only to the demand
at market, and advancing from the Treasury, in the first instance, what these may prove deficient, to be replaced by subsequent sales, rests for the determination of the Legislature. If
indulgence for the funds can be admitted, they will probably
form a resource of great and permanent value; and their embarrassments have been produced only by overstrained exertions to provide accommodations for the Government of the
Union.

[P. 100, DOCUMENTARY HISTORY OF . . . THE CAPITOL . . .]

JEFFERSON TO CONGRESS

COMMUNICATED TO CONGRESS, *January* 11, 1802.

TO THE PRESIDENT OF THE UNITED STATES:

The memorial of the Commissioners appointed by virtue of an act of Congress entitled: "An act for establishing the temporary and permanent seat of Government of the United States," respectfully showeth:

COMMISSIONERS' OFFICE, *December* 4, 1801.

.   .   .   .

The act of Congress authorizing the President to locate a district for the permanent seat of the Government of the United States; the actual location of that district; the grant of lands for a federal city; the power given by the President to the Commissioners to sell that part of the land so granted, which was placed at his disposal; the sale of six thousand lots to Morris & Greenleaf, by agreement dated 23rd December, 1793; the modification of that agreement by another, entered into in April, 1794; the failure of those gentlemen to fulfill their contracts, and the various measures pursued to obtain money to carry on the public buildings, are recited in the above-mentioned representation; and copies of the legislative acts, deeds and other writings therein referred to are annexed, and the whole printed for the use of members of Congress. The property belonging to the public is therein stated to consist of twenty-four million six hundred and fifty-five thousand seven [hundred] and thirty-five square feet of ground in the City of Washington, equal to four thousand six hundred and eighty-two lots, of five thousand two hundred and sixty-five square feet each, exclusive of lots which bind on navigable water; these form fronts to the extent of two thousand and forty-three feet, and on them are four wharves in a useful state.

.   .   .   .

Your memorialists readily admit that the public property remaining for sale is not, on an average, equal in value to that which has been sold; yet as great abatement was in many instances made in the price of lots, in consideration of building contracts, and as inducements to purchase in the city have much increased, they conceive those on hand may, in the course of a few years, be disposed of at least to as great advantage as those already sold; but if the law authorizing a loan for the use of the City of Washington should be carried strictly into effect, your memorialists are apprehensive that this property must be, in a great degree, sacrificed.

[Pp. 332–333, U.S. v. MORRIS, Vol. 6.]

COMMISSIONERS TO JEFFERSON

Commissioners Office 22nd *January* 1802.

Sir

The term having expired during which the first and third Articles of the Terms and Conditions, declared by the President of the United States on the 17th October 1791 for regulating the materials and manner of building and improvements on the Lots in the City of Washington, have been suspended — We have taken the subject into consideration and are of opinion that it may be expedient to extend the indulgence last given to the end of the present year, with this difference that no wooden building covering more than 320 Square feet, or more than 12 feet high from the Sills to the eve, shall be permitted; houses of that discription will be sufficient for Tradesmen or others of small property for whose encouragement and accommodation alone we should think it adviseable to permit Wooden buildings of any dimensions to be erected in the City. We inclose a

writing agreeably to former precedents for your signiture
should you approve of the measure proposed.

> We are &c.

> > W^M THORNTON
> > A. WHITE
> > T. DALTON

PRESIDENT OF THE UNITED STATES.

[Pp. 124–5, COMMISSIONERS' LETTERBOOK, Vol. 6, 1800–02, in the National Archives.]

COMMISSIONERS TO JEFFERSON

Commissioners Office 8th *February* 1802.^46

Sir

We received by last post, a letter from the Governor of Maryland, and not having it in our power to pay the interest due to
that state, we have agreeably to the Governors request transmitted his letter with the enclosures to the President of the
United States. We are &c

PRESIDENT OF THE UNITED STATES.

[P. 126, COMMISSIONERS' LETTERBOOK, Vol. 6, 1800–02, in the National Archives.]

DANIEL CARROLL TO JEFFERSON

Washington Feby 8th 1802

THE PRESIDENT OF THE UNITED STATES

Sir/

In consequence of an application to the Com^rs of Washington

46 Feby 9th 1802   In the recess of the Board a letter was received from the Governour of
Maryland dated 2^d instant, enclosing a letter to him of the same date
from the Treasurer of the Western Shore, and a resolution of the Assembly passed 23^d Decr 1799 which first mentioned letter, with the enclosures, was yesterday transmitted to the President of the U. States
agreeably to the request of the Governour, and a letter written to the
President enclosing the same.

[P. 269, Proceedings of the Commissioners, VI, 1800–02, in the National Archives.]

by Mr. Barry in the year 1800 for the removeal of the houses of
Mrs Fenwick, situated in south Capitol street, and a valuation
being had to that effect, & Mrs Fenwick having gone to a considerable expence in building a new house, under the expectation of receiving that valuation, which has since been refused
her by the Comm^{rs}, as will appear by the inclosed letters. In
the mean time her enclosures were removed, her garden broken
up, & much incommoded in other respects. — I beg leave to
submit the letters and valuation to you, & beg if you see proper,
you will direct payment to be made —. I have the honor to be
          Sir
                    Your M^{o} Ob^{t} Servt
                              DAN^{L} CARROLL OF DUD^{N}

[Ms., *Jefferson Papers*, Library of Congress.]

COMMISSIONERS' NOTE

Feb? 9th 1802   The President of the U. States having in person
                returned the letter from the Governour of Mary-
                land with the papers accompanying it, which
                were transmitted to him yesterday, and having
                recommended that the same should be com-
                municated to the Com^{ee} to whom his Message
                of 11th Ult? was referred; the same were accord-
                ingly enclosed in a letter to Joseph N. Nicholson
                Chairman of the said Com^{ee}

[P. 270, PROCEEDINGS OF THE COMMISSIONERS, VI, 1800–02, in the National Archives.]

COMMISSIONERS' NOTE

Feb? 9th 1802   A Note of this date received from the President
                of the U. States enclosing a letter to him from
                Daniel Carroll of Dud^{gtn} dated 8th instant, with
                several letters which have passed between the

Commissioners, Mr Carroll and Mrs Fenwick on the subject of removing her houses, also the valuation of those houses by Messrs Harbaugh and Duncanson.

[Pp. 269–70, PROCEEDINGS OF THE COMMISSIONERS, VI, 1800–02, in the National Archives.]

COMMISSIONERS TO JEFFERSON

Commissioners Office 9.th *February* 1802.

Sir

We have just received your Note with Mr Carrolls letter to you, and several letters which had passed between the Commissioners, Mr Carroll and Mrs Fenwick respecting the removal of Mrs Fenwicks houses. Our Sentiments of that measure are fully expressed in those letters, and we have not changed them; they would remain the same, if we had the sole authority in the case, which we do not conceive we have. By the Deed of Trust the Original Proprietors are entitled to retain the buildings, when the arrangements of the Streets &c will conveniently admit of it; but if the arrangements of the Streets will not admit of retention *and it shall become necessary* to remove such buildings; then the Proprietor shall be paid the just valuation thereof; It is not said who shall have the power to judge of that necessity; but it seems from implication to result to the President who alone had the right to lay out the City; there is no act which even by implication vests the Commissioners with power over the subject. The facts in Mr Carrolls case fully appear from the communications he has made to you, which you will receive inclosed. We are &c.

A. WHITE
T. DALTON

PRESIDENT OF THE UNITED STATES.

[Pp. 126–7, COMMISSIONERS' LETTERBOOK, Vol. 6, 1800–02, in the National Archives.]

JEFFERSON TO DANIEL CARROLL

Washington Feb. 11. 1802

Sir

Immediately on the receipt of your letter on the subject of mrs̄ Fenwick's case, I referred it, with the papers accompanying it, to the Commissioners. their answer, with the same papers, is now inclosed. You will observe they do not consider a question on the demolition or removal of a house, as decided by their first proceedings on the subject; nor will they give the final order for it: and that the house having never in fact been demolished or removed, it's demolition or removal is not to be paid for. my means of proceeding with the board of Commissioners has been as if it were two houses of legislation. Where both concur affirmatively the thing is to be done. Where neither disagrees, nothing can be done. the board having negatived this proposition, it would have been useless for me to enter into the consideration of it, or to make up any opinion on the subject. Accept assurances of my esteem & respect.

TH: JEFFERSON

DANIEL CARROL ESQ.

[Ms., *Jefferson Papers*, Library of Congress.]

COMMISSIONERS TO JEFFERSON

Commissioners' Office
11 *Feb'y,* 1802

Sir:

In compliance with your wishes, as intimated to us, we transmit to you copies of the acts of Congress the late President Washington and Adams directing the conveyance of the streets and public appropriations in the city of Washington to the commissioners, agreeably to the act of Congress intituled "An act for establishing the temporary and permanent seat of Government of the United States."

We are, &c.,

A. White
T. Dalton

PRESIDENT OF THE UNITED STATES

[P. 228, U.S. v. MORRIS; p. 128, COMMISSIONERS' LETTERBOOK, Vol. 6, 1800–02, in the National Archives.]

L'ENFANT TO JEFFERSON

City of Washington March 12th 1802

Sir

Under the apprehension of Impropriety in the liberty I took of adressing you, in november ult^{mo}, but remaining Ignorant whether resting as I Dec^d requested leave to rest on you for Settlement of the business the subject of two repeated memorials to Congress be agreable to you: — the difficulties which this uncertainty set me under with regard to the Committee of claims to whom my memorials stand refered since the begining of this Congress (I having consequent to the wish Imparted to you and to the dependance I place in your goodness, beged the chairman of that Committee would delay their proceeding upon) forces on me the necessity to renew the Sollicitation to you.

From dispositions testified by my last address I promised to myself that such Settlement as I feel entitled to wait from government, might have been effected in some other ways than through a Committee of claims, which (besides, that, I fear from their having once already reported against the memorial) truely to my mind made it a disgracefull reflection that a recompense merited should be made necessary to claim.

of this however, Sir, your Judgement best will determine, and I only advert to the circumstance to speak of my embarrassement on the Subject and how seeing the session of Congress fast approaching to its close now add disquietude to the apprehension of having mistaken in the manner of late request to you ——— well persuaded nevertheless but you will excuse where the Intention was purely to prove my respect and esteem of your natural disposition: — encouraged by this hope I have here recalled to your mind all matters before stated — and beg you to believe that the request which I made to you appeared to me proper because more flatering to my embition to obtain my prayer through your Favour

> with great respect
> I have the honor to be

Sir — your Excellency

> most obedient and
> humble Servant.

> P. CHARLES L'ENFANT

HIS EXCELLENCY THOMAS JEFFERSON
President of the United States

P.S. having your Statement inclosed in the late address.

[Ms., *Jefferson Papers*, Library of Congress.]

JEFFERSON TO L'ENFANT

Washington Mar. 14. 1802.

Sir

Your letter of the 12th is at hand. immediately on the reciept of the former one I referred it to the board of Commissioners, the authority instituted by law for originating whatever proceedings regarding this city have been confided by the legislature to the Executive. their opinion, which I approved, was that they could only repeat you the offer formerly made with the approbation of General Washington, and they undertook to do this. for any thing else, the powers of the legislature are alone competent, and therefore your application to them was the only measure by which it could be obtained. Accept my respects & best wishes.

TH: JEFFERSON

MAJ^R LENFANT.

[Ms., *Jefferson Papers*, Library of Congress.]

DANIEL CARROL TO JEFFERSON

Washington March 28th 1802

THE PRESIDENT OF THE UNITED STATES

Sir/

Since you did me the honor the other day to mention the subject of the Canal from the falls of Pot° to the Eastern branch, I have thought much on the subject, & satisfied you will excuse the liberty I am now taking, have determined to address you a few lines — I see innumerable difficulties attending the plan you proposed, one which you mentioned, the want of funds, The ground where you proposed introducing the Canal into the City to wit, Pens.^a avenue I do suppose, must be about thirty feet, above the level of water struck in Geo Town, & would continue to that height, or nearly until you would come to the south of the Presidents house, shoud this be correct or nearly so, I apprehend to remove such a body of earth, to so great a depth, would be attended with an expence that would not be encountered. I am allso satisfied to take the canal along tiber, creek & introduce it into the eastern branch by new Jersey avenue, would cost considerably less, than taking through Geo Town, independant of the high ground on Pens^a avenue — With high respect I am
    Sir
        Your Mo ob^t Servt

DAN^L CARROLL of Dud.^n

[Ms., *Jefferson Papers*, Library of Congress.]

JEFFERSON TO THE SENATE

JEFFERSON'S MESSAGE TO THE SENATE

April 5, 1802

Gentlemen of the Senate:

Since my message of January 6th, to the Senate, I have received information that Thomas Sim Lee, therein named as a Justice of the Peace for the county of Washington, had resigned that office; and that Benjamin Stoddart and William Hammond Dorsey, therein also named as Justices for the same county, had declined qualifying. This renders it necessary to withdraw their nominations for re-appointment, which I hereby do; and I nominate in their stead Anthony Reintzell, John Oakley, and Isaac Pierce, to be Justices of the Peace for the said county.

In the same message, of January 6th, the name of John Laird was inserted by mistake, instead of that of Benjamin More, who (and not John Laird), had been commissioned and qualified as a Justice of the Peace. I therefore beg leave to correct the error, by restoring to its place the name of Benjamin More, and nominating him to be a Justice of the Peace for the said county, and by withdrawing that of John Laird.[47]

I learn also, from the county of Alexandria, that William Fitzhugh, Richard Conway, and Thomas Darne, named in the said message as Justices for that county, have declined qualifying. I therefore withdraw their nominations; and I nominate in their stead, George Slacum, Presly Gunnell, and John Dundas, to be Justices of the Peace for the said county of Alexandria.[48]

[JOURNAL OF THE EXECUTIVE PROCEEDINGS OF THE SENATE, I, 417-18, 423.]

[47] On April 27, 1802, the Senate confirmed the following nominations of Justices of the Peace for the District of Columbia, Washington county: Daniel Reintzell, Daniel Carroll, Cornelius Coningham, Thomas Peter, Robert Brent, Thomas Addison, Abraham Boyd, John Mason, William Thornton, Joseph Sprig Belt, Thomas Corcoran, Anthony Reintzell, John Oakley, Isaac Peirce, Benj. Moore.

[48] On April 27, 1802, the Senate confirmed the following nominations for Justices of the

ALEXANDER WHITE TO JEFFERSON

Rec.^d Apr. 13.

Commissioners Office 13th *April* 1802

Sir

In consequence of what you were pleased to mention this morning I send a rough sketch of a Resolve respecting a subject which I do not feel myself competent to act on. I have examined the Essays of Nicholas King while he was in the employ of the Commissioners, and acting under the auspices of Doctor Thornton, from which it appears that their Idea was to carry a Water Street 80 feet wide through the whole extent of the Patowmac and Eastern Branch, one hundred feet distant from the Channel, having all the space between that and the shore which in some instances I am inclined to believe is not less than one thousand feet, under water until it shall be filled up. I do not see the propriety of this, and have drawn the Resolve in such general terms, that without deviating from it, the President may direct the Street to be laid out in any manner he may think most proper.

I shall with great pleasure facilitate your views, but unless I can get away on Saturday next it will subject me to considerable inconvenience — I am with sentiments of the highest respect

    Sir

      Your most Ob.^t Servt

ALEX.^R WHITE

PRESIDENT OF THE U. STATES

[Ms., *Jefferson Papers*, Library of Congress.]

Peace for the District of Columbia, Alexandria county: George Gilpin, Francis Peyton, Charles Alexander, George Taylor, Jonah Thompson, Abraham Faw, John Herbert, Cuthbert Powell, Jacob Hoffman, Elisha Cullen Dick, Alex. Smith, Peter Wise, Jun., George Slacum, Presly Gunnell, John Dundas.

ALEXANDER WHITE TO JEFFERSON

[*April* 13th 1802]

Resolved, as the opinion of the Board that a Plan of the City of Washington on which the public appropriations, as they are described in the several Acts of the President of the U States directing the conveyance thereof to the Commissioners; the Squares or Parcels of ground which have been divided, or prepared for division, as building lots; and the Streets as actually laid out on the ground, shall be plainly and distinctly delineated — ought to be engraved, and published under the sanction of the President of the U. States — And that a Street round those parts of the City which bind on navigable water ought also to be designated on such plan so that the same, in such parts as are covered with water, may hereafter be made, agreeably to an established Rule —

[Ms., *Jefferson Papers*, Library of Congress.]

COMMISSIONERS TO JEFFERSON

Commissioners Office June 1. 1802

Sir

This being the expiring hour of Office we leave the Books Plans Papers Instruments and other articles belonging to the Commissioners Office in the Custody of Mr Munroe our Clerk, to be delivered to the Superintendant when appointed by the President, except the Books and vouchers requisite to compleat the accounts in conformity to the act of Congress; which accounts have been commenced & progressed in as far as our time would allow. We are &c.

W^M THORNTON
A. WHITE

PRESIDENT OF THE⎫
UNITED STATES   ⎬

Mr. Daltons indisposition has prevented his attendance for a few days.

[P. 142, COMMISSIONERS' LETTERBOOK, Vol. 6, 1800–02, in the National Archives.]

JEFFERSON PROCLAMATION

COMMISSION OF APPOINTMENT OF MAYOR

THOMAS JEFFERSON, *President of the United States of America,*

To all to whom these presents shall come Greeting:

Know ye, That reposing special Trust and Confidence in the Integrity, Ability and Diligence of Robert Brent, of the City of Washington, I do in pursuance of the powers vested in me by the Act of Congress entitled "An Act to incorporate the inhabitants of the City of Washington, in the District of Columbia" hereby appoint him the said Robert Brent, Mayor of the said City of Washington, and do authorize him to exercise and fulfil the duties of that office according to law; and to Have and to Hold the same with all the powers, privileges and authorities thereto, of right appertaining unto him the said Robert Brent for the term of one year from the day of the date hereof, unless the President of the United States for the time being should be pleased sooner to revoke and determine this Commission.

In Testimony whereof, I have caused these Letters to be made Patent, and the Seal of the United States to be hereunto affixed.

Given under my hand, at the City of Washington the first day of June in the year of our Lord one thousand eight hundred and two; and of the Independence of the United States of America the twenty-seventh.

[SEAL]   TH: JEFFERSON.

By the President:

JAMES MADISON, *Secretary of State.*

[RECORDS OF THE COLUMBIA HISTORICAL SOCIETY, Vol. 2, pp. 240–41.]

JEFFERSON TO ROBERT BRENT

Washington, June 3, 1802.

Dear Sir:

The Act of Congress incorporating the city of Washington has confided to the President of the U. S. the appointment of the Mayor of the city. As the agency of that officer will be immediately requisite, I am desirous to avail the city of your services in it, if you will permit me to send you the commission. I will ask the favor of an answer to this proposition.

Will you also do me that of dining with me the day after tomorrow (Friday) at half after three? Accept my friendly and respectful salutations.

TH: JEFFERSON.

TO ROBERT BRENT, ESQ.

[RECORDS OF THE COLUMBIA HISTORICAL SOCIETY, Vol. 2, pp. 239–40.]

ROBERT BRENT TO JEFFERSON

Washington, June 3d, 1802.

Dear Sir:

I have had the honor of receiving your favor of this date, asking my acceptance of the appointment of Mayor under the late Act of Congress for incorporating this city.

Altho I feel great diffidence in the talents I possess for executing that duty, in a manner which may afford general satisfaction, yet feeling it a duty to contribute my feeble aid for the public service, I will venture upon its duties.

I beg you Sir to accept my thanks for the honor, which you are about to confer on me and for the obliging manner in which you have been pleased to communicate it.

I will, with pleasure, accept your polite invitation to dinner on Friday next. With sentiments of much respect and esteem I have the honor to be Sir, Your Obt. Ser.

ROBERT BRENT.

[Reply to President Jefferson's letter of June 3, 1802. Taken from RECORDS OF THE CO-LUMBIA HISTORICAL SOCIETY, Vol. 2, p. 240.]

DANIEL BRENT TO JEFFERSON

June 7th 1802

Sir/

Agreeable to your desire, I have spoken to mr. Hadfield to furnish a plan for the Jail. this he has promised to do, which when done shall be sent in to you —. I transmit herewith several plans which have been handed to me & from which some useful hint may perhaps be taken —. With sentiments of the highest respect I am Sir y^r Ob^t Servt.

DANIEL C. BRENT

[Ms., *Jefferson Papers*, Library of Congress.]

ALEXANDER WHITE TO JEFFERSON

Woodville 10.th *June* 1802

Sir

In the last conversation I had the honour to hold with you, you observed that you had not expected anything further would have been paid to the Commissioners on account of the Square conveyed to the U. States for the Site of Marine Barracks — This has occasioned me to reflect on what passed between us on that subject previous to the purchase; and if my memory does not fail me, the idea originated with you, having in view principally the putting the streets in a better state. Some doubt seemed to be entertained of the strict right thus to apply the money, and I was asked if I could not find an apology to excuse us to Congress. At our next meeting I stated that the Commissioners had expended much larger sums on objects authorised by the guarantee Law, than had been raised by the sale of property pledged and therefore I conceived the money proposed to be expended on the streets was entirely clear of the guarantee — It was then suggested as a doubt, whether money granted by the Proprietors of the soil for erecting the public buildings, could be applied to making Streets — To which I answered, that the Land being granted for the purpose of a City, and the President being authorised to lay it off in such Streets &. as he should deem necessary, it appeared to be a matter of course, that the Streets should be opened and rendered passable; the President being Judge of the degree of repair into which they should be put, having regard to the means in his hands, and the various objects to which these means were applicable — On this explanation I thought all difficulties were removed, except that existing appropriations did not warrant the expenditure of a larger sum than $4,000; the Com.^{rs} certainly counted on the receipt of the balance whenever an appropriation could be made, and regulated their operations accordingly. The Secretary of the Navy recommended the appropriation which no doubt would have been made had his letter been laid before the Committee of Ways and Means; for want of this sum we found ourselves much embarrassed at the expiration of our office; and I consider it as the principal fund on which Mr Munroe can rely to take up our Note in Bank, and to pay other pressing demands.

I would likewise observe that a purchase by the U. States of City property from the Com.^{rs} is not unprecedented. During the former administration the Secretary of the Navy, and my Colleague Scott were anxious to obtain a donation of City Land for the Navy Yard, but finding me inflexible (although a majority of the Board would have complied) the Secretary thought proper to come forward with $4000 and make a purchase.

I have taken the liberty thus to recapitulate the circumstances attending this case, and to state the influence they had on the conduct of the Board, in hopes, that you will be of opinion, that an appropriation ought to be made, which I have no doubt will be done, unless it should be known that the Presidents opinion is unfavourable to the measure — With anxious wishes for the prosperity of our infant City — I remain with sentiments of the highest respect

   Sir

     Your most Ob^t Servt

          ALEX^R WHITE

PRESIDENT OF THE U. S.

[Ms., *Jefferson Papers*, Library of Congress.]

DANIEL BRENT TO JEFFERSON

          June 26th 1802

Sir,

Mr Hadfield yesterday furnished me with the Plans and specifications, herewith sent, which are submitted for your inspection and directions. I think in some few instances he ought to have been more particular; this however can be easily rectified. The Jack Rafters are I think too far apart, they ought not be more than nine Inches from center to center. From Blagden's note to me, you will see, nearly, the quantity of free Stone necessary, as also the price. Mr Hadfield having changed the plan of the Steps a little and added some for the chimnies, the quantity is not accurately ascertained. There is no public Stone proper for the Stairs; this can quickly be obtained from the quarries.

I have thought the Ground I pointed out to you, as laid down in the printed Plan of the City for the Court-House, Jail and

Gardens, consisted of three distinct Squares & were intersected by the Streets E & F; but M.ʳ Munroe informs me that it is one entire appropriation, and that no Street in the real Plan of the City passes through that or any other public appropriation: this I consider a lucky circumstance, for upon examining the Ground on yesterday, I found by placing the Jail in the center of the supposed Square from east to West, and forty feet from E Street, that it will be thrown into low Ground, whereas, as no Street passes through the appropriation, by fixing the front upon a line with E Street, we shall have excellent Ground. At 12 Oclock when I suppose you are about to ride out, I will call, and if convenient to you, will point out the Ground more correctly. With Sentiments of high respect,

> I am Sir,
>
> Y.ʳ Mo: Ob.ᵗ Serv.ᵗ
>
> DANIEL C. BRENT

PRESIDENT OF THE UNITED STATES

[Ms., *Jefferson Papers*, Library of Congress.]

ALEXANDER WHITE TO JEFFERSON

Woodville 13.ᵗʰ *July* 1802

Dear Sir

I am favoured with yours of 5.ᵗʰ instant. In the course of the summer or autumn I intend to visit the Cavities of Ice, and to make more particular observations than heretofore. Should I in the mean time obtain information which may deserve attention I will communicate it. I am much surprised at Hobans conduct —; his agreement with the late Commissioners, as entered in their Journal, ought perhaps to have been more explicit — but I believe it does not express that he should continue in pay till the buildings should be finished. A stipulation which I should have considered so improper, would hardly have escaped my recollection, but we need not depend on memory. the writing will speak for itself. Some years ago both my Colleagues were desirous of getting Hoban out of the way; and amazing exertions were made to find something in his conduct which would justify them in dismissing him. I believe he would then have disputed their right, but I did not understand, either on that occasion, or on a subsequent one, which I am about to mention that he expected to receive his salary after the works should cease. Towards the close of the year 1800 it was proposed to notify him that his services would not be required after a certain day, upon a supposition that there would be nothing further done towards carrying on the building till Congress should take order therein. He made no objection to this in conversation with me but the shortness of the notice — the time was then prolonged; and a letter written to him amounting to a discontinuance, and there the matter rested till after you came into office, and ordered the works to be proceeded on. After which we continued his salary by an order, implying according to my remembrance, that it had been discontinued, but the minutes will show how far I am accurate. I made no note of this transaction.

Our Harvest is productive beyond example, and the weather generally favourable, though we have at times been interrupted by showers, which promote vegetation in a great degree, but have not been sufficient to affect the Springs or Wells —

I wish you all the pleasure, during your retirement, which domestic life affords, and remain with sentiments of real regard

       Dear Sir

         Your Ob^t Servt

                          ALEX^R WHITE

THO^S JEFFERSON ESQUIRE
   P. U.

[Ms., *Jefferson Papers*, Library of Congress.]

Thornton to Jefferson

Washington 28th *July* 1802
rec^d July 31

Sir

The Secretary of State received the enclosed this morn^g which he desired me to forward to the President.

I found on my arrival at Mount Vernon, that I was precluded from the pleasure I anticipated in purchasing for you the Terrestial Globe, which formerly belonged to General Washington; & which you wished to possess, as a Relick. — It was considered as belonging to the Library, &, consequently, the Property of Judge Washington, but the Legatees made him pay dearly for another Globe, which he considered himself in Duty bound not to part with. I mean the Head of the Testator; & this, after I had informed them, that as many Heads of him as there were Heads in the Army he commanded could be had for two or three Guineas each. The Judge did not know this, but declared he would give what any other Gentleman would give. Upon this a young man was advised (as I heard him afterwards acknowledge) to bid 250 Dollars, and the Judge was accordingly obliged to give that Sum. — I was sorry that the Heirs of such a man should have acted so unworthily —. But it was unknown to some of them. The Legatees then retired to a chamber & *cast Lots for his Garments!* There was something in the whole Scene, & in the general Proceedings that shocked me. But it was a Scene, which, although devoid of Feeling, *was not without Interest.*

Accept,
Sir,
my sincerest good wishes
& highest Consideration. —

WILLIAM THORNTON

PRESIDENT OF THE UNITED STATES

[Ms., *Jefferson Papers*, Library of Congress.]

DANIEL BRENT TO JEFFERSON

Washington, Aug.ᵗ 3ᵈ 1802
rec.ᵈ Aug. 5

Sir,

Enclosed is a copy of a Letter from Mʳ Hadfield which I think proper to communicate to you and to request your directions on the subject.

As I understood it to be a direction from you to me, that the Grates should be fixed in Iron frames, I have contracted for them so to be done, and contrary to the opinion and wishes of Mʳ Hadfield, who insists upon his Plan as the best. The article respecting the Ironwork of the Windows, is thus expressed — "all the windows in the ground Story except in the goalers Room, to have double Grates of eight cross Bars each — four upright & four horizontal — all the windows above, except the goalers Room, to have only one cross grate of eight Bars — the windows of the goaler's Room above and below, to have only four upright Bars in each — all the horizontal bars to be one inch and one inch & a quarter thick, and the upright Bars three Inches broad, and three quarters of an Inch thick, to be punched through so as to receive the horizontal Bars — all the Bars to be fixed in an Iron frame, each going through, and well rivetted — the frame to be sunk into the Stone it's whole thickness — the frame is to be three Inches broad, and three quarters of an Inch thick."

I am not attached to this mode, and am ready to adopt any that may be thought better; but I do not think myself at liberty to make a change without your directions — this change, if deemed proper, will not delay the work — with respect to the Doors, I shall have them iron sheeted, agreeably to your former Instructions. As to the Roof, I should prefer the substantial parts of good white Oak — The Rafters and Lathing, I think may with safety be of good pine or yellow Poplar — the Roof of course will be much lighter, and I think, will last as long —

We shall commence to lay the foundation on about Monday next — the granite which the undertakers have already got down from the falls, I am told, is of a very excellent quality.

I am, with Sentiments of high respect,

   Sir,

     Y.ʳ Mo: Ob.ᵗ Serv.ᵗ

          DANIEL C. BRENT

PRESIDENT OF THE UNITED STATES

[Ms., *Jefferson Papers*, Library of Congress.]

THOMAS MUNROE TO JEFFERSON

THOMAS MUNROE, SUPERINTENDENT, TO THE PRESIDENT

Washington 13th *August* 1802.

Sir:

Mr. King, the late Surveyor of the City, and his Son Robert having this morning informed me that they shall on Sunday next sail for England in a vessel lying at Alexandria — and that several persons have applied to them within the last day or two to lay off lots & give levels, and other necessary information relative to buildings, which it will not be in their power to do before their departure, and as some inconvenience may arise from the want (even for a short time) of a person to perform these particular duties, I have deemed it proper to communicate the circumstances for your direction on the subject.

Mr. King, the younger, tells me there are upwards of seventy houses now building, & about to be commenced in the City; if so, many applications will be made by the builders for information similar to that heretofore given by him under his appointment from the Commissioners to regulate the lines and levels of Lots, and to carry into effect the general regulations for building declared by the President on the 17th of October 1791.

I fear the State of the Surveying Department generally is more irregular and confused, and will require much more attention and labor to adjust & compleat it than has been supposed. Some inconvenience has lately been experienced & complained of from the want of a Surveyor properly qualified to attend the Office. Several of the Lots advertised for sale on the 30th Inst I find have not been calculated and their contents in square feet ascertained, nor have the divisions of all the squares been perfected. I think we cannot do well without a Surveyor at the Sale. Various cases have occurred at all past sales which required the services of one. If there be any documents or materials which may be deemed useful in correcting the plate for a permanent plan of the City they can be more conveniently collected during the present & next two months, than at a later period, in case you should honor me with any directions on the subject.

With sentiments of the highest respect,
I have the honor to be Sir,
Yr Mo Ob Servt,

THOMAS MUNROE.

[Pp. 2270-1, U.S. *v.* MORRIS, Records, Vol. VII.]

JEFFERSON TO THOMAS MUNROE

[TO T. MUNROE]

Monticello, August 16, 1802.[49]

Sir,

Yours of the 13.th is this moment received, informing me of the vacancy in the office of Surveyor of the City, by the departure of the late Surveyor, and of the necessity of an immeadiate appointment. According therefore to what had been proposed in that event taking place, I presume it is proper to appoint Mr

[49] Copy made from the original in the State Department on Aug. 1, 1890.

Nicholas King, to that place. I believe his appointment was heretofore *made by the Comm.^rs* with the approbation of the President, but that the appointment had only their signature. if so, yours is now to supply that, and consequently, you will get the final authority to Mr Nich.^s King to act. should I be mistaken in this and should a commission signed by the President be requisite then let such an one be forwarded to me for signature, and desire him to act in the meantime under the authority of this letter, that nothing may suffer. Accept my best wishes and respects.

TH: JEFFERSON.

[Ms., *Letters of the Presidents of the U. S. to the Commissioners of Public Buildings and Grounds,* original in Manuscripts Division, Library of Congress, photostat in National Archives.]

THOMAS MUNROE TO JEFFERSON

Washington, 24th *August* 1802.

Sir:

I have the honor of enclosing a letter which I yesterday received from Mr. Nicholas King.

The Commissioners have always heretofore appointed the Surveyor by Letter, or by entry in the minutes of their proceedings; but in case Mr. King's proposition respecting Salary shall be acceded to, a short Letter of appointment from the President would, I have reason to believe, be more agreeable to him than if it were otherwise conferred, and if there be no objections to his being gratified it will be quite as agreeable to me as any other mode of appointment.

I have the honor to be with the most respectful consideration, Sir,

Yr Obt Servt

THOMAS MUNROE.

PRESIDENT OF THE UNITED STATES.

[P. 2271, U.S. *v.* MORRIS, Records, Vol. VII.]

JEFFERSON PROCLAMATION

THOMAS JEFFERSON PRESIDENT OF THE UNITED STATES

To all whom it may concern. Greeting.

Whereas a Committee appointed by and in behalf of the Citizens and House holders in that part of the City of Washington which lies west of the President's house have solicited that the open space of Ground between Square numbered seventy eight and one hundred and one, bounded by Pennsylvania Avenue, I Street north, and twentieth street West may be appropriated as a site for a Market in which solicitation of the original proprietor of the Ground within said space has joined and united with said Committee, and the said Committee having certified that all the owners of property and Inhabitants contiguous to the said Space two, who are absent excepted, anxiously wish that the same space may be appropriated as aforesaid.

I do therefore declare and make known that the said open space be, and the same hereby is appropriated and granted as a site for a Market during the pleasure of the proper authority and subject to the rules and regulations such Authority may have ordained and established, or shall hereafter ordain and establish.

Given under my Hand at the City of Washington aforesaid this tenth day of November in the Year one thousand eight hundred and two.

Th: Jefferson

[*Letters of the Presidents of the U. S. to the Commissioners of Public Buildings and Grounds*, original in Manuscripts Division, Library of Congress, photostat in National Archives.]

Rt. Smith to Jefferson

Navy Department, 8th *December*, 1802.

Sir:

I have the honor to enclose two copies of a report made to

me by B. H. Latrobe, Esq. on the subject of a dry drock at this place, of a size sufficient to contain twelve frigates of forty-four guns, in which report he mentions the site that would, in his opinion, be the best; the works necessary to be erected, accompanied by drawings, the means of supplying the dock with water, and the probable period it would take to complete the works, to which he has subjoined the necessary estimates, exhibiting the probable cost.

I also enclose two copies of a report made to me by Captain Tingey, in pursuance of instructions to examine the streams of water in the neighborhood.

I have the honor to be, with the greatest respect and esteem, sir, your most obedient servant,

Rt. Smith.

THE PRESIDENT UNITED STATES.

[P. 104, DOCUMENTS, Legislative and Executive, of the Congress of the U. S., AMERICAN STATE PAPERS, Vol. 23.]

NOTE: The report by Latrobe is on pages 105–7, same volume.

LATROBE TO JEFFERSON

EXTRACT OF A LETTER FROM B. HENRY LATROBE
TO THE PRESIDENT DATED

Philadelphia. December 15.th 1802.

Sir/

Capt Dale, of the U.States Navy, called upon me this morning, and in conversation upon the Naval Arsenal or Dry-docks proposed by you to be erected at the Federal City, which he most warmly approved, — he informed me that the Swedish Government had lately concieved the idea of adopting the same means of preserving their Navy in times of peace. The Swedish Admiral Söderstrom described to him the situation of the Dock which was then in the progress of construction. It was intended to contain eight ships of 74. guns, and another was projected to contain 12, in all making provision for 20. ships of the line. The situation was remarkably favorable. Deep water close to a perpendicular rock, which can be easily wrought, gives the opportunity of excavating the Dock, the rock forms the wall, and the roof is laid over, at such a height that the ships go in with their lower masts standing. Capt Dale did not exactly know how the ships were worked into the dock, but from his description of the situation I presume they are tide-docks.

Admiral Söderstrom said, that the vessels were to be washed with fresh-water, perfectly drained, and opened to a circulation of air, and that he had no doubt of their remaining in perfect repair in the dock for a century, and gave many reasons for his opinion which were convincing.

[Copied from ms. *Records of the Senate,* in the National Archives; published in AMERICAN STATE PAPERS, Vol. 23, p. 108.]

THOMAS MUNROE TO JEFFERSON

Superintendent's Office, Washington, December 20, 1802.

Sir:

Pursuant to the sixth section of the act of Congress of last session entitled "An act to abolish the board of commissioners in the city of Washington, and for other purposes," and under your direction of the 16th of June last, I proceeded, with all possible diligence, to prepare a statement of all the lots of the description in the said section mentioned; and on the 19th of that month advertised the same for sale on the 30th day of August then next ensuing; which advertisement was published according to law; and on the day appointed the said sale commenced, and was continued, by adjournment, until the 29th day of October last; during which time the whole of the said lots were sold, and produced the sum of $26,848 10; of which I paid away, agreeably to the fourth section of the above-recited act of Congress, the sum of $2,249 03, (together with $2,563 85, which arose out of other funds of the city,) for debts which had been contracted by the late commissioners in their capacity as such, the payment whereof was not specially provided for by the aforesaid act of Congress; and the balance, to wit, $24,599 07, was applied, as directed by the said act of Congress, towards the payment of the loan of $50,000 by the State of Maryland.

It may not be improper here to mention that very few, if any, of these lots produced, by the resale thereof, the amount of the original purchase money due thereon; that the deficiency is very considerable, and that it is not probable the debtors will be able to pay more than about $10,000 thereof. Some, however, who are deemed able to pay, contend that they cannotbe compelled to make payment, because, they say, the act of the Maryland Legislature of 1793, chap. 58, which authorizes a resale in case of default in payment, does not admit of reselling more than once; and that, if the power of resale be exercised, the original purchaser is not bound for any deficiency, more than once; and that, if the power of resale be exercised, the original purchaser is not bound for any deficiency, as the public or city agent had a choice of two remedies, to wit, a suit or release; and, having elected to resell, they have not a right to use both remedies, and to resort to a suit for the deficiency. This doctrine is particularly insisted on in the case of an endorser of the note of a deceased purchaser, at a resale; in which case a second resale has been made, and a considerable deficiency has in consequence happened. The endorser now says he is ready and willing to pay the amount due on the lots, as purchased by his principal, upon the same being conveyed for his indemnity. Before I adopt any compulsory measure on this subject, I have supposed it to be proper to submit the circumstances for the consideration and opinion of the proper law officer, and to pray the instructions of the President in the premises.

The number of lots which were thrown into the market at

the public sale, directed by the act of Congress before recited, being much greater than the demand, and the positive and unconditional obligation imposed by that act of Congress to sell the whole of them within a limited time, not only subjected those lots to great sacrifices and disadvantages in the sale thereof, but has also materially injured the private sales of all the other public lots, in the sale of which the President might exercise his discretion. Of this description of lots, however, I have sold five, which have produced $1,531 43, cash.

In my accounts from 1st June last to the 1st ultimo, prepared for the Treasury Department, it appears that, in addition to the receipts and expenditures hereinbefore stated, I have received —

From the late board of commissioners, being the balance which remained in their hands when the commission ceased, 1st June last,..	$110 59
For lots purchased prior to 6th May, 1796, voluntarily paid by the purchasers before the public sale on 30th August last,...	1,274 28
For balance of purchase money for lots sold by the commissioners since 6th May, 1796,...............................	109 93
And from sundry persons, for small balances which were due to the city on accounts other than for lots sold,..............	320 73
Making...	$1,815 53

Which has been expended as follows, viz: $374 60 for expenses attending the aforesaid public sale of lots; and $408 51 for other expenses necessarily incurred in the execution of the duties of the office of superintendent; the balance, to wit, $1,032 42, is included in the sum of $2,563 85, hereinbefore stated to have been paid for debts contracted by the commissioners.

The receipts and expenditures since 1st ultimo amount to $36 80 only.

The debts now due to the city, and considered as good, exclusive of the deficiencies on the lots resold for default of payment, amount to upwards of $13,000. Of these deficiencies it is thought (as is before stated) the debtors will be able to pay about $10,000. The property of the city, (besides the debts,) as stated in the representations of the late commissioners to the President, on 28th January, 1801, and 4th December, 1801, estimating the lots at the average prices of those previously sold under the condition of improvement (which were much lower than the unconditional sales by individuals,) amounted to $884,819 88, out of which lots have been since sold to the amount of $9,886 24 only, for about the prices at which they were estimated.

Besides the debts and property before mentioned, there is due to the city (including interest) upwards of $100,000; $80,000 (principal) whereof is for the one thousand lots mentioned in the commissioners' representations to have been conveyed to Messrs. Morris and Greenleaf, under the circumstances therein particularly detailed, and concerning which a bill has been filed in the high Court of Chancery of the State of Maryland. The balance, between 4 and $5,000 principal, is due for valuable water lots, originally bought by James Greenleaf, and resold in the usual manner for default of payment, and for which the second purchaser has always been ready to pay the purchase money, but has been prevented by an injunction of the Chancellor of Maryland, on a bill filed, by Mr. Greenleaf's trustee. This bill, as well as that filed with regard to the one thousand lots, is still pending, and the counsel for the city are of opinion the decisions in both cases will be favorable to the public interest.

The debts due and to become due from the city (except for the advances from the Treasury of the United States, and the two loans by the State of Maryland, of $100,000 each) are very inconsiderable; and it is hoped that the large fund hereinbefore stated (by the future sales of the property being made commensurate only with the demand therefor, agreeably to the provision contained in the 5th section of the before-recited act of Congress) will not only be adequate to the indemnity of the Government for its liberal patronage, but will also yield a surplus for the use of the city.

The state of the public buildings, directed to be reported, is the same as at the last session of Congress, or not materially changed. The private buildings, then seven hundred and thirty-five in number, have since increased a few more than one hundred.

The before-mentioned representations of the commissioners in January and December, 1801, and the documents accompanying them, which were laid before Congress, being very full and minute on the affairs of the city, prior to their respective dates, I beg leave to refer to them; but if there be any thing which you, sir, deem necessary, and which those representations and the present do not embrace, it will afford me much pleasure to communicate it.

I have the honor to be, with sentiments of the greatest respect, sir, your most obedient servant.

THOMAS MUNROE.

THE PRESIDENT OF THE UNITED STATES.

[Pp. 337-8, AMERICAN STATE PAPERS, Miscellaneous, Vol. I; this is the superintendent's report accompanying Jefferson's message to Congress of January 24, 1803.]

JEFFERSON TO CONGRESS

Communicated to Congress, December 28, 1802.

Gentlemen of the Senate and of the House of Representatives;

In my message of the 15th instant, I mentioned that plans and estimates of a dry dock, for the preservation of our ships of war, prepared by a person of skill and experience, should be laid before you without delay: these are now transmitted; the report and estimates by duplicates, but the plans being single only. I must request an inter-communication of them between the Houses, and their return when they shall no longer be wanting for their consideration.

TH: JEFFERSON.

[P. 104, AMERICAN STATE PAPERS, Vol. 23. DOCUMENTS, Legislative and Executive, of the Congress of the United States, from the First Session of the First to the Second Session of the Eighteenth Congress, inclusive: Commencing March 3, 1789, and ending March 5, 1825.]

JEFFERSON PROCLAMATION

BY THE PRESIDENT OF THE UNITED STATES

Whereas by the first Article of the Terms and Conditions declared by the President of the United States on the seventeenth day of October 1791 for regulating the Materials and manner of Buildings and Improvements on the Lots in the City of Washington, it is provided that the outer and party walls of all Houses in the said City, shall be built of Brick or Stone" — and by the third Article of the same terms and Conditions it is declared, that the wall of no house shall be higher than 40 feet to the roof in any part of the City, nor shall any be lower than 35 feet on any of the Avenues; And Whereas the above recited Articles were found to impede the Settlement in the City of Mechanicks and others whose Circumstances did not admit of erecting houses authorized by the said Regulations, for which cause the operation of the said Articles has been suspended by several Acts of the President of the United States from the fifth day of June 1796 to the first day of January 1803 and the beneficial effects arising from such suspensions having been experienced — it is deemed proper to revise the same, with the exception hereafter mentioned. Wherefore I Thomas Jefferson President of the United States do declare that the first and third Articles above recited shall be, and the same are hereby suspended until the first day of January 1804, and that all Houses which shall be erected in the said City of Washington previous to the said first day of January 1804 conformable in other re-

spects to the regulations aforesaid shall be considered as lawfully erected, except that no wooden house covering more than
320 square feet or higher than twelve feet from the Sill to the
Eve shall be erected — nor shall such house be placed within
24 feet of any brick or Stone house.

Given under my hand this 15th January 1803 [50]

TH: JEFFERSON

[*Letters of the Presidents of the U. S. to the Commissioners of Public Buildings and Grounds,* original
in Manuscripts Division, Library of Congress, photostat in National Archives.]

DANIEL BRENT TO WASHINGTON

Washington, January 21, 1803.

Sir:

I now enclose you the account and copies of the contract and
bill of particulars respecting the jail directed at the last session
of Congress to be built in this city.

Although every effort was made to complete the plan adopted
for the sum appropriated, it could not be done; it was then determined to finish only certain parts of the building, and to
keep the amount for such as should be finished within the appropriation. Messrs. Huddlestone and Nesmith contracted to
complete all the building except the interior of the west wing
and the iron grated doors, which were at first contemplated to
be put in for the sum of $7,426; and Mr. George Hadfield,
whose plan was adopted, was appointed to superintend the
erection of the building. An estimate of the sum necessary to
complete the west wing in the same manner as the east wing is
herewith transmitted, which amounts to the sum of $2,577,[51]

[50] This order suspending the original Articles was repeatedly published throughout
Jefferson's administration.
[51] *Estimate of the expense necessary for finishing the interior of the west side of the new jail in the
city of Washington.*

Digging foundation, and removing the earth,.	$34 00
All rough stone work, materials and labor included,.	565 00
All brick work, materials and labor included,.	286 00
All plastering, materials and labor included,.	96 00
All freestone work and lead, stone not included,.	301 00
Finishing pediment,.	13 00
All carpentry and joinery materials, and labor included,.	700 00
All iron work,.	502 00
Clearing away the rubbish from the south side and the ends,.	80 00
	$2,577 00

GEORGE HADFIELD.

leaving out all the iron grated doors. If a kitchen should be built, (and one is absolutely necessary,) the further sum of about $300 will be wanted.

The contractors have completed their work, except a few articles, which will be done. In the sixth article of the contract, it is stipulated, that such alterations or additions to the mode of building the jail as could not be adjusted by the parties, were to be left to reference; some alterations were considered as proper, and directed by the superintendent, and one respecting the cell doors was directed by me. The contractors claim for extra work the sum of $1,098; on this subject, however, there is a considerable difference between the superintendent and them. They claim for many things as extra work which he does not admit to be extra. There is also a difference of opinion between them on the amount of the deduction that ought to be made in the iron work. If he is correct in his opinion, there remains the sum of $449 for extra work only to be examined, which will be seen by a reference to his letter to me, a copy of which is sent.[52] The contractors, under the sixth article of the

[52]

Sir: *City of Washington, January* 19, 1803.

The new jail is now ready for your reception, as completed agreeable to contract, except in a few articles, which the present season has prevented being done, and which, by agreement, may be finished at any future period; for which purpose I shall note them hereafter. The building, I presume, is executed throughout with fidelity to the contract; the execution is plain, but the work is strong, substantial, and firm.

An expense for some extra articles has unavoidably accrued, either for work which

contract, claim a right of reference upon those subjects. If all these claims should be established, and Congress determine to finish the jail and build the kitchen, the sum of $3,702 66, in addition to the sum of $272 34 of the sum appropriated, which is in hand, will be requisite.

When I appointed Mr. Hadfield the superintendent, I agreed to give him for his services the sum of $200, and this is the amount of his claim against me; but he states that he thinks this sum too small a compensation for his trouble. He has, in drawing plans, making out bills of particulars and estimates, and superintending the work, been closely engaged for seven months, so that two dollars per day for his services cannot be thought unreasonable; and I must do Mr. Hadfield the justice to say, that I think the sum of $200 is not a sufficient compensation for his trouble, and I believe he has been very attentive. If it should be thought proper to come up to Mr. Hadfield's idea, the sum of $220 more will be wanted on his account.

With sentiments of the highest respect, I am, sir, your obedient servant,

DANIEL C. BRENT.

THE PRESIDENT

[Pp. 338–9, AMERICAN STATE PAPERS, Miscellaneous. DOCUMENTS, Legislative and Executive, of the Congress of the United States, Vol. I.]

---

has been thought greatly advantageous to the building, or other contingencies not to be foreseen but during the progress of a building; in consequence of which, and also of a clause in the contract providing for additional work, the contractors bring in an extra claim of $962; $253 of which I reject as unfounded; the remainder $709 are for iron work, and other articles ordered for reasons as above mentioned; a deduction in your favor must be made for the omission of the iron frames, which I calculate ought not to amount to less than $260; in which case the remaining sum for extras to be examined would be $449.

I presume, sir, that if you approve of the building, you might receive it, and close the contract with the undertakers, to prevent delay, leaving the business of extra claims to any time afterwards.

I remain your obedient servant,

GEORGE HADFIELD.

D. C. BRENT, ESQ.

JEFFERSON TO CONGRESS

JEFFERSON TO THE SENATE AND HOUSE OF REPRESENTATIVES

January 24, 1803

I transmit a report by the superintendent [Thomas Munroe] of the city of Washington on the affairs of the city committed to his care. By this you will perceive that the resales of lots prescribed by an act of the last session of Congress did not produce a sufficiency to pay the debt to Maryland, to which they were appropriated; and, as it was evident that the sums necessary for the interest and instalments due to that State could not be produced by a sale of the other public lots, without an unwarrantable sacrifice of the property, the deficiencies were of necessity drawn from the treasury of the United States.

The office of surveyor for the city, created during the former establishment, being of indispensable necessity, it has been continued; and to that of the superintendent, substituted instead of the board of commissioners, at the last session of Congress, no salary was annexed by law. These offices being permanent, I have supposed it more agreeable to principle that their salaries should be fixed by the Legislature, and therefore have assigned them none. Their services to be compensated are from the 1st day of June last.

The marshal of the District of Columbia has, as directed by law, caused a jail to be built in the city of Washington. I enclose his statements of the expenses already incurred, and of what remains to be finished. The portion actually completed has renedered the situation of the persons confined much more comfortable and secure than it has been heretofore.

[Pp. 337–38, AMERICAN STATE PAPERS, DOCUMENTS, Legislative and Executive, of the Congress of the U. S., I, 1834; the superintendent's report; also p. 103, DOCUMENTARY HISTORY . . . OF THE CAPITOL.]

DANIEL BRENT TO JEFFERSON

Feby 17.th 1803

Rec.^d Feb. 17

Sir/

It is difficult to ascertain the quantity of stone that can be raised in a given time by a given number of hands, because the rock is buried in the earth from 5 to 15 feet, & it cannot be known whether it is good or will cut well, untill the earth is removed, the removing of which constitutes a considerable portion of the labour in quarrying; & it not infrequently happens that the rock either is not good or will not cut, & the labour & time taken up in removing the earth is lost.

In the year 1797 a company I was concerned in delivered at the City wharf 900 Tons of stone, & I think more than 100 Tons remained in the quarry — this was done by about 26 hands, hired by the year, includeing, in that number, 2 Overseers, 1 blacksmith & his striker, 1 cooke, 1 shipper & 3 watermen; in addition to this labour we, in the summer hired hands by the month. Not haveing the weekly returns of the hands here, I cannot state the amount of this labour, but from my best recollection I am *confident* it did not exceed that of 10 hands by the year, & I think less than that of five. —

It is proper to observe: that every thing was well prepared to commence with the year — no time was lost, that the hands hired by the year were well experienced in quarrying, & were chosen from the best of those who had been accustomed to that work — that I think as many equally good hands cannot be got at present that more stone cou'd then be raised in that quarry, than any other on Aquia creek, as there was less dirt to remove, & the stone cut better — I have writ to Virginia on this subject & so soon as the answers return you shall know the result. I have to apologize for not sending in this evening, but,

I was kept up almost the whole of Tuesday night. with mo^t respect I am Sir Y^r Ob^t Servt

DANIEL C. BRENT

[Ms. *Jefferson Papers*, Library of Congress.]

JEFFERSON TO LATROBE

THE PRESIDENT TO BENJAMIN H. LATROBE

March 6, 1803

Sir: Congress has appropriated a sum of $50,000, to be applied to the public buildings under my direction. This falls, of course, under the immediate business of the superintendent, Mr. Munroe, whose office is substituted for that of the board of commissioners. The former post of surveyor of the public buildings, which Mr. Hoban held until the dissolution of the board at [$1,700 a year], will be revived.

If you choose to accept it, you will be appointed to it, and would be expected to come on by the 1st of April. Indeed, if you could make a flying trip here to set contractors at work immediately in raising freestone, it would be extremely important, because it is now late to have to engage laborers, and the quantity of freestone which can be raised, delivered, and cut in the season is the only thing that will limit the extent of out operations this year.

I set out to-morrow for Monticello, and shall be absent three weeks, but shall be glad to receive there your answer to this.

Accept my friendly salutations and regards.

P.S. — On the raising of freestone be pleased to consult Col. D. H. Brent, who can give you better information and advice on the subject than any other person whatever, having been much concerned in the business himself.

[Glenn Brown, HISTORY OF THE UNITED STATES CAPITOL, I, 32.]

JEFFERSON TO LATROBE

THE PRESIDENT TO BENJAMIN H. LATROBE

March 6, 1803

Dear Sir: The letter in which this is inclosed being a public one, and to be produced whenever necessary as a voucher, I have thought that it would be useful to add a word in one of a private and friendly nature. From the sum of $50,000 we shall take between $5,000 and $10,000 for covering the north wing of the Capitol and the President's House.

The residue of $40,000 to $45,000 will be employed in building the south wing, as far as it will go. I think it will raise the external walls as far as the uppermost window sills, being those of the entresols, and I have no doubt Congress at their next session will give another $50,000, which will complete that wing inside and out in the year 1804 . . . Should you think proper to undertake it, if you come on here on a flying trip, as suggested in my other letter, you can advise with Mr. Munroe, who will set into motion whatever you may desire, and if you can be here finally the first week in April you will find me here, and everything may be put under full sail for the season.

Accept my best wishes and respects.

P.S. — I think a great deal of sheet iron will be wanting.

[Glenn Brown, HISTORY OF THE UNITED STATES CAPITOL, I, 32–33.]

THOMAS MUNROE TO JEFFERSON

Washington 14th *March* 1803

Sir,

I recd, on the 10th Instant, the Letter which you did me the honor to write from Col Wrens on the 7th — We are proceeding with diligence in our operations on Pennsylvania Avenue according to your directions. It seems to be a very general opinion here that without the trees are boxed, or otherwise protected from the horses and cattle a great many, if not all of them will be barked and destroyed — several instances have been pointed out to me where they were planted last year, and all destroyed.

A man near the Avenue says he had twenty or thirty destroyed by a neighours horse in one night — I should not myself suppose that we should lose more in that way than we could easily replace —. Do you, Sir, think that a coat of whitewash, which I am told they give to the young trees in the English Deer Parks would have any good effect, or be advisable as a protection against cattle? A person who thinks boxing absolutely necessary says each tree will cost One dollar, when completed, that is, the tree itself, planting, boxing painting and box, and doing everything else relating to it. —

The Stakes to tie the trees to, which it is said will probably cost nearly as much as the trees, would as is said, be unnecessary, if boxes were used, but the expense of boxing would I imagine be at least double.

Dr Thornton, Mr King and myself have conversed on the manner of laying off the lines and planting the trees — The three modes illustrated by the enclosed sections — were suggested — I mentioned the plan No. 3 as the one which I believed you had designed, and would, I thought, adopt, but as no inconvenience would arise from the delay of submitting the other two plans to you I got Mr King to make the sketch — The row on each side of the footways nearest the Houses which we are proceeding in will at all events be right and comfortable to either plan — I shall get the trees from Mount Vernon, and Genl Masons Island & I expect from the samples I have seen, they will be of a good size, price twelve & a half Cents each. Genl Mason is one of those who think they will not do without boxes.

I have just recd the enclosed letter from the Committee Appointed at a meeting of the Contributors to the Theatre contemplated to be built here They are very anxious, on acct. of the building season having arrived, to receive an answer so soon as the convenience of the President and the important subjects of his consideration will admit — The spot solicited is that coloured yellow in the space called "Bank square" in the sketch herewith sent. — Perhaps part of the public ground on the south side of the Avenue nearly opposite would suit as well or better as a grant of the site asked for may be objectionable on the ground of its having been generally supposed to be designed for another purpose. — I have taken the liberty of forwarding herewith a plan of the City as it is possible you might not have one at Monticello.

I Have the Honor to be with perfect respect & Consideration, Sir,

> Yr mo Ob Servt
>
> THOMAS MUNROE

PRESIDENT OF THE UNITED STATES

[Pp. 277–8, U. S. v. SMITH.]

JEFFERSON TO LATROBE

March 15. 1803.

Sir

The legislature of the US. having made provision for the repairs and construction of the public buildings at Washington it becomes necessary to revive the office of Surveyor of the public buildings who was formerly charged with the immediate direction of them under the superintendance of the board of Commissioners. You are therefore hereby appointed to that office with the salary of seventeen hundred Dollars a year which was allowed to him, to commence from this day.

> TH: JEFFERSON

TO B. HENRY LATROBE ESQ.

[Ms., *Jefferson Papers*, Library of Congress.]

JEFFERSON TO THOMAS MUNROE

Monticello Mar. 21. 1803.

Dear Sir

Your letter of the 14.th was recieved on the 18.th and this goes by the return of the first post, that which brought it not affording time for an answer. N.º 2. in the draught m.^r King was so kind as to send me is exactly what Dr Thornton explained to me as the original design except that he did not mention the two middle rows of trees but only the two outer ones on each side. and, omitting the two middle rows, I think this the best design. it will then stand thus.

one reason of preference is that this agrees with the present disposition of the Pensylvania avenue. it will allow us also next autumn either to plant our oaks, elms &^c in the same lines with the lombardy poplars, giving to these trees of large growth a distance suitable to their size, or we may plant them midway at a.a. so as to make a shaded mall of 41. f. breadth, or pass a canal along the middle at a.a. at a future day, or a gravel walk, or anything we please. as you have already planted the rows b.b. you will therefore be pleased to plant c.c. at 33. f. distance from b.b. or at 4. f. distance from the gutters. The stakes may be omitted, and as my return will be so soon, the boxing or other guard may then be the subject of consultation.

Until the organisation of the district of Columbia, when a better directory for the city than the President of the U. S. will probably be provided, I am unwilling to do any thing which will bear delay, and especially to change any original destination of the public grounds. and as I shall be with you within one week after you recieve this, the object of the committee for the Theatre shall be considered immediately on my return. be pleased to mention this to them and to accept my friendly salutations.

TH: JEFFERSON

M.ᴿ MUNROE

[Ms. *Jefferson Papers*, Library of Congress.]

JEFFERSON TO CARROL, DANIEL BRENT, AND MINIFIE

Washington May 28. 1803

Gentlemen

I have received your letter of the 24ᵗʰ proposing the application of any public monies that may be under my controul & which could with propriety be so used, to the improvement of the Pensylvania avenue from the capitol to the bridge now to be built over the Eastern branch. the funds of the city formerly applicable to such objects, are now appropriated by law to the reimbursement of the monies lent by the US. to the Commissioners. the only remaining fund under my direction, which has any relation to the city, is the sum of 50,000 D. appropriated by a law of the last session to 'such repairs or alterations in the capitol & other public buildings as may be necessary etc. and also for keeping in repair the *highway between* the capitol & other public buildings.' these are the words of the law, and you will be sensible that they are descriptive of the Pensylvania avenue between the capitol & the public buildings on the President's square exactly, and of no other highways, and as they were expressly explained to me by the member who moved the insertion of these words, and by others. sincerely desirous of promoting the interests of the city and of Georgetown (for their contiguity & other circumstances identify them in their relation to the government) I should have been happy to have it in my power to improve their communications with each other & with the country round about them: but no such power has been given to me. Accept assurances of my great respect & consideration.

TH: JEFFERSON

DAN.ᴸ CARROL of Dudⁿ.⎫
DAN. BRENT   ⎬ Esquires. Directors of the Eastern
CHAˢ MINIFIE   ⎭   branch bridge co.

[Ms., *Jefferson Papers*, Library of Congress.]

NICHOLAS KING TO JEFFERSON

TO THE PRESIDENT OF THE UNITED STATES

Surveyor's Office, 25th *September*, 1803.

Sir:

The act of Congress establishing the temporary and permanent seat of the government of the United States, and the deeds of trust from the proprietors of the lands on which the city of Washington is located, having given to the President the power, and left to his judgment the manner of laying out the city, I take the liberty of presenting a statement of the progress made in the surveying department, and in the execution of the plan; also, the difficulties or obstructions which have occurred, and what appears to be yet necessary to be done under the trust and powers vested.

The subject is important to those who have conveyed their property on special trusts, and to the purchasers of lots, which have either been assigned to the original proprietors, or to the public, and by them sold. And it becomes necessary to have a recurrence to many of the early transactions in the city, since the sources of most of the present difficulties may be traced to that period.

The act of Congress for establishing the temporary and permanent seat of the government of the United States, which passed on the 16th of July, 1790, and the act to amend the same, passed on the 3d March, 1791, direct the location of the district. They authorized the President to appoint commissioners, who, under his direction, were to survey and define its limits; they give power to purchase or accept such quantity of land on the eastern side of the Potomac, as the President should deem proper, for the use of the United States; and according to such plans as the President should approve, the Commissioners were to provide suitable buildings for the accommodation of Congress. For defraying the expense of such purchases and buildings, the President is, by these acts, authorized to accept grants of money.

After locating the district, the President proceeded to fix on a place within its limits for the immediate residence of the Government, and the sites for public buildings. He selected the most eligible situation, determined the extent required for the city, and met the proprietors of the lands it covered at Georgetown on the 12th April, 1791, where he made them certain proposals, and explained his ideas on the subject. The owners of the lands generally came into the measure; and an agreement was drawn up and signed, which formed the basis of the deeds of trust, which they separately executed almost immediately afterwards to Thomas Beall, of George, and John M. Gantt.

By these deeds the proprietors conveyed all their lands within the proposed limits for a Federal city, to be laid out with such streets, squares, parcels, and lots, as the President of the United States should approve.

The trustees were directed to convey to the commissioners and their successors in office, "for the use of the United States, forever, all the said streets, and such of the said squares, parcels and lots as the President should deem proper, for the use of the United States." The residue of the lots into which the lands conveyed should be laid off, are directed to be divided equally — one half to be assigned to the original proprietor of the land, the other moiety "to be sold at such time or times and on such terms and conditions as the President of the United States, for the time being, shall direct." And the produce of the sale of the said lots, when sold as aforesaid, in the first place to be applied to the payment in money for so much of the land as might be appropriated to the use of the United States, at the rate of 25 pounds per acre, not accounting streets as part thereof. This being so paid, or in any other manner satisfied, "then the produce of the same sales or what thereof may remain as aforesaid, in money or securities of any kind, shall be paid, assigned, transferred and delivered over to the President for the time being, as a grant of money, and to be applied for the purposes, and according to the act of Congress aforesaid." Another of the trusts in, that the proprietors shall retain the grounds on which their farm buildings stand, if the arrangements of the streets, &c., allow it, on paying therefor at the same rate they were to receive for the lands appropriated to the use of the United States. The proprietors also reserved to themselves the timber and wood growing on their grounds, except such as the President thought proper to retain, and for which they were to receive a compensation.

On the 19th December, 1791, the Legislature of Maryland passed an act concerning the Territory of Columbia and city of Washington, subjecting the lands of all other persons in the city, to the same terms and conditions as those conveyed by Notley Young and others, in trust to T. Beall and Jno. M. Gantt; and directing the mode of division where parties do not attend or are otherwise incapacitated from making the division with the commissioners. The fifth section declares "that all the squares, lots, pieces and parcels of land within the said city which shall have been or shall be appropriated for the use of the United States, and also the streets shall remain and be for the use of the United States; and all the lots and parcels which have been, or shall be, sold to raise money, as a donation as aforesaid, shall remain and be to the purchasers according to the terms and conditions of their respective purchases. And the twelfth section gives to the Commissioners, for the time being, "until Congress shall exercise jurisdiction within the District," the power to license the building of wharves in the waters of the Potomac and the Eastern Branch, adjoining the said city; of the materials, in the manner and extent they may judge durable, convenient, and agreeing with general order. But no license to build a wharf before the land of another, nor any wharf to be built in said waters, without license, or different therefrom. It also gave them the power to make regulations for the discharge and laying of ballast from the ships lying in the Potomac, above the lower line of the territory, and Georgetown, and in the Eastern Branch. Also, for landing and laying materials for building the said city, for disposing and laying earth dug out of wells, cellars and foundations, and for ascertaining the thickness of the walls of houses, and for enforcing the same by penalties, to be collected and applied as a donation, under the act of Congress.

These recited acts of Congress and of the Assembly of Maryland, with the deeds of trust, are the sources of authority under which the President and Commissioners have acted in laying off the District of Columbia and the city of Washington.

Previous to the meeting of the President with the proprietors of the lands in Georgetown, measures have been taken by him for the location of the city; the ground had been surveyed, and a plan, or the outlines and principal features thereof, made by Major L'Enfant. For, in a letter written by Messrs. Scott and Thornton, two of the commissioners then in the city, to Mr. White, the other commissioner, then in Philadelphia, dated 16th March, 1798, and in answer to one by which Mr. White communicated to them the opinion of President Adams, in favor of placing the executive offices near the Capitol, they say: "When the late President of the United States called together the original proprietors who granted the soil on which the Federal city was to be erected, he laid before them a plan with the present appropriation for the Capitol and President's House, and the offices of the several Departments contiguous to the latter; and, under the faith of these appropriations, thus publicly declared, the proprietors agreed to make the several grants which afterwards took place. These two appropriations, viz: for the Capitol and President's House, the only ones made until the year 1796, were published on the engraved plan, promulgated by the President, and were declared to be sanctioned by him at all the public sales at the early periods of the city." "When the President has under the deed of trust, once executed his power, by establishing a public appropriation how far he can afterwards change or abolish it, or how far a court of equity will countenance and sanction sales, made by the Commissioners, of lots apparently contiguous to some great national building, which is afterwards abolished or changed by the President, are questions worthy of consideration, and will no doubt, be weighed before they are acted upon."

The appointment of the first commissioners took place in January, 1791. They proceeded to the survey, and planted the corner-stone of the District at Jones' Point, on the 15th of April, after which they directed the staking and laying off, on the ground, the plan of the Federal City; the appropriations for public use, and squares for buildings, commencing with those parts most immediately wanted for public buildings, or for division with the proprietors and sale. The following advertisement was published by them, dated Georgetown, 30th June, 1791:

"The President having approved the sites of ground for the public buildings, to be erected in pursuance of the act of Congress for establishing the temporary and permanent seat of the

Government of the United States, the commissioners appointed
in virtue of that act will meet at Georgetown, on Thursday, the
17th of October, next and proceed to sell, at vendue, a number
of lots in the best situations in the city," &c.

While preparing for this sale, Mr. Ellicott, the acting surveyor under Major L'Enfant, presented, on the 8th September,
1791, some observations respecting it. He dissuades them from
making the first sales in the immediate vicinity of the President's House and Capitol, as that property would increase in
value by the erection of the public buildings, and advises them
to sell between the President's House and Georgetown, and in
Funkstown, and on the Eastern Branch, where a town and
navigable waters presented great inducements to purchasers.
On the 17th of October, 1791, the squares No. 128 (166 on the
engraved plan,) 127, 105, 106, 77, 78 and 79, were divided between the commissioners and proprietors. Other squares in
that neighborhood were also divided about the same time.

On the 8th of September certain queries, respecting the city
and territory, were discussed by the Commissioners and the
Secretary of State, and decided upon. The day following, the
commissioners wrote to Mr. L'Enfant, (then in Philadelphia,
preparing the plan for publication,) informing him of the name
of the city and territory; how the streets on the map were to be
designated, and requesting him to show on it the post road. In
a post-script to the letter, it is added "if you have no contrary
directions, we wish 10,000 of the maps to be struck, on the best
terms, and as soon as possible, leaving any number the President pleases to his order. One half of the residue to be left in
Philadelphia, and the other half transmitted to us." On the
24th of the month the commissioners came to a resolve "that
Major L'Enfant be instructed to direct 300 copies of the plan of
the Federal City to be transmitted to such parts of the Northern
States as he shall think proper, and that he keep the remainder,
subject to the directions of the President."

The public sale of lots advertised by the commissioners commenced on the 17th of October, and continued on the 18th and 19th, when lots were sold in the squares No. 78, 79, or 101, 105, 107, 126 and 127. At this sale plats of that portion of the city were shown to the purchasers, with the President's square delineated thereon, to prove the eligibility of situation, and appreciate the property sold. As soon as the sales had closed (21st October, 1791,) the commissioners informed the President thereof by letter, stating the prices and amount of lots sold, and that they had consulted Major L'Enfant and Mr. Ellicott as to the time against which things would be in readiness for another sale. "They expected it to be in the middle or last of June, though we wish it to be earlier, because of the ideas strangers have of coming southward so late as July. Yet it is our present intention not to publish a further sale till we see the *plate in circulation*, and the work so far completed that everybody may have a chance for the object of their choice, and no way have cause of complaint that the whole circumstances are not before them. We have been under some difficulties from the imperfect state furnished and which has subsisted, but we wish to avoid the like in future."

When the President met the National Legislature on the 25th of October, 1791, he made the following communication to them on the subject of the District, in the speech he delivered:

"Pursuant to the authority contained in the several acts on that subject, a district of ten miles square, for the permanent seat of the Government of the United States, has been fixed and announced by proclamation; which District will comprehend lands on both sides of the river Potomac, and the towns of Alexandria and Georgetown. A city has also been laid out agreeably to a plan, which will be placed before Congress, and as there is a prospect, favored by the rate of sales which have already taken place, of ample funds for carrying on the necessary public buildings, there is every expectation of their due progress."

This plan was placed before Congress during the session, as appears by the following accompanying communication or message:

United States, Dec. 13th, 1791.

"Gentlemen of the Senate and of the House of Representatives:

"I place before you a plan of the city that has been laid out within the district of ten miles square which was fixed upon for the permanent seat of the Government of the United States.

"GEO. WASHINGTON."

At this time Mr. L'Enfant was in Philadelphia, and the field operations carried on in the city by his agents. Under an impression of being insubordinate to the commissioners, and employed by the President to carry the plan into execution, he seldom consulted the board in its progress, but gave what he considered proper instructions to those in his employ during his absence. Serious differences arose between them as to the extent of their powers; they came to a crisis in January, 1792, while Mr. L'Enfant was in Philadelphia. His agent Mr. Roberdeau, was compelled by the commissioners to desist from digging the foundation of the Capitol, commenced under the Major's orders, and discharged from the public employ.

Mr. L'Enfant's irritation at this conduct led to his dismissal, and prevented the publication of that plan by which the operations in the city had been till then conducted. In this disadvantageous predicament, Mr. Ellicott was instructed by the President to prepare a plan for publication, using such materials as he possessed, and the information he had acquired while acting as surveyor in the city. Major L'Enfant having refused to give up the original plan, a plan was drawn by himself and brothers, without Mr. L'Enfant's aid, and ready for engraving by the 14th of March, 1792. He informed the commissioners that it differed from the plan acted upon in some instances, but, in his opinion, was more adapted to the nature of the ground. Two copies of this plan were placed in the hands of the engravers, one in Boston the other in Philadelphia, and every exertion made to have the printed copies in circulation previous to the sale of lots contemplated in the summer of that year. While the plan by Mr. Ellicott was in a state of progression, several alterations from Mr. L'Enfant's plan, which proceeding in the survey suggested, were proposed to the President, and which he disapproved, as appears by a letter from the Secretary of State to the commissioners, dated the 20th of April.

The first proof sheet from the Boston plate was transmitted to the Commissioners early in July, and considerable uneasiness existed with them a month afterwards, on account of not having received the plans. The Boston impressions only could be exhibited at the second public sale of lots which commenced in October, 1792, as it was the 13th of November before the Philadelphia plans were in Washington.

The difference between these engraved plans and that of Major L'Enfant's could not be generally known farther than in the immediate vicinity of the sales made in October, 1791, for no more of the plan was then communicated to the purchasers than was necessary to show the situation relatively to the appropriation for the President's House, and have an influence on their value. It was the only public ground near the lots then exposed for sale, and lay principally in the hands of Mr. Samuel Davidson. He, therefore, was the only proprietor whose interest was known to be effected to any extent by the alterations made in the plan. Certain squares were omitted, which existed in the plan by which the first sales were made, and which the President of the United States had communicated to Congress as the plan of the city. Other squares, for building lots, although retained in Mr. Ellicott's plan, were curtailed considerably in extent. These deviations were by Mr. Davidson considered as infractions of the compact made from the Executive, and ommissions which Mr. Ellicott was not justified in, after the public faith was pledged by the first sales, by the maps then exhibited, and by the declaration of the President to Congress. He contended that this act of the President was the full execution of the trust vested in him by the deeds to declare the squares wanted for the use of the United States, particularly as no intimation of such change was given to him, but on the contrary possession of the President's square was actually and formally taken by the commissioners under L'Enfant's plan, and prior to Mr. Ellicott's undertaking to make one. One half of the lots or squares so omitted were his under the deed of trust, and the most valuable of his lands. He therefore protested against the alteration when the plans came to hand, and has ever since claimed the re-introduction of them agreeably to the first plan. That his claim might receive no injury by the property coming into other hands, at the public sale in October, 1792, he divided with the commissioners the squares adjoining the appropriation by whole squares instead of lots, as was at that time customary. The squares numbered 167 and 186 were assigned to him as original proprietor, and the squares numbered 221 and 200 were declared subject to sale under the deed of trust. At the sale square No. 221 was offered, and although so large an original proprietor he became the purchaser. The square No. 200 was sold at private sale after the close of the public sale, in single lots and at different times. On the settlement of the account between Mr. Davidson and the commissioners, in 1794, the annexed instrument was executed. (A.)

No determination on Mr. Davidson's claim has yet been had, though so material to him and the public. Remaining in the present state deprives him of the use or disposal of his adjoining property, and retards the improvement of one of the most eligible parts of the city.

For the elucidation of this dispute, I annex the following plats or sections. No. 1, copy of part of a plan supposed to be that sent to Congress, and received by the late Commissioners from the Secretary of State's office. No. 2, copy of a plan shown at the first sales. No. 3, copy of part of a plan in my office, said to be taken from Mr. L'Enfant's plan as executed on the ground by Mr. Hallet, an architect at that time, employed by the commissioners; and No. 4, a plan of the President's square, agreeably to Mr. Davidson's claim.

The publication of the engraved plans was considered by the Executive as "giving the final and regulating stamp to the city of Washington," defining the limits of property, and exhibiting the advantages and choice of situations to those who by purchase or otherwise should become interested in the future Metropolis of the Union.

It was circulated by the commissioners in the United States as the plan of the city; it was forwarded to most nations of Europe from the office of State, and through the agents of the United States. In the sales made by the commissioners in their negotiations for loans for the purpose of carrying on the public buildings, this plan was exhibited, and referred to and the advantageous disposition of the streets, the appropriations for the United States and for the city were held forth as inducements to purchasers, and examples of its superiority over the other cities in the United States, as regarding the convenience and health of the citizens, or the beauty and ornament of the place.

The specific appropriations, or the uses to which these appropriations were to be applied, appeared in Major L'Enfant's plan, but are not put upon the engraved plan, except for the Capitol and President's house. Yet in the sales that have been made, both by the commissioners and the original proprietors, the designation of these spaces have been spoken of as inducements to purchasers, many of whom have selected their property accordingly.

In a letter from the commissioners to Mr. Ellicott, dated in June, 1792, they informed him of the postponement of the public sale to the 8th of October, much later than they had contemplated, partly to give time for the completion of a greater progress of the work, and because "they were anxious that everybody may be able to procure their fancy as to any part of the city."

In the progress of laying off the city on the ground very many alterations from the engraved plan have been made, and most of them since the large sales to Greenleaf and Morris, and the public sales in 1792, when that plan was put into circulation. — (D) Upwards of one hundred and thirty building squares have been introduced, which are not in the published plans, lying generally in those open spaces at the intersection of avenues and streets. Besides taking away much of the characteristic beauty of the plan, they deprive a great number of the lots of the advantages which these open areas gave. They had been generally inserted to gratify proprietors, to whom the acquisition of an additional lot was more desirable than either the beauty or health of the city, to which these open spaces would have so much contributed. Besides the introduction of new squares, numberless other alterations have been made in the number and direction of the streets, the dimensions of the building squares and public appropriations. Many of the latter have been contracted, either by introducing new building squares upon them, or extending the fronts of those by which they are surrounded. The alteration in the President's square is the only one which took place previous to the publishing of the plan, and that was to the disadvantage of the proprietor; the other alterations are since the publication, and give the proprietors a greater number of building lots than the plan contemplated.

Although the engraved plans, as well as Major L'Enfant's, carried the streets to the navigable water, exhibiting how the improvements and streets on the flats, which must be filled up to arrive at the channel, were to take place, it has been laid out upon the ground and acted upon in sales no farther than the bank of the river. As it regards the future health of the city, the convenience of the mercantile interest, and the designation of the limits of property, and the rights acquired by purchasers of lots in the vicinity of the water, it is of importance that this part of the plan be established before many wharves are built, or much property involved in the decision. It will be observed that all the plans exhibit a street in front of the building squares, beyond which wharves only are allowed. In the plan engraved at Boston, this line of the street is shown, but the extent of the building squares between it and the bank of the river are left open for decision as the laying off the city progressed. In the Philadelphia plate, the plan is perfected to the channel, and those squares defined.

That there should be one continued street on the water side of the city, in which the others terminate, beyond which no house or building which may impede the access of air, or be the cause of a nuisance, will be allowed, seems of indispensable necessity in this climate and the permanent seat of the Government. To the neglect of this precaution, many intelligent men attribute those autumnal fevers which ravage our seaports, and suspend commercial industry in the most favorable time of the year. The Maryland Legislature gave to the commissioners, until the assumption of jurisdiction by Congress, extensive powers on this subject. It excited considerable attention in 1795, for, in the month of February, in a letter to Governor T. Johnson, the commissioners say, "the board have already informed you, by their letter from Georgetown, of the 15th instant, of their determination to suspend any further sales on square west of square 4, until they see the President, or know his determination on a Water street on Rock Creek." On this subject, nothing was decisively done, from the publication of the plan in 1792, to July 1795. In laying off the city they stopped, as before observed, on the bank of the river; sold the lots on the high ground with a water privilege, without defining either what the privilege is, or the extent or direction in which the purchasers were to wharf and improve.

On the 20th of July, 1795, the commissioners published the regulations (B,) which instead of defining, have thrown additional obstacles in the way. The permission there given to wharf and build as far as those interested please, not interfering with the channel, may subject the city to all the evils of docks, slips, and receptacles of filth, which ought to be so carefully guarded against, and which the published plan did prevent. For, although the squares on the ground and vicinity of the river, as they have been divided and sold, differ in many respects from the engraved plan, yet that plan establishes the principle of a Water street, beyond which wharfs only, but no buildings can be erected; and, as no channel line has been fixed, or depth of water to wharf to, the regulation is incompetent to benefit the city. Persons wharfing are directed to leave a space for a street wherever the general plan of the city requires it, yet the engraved plan has been so far departed from as to be useless as a guide, while the office plans have never been carried to the extent necessary to determine where those spaces for streets must be. The regulations further direct that where no streets intersect the wharf, the maker of it shall leave a space of 60 feet at the termination of every 300 feet of made ground. Whether these 60 feet streets are in addition to those in the engraved, or some other plan, cannot by individuals be ascertained, nor would the Board of Commissioners ever give information on the subject. Besides, the purchasers never knew where these 300 feet were to be measured from, for if it were from the last street on the land, it would not agree with other streets which are laid out; if from the shore or bank of the river, as the words "made ground" imply, the street would have all the indentings and curves of the bank. In some places it would be on the edge of the channel, at others in the channel; or, where there is a great distance from the bank to the deep water, there may be a considerable space to wharf and build upon, beyond the street directed to be left.

In the month of October, two of the Board of Commissioners gave permission to Mr. Barry to build upon and occupy exclusively that part of Georgia avenue in front of square 771, notwithstanding the regulations they had so recently made. — (C.) An inspection of any of the maps will show the importance of this avenue to the commercial interests of the city. Its continuation is designated on them, and the quantity of earth from eastern fork of the canal, which must be there deposited, will make it all firm ground. This act of the board was protested against by one of the members. — (C.) Notwithstanding the permission given to Mr. Barry, the commissioners in other instances, deny their power to do so. (See their letter to Mr. Law, on the 30th November, 1795, a copy of which is subjoined, E.) In the year 1798, there was a farther change in the opinion of the Board, for, in answer to the request made by the attorney of Mr. Peter, (one of the original proprietors of lands in the city lying on the Potomac, near Georgetown,) to know the extent of wharfing and water privileges attached to what were called water lots, and assigned to him on division, they say: "When the Commissioners have proceeded to divide a square with a city proprietor, whether water or other property, they have executed all the powers vested in them to act upon the subject. It appertains to the several courts of the State and of the United States to determine upon the rights which such division may give; any decision by us on the subject would be extrajudicial and nugatory." It is unnecessary to comment on sentiments like these, or state their effect on the minds of persons wishing to improve, yet cautious as to title, and the rights they acquire.

Perfecting this part of the plan, so as to leave nothing for conjecture, litigation, or doubt, in the manner which shall

most accord with the published plans, secure the health of the
city, and afford the most general convenience to the merchants,
requires immediate attention. The extent of the powers yet
unexecuted, and the consequence of the official acts of the Commissioners will require some consideration.

A few remarks, which an attentive examination of the plans,
existing circumstances, and what appears to be the permanent
interest of the city have suggested, are here respectfully submitted, under an impression of their utility in any decision
which may take place.

Whether the malignant fever, to which the large towns situated on the navigable waters of the United States are frequently
subjected, are of local origin or imported is not, as it relates to
this city, a fact of so much importance as that generally conceded of its propagation and virulence, depending upon the
state of the atmosphere. That it is invariably most alarming
and destructive in those situations which become the receptacle
of the filth of the city, whether brought by the rain along the
streets, or discharged through the common sewers. It is in the
vicinity of the water, where the docks, slips, and other artificial
obstructions to the regular and free current or stream of the
river, retain the accumulated filth between the wharves that the
air is vitiated. The mud and faeces are there exposed to the
putrifying heat of the mid-day sun, for even at high water there
is no current to carry it off into the stream. This erroneous
mode of wharfing seems to have been introduced when immediate interest only was considered, and without an anticipa-
tion of the growth and population to which the towns were
destined to arrive. The dreadful consequences are now suffered,
when a radical cure will be attended with enormous expense.
Happy may it be for the future inhabitants of the city of Washington if it profit by the experience of others, and before it is too
late, adopt a system of improving the waters property, which,
without lessening the commercial advantages of the plan, shall

effectually remove the impurities brought into the river.

The principle adopted in the engraved plan, if carried into effect and finally established in the plan now laid out upon the ground, when aided by proper regulations as to the materials and mode of constructing wharves for vessels to lay at and discharge their cargoes on, seems well calculated to preserve the purity of the air.

The other streets of the city will here terminate in a street or key, open to the water, and admitting a free current of air. It will form a general communication between the wharves and warehouses of the different merchants; and, by facilitating intercourse, render a greater service to them than they would derive from a permission to wharf and build at pleasure. The position of this Water street being determined, it will ascertain the extent and situation of the building squares and streets on the made ground, from the bank of the river, and bring the present as near to the published plan as now can be done. It will define the extent and privileges of water lots, and enable the owners to improve without fear or infringing on the rights of others.

Along the water side of this street the free current or stream of the river should be permitted to flow, and carry with it whatever may have been brought from the city along the streets or sewers. The wharves permitted beyond this street to the channel may be stages or bridges with piers, and sufficient waterways under them. And on the wharves so erected it would seem proper to prohibit the erection of houses, or anything obstructing a free circulation of air.

Annexed are the following explanatory maps:

No. 5. The plan first published from the Boston plate, and circulated at the sales made in the fall of the year 1792.

No. 6. The plan from the plate engraved in Philadelphia, and published shortly after the other.

No. 7. Another of the Philadelphia engraved plans, on which

is exhibited the alterations from that part of L'Enfant's plan where the sales were first made; the alterations which have been made since the publication of it by the Commissioners; and that part of the city, in the vicinity of the water, where the Commissioners have declined acting or establishing it, and which yet remains to be done.

No. 8. A map transmitted by the proprietors to the executive, showing the state in which the map was left by the Commissioners, in the vicinity of the Eastern Branch, as a proof of the necessity of some other determination being had on the subject than the published regulations.

On the introduction of new building squares, (not the public appropriations,) which have been laid out by the Commissioners since the publication of the engraved plan, the alterations in the situation of the canal, and the number and direction of streets, I can only observe that however it may have mutilated the design and lessened the advantages of the plan, there seems a necessity for retaining them, for the squares have been divided with the proprietors, placed on record, and in many instances sold to many individuals unconscious of doubts existing as to the powers of those by whom they were laid off. To strike them out of the present plan might be highly injurious to individuals, without being attended with an equivalent advantage to the city. Their introduction has been so inimical to the faith pledged by the circulation of the printed plans, as to call for the establishment of a final and complete plan, from which no future deviation can be made to gratify individual proprietors, at the expense of former purchasers or the health of the citizens. These spacious avenues and streets and open areas or public spaces, at the intersection of streets and avenues, (so ornamental and conducive to the purity of the air,) which yet remain ought to be forever secured to the city.

The extensive appropriations for the public buildings of the United States and the city, for public walks, markets and other important purposes ought to be held agreeably to the intention of the donors, and the views with which they were selected, in order to acquire and secure the public confidence, so necessary to our growth and prosperity. This can only be done by the President or Congress sanctioning a definitive map. The surveying is now so far completed that it can be done with the utmost precision, and every foot of ground within the limits of the Federal city, with its appurtenant privileges, may be so defined as to prevent litigation or doubt on the subject. If it is not done at this time the evils will increase and every year add to our difficulties. Even now, from the various decisions or neglects, alterations or amendments which have heretofore taken place, some time and investigation may be necessary in the arrangement of a system which shall combine justice with convenience. If this decision is left to a future period and our courts of law, they can have only a partial view of the subject, and any general rule they may adopt may be attended with serious disadvantages.

I am, sir, with the greatest respect, yours truly,

NICHOLAS KING,
Surveyor of the City of Washington.

[Pp. 297–310, U. S. *v.* MORRIS, Vol. 6.]

BLAGDEN TO JEFFERSON

The mode stone cutters practice fore the valuation
of columns, in stone similar to that got at Aquia

1st   The stone in a quarried state per foot cube

Add Workmanship	$	
Base if the Attic.............	1/40	per foot superficial
if tuscan..............	1/ —	d°
Capital...............	1/40 —	d°

Shaft suppose in three pieces. first block including cincture and third the astragal at $/50 per foot Super.

Fore the circumferance of base girt the upper toras and capital the upper part of Avolo

Girt the shaft at bottom and that multiplied into the height including cincture and astragal

The above prices is fore a column of two feet diameter, setting will be an extra expence.

GEO BLAGDEN

Washington

27 Sept.ʳ 1803

[TO THE PRESIDENT]

[Ms., *Jefferson Papers*, Library of Congress.]

STODDERT TO JEFFERSON

Geo Town 12 *Oct.* 1803.

Sir

The attention the City of Washington has constantly experienced at your hands, leads me to hope, that any honest plan which promises advantage to the City, and which can injure nobody, will have your countenance.

Washington suffers more than any other place, for want of active capital. Men of money, have not shown a disposition to move to Washington with their money; nor is it probable they will, until they see that capital can be had without them. The City never can flourish, until active capital, without which there can be no enterprize, shall by some means, be introduced.

It was from considerations like these, that an effort was made last session of Congress, to get an insurance Company incorporated, on a plan similar to the one, I have now the honor to enclose. After passing the house of Rep.ˢ by a large majority it failed in the Senate, by one or two votes. I think it failed because some members did not understand it — and perhaps it was taken up at too late a period of the Session.

The remarks that accompany the bill, were made for the people of the City & Town — I enclose them, not under the impression, that the subject is not already well understood by you. — Nor have I taken the liberty thus to obtrude upon your time, from an expectation, or even a wish, that you should make this thing of sufficient importance to notice it to Congress.

I have the honor to be

With high respect Sir Y.^r

Mo Obed. Servt

BEN STODDERT

[Ms., *Jefferson Papers*, Library of Congress.]

JEFFERSON NOTES

NOTE. for many of the facts & documents here stated reference must be had to State papers. Dec. 17. 1800. Jan. 30. 1801. Apr. 8. 1802.

1803. *Oct* 12

Questions arising from time to time What is the plan of the city of Washington? have not unauthoritative alterations been made in it? how do these alterations affect the rights of individuals? it becomes necessary to review the facts on which they depend, to deduce principles from these, & to apply them to individual cases.

Act of Congr. 1790. c. 28.   prescribes to Commissioners, under the direction of the Pres. of the US. to survey, & by metes & bounds define & limit the territory Etc. to purchase or accept land, as the Pr. US. shall deem proper, for the use of the US. and to provide suitable buildings for the accomodation of Congress, & of the President, & for the public offices of the govt̄ of the US. according to such plans as the Pr. shall approve. the Pr. is authorised to accept grants of money for defraying the expence of such purchases & buildings.

1791. Apr. The proprietors of the lands on which the city is laid, convey to trustees as follows, the lands to be laid out, with such streets, squares, parcels & lots as the Pr. US. for the time being shall approve. the trustees to convey to the Comm.ʳˢ for the time being, for the use of the US. all the streets, & such squares, parcels & lots, as the Pr. shall deem proper for the use of the US. the residue of the lots to be divided one half to the proprietor, the other half to be sold on such terms & conditions Etc. as the Pr. US. shall direct the trustees to convey to the purchasers, & the proceeds of the sales to be applied, 1.ˢᵗ to pay the proprietor for the lots, squares & parcels appropriated to the use of the US. at £ 25. per acre, the balance to the President as a grant of money, & to be applied for the purposes & according to the act of Congr. the conveyor to possess & occupy, until the same shall be occupied under the said appropriations for the use of the US. or by purchasers: & to cut & take the trees, timber & wood, except such of the trees & wood growing as the Pr. or Comm.ʳˢ may judge proper & give notice shall be left for ornament; for which a just value to be paid the trustees, at the request of the Pr. US. for the time being, to convey all the lands here conveyed to such person as he shall appoint subject to the trusts.

Oct. 17.   The first sale of lots took place. squares 77. 78. 79. 105. 106. 107. 127. 128. were divided, & were sold.

it is to be observed that none of these touch the Pr's square, either as then projected, or afterwards established.

Oct. 25.
1791.

President Washington informs Congress of the state in which the business then was, to wit, that the district was located, & a city laid out on a plan which he should ~~communicate~~ place before them. and Dec. 13. he communicated to them L'Enfant's projet, & after time given for inspection, he withdrew it.

Dec. 19.

The legislature of Maryland pass an act. by §. 5. all the squares, lots, pieces, & parcels of land within the city, which have been or shall be appropriated for the use of US. & also the streets, shall remain & be for the use of the US. and all the lots sold shall be to the purchasers according to the conditions of purchase. the Comm^rs for the time being, shall from time to time, until Congress shall exercise the jurisdiction, have power to license the building of wharves adjoining the city, in the manner, & of the extent they may judge ~~proper~~ convenient, and agreeing with general order; but no wharf to be built before the land of another, nor without licence. they may direct as to ballast, materials for building, earth from cellars Etc. the thickness of walls, under penalties not exceeding £10. grant licences for retailing spirits.

Mar. 14.
1792.

Pr. Washington having employed Ellicot to prepare the plan of the city for engraving, ~~towards which~~ the groundwork of which was L'Enfant's projet ~~was taken as the groundwork, but~~ with several alterations ~~made with his approbation,~~ approved by him. and particularly with an omission of the specific appropriations of the public squares,

proposed in the projet being which, except those of
the Capitol & President's square were struck out
and left for future determination as the uses should
occur, except these of the Capitol & President's
square. Ellicot now compleated it: and it was put
into the hands of engravers at Philadelphia & Boston to be engraved.

Apr. 20.   The commissioners having proposed to the President some further alterations, the Secretary of
state informs the Comm.^{rs} that the Pr. declined
making any alterations in the city, in consideration
of the expediency of fixing the public opinion on
the thing as stable & unalterable, the loss of work
done if altered, the changing all the avenues which
point to the Capitol, removing the two houses to a
still greater distance, change in the engraving Etc.
[it may be conjectured that one of their proposed
alterations was the removal of the Capitol East-
wardly to the highest part of the ground to save the
digging down that.]

Oct. 8th A sale of lots takes place, at which the Boston
engraved plan was exhibited. in this the lines next
to the water are omitted.

At this sale a division took place between the
Comm.^{rs} & Davidson, squares 167. & 186. are assigned to Davidson, & 200. 221. to the US. Davidson becomes the purchaser of 221. and 200 is sold
to others and he recieves paiment at the rate of £25.
per acre for every foot of the residue of the Pr's
square, & consequently for the very ground he
since reclaims. on this occasion the Comm.^{rs} &
Davidson enter into a written agreement that if any
squares for buildings or other appropriations, except as a public square, are hereafter made on

Davidson's part of the Pr's square, bounded on the W. by 17.th street, N. by H. street, E. by 15.th S. by Dav. Burnes's line (except the two squares 167. & 221. already established & laid off, the s^d Saml Davidson should be entitled to his dividend thereof.

July 20. 1795.

The Comm.^{rs} published regulations respecting wharves (expressing it to be under the authority given them by the act of Maryland.) they permit the proprietors of water lots to wharf as far out as they think proper, not injuring or interrupting the channel, leaving space where the plan of the streets requires it, and 60. f. at every 300. f. for a street where the plan indicates none.

Oct. 5. 1795.

They permit m̄ Barry to wharf across the Georgia avenue. at various times they sell lots on the bank *with a water privilege*, viz. N.ºs 1.2.3.4.5.6.7. 17.18. square N.º 8. sold to m̄ Templeman. Genl

Mar. 2. 1797.

Washington executes an instrument of directions to the Trustees to convey to the Comm.^{rs} all the streets as delineated in a plan said to be annexed, and 17. spaces of ground, as therein specially designated, for public reservations. by accident the plan was not annexed, but this annexation was supplied by President Adams July 23. 1798.

Other ~~reservations~~ appropriations of the reserved squares have been inferred from President Washington's letters of Oct. 21. & Dec. 1. 1796. to wit of the 4.th reservation for an University and of the 13.th for a Marine hospital. but the uncertain language of those letters is decided negatively by his subsequent omission of these appropriations in the Plan & Declaration of 1797. The 7.th reservⁿ & the angular space between 78. and 101. have been regularly appropriated for a market.

Apr.
1799.

President Adams ~~appropriated~~ designated the 14.th reservation to a Navy yard, & it has been assumed for that purpose: but the appropriation has not yet been formally made.

Feb. 27.
1801.

Congress assume the jurisdiction of the territory.

May 3.
1802.

Congress establish a corporation, giving them powers which in various instances abridge or supersede those of the Commissioners.

From these facts the following legal deductions may be drawn.

The power of the President to establish the plan of the city is derived solely from that part of the deeds of the proprietors which requires the trustees to convey to the Commissioners *such streets and squares as the Presid.^t should deem proper,* for the use of the US. these having left him free as to the time & form of executing this power, we are to seek for those acts, words, or instruments proceeding from him which did amount in law to a full execution of his power, or a compleat declaration of all the streets and squares reserved; premising that it was not requisite that he should execute his power all at once, but by successive acts as he should find best.

1. The sales and divisions of squares & lots made by his authority, were an execution of his power as to do much of the plan as limited them, & their limits would thenceforward be established & unalterable. but these did not determine his power as to other parts not conveyed or divided.

2. His message to Congress of 1791. and communication of a first projet of the city by Lenfant, was merely a matter of information of the progress

of the business and not a determination of it. his letter of Feb. 20. 1797. to the Comm.^{rs} explicitly declares this, his subsequent alterations shew it, and the solemnity of his instrument of directions to the trustees for a more extensive execution of his powers when he thought the business ripe for it, are a conclusive proof of his intentions.

3. This direction of 1797. Mar. 2. to the trustees to convey streets & squares according to the plan annexed, was plainly intended as a solemn execution of his powers, and conclusive on him & his successors, as far as it went: and the plan therein referred to, the annexation of which was supplied by President Adams, taken in conjunction with the explanatory instrument of directions, may be considered to be the established plan of the city so far as it went. ~~some designations in it, inconsistent~~ it appears indeed to have been made on a survey not accurate in every part, so that certain designations in it could not be applied to the ground, & were liable either to correction from that, or to nullity. Such portions of the power as were not executed by this instrument, remained of course in the President. such were the future appropriations of the areas reserved except the Capitol & President's squares: and the destination of many angular points formed between the intersections of streets, and the building squares delineated in the plan. these being left vacant in the plan, & not disposed of in the act of Mar. 2. 97. were left to be acted on thereafter. some of them have been since been reserved & paid for, others divided as building squares; others still remain to be divided or reserved & paid for.

This plan of Pr. Washington's is controuled by another circumstance. by the common law of England, presumed to be unaltered in Maryland in this particular, the property, tam aquae quam soli, of every river, susceptible of any navigation probably, but certainly of every one having flux & reflux, is in the king, who cannot grant it to a subject because it is a highway except for purposes which will increase the convenience of navigation. the ordinary low water mark is the limit of what is grantable by the crown to an individual. accordingly the grants from the crown, on such rivers, are ordinarily limited by the river: and so probably were the grants to the proprietors on the Potomak & Eastern branch. in the only deed I can recur to, that of Abraham Young, I observe he bounds his conveyance *by & with the waters of the Eastern branch & Potomak river;* and if the other proprietors have not done the same, the law has done it for them. the bed of the river vested, on the revolution in the states of Maryland & Virginia, & by their cessions was transferred to the US. but no act of the US. authorised the Pr. to lay out or establish the plan of a city. he recieved that authority only from the proprietors, & consequently it could extend no farther than their right extended, to the water edge. whatever parts of the plan therefore went beyond the water edge, were null for want of authority to lay them there.

Let us now proceed to examine the alterations which have been made and the effect they have on the rights of individuals.

1. The alteration pretended by m͞r Davidson, is no alteration at all. the building squares he claims

were never established as such. they appeared indeed in the first project of Lenfant, but never were
authorised by any act of the President's. this is
proved by m͞r Davidson's own agreement with the
Comm.͌ˢ in which the provision that '*if* any building squares other than 167. & 221 should afterwards be established on his part of the Pr's square,
the limits of which are there distinctly specified, he
should have his dividend of them,' admits there
were none then and he recieves paiment at £25. an
acre for the residue on the footing of a public
square. it is proved by the authentic plan established in 97. and the written directions, reserving
the ground expressly for the public use. it is explicitly declared by President Washington in his
letter of Feb. 20. 97. and is said to have been also
declared by Pr. Adams. it is impossible for any
thing to be more definitively decided, and I will
venture to affirm that there exists no where a power
to alter it, not even in Congress. for as the Proprietors were masters of their property, to give, or not
to give, so were they of the conditions and limitations on which they would give. having more confidence in the cordiality of the then President, than
in that of Congress, towards their new city, they
preferred placing under his discretion even what
they should give for the use of the US. they trusted
that all the material powers would be executed in
his time, as in fact they were, & by himself. as to
trusts thus submitted to the President, Congress
cannot legislate. e.g. they cannot change the location direction or dimensions of streets or squares or
otherwise alter the plan of the city, appropriate
squares or building lots, alter the conditions of con-

veyance, as by authorising wooden houses [53] etc. on
the other hand they have the right to legislate over
every thing ceded to them by Maryland. but that
cession contained an express reservation of all individual rights. they have the legislation over the
bed of the river, may regulate wharves, bridges
Etc. built into or over it, Etc.

2. the conversion into building lots of the angular spaces left vacant in the plan and declaration of
97. have been called alterations, but they are not:
they are only successive & supplementary execu-
tions of the power; the location of the bed of the
canal in 1795. and the establishment of more building lots on Nottley Young's ground than appear in
the engraved plan, was previous to the plan and
declaration of 1797. and expressly established by
them. the actual location of squares 728. 729. being
different from what they appear to be in the engraved plan, have been deemed alterations. so also
the establishment of building squares in a space in
Hamburg South of 104. which appears vacant in
the engraved plan. but these are errors of the engraved plan; all of them having been laid off before
it was engraved, altho it escaped Ellicot's notice.

3. When the Plan & Declaration of 1797. were
established, the whole of the delineations had not
been actually made on the ground. hence it happened that when they came to be made, they were
found impossible & inconsistent with the ground.
thus the 15th & 16th reservations were intended for a
market with a canal leading to it from the river.
the actual ground was found too far withdrawn

[53] qu. whether some of the provisions in the act of 1802 ch. 41. respecting the canal
do not rest merely on the assent of the President given to that act, & how far they
could be revoked?

from the river, & that a canal could not be drawn
to it. they were therefore corrected by being converted into building squares 852. & 881. and the
reservation was located between them & the river.
[it is not said that these alterations were before the
authentic plan, and make a part of that plan.]

4. The plan & Declaration of 97. were void as to
so much of them as projected beyond the water
edge, beyond which the President's power did not
extend.

5. The bed of the river being vested in the state
of Maryland, & by them ceded to the US. with a
reservation of the right of legislation until it should
be assumed by Congress, the alienations of the
right of wharfing so far as they were actually made
by the Commissioners before Feb. 27. 1801. consistently with the act of Maryland, were valid. but
their regulations of July 20. 1795. did not convey a
general right to all purchasers of Water lots. it was
no more than an advertisement, which they were
free to depart from at any time before actual sale.
the deed of conveyance is the only thing which
could convey the right actually. the Commissioners
possessed, as to wharves, not a mere naked power,
but a power coupled with an interest: and could
therefore vary their terms as a private individual
may at any time before an actual contract.

On the whole the Question now recurs, What is
the Plan of the city of Washington.

It is, as to it's main part, the Plan and Declaration of 1797. 1.st emarginated as to so much as projected beyond the water edge. 2. with such
wharves added as the Comm.^{rs} validly authorised
before 1801. [3. with the alterations of the 15.th &

16.th reservations & of squares 852. & 881.] qu? 4. with the insertion of such angular spaces as have been reserved or converted into building lots. 5. the insertion of the appropriation for a market & the 14.th to a Navy Yard.

TH: JEFFERSON
Oct. 12. 1803.

Oct. 18. 1803. Since writing the above I have seen the opinion of m̄ Charles Lee, while Attorney Gen! on the subject above considered and I concur in most of it's contents. in the following particulars however, I do not.

1. he supposes the Pr's sanction will be necessary for such streets as shall be reclaimed from the water. I think that power rests with Congress.

2. he quotes these words of the constitution, to wit, 'Congress shall have power to dispose of and make all needful rules & regulations respecting the territory or other property belonging to the US.' and supposes they give Congress a power over the squares reserved for the US. but they can have no power over them further than the proprietors have granted. the US. are the cestuy que trust, the President (not Congress) is the trustee. the only question in the case of the Queen of Portugal is whether a lot appropriated for the residence of her minister is appropriated to a public use?

3. he thinks the angular spaces are public ways. I do not think any act of the President's has made them so.

4. he thinks the Pr. could sell a public square & lay out the money in other grounds for the same purpose. I think that having declared it reserved for

public use, he has so far executed his power, & cannot afterwards alien it for private use.

[Ms., *Jefferson Papers*, Library of Congress.]

Thomas Munroe to Jefferson

THOS. MUNROE, SUPERINTENDENT TO THE PRESIDENT

Superintendent's Office Washington, 18th *Feb.* 1804.
Sir:

The enclosed representation having been this day delivered
.to me, to be laid before you, it may not be improper for the
following observations to accompany it.

A man by the name of Jenkins, tenant of Samuel Davidson
an original proprietor, claims the right of retaining possession
of the part of the City mentioned in the representation under
that part of the Deed of Trust, of which the enclosed is a copy,
and accordingly keeps the same enclosed as a Corn-field — the
Cattle, horses and hogs of the Citizens get into this field, and it
is said Jenkins frequently kills them. Several applications have
been made to me for prompt redress under your Authority,
and I have told the Applicants they must resort to the Judicial
authority, it being the Opinion of the Attorney of the District
"that so soon as appropriations & designations were made by
the President, whether for streets or other public purposes, and
so soon as Lots were sold to individuals, from that moment did
the right of the Original proprietor to possess the land so disposed of cease."

I have frequently communicated this to Davidson, Jenkins,
and the persons who have made complaints, as long ago as
April last, but Jenkins still keeps up his enclosures and justifies
it under his landlord's construction of the deed of Trust; altho'
he admits the streets are designated by the plan of the City, and
that lots have been sold in their vicinity; but he contends, these

lots must be required for actual improvements & that the streets must become necessary for the convenience of the improvers of the lots, or of the public in such degree as to make it manifestly necessary that the Original proprietor should relinquish his possession.

I have always suggested that these streets were notoriously known as such, and that the plan of the City was a sufficient designation of them; but perhaps you, Sir, may deem it proper to make some declaration on the subject to be published that the Court may have the less hesitation in acting, & Offenders have better information.

I have the honor to be with the utmost respect, Sir,

Yr. mo Ob Hum Servt

THOMAS MUNROE.

[Pp. 2271–2, U. S. v. MORRIS, Records, Volume VII.]

LATROBE TO JEFFERSON

Report on the public Buildings. Feb.ᵣ 20.ᵗʰ 1804.
8 Cong: L. 1 Sess.
Accompanying the Presidents message of 22 Feb: 1804.

TO THE PRESIDENT OF THE UNITED STATES

Washington, Feb.ᵣ 20.ᵗʰ 1804

Sir,

On the 4.ᵗʰ of April 1803, I had the honor to lay before you, a general report, on the State of the public Buildings in this City. I now beg leave to submit to you an account of the progress that has been made in the works directed by you in consequence of that report: and in order more clearly to explain the subject, I beg to recapitulate concisely what I formerly stated.

I. *On the North Wing of the Capitol.*

On a careful Survey of the North wing of the Capitol it was
found, that the want of Air & light in the Cellarstory, had began to produce decay in the Timbers, — that the roof was
leaky, & the cielings & walls of several of the Apartments were
thereby injured, — that it would be impossible to render the
Senate Chamber, the extreme coldness of which was matter of
serious complaint, more warm and comfortable without the
construction of stoves or furnaces below the floor for which purpose it would be necessary to carry up additional flues, and to
remove a very large quantity of rubbish from the Cellars: —
and that the Skylights were extremely out of repair.

During the course of the last Season therefore openings have
been made into all the Cellars, the decayed timbers have been
replaced where immediately necessary, — the floors that required it have received additional support, the Senate Chamber has been rendered more comfortable by the introduction of
warm air, — by the erection of a stove, — by the exclusion of
cold air from the Cellar by plaistering, — and should the plan
adopted after the experience of the present Session be approved, another Stove is ready to be put up. — All the Cellars
have been cleared and the rubbish removed. In respect to the
roof, the best repairs which could be made without unroofing
the whole wing, have been made, and the leaks rendered of less
importance: — but the early meeting of Congress, and the
magnitude, & the doubtful completion as to time, of a thorough
repair by taking off the whole upper part of the roof, induced
me to postpone this operation. Every preparation however is
made, and the lead which covers so great a part of the roof will
contribute greatly to defray the expense of this thorough repair.

The skylights have also been *only repaired*, but it is necessary
to substitute in their room Lanthorn lights, with upright Sashes
and close tops. This Work has also been deferred, and for the
same reasons.

General repairs of those parts of the building which were hastily and slightly executed previously to the removal of the seat of Government were also necessary, and they have been made.

II. *On the South Wing of the Capitol*

On the 4th of April 1803, it was necessary to report to you, — that on opening, in order to examine the Walls of the Cellar story of the South wing of the Capitol the workmanship was found to have been so unfaithfully performed, as to render it absolutely necessary to take them down to the foundation, and that even the greatest part of the Materials were too bad to be used again. — Previously therefore to the commencement of the work upon this Wing all the old external Walls were removed. The new Work was executed with the best Materials and in the most durable manner, that could be devised. — Great disadvantages were encountered at the commencement of the Season. The long intermission of public Work, had scattered the Workmen, and the supply of materials was difficult and tardy. The work however which has been done, is considerable. The Walls have been raised to nearly half the heighth of the Ground story. The preparations for further progress, — should the Legislature direct the same, are also great, and materials are now collected on the Spot nearly sufficient, and already prepared to finish the external Walls of the lower story. The rapidity and greater occonomy with which the work will in future proceed are also an advantage gained. A System for the supply of materials is now organized, — a great number of excellent Workmen are collected, and the expense of Machinery, Scaffolding, & utensils defrayed.

The Hall in which the House of Representatives are now assembled was erected as part of the permanent building. I am however under the necessity of representing to you, that the whole of the Masonry from the very foundation is of such bad

workmanship and materials, that it would have been dangerous
to have assembled within the building, had not the Walls been
strongly supported by shores from without. — For easy examination the Wall has been opened in several places, and an actual inspection will immediately explain the state in which it is.

Besides the Work done to secure the present Building, — it
has been lighted in the best manner which the construction of
the roof will admit, — in order to remedy the diminution of
light by carrying up the external Walls. — The increase of the
number of the Members of the House this Session, rendered it
necessary to take up the Platform, and to enlarge the space for
seats. This has also been done, & forms part of the Expenditure
of the Season.

In my former report, I took the liberty to suggest the propriety of considering whether any & what improvement of the
original plan of the Work, might be necessary for the better
accomodation of the House of Representatives in the South
Wing of the Capitol, so as to bring the Offices attached to the
house nearer to the Legislative Hall. The attention You have
already been pleased to give to this subject encourages me to
suggest the necessity of an ultimate decission previously to the
Commencement of the Work of the ensuing Season.

III. *The President's house*

Agreeably to Your desire that the Monies appropriated by
the Legislature should be devoted as much as possible to the
erection of the Capitol & to the accomodation of the Legislature, — the expenditure on the President's house has been kept
as low as possible.

In my former report to You on this building I stated, — that
the Roof & gutters were so leaky as to render it necessary to
take off all the Slating; to take up all the Gutters & to give them
much more current; and to cover the building with Sheet iron,

as uniting Safety against fire with Acconomy; — To strengthen & tie together the roof which having spread, has forced out the Walls; — to put up the Stair case, which was already prepared; to sink a Well for the purpose of procuring good Water, of which the house was in absolute Want — to glaze those Apartments which required it, & to complete some accomodations wanted in the Chamber story.

All these Works, except the complete repair of the roof have been done. The work on the roof is however in progress, and the funds remaining in hand are estimated to be sufficient to complete this object.

The Superintendant of the City has favored me with the necessary information to give the following Statement of Expenditures, up to this day.

1. The expenditure of monies out of the fund of 50,000$, on the roads, and on objects not placed by You under my direction,　　4,832.63

2. On the North wing of the Capitol,　　　　　　　$
   a. In repairs........................　1.513.22½
   b. On the Senate Chamber...........　1.168.34½
   　　　　　　　　　　　　　　　　　　　　　　　2.681.57

3. On the South Wing
   a. Repairs &c of the Hall of Representa-
      tives.............................　555.13½
   b. Materials, Labor, & Superintendance } 31.190.23½　31.745.37
      of the Work of the South Wing..... }
      　　　　　　　　　　　　　　31.745.37

4. On the President's House.
   Repairs, and Works enumerated above................　2.251.67
5. Balance, estimated to be sufficient to discharge unsettled & ⎞
   outstanding acc.ts — to complete existing contracts of last ⎬ 8.488.76
   Season — to pay advances on new Contracts, & prepare to ⎟
   lay in a Stock of new materials...................... ⎠
   　　　　　　　　　　　　　　　　　　　　　　50.000 —

The above statement, collected in many instances from running, and unsettled accounts, is necessarily liable to corrections in detail, — which cannot however in any case, materially affect the results stated.

The Season is now at hand in which preparations for the Work of the present Year should be made. I therefore respectfully submit the premisses to Your consideration, — and am
        Your faithful humble Serv.ͭ

B. Henry Latrobe
*Surveyor of the public Buildings
of the United States at Washington.*

P.S.   I beg leave to add, that to compleat the Work *in freestone* of the South wing, — which is the most expensive part of the building, the Sum of 30.000$ will be Sufficient, according to the best Estimate which can be made.

[From the original ms. in the National Archives, incomplete text in DOCUMENTARY HISTORY . . . OF THE CAPITOL, pp. 104–6.]

MESSAGE TO CONGRESS

THE PRESIDENT TO THE SENATE AND HOUSE OF REPRESENTATIVES

February 22, 1804

I communicate to Congress, for their information, a report of the surveyor of the public buildings at Washington, stating what has been done under the act of the last session concerning the city of Washington on the Capitol and other public buildings, and the highway between them.

[P. 104, DOCUMENTARY HISTORY . . . OF THE CAPITOL.]

LATROBE TO JEFFERSON

Washington, February 27, 1804.

THE PRESIDENT OF THE UNITED STATES

Dear Sir: I judged very ill in going to Dr. Thornton. In a few peremptory words he in fact told me that no difficulties existed in his plan but such as were made by those who were too ignorant to remove them, and though these were not exactly his words, his expressions, his tone, his manner, and his absolute refusal to devote a few minutes to discuss the subject, spoke his meaning even more strongly and offensively than I have expressed it. I left him with an assurance that I should not be the person to attempt to execute his plan, and had I been where I could have obtained immediate possession of pen, ink, and paper, I should have directly solicited your permission to resign my office.

I owe, however, too much to you to risk by so hasty a step the miscarriage of any measure you may wish promoted, and I shall devote as before my utmost endeavors to execute the disposition in the committee, to which I am summoned to-morrow morning, in favor of the appropriation.

In respect to the plan itself, it is impossible to convey by words or drawings to the mind of any man the impression of the practical difficulties in execution which twenty years' experience creates in the mind of a professional man. I fear I have said too much for the respect I owe your opinions, though much too little for the force of my own convictions. The utmost praise I can ever deserve in this work will be that of *la difficulté vaincue*, and after receiving your ultimate directions all my exertion shall be directed to gain this praise at least.

My wish to avoid vexation, trouble, and enmities is weak compared to my desire to be placed among those whom you regard with approbation and friendship.

If you, therefore, under all circumstances, conceive that my services still be useful, I place myself entirely at your disposal.

In order to pass my accounts it will be necessary to produce a regular appointment from you to my office. May I beg you to give the necessary directions for this purpose? I ought to leave Washington on Wednesday morning. I am, etc., etc.

[THE JOURNAL OF LATROBE, pp. 119–121.]   [B. H. LATROBE]

JEFFERSON TO LATROBE

Washington, February 28, 1804.

Dear Sir

I am sorry the explanations attempted between Dr. Thornton and yourself, on the manner of finishing the chamber of the House of Representatives, have not succeeded. At the original establishment of this place advertisements were published many months offering premiums for the best plans for a Capitol and a President's house. Many were sent in. A council was held by General Washington with the Board of Commissioners, and after very mature examination two were preferred, and the premiums given to their authors, Doctor Thornton and Hobens, and the plans were decided on. Hobens' has been executed. On Doctor Thornton's plan of the Capitol the north wing has been extended, and the south raised one story. In order to get along with any public undertaking it is necessary that some stability of plan be observed — nothing impedes progress so much as perpetual changes of design. I yield to this principle in the present case more willingly because the plan begun for the Representative room will, in my opinion, be more handsome and commodious than anything which can now be proposed on the same area. And though the spheroidical dome presents difficulties to the executor, yet they are not beyond his art; and it is to overcome difficulties that we employ men of genius. While, however, I express my opinion that we had better go through with this wing of the Capitol on the plan which has been settled, I would not be understood to suppose there does exist sufficient authority to control the original plan in any of its parts, and to accommodate it to changes of circumstances. I only mean that it is not advisable to change that of this wing in its present stage. Though I have spoken of a spheroidical roof, that will not be correct by the figure. Every rib will be a portion of a circle of which the radius will be determined by the span and rise of each rib. Would it not be best to make the internal columns of well-burnt brick, moulded in portions of circles adapted to the diminution of the columns? Burlington, in his notes on Palladio, tells us that he found most of the buildings erected under Palladio's direction, and described in his architecture, to have their columns made of brick in this way and covered over with stucco. I know an instance of a range of six or eight columns in Virginia, twenty feet high, well proportioned and properly diminished, executed by a common bricklayer. The bases and capitals would of course be of hewn stone. I suggest this for your consideration, and tender you my friendly salutations.

[TH: JEFFERSON.]

[Pp. 13–15, WRITINGS, Memorial Edition, Vol. XI.]

LATROBE TO JEFFERSON

Newcastle, March 29, 1804.

THE PRESIDENT OF THE UNITED STATES,
    WASHINGTON.

Dear Sir: I herewith transmit to you a separate roll containing drawings, being the plans and sections of the south wing of the Capitol according to the ideas which I explained to you when I had the favor of seeing you last. I fear, however, that these and any other preparations for proceeding with the public works may be useless, for by a letter from Mr. Lenthall I learn that the appropriation bill has passed the Senate with an amendment enjoining the removal of Congress to the President's house. This amendment must either be fatal to the bill when returned to the House of Representatives or divert the expenditure of the appropriation from the Capitol to I know not what sort of an arrangement for Congress and for the President, if it should pass into a law.

However, as it is impossible to think or speak with legal respect of the years in such a measure, or to suppose that such a law should pass both houses, I will take the liberty to explain the drawings as concisely as I can.

[B. H. LATROBE.]

[THE JOURNAL OF LATROBE, p. 122.]

JEFFERSON TO LATROBE

Monticello Apr. 9. 04.

Dear Sir

I received three days ago your favor of Mar. 29 and have taken the first leisure moment to consider it's contents & the drawings they refer to, and I approve generally of the several distribution of both the floors, with some exceptions which shall be noted below. But we must for the present defer whatever is external in the North wall of the South wing, that is to say, the vestibule, the speaker's chamber, the withdrawing room, for the members and the coridor & staircase between them; 1st because all our efforts will be not more than sufficient to finish the South wing in 2 summers & 2dly for a more absolute reason that the object of this appropriation is to finish the wing. there having been no idea in the legislature of doing any ~~thing~~ part of the middle building. For the present, a temporary staircase may be put up in the place of the Vestibule & upper coridor. I perceive that the Doric order for the Representative's chamber must be given up on account of the difficulty of accomodating it's metop[e] & triglyph to the intercolonnations resulting from the periphery of the room: and as the Senate chamber is Ionic, we must make this Corinthian, & do the best we can for the capitals & modillions. I suppose that this will be the best. The following are the exceptions, or rather the doubts, as to some of the details of the plans. I have approved the Speaker's chamber & Drawing room for the members: would it not be better to assign for the [illegible] the Sergeant's room, & for the [illegible] [illegible]? on the lower floor would it not be better to convert the lobbies of the [illegible] & representatives rooms, opening from the Antichambers, and let the entry to the staircase [illegible] [illegible] be directly thro' the corner window adjacent to it? a [illegible] [illegible] [illegible] [illegible] refer [illegible] I think less than the semicircle would be enough. I return you the drawings and pray you to push the works with all the force which can be employed in the order proposed in my last letter to you. Accept my friendly salutations & assurances of respect.

TH: JEFFERSON

Mᴿ. LATROBE

[Ms., *Jefferson Papers*, Library of Congress.]

JEFFERSON NOTE

An Estimate fore a Tuscan Column whose diameter is 14 Inches — to stand on a Sub plinth one diameter in height. The shaft in one entire stone including Cincture and Astragal

	$
Stone will cost..................	17.50
Workmanship on Dᵒ..............	25 ..
	$42.50

Such a column, including it's base and capital measures about 34. square feet superficially. which is $73\frac{1}{2}$ cents a square foot.

14ᵗʰ *June* 1804
GEO BLAGDEN

One of my Doric columns measures 99.5 sq. f.

it's workmanship at that rate is 73. D.

[Th. Jefferson's marginal comments.]

M.ᴿ JN.ᴼ LENTHALL

[Ms., *Jefferson Papers*, Library of Congress.]

JEFFERSON TO THOMAS MUNROE

MUNROE THOS. July 14, '04, DAVIDSON CASE

Washington July 14—'04.

Sir:

In answer to your letter covering Mr. Davidson's on the subject of the claim he sets up to certain grounds near the President's house, I did receive an early application from him on the subject as he states; but it was very long before I got all the materials which were necessary to enable me to make up a satisfactory judgment on that & the many other questions respecting the city which had accumulated. In Oct. 1803, I took up the cases, and gave them all the time and consideration which their difficulty required, and communicated the result to you. I do not recollect, however, whether I gave you a copy or only the reading of it.

With respect to Mr. Davidson's case, I found that Gen'l Washington had decided it in his letter of Feb. 20, '97, wherein as to the matter of right he is clear & decisive against the claim and as to the question of indulgence he leaves it to the commissioners who would not agree to give it. On a full view of all the circumstances & documents respecting the case I thought Genl. Washington's decision perfectly just, and I think Mr. Davidson's error proceeds entirely from his considering L'Enfant's draught as the first plan; whereas it was only the first proposition prepared for, & subject to, future modifications. The Plan & declaration of 1797 were final so far as they went: but even they left many parts unfinished, some of which remain still to be declared. The sale in Oct., 91, of a few lots would certainly fix so much of the plan as respected those lots, but no farther. None of these touched the President's square and consequently could not fix that. Mr. Davidson's own agreement with the Commissioners provides that "if any building squares other than 167 & 221 should afterwards be established on his part of the President's square (the limits of which are there distinctly specified, as declared in 1797) he should have his dividend of them;" this is a solemn admission under his own hand in Oct., 92, that none were then established. I state these only as my reasons for concurring with Genl. Washington in his decision of Feb. 97, a copy of which I will pray you to send to Mr. Davidson. Accept my best respects.

TH: JEFFERSON.

MR. MUNROE.

[Pp. 2272–3, U. S. *v.* MORRIS, Records, Vol. VII.]

LATROBE TO JEFFERSON

TO THE PRESIDENT OF THE UNITED STATES

The Report of the Surveyor of the public buildings of the United States at Washington.

Washington Dec. 1st 1804.

Sir,

In reporting to You on the manner in which the work on the public buildings of the United States has been conducted during the Year 1804, I cannot avoid expressing my regret that a sensible portion of the appropriation by Congress has necessarily been expended in pulling down or repairing what was done insufficiently, previously to the Year 1803.

The application of the public money to the separate objects of the President's house, & the Capitol, including the alteration, removal, reerection or repair of the works, will be separately stated in the accounts of the superintendant of the city to be rendered to the Treasury. But as these accounts will not be closed untill the 1ˢᵗ of January 1805, he has furnished me with the following statement, up to the present day, of payments in the present year out of the Appropriation for 1804, and a Balance of the Appropriation of 1803 not expended in that year viz! —

		$
Capitol, including all alterations additions repairs in north wing (except fitting up Representatives chamber)		44,548.20
For Fitting up Representatives chamber................		689.23
Presidents House.....................................		11,928.29
Payments on Acc! for sundry materials, on Acc! of the particular Application whereof has not yet been rendered		500.
		57,665.72

1. *The Presidents' house*

It is well known that the Presidents house was inhabited before it was finished; — and that it still remains in a state so far from completion, as to want many of those accomodations which are thought indispensible in the dwelling of a private citizen. Of the inconveniencies attending the house, the greatest was the leakiness of the roof, which had indeed never been tight. The rain water which entered the building in every part, had injured the furniture exceedingly, and ruined many of the cielings. This important defect arose from two principal causes: — The very injudicious manner in which the gutters, and the troughs conveying the water to the Cistern were constructed, — and the badness of the Slating.

The Gutters are of lead. — The Sheets were soldered together; the fall or current of the gutters was much too small: — the openings in the roof through which the water passed into the trough, were so contracted as to be incapable of discharging the water of a moderate rain, consequently it overflowed & found its way into the building: — the troughs were of boards, lined with lead, soldered at the joints, & laid with very little current: and all the lead was of bad quality & badly cast. All &

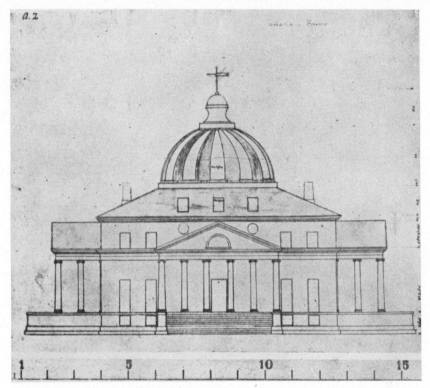

*Design for President's House, by Thomas Jefferson 1792 (exterior), submitted anonymously.
Courtesy Fine Arts Division, Library of Congress—20¾" x 17½".*

View of the White House, showing the terraces designed by Thomas Jefferson.

Ellicott's map of Washington, 179.

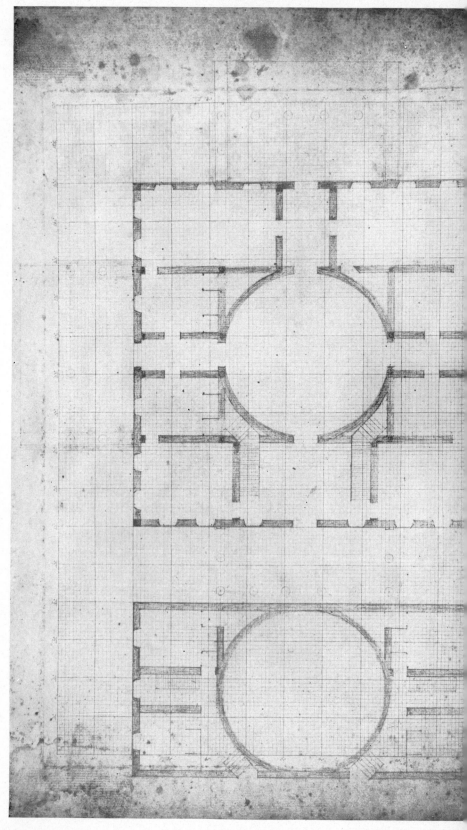

Design for President's House, Washington—by Jefferson—1792—(interior) (Thomas

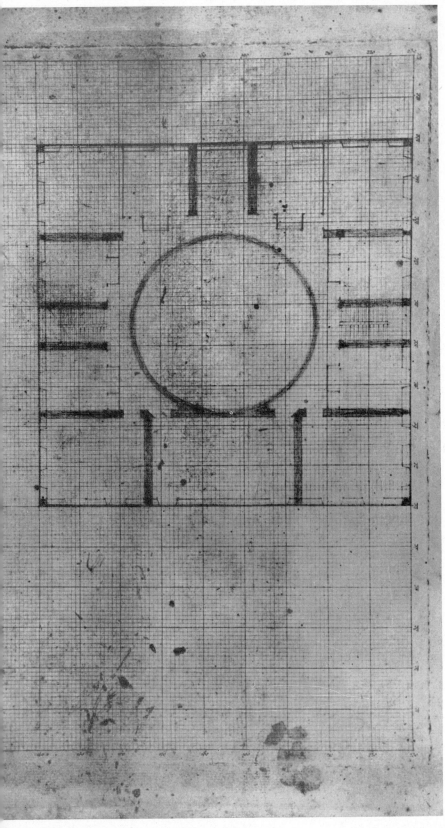

*ection)—Fine Arts Division, Library of Congress—30½″ x 21″.

The floor of the house is on a level with the enriched band.

enriched band   9
Story - - - - 11 - 3.5
Plinth - - - -   8.
                  12 - 10.5

Terrace floor   9. 1.5
shutterns & shutny -   1.
ridge joint in the middle   1 - 0.
                            1 - 2.5

Cornice 13½ = (in) 11   ⅞ ⅞
Frize   2.6½ (in)   6.6   1 - 2.5
architrave 35   8.8
            1 - 4.5   2 - 2.A
column 7 diam. 9 - - - - 8 - 7.6
subplinth = plinth of house - - -
                                    11 - 0.
                                       8.
                                   12 - 10.5

intercolumniation 6 diam. 7 - 6.5   ÷ 7 = 15.857
                  1 diam.   1 - 2.1
cent. to cent. of column 7 diam. 8 - 9.5

A section across the Western Offices.

cont. of the floor of President's house

ridge joint
gutter joint
ceiling of the rooms

                                5 - 10.5
                                   6 ÷
                                2 - 11.
                                   1 ÷

A section longitudinal of the eastern offices, now

Floor of the Terras in the Level of Plan of Pr's House.

17 - 7²

8 - 9,6

Lower Floor of Treasury office

Jefferson's plan of colonnades and dependencies for the President's House—about 1840. (Thomas Jefferson Coolidge Collection)—Fine Arts Division, Library of Congress—15¾" x 11¼".

The Jefferson pier, marking the intersection of the Capitol and White House axes on the L'Enfant Plan of 1791.

each of these causes occasioned leakage in the Gutters & troughs. It requires very little theory or experience to know that, wherever solder is used in leaden Gutters, leakage is inevitable. In Water Cisterns, & pipes, solder is necessary, and the joints made with it are sound & permanent, — the temperature of the Water they contain not being subject to great variation. But in gutters & flats, alternately exposed to the scorching sun, & to severe frost, — the use of solder is everywhere inadmissible, — but peculiarly so in our climate. It is besides very expensive, & in no well constructed building is it necessary. In the president's house, five feet of additional current was easily procured, — and by that means the new gutters were laid without solder, and with proper grovings & drips.

The first part of the season was so uncommonly wet, that no very early measures could be taken to make a thorough repair of the roof. The attempts at temporary repair, made with a view to save the furniture & cielings of the house, did not succeed, and tended only to prove the absolute necessity of a complete alteration of the whole system of guttering, and of providing new lead for the whole building. Such a general repair is always troublesome and difficult, and was much more expensive than it would have been to have executed the work right at first. It is now finished, and the roof is free from leaks. It will, I have no doubt, remain so.

The second Cause of leakage was the Slating. — The quality of the Slate was bad, — but their size, especially towards the ridge, was more injurious than their bad quality. The upper courses, for a considerable distance down the roof did not show more than from 2 to $2\frac{1}{2}$ inches in width, and a large majority of these Slates were only from $1\frac{1}{2}$ to 3 inches in breadth. Slated roofs are always very difficult to repair, but such a roof could not be repaired at all; and there were also other reasons, which rendered it necessary at all events to remove so heavy a covering as Slate.

I am uninformed why the particular mode of construction which renders this roof so heavy & so high was adopted. If strength was proposed, capable of bearing a covering of Slate laid in mortar, it has not been attained, — for the framing has every where given way, — and at the Eastern end of the house, where there are no internal Walls it has failed so much as to force out both the front & the back Walls very considerably. It appeared therefore necessary, in the first place, to secure the timbers as well as the Walls by strong ties of Iron; — which being fixed, — both are now perfectly safe. — In the next place it became highly proper to take off the load of Slates & mortar, even had they not leaked; — for they seemed to be the principal cause of the failure of the framing. — In the covering which was to supply the place of Slate, — *lightness* was the principal requisite: but safety from fire, & occonomy were also necessary considerations. Shingles & tiles were therefore out of the question, — as well as lead; — and the choice was confined to Copper, — Tin, — & painted Sheetiron. Of these, Sheet Iron was by far the cheapest, — and with a little attention to its painting, quite as permanent, as the two former. — 100 superficial feet of Slating in Mortar weighs about 15 Cwt, — of Sheet Iron, exactly 147#. So that the building, — the roof containing 12.600 superf! feet, could be relieved of a weight of about 82 Tons. — These reasons induced the adoption of a Sheet iron roof, which has accordingly been put on.

The repair or rather the total renewal of the roof of the Presidents house, — forms the principal part of the expense of this building for the season. It has however been further requisite to make a new drain from the house, of such dimensions & construction, as to prevent it from being filled up as before, and the building from being flooded from the circumjacent grounds. The cost of this improvement, — and the finishing of one of the Chamber apartments in the Second story, bears a small proportion to the former Sum.

2. *The Capitol*

In my former reports to You, I stated the propriety of reconsidering the plan of the South wing of the Capitol; and on the reasons given in that Report, and in a letter to the Chairman of the Committee of the house of representatives appointed to enquire into the subject, the place, which has been the Ground work of all that has been done during the Season, was approved and adopted. By the arrangements of this new design, the House of Representatives will sit on the principal story of the building the whole of the Ground Story being appropriated to the offices of the house: a situation the most contiguous which could be obtained, and far preferable for Offices to the North wing, or the Attic Story.

Various causes have conspired to prevent our carrying up, this Season as large a Mass of building as was expected. The first & principal of these have been the time, labor, & expense of pulling down to the very foundation all that had been formerly erected. Bad as the workmanship appeared before the Walls were taken down, — the measure of removing them entirely was still more justified by the State in which they were found to be on their demolition. Even the materials, with exception of the bricks, were not of any important value to the new work. The stone was fit only to be used as common rubble, and most of the Timber, was in a state of decay, from the exclusion of Air.

Another cause of delay in preparation, and an important one, was the late period at which the appropriation was made. The extreme wetness of the beginning of the Season, and the floods which filled up some of the quarries, & retarded the working of others, afterwards operated much against the progress of the buildings, and threw great difficulties in our way. After the work had begun, we were again interrupted by the sickness which prevailed, and which at one time threatened, —

by depriving us of many of our best workmen, — to put a total stop to the work.

Under all these inconveniences, and others arising from the nature of the building itself, the work has been carried on. The best mode of proceeding would undoubtedly have been to have carried up the interior with the exterior walls. But the former building stood within the area of the Wing. Had the external walls been suffered to remain on the level at which the work was closed, at the end of the Year 1803, till the inner building could be removed, and the internal Walls carried up, — little progress could have been made in the former, during the present Season, & the Stonecutters would have been idle. It was therefore thought best to carry up all the external walls by themselves, — thereby forwarding the more slow progress of the ornamental work in freestone, & to construct them in such a manner as to prepare for good bond with the interior work, & for the support of the Vaults, the pressure of which they will be required to resist. Thus has the work been raised to the level of the Selles of the Attic windows externally, and by far the most tedious expensive part of the work in freestone has been completed, excepting the Cornice and the Capitals of the Pilasters. Of the Cornice a large portion is also wrought, & of the 30 Capitals, 16 are finished.

Of the interior parts of the building all the foundations are laid, and brought up to the floor of the Cellar story on the North side, and although they do not appear to view, the work done in them is very considerable. The whole South half of the Cellar Story is Vaulted, and ready to receive the Walls of the Basement or Office story.

Preparations to a very great extent have already been made, in order to proceed vigorously with the building as soon as the will of the national legislature shall be known to that effect, and the Season will permit. All the freestone for the external walls, Entablature, & Ballustrade is provided, and the greatest part of it on the Spot. For the internal Colonnade all the Stone is ordered, — most of it quarried, & much already brought to the building. Early in the Season the public Quarry on the Island in Acquia Creek was opened, and much useful Stone quarried: and it would have been much to the advantage of the public, had the extent of the appropriation permitted us to have prosecuted this work. But it was found that to clear out the rubbish of former workings, and to provide for the conveyance of the Stone to the water-side, — altho' ultimately a measure of occonomy, would have made too large a deduction from the funds required to carry on the building itself, and contracts for stone with individuals were therefore preferred.

In the arrangements for erecting so large an edifice as the South wing of the Capitol, and for pulling down or repairing extensive works of former construction, it was not easy, — perhaps it was impossible, so to proportion all the various contracts and engagements for Labor & materials to the funds appropriated to this ultimate liquidation, as to keep within their limits, and at the same time to make exertions equal to the public expectation, arising out of their extent.

In the present instance, — the contracts which are made, and which are in the progress of their completion will exceed in amount what remains of the appropriation of last Year. I must however at the same time observe, — that the stock of materials wrought and unwrought, which are now actually at the building, exceed greatly this deficiency. Should the National Legislature, on view of the solid, permanent, and incombustible manner in which the work has been executed, and on consideration of the evidences of fidelity to their duty which those engaged in the Labor of the work have every where exhibited, — think proper to proceed with the completion of the building, — it would much tend to the early occupation of their house, by the house of representatives if an appropriation exceeding 50.000 dollars were made for the next Season. Such an appropriation, while it would give larger limits to the exertions which might be made, would by no means disturb that system of occonomy which has hitherto been pursued; — but would rather conduce to the more advantageous & provident purchase of all our materials. And it is especially to be considered, that too early & extensive provision cannot be made for those parts of the work, which must necessarily be of wood. — The time is now at hand at which further delay would be injurious & expensive, — and should the Sum necessary for this provision, added to the arrears which are or will become due on outstanding contracts, be defrayed out of a future appropriation of only 50.000 Dollars, the progress of the Solid parts of the building will be materially injured, and must to a certain extent, be put off to another season beyond the next.

In my letter of the 28th of Feb^{ry} 1804 to the Chairman of the Committee of the house of representatives to whom the Subject of the public buildings was referred, — I presumed that three annual appropriations of 50.000 Dollars each would be sufficient to finish the South wing of the Capitol. — This estimate was given, under statement of the extreme difficulty of estimating a work of this kind. — One of these appropriations of 50,000 Dollars has been granted. — But from the detail of the statements I herein submit to you it will appear, that the whole of it could not possibly be made applicable to the actual *progress* of the work on the Capitol.

Having thus endeavored correctly, & minutely to report the progress of the work on the public buildings during the past Season, I now most respectfully submit to You all the views of the past, and for the future which the facts suggest.

B. Henry Latrobe,
Surveyor of the public buildings of the United States
at Washington.

[Original ms. in Senate Archives; published incompletely in DOCUMENTARY HISTORY . . .
OF THE CAPITOL, pp. 111–14.]

JEFFERSON TO CONGRESS

THE PRESIDENT TO THE SENATE AND HOUSE OF REPRESENTATIVES
December 6, 1804

I communicate for the information of Congress, a report of the surveyor of the public buildings at Washington, on the subject of those buildings, and the application of the monies appropriated for them.

[P. III, DOCUMENTARY HISTORY . . . OF THE CAPITOL.]

LATROBE TO MAZZEI

Washington, March 6, 1805.

PHILIP MAZZEI, ESQ.

Sir: By direction of the President of the United States I take the liberty to apply to you for your assistance in procuring for us the services of a good sculptor in the erection of the public buildings in this city, especially of the Capitol.

The Capitol was begun at a time when the country was entirely destitute of artists, and even of good workmen in the branches of architecture, upon which the superiority of public over private buildings depends. The north wing, therefore, which is carried up, although the exterior is remarkably well finished as to the masonry, is not a good building. For two or three years after the removal of Congress to this city the public works were entirely discontinued. In the year 1803, however, they were resumed, and under the patronage of the present President and the annual appropriations by Congress the south wing of the Capitol has been begun and carried on. It is now so far advanced as to make it necessary that we should have as early as possible the assistance of a good sculptor of architectural decorations. In order to procure such an artist the President of the United States has referred me to your assistance, and to enable you to make choice of the person most likely to answer our purpose I will beg leave to describe to you the nature of the work we require to be done. The principal sculpture required will be of twenty-four Corinthian capitals, two feet four inches in diameter at their feet, and open enriched entablatures, of 147 feet (both English measure) in length. There are besides five panels (tavole) enriched with foliage and an eagle of colossal size in the frieze, the distance between the tips of the extended wings being twelve feet six inches.

The material in which this is to be cut is a yellowish sandstone of fine grain, finer than the peperino or gray sandstone used in Rome — the only Italian sandstone of which I have any distinct recollection. This stone yields in any direction to the chisel, not being in the least laminated nor hard enough to fly off (spall) before a sharp tool. It may, therefore, be cut with great precision. The wages given by the day to our best carvers are from $3 to $2.50, or from about $750 to $900 per annum. They are considered good wages, but the workmen who receive them are very indifferent carvers and do not deserve the name of sculptors. My object is to procure a first-rate sculptor in the particular branch of architectural decorations. He should be able to model and bring with him another good though inferior workman as his assistant, to whom we could pay from $1.50 to $2 per day.

It is not my intention to confine you to these prices, but to leave it to you to do the best you can for the public interest both as to the excellence of the talents and the moderation in the wages of the person you may be pleased to select. Should you even (which I do not think improbable) find a man of superior merit willing to come hither on lower terms than those we pay to our very indifferent carvers, it were well to contract with him at the terms with which he will be perfectly satisfied, as he may depend on receiving such an addition to his stipulated salary if his conduct merits it as will place him in proper relation as to salary as well as to abilities with our other workmen. There are, however, other qualities which seem so essential as to be at least as necessary as talents. I mean good temper and good morals. Without them an artist would find himself most unpleasantly situated in a country the language and manners of which are so different from his own, and we should have no dependence upon a person discontented with his situation. For though every exertion would be made on my part to make his engagement perfectly agreeable to him, the irritability of good artists is well known and it is often not easily quieted.

The American consul at Leghorn, who does me the favor to forward this to you, will provide all the expenses and make the arrangements necessary to the voyage of the persons you may select. I think it necessary that he should enter into a written contract to remain with us two years. We will pay all their expenses hither, their salary to commence on the day on which they shall be ready to leave Leghorn, and any reasonable advance to enable them to wind up their affairs at home should be made to them. Single men would be preferred, but no objection would be made to married man, whose family may come over with him. On expiration of the time, and should he choose to return, the expenses of the voyage will also be paid to him on his arrival again in Italy and not before. But this stipulation should not be made unless absolutely demanded. I have a further favor to ask which I hope will give you less trouble than the preceding. It is proposed to place in the Chamber of Representatives a sitting figure of Liberty nine feet in height. I wish to know for what sum such a figure would be executed by Canova in white marble, and for what sum he would execute a model in plaster (the only material I believe in which it could be brought hither), to be executed here in American marble from the model.

If Canova should decline the proposal altogether, as he must now be an old man, what would be the price of such a statue and such a model by the artist he should recommend as in his opinion the nearest to himself in merit?

Although I have not the honor to be personally known to you, I shall not take up your time by apologies for giving you this trouble.

The time is already approaching when our vines and our olives will spread your name and our gratitude over a great portion of our country. Let us also owe to your kindness the introduction of excellence in the most fascinating branch of art.

With true respect, etc.,

B. H. LATROBE.

[Pp. 3–4, ART AND ARTISTS OF THE CAPITOL OF THE UNITED STATES OF AMERICA, by Charles E. Fairman.]

JEFFERSON TO THOMAS MUNROE

Th: Jefferson presents his compliments to m͞r Munroe. he recieved some time ago a parcel of sheet iron from m͞r Latrobe but, without knowing exactly how much, he had supposed it double the quantity stated in the papers furnished by m͞r Munroe, at least he thinks he ordered double the quantity. nevertheless presuming this to be what was furnished him, & which was ordered on his private account, he will answer it to m͞r Lenthall. he returns the account in the name of the Superintendent, and retains that stated against himself. he presumes it was stated in both forms, to meet the case either the one way or the other as it should be.

Apr. 24. 05.

[Letters of the Presidents of the U. S. to the Commissioners of Public Buildings and Grounds, original in the Manuscripts Division, Library of Congress, photostat in National Archives.]

JEFFERSON TO THOMAS MUNROE

Th: Jefferson presents his compliments to m͞r Munroe. he has this moment seen a wooden house building in E. street near m͞r Hobens' which seems indubitably beyond the limits allowed. he prays him to have it examined, & if found unlawful, to have injunctions instantly served on all liable to them.

Apr. 26. 05.

[*Letters of the Presidents of the U. S. to the Commissioners of Public Buildings and Grounds*, original in Manuscript Division, Library of Congress, photostat in National Archives.]

JEFFERSON TO THOMAS MUNROE

TH: J. TO M͞R MUNROE

I do not know whether it is the practice here to issue a sub-poena of injunction without a bill filed. if it is, it would be best to take out one immediately against the master Carpenter & the owner or employer. if it is not the custom, then the case should be stated by letter immediately by post to the Atty of the District, & a bill desired from him without delay. the evasion of putting 2 frames together is too palpable to need consultation.

Mr. Gallatin wishes you to call on him, to explain to him exactly the situation of the High-way fund, & the manner in which you have given in your accounts.

[April 26. 1805.?]

[*Letters of the Presidents of the U. S. to the Commissioners of Public Buildings and Grounds*, original in Manuscript Division, Library of Congress, photostat in National Archives.]

JEFFERSON TO THOMAS MUNROE

Th: J. presents his compliments to m͞r Munroe; he is so much engaged as to be unable to read the inclosed with attention, but has no doubt it is sufficient to obtain the injunction on; & should it need anything material afterwards, it can be amended.

May 1. 05.

[*Letters of the Presidents of the U. S. to the Commissioners of Public Buildings and Grounds*, original in Manuscript Division, Library of Congress, photostat in National Archives.]

LATROBE TO JEFFERSON

THE PRESIDENT OF THE UNITED STATES

Wilmington, Del., May 5, 1805.

Dear Sir: I herewith transmit to you two sheets containing the drawing of the buildings proposed to connect the President's house with the public offices on each side. The height of the story indispensably necessary in the fireproof of the Treasury, of which I by this post also transmit a plan to the Secretary of the Treasury, as well as the general appearance and the connection of the colonnade with the offices at different heights, have induced or rather forced me to make the colonnade of the exact height of the basement story. This throws up the blocking course to the window of the President's house and gets over all difficulties.

[B. H. LATROBE]

[THE JOURNAL OF LATROBE, p. 127.]

THOMAS MUNROE TO JEFFERSON

T Munroe presents his best respects to the President — He did not until Saturday meet with a suitable person to top the trees — a beginning was made on that day (Holt the Gardner having previously given it as his Opinion that it might, at almost any time of the year, be done with safety.) Some persons, however, yesterday mentioned that the sap was too much up, and that many of the trees would be killed if topp'd or trimm'd at this advanced period of the season — TM cannot think so, but not being so well informed on the subject as many others, and being unwilling to run any risk, respectfully asks the Opinion of the President whose experience & knowledge of these things he presumes enable him to say with certainty whether there ought to be a doubt entertained about it

Monday morning 13 *May* 1805

I think they may safely proceed

TH: J.

[*Letters of the Presidents of the U. S. to the Commissioners of Public Buildings and Grounds*, original
in the Manuscripts Division, Library of Congress, photostat in the National Archives.]

ROBERT BRENT TO JEFFERSON

City of Washington August 6th 1805

Dear Sir

At a meeting in the Capitol this day of the Board of Trustees
of the public Schools established by an act of the Corporation
of this City, you were unanimously appointed president of the
Board; and it is with peculiar satisfaction that I fulfil the Instructions of the meeting in communicating this circumstance
to you.

I have the honor to be with
respect & Esteem Dear Sir
Your Obt Servt

ROBERT BRENT *Chairman*

[Ms., *Jefferson Papers*, Library of Congress.]

JEFFERSON TO LAMBERT

Th: Jefferson returns his thanks to m̄r Lambert for the
pamphlets he has sent him and for the testimony they contain
of his respect. he has much confidence in the accuracy with
which he has ascertained the geographical position of our capital, and on account of the importance of a just ascertainment of
our first meridian, hopes it will be still pursued by himself &
others familiar with the practice as well as the theory of the
subject. he presents him his salutations & respects.

Monticello. Aug. 12. 05.

[Ms., *Jefferson Papers*, Library of Congress.]

JEFFERSON TO ROBERT BRENT

Monticello, August 14, 1805.

Sir:

A considerable journey southwardly from this has prevented my sooner acknowledging letters from yourself, from Mr. Gardiner, and from Mr. S. H. Smith, announcing that I had been elected, by the City Council, a trustee for the Public Schools to be established at Washington, and, by the Trustees, to preside at their Board.

I receive, with due sensibility, these proofs of confidence from the City Council and from the Board of Trustees, and ask the favor of you to tender them my just acknowledgments.

Sincerely believing that knowledge promotes the happiness of man, I shall ever be disposed to contribute my endeavors towards its extension; and, in the instance under consideration will willingly undertake the duties proposed to me, so far as others of paramount obligation will permit my attention to them.

I pray you to accept my friendly salutations, and my assurances of great respect and esteem.

TH: JEFFERSON.

ROBERT BRENT, ESQ.,
    Chairman &c.

[P. 003, HISTORY OF THE PUBLIC SCHOOLS OF WASHINGTON CITY, District of Columbia, From August, 1805, to August, 1875, written, at request and published by order of the Board of Trustees of Public Schools, for the National Centennial Year, 1876, By Samuel Yorke At Lee.]

JEFFERSON NOTE

Honored Sir

We whose names are hereunto subscribed having been appointed a Committee for the purpose of devising means to remove the great grievance which the citizens of the Eastern District of the City labor under for the want of a market in that

District, do humbly request that you will grant us permission to erect a markethouse of the Square west of Square 881, which is designated on the original plan of the City a Market Square
We are with veneration and respect
Sir, your obedient Humble Servants

ROB.ᵀ ALEXANDER
ADAM LINDSAY
WILLIAM PROUT

Mr. Munro will be pleased to report to me on the reasonableness of this application.

TH: JEFFERSON
Oct. 27. 05

[*Letters of the Presidents of the U. S. to the Commissioners of Public Buildings and Grounds*, original in Manuscripts Division, Library of Congress, photostat in National Archives.]

PROCLAMATION

I THOMAS JEFFERSON PRESIDENT OF THE UNITED STATES

Do hereby declare and make known that the public reservation in the City of Washington numbered sixteen, being bounded on the north by K street south, on the south by L street south, on the west by Sixth street East and on the East by an Alley sixty feet wide which bounds square numbered Eight hundred and eighty one, be and the same hereby is appropriated as an for the site of a public market during the pleasure of the proper authority, and subject to the rules and regulations such authority shall have ordained and established or may hereafter ordain and establish.

Given under my Hand at the City of Washington this twenty eighth Day of October in the year One thousand eight hundred and five.

TH: JEFFERSON

[*Letters of the Presidents of the U. S. to the Commissioners of Public Buildings and Grounds*, original in the Manuscripts Division, Library of Congress, photostat in the National Archives.]

JEFFERSON TO CONGRESS

THE PRESIDENT TO THE SENATE AND HOUSE OF REPRESENTATIVES
December 27, 1805

I lay before Congress a report of the surveyor of the public buildings, stating the progress made on them during the last season, and what may be expected to be accomplished in the ensuing one.

[P. 115, DOCUMENTARY HISTORY . . . OF THE CAPITOL.]

JEFFERSON TO THOMAS MUNROE

Washington Feb. 23. 06.

Sir

I return you the inclosed proclamation, & to avoid an innovation which might produce uneasiness, I believe it will be best to continue it in it's usual form.

With respect to inclosures, so long as the former proprietors keep up an inclosure, & the streets in it are not pressingly wanted for the public, we will permit them to remain. but whenever the owner has once taken away his inclosure, we must never permit it to be put up again, except in squares, leaving all the streets open. by attending strictly to this we may in time get the whole site of the city cleared of the right of occupation. Accept my salutations.

TH: JEFFERSON.

[*Letters of the Presidents of the U. S. to the Commissioners of Public Buildings and Grounds*, original in the Manuscripts Division, Library of Congress, photostat in the National Archives.]

JEFFERSON TO THOMAS MUNROE

Th: Jefferson, with his compliments to M.ʳ Munroe, incloses him a letter to John Davidson for his perusal & to be forwarded, retaining a copy with the original now inclosed, for the use of his office.

Mar. 30. 06.

[*Letters of the Presidents of the U. S. to the Commissioners of Public Buildings and Grounds*, original in the Manuscripts Division, Library of Congress, photostat in the National Archives.]

JEFFERSON TO DAVIDSON

Washington 30th *March* '06

Sir,

The circumstance which has drawn attention to the re-inclosure of the City Lots was this observation that great obstructions were made to the outlets of the City by extensive inclosures in the north Eastern quarter; which too are not employed in raising garden stuff or grass or any other article which might accommodate the City, but are worn down in Indian Corn and then turned out incapable of bringing any thing — therefore it was thought best that as fast as the occupiers voluntarily withdrew their inclosures that they should not be reestablished, as the open grounds employed as a common in grass for the support of the cattle of the poor who depend much on them for subsistence are of more value to this City than inclosed and worn down with Indian corn. Observing however that the grounds you wish to re-inclose between K street, Massachusetts Avenue, 11th & 14th streets will not stop any important outlet and desirous of yielding every indulgence to proprietors not inconsistent with the general good permission is given to reinclose those grounds — always subject however to have the streets opened when the convenience of the City shall require it —

Accept my salutations & assurances of esteem

TH: JEFFERSON

MR SAML DAVIDSON

[*Letters of the Presidents of the U. S. to the Commissioners of Public Buildings and Grounds*, original in the Manuscripts Division, Library of Congress, photostat in the National Archives.]

Breckenridge to Jefferson

Washington, April 5, 1806

Sir:

I have examined the memorial and accompanying documents of S. Davidson, which you were pleased to transmit to me some time since for my opinion, and have received from Mr. Davidson such explanations and elucidations of the subject, as he thought proper to give.

I understand his statement and cause of complaint to be this: that a plan of the City of Washington, designed by Mr. L'Enfant in 1791 (and which is hereunto annexed and marked No. 2), ought, so far as regards the President's Square and adjoining lots, to be considered the plan of the City; that by successive acts and declarations of President Washington, and those acting under him, this plan was sanctioned, and sales partially made under that sanction; that in 1792 Major Ellicott, under the authority of President Washington, altered the plan designed by L'Enfant, materially, to the prejudice of Davidson and of the City, by omitting to include as building lots four several parcels of ground, painted yellow in the annexed plan of L'Enfant, lying north of the President's House, and that thereby he is deprived of a moiety of this ground, to which he would have been entitled, under the plan of L'Enfant and under the deeds of trust made by him, Davidson, to the trustees of the City.

Opinion.

Two questions naturally occur in the examination of this case: 1st. What powers did the President possess to establish the plan of the city? 2nd. How and when has he exercised these powers? (1) The Power of the President to establish the plan of the city is derived solely from the deeds of the proprietors. These require the trustees to convey to the Commissioners "such streets, squares, parcels, and lots, as the President shall deem proper for the use of the United States." No time being limited in which this power should be exercised by him or under his authority, it follows, that it rested in his discretion to execute it from time to time as circumstances might require. The manner in which the power should be exercised being also undefined, its execution is to be sought for in the declaration, acts or instruments, by which it is manifested. When such execution is clearly manifested by any such act, it is, I conceive, a complete exercise of his power, and so far as that act extends is irrevocable by himself and binding on his successors.

This leads to an examination of the 2nd point, how far, and in what manner, the power has been exercised? In October, 1791, President Washington informs Congress that the District was located, and City laid out, a plan of which should be laid before them.

In December following he communicated to them the plan of L'Enfant, and after time given for its inspection, he withdrew it. This communication of the plan was intended merely as a matter of information, and to shew in what state the business then was. All his subsequent acts and declarations conclusively prove that this plan had not then received his sanction. Major L'Enfant having been dismissed, Major Ellicott was in 1792 employed to prepare a plan, which he accordingly did; and although the ground work of the plan was the design of L'Enfant, yet President Washington declares that many alterations deemed essential were made in it with his approbation, particularly in the public squares, which except those of the Capitol and President's House, were struck out of L'Enfant's design, and were left to future determination. This plan, thus compleated, was sent to Philadelphia to be engraved, was accordingly engraved, was promulgated throughout the United States, and, to use the expression of President Washington, was thereby intended to receive "its final and regulating stamp."

In October, 1792, a sale of lots took place, at which this engraved plan was exhibited. At this sale a division was made between the Commissioners and Mr. Davidson, and the squares 167 and 186 were assigned to him; and squares 200 and 221 to the United States. Mr. Davidson became the purchaser of 221; and 200 was sold to others, and he received payment at the rate of £25 pr. acre, in conformity to the deed of trust, for the residue of the President's Square.

In February, 1797, the President in answer to a letter written to him by the Commissioners, enclosing a memorial from Mr. Davidson upon the subject of complaint now under consideration, explicitly declares that the transmission of L'Enfant's plan to Congress, was not considered by him as an adoption of it; that he considered it as then remaining under his control; that many errors were afterwards discovered in it and corrected; that he had so often expressed his unwillingness to depart from the engraved plan, in every instance where it could be avoided, that he hoped no repetition of this sort would have been made by any of the proprietors.

In March, 1797, President Washington executes an instrument of writing in which he directs the trustees to convey to the Commissioners all the streets as delineated in a plan said to be annexed. This by accident was not annexed; but is said by the Commissioners to have been annexed and sanctioned by President Adams in 1798. Nothing it appears to me can be more conclusive to shew the intention of President Washington than the foregoing facts; that so far from omitting by mistake to establish, as building lots, the ground in controversy, exhibited in L'Enfant's plan, he evidently intended to exclude those lots from the engraved plan. That Mr. Davidson did not himself consider this portion of L'Enfant's plan to have been retained, much less sanctioned by President Washington, is manifest by a written contract entered into between him and the Commissioners, on the 9th of January, 1794, in which it is agreed that if any new square or squares for buildings, or other appropriation for buildings, or other appropriation except as a public square is hereafter made on his, said Davidson's part of the President's Square, bounded on the west by 17th street west, on the north by H street north, on the east by 15th street west, and on the south by D. Burnes' line (except the two squares of 167 and 221 already established and laid off), that then the said Davidson is and shall be entitled to his dividend of such square or squares or other appropriation agreeably to his deed of trust.

I am, therefore, of opinion on this part of Mr. Davidson's memorial, that the plan of L'Enfant, so far as respects the lots which he now claims, as building lots, was never established as such by President Washington; that although they appeared in the plan of L'Enfant, yet they were struck out of the plan which was afterwards drawn by Mr. Ellicott, engraved by order of the President, and declared by his successive acts to be the plan of the City which he would not depart from in any instance, where it could be avoided. So completely have the powers vested in President Washington been exercised in settling definitively the plan of the city, so far, at least, as regards that portion of it now under consideration, that in my opinion there rests nowhere a power to alter it. The proprietors of the soil had a right to annex such conditions and limitations to their grants as they judged proper. The President, who was their trustee, has executed, so far as regards the present question, his trust. He has determined the plan. He had the exclusive power to do so. He has completely expended that power, and it is unalterable, not only by his successors but by Congress itself.

I cannot discern any just foundation for the claim which Mr. Davidson sets up to a portion of the grounds allotted to the War Office. It appears from a certificate from the Commissioners dated 29th January, 1794, that he has actually received from them at the rate of £25 pr. acre for the President's square, including the very ground in which he now claims an interest.

The memorial and accompanying papers are all returned and I have the honor to be

Most respectfully, Sir,

Your most obedient Servant,

JOHN BRECKENRIDGE.

THE PRESIDENT OF THE UNITED STATES.

[Pp. 2273–2276, U. S. v. MORRIS, Records, VII.]

KING TO JEFFERSON

NICHOLAS KING TO JEFFERSON

September 25, 1806.

[refers to plans and regulations by the Commissioners on July 20, 1795]

Perfecting this part of the plan, so as to leave nothing for conjecture, litigation or doubt, in the manner which shall most accord with the published plans, secure the health of the city, and afford the most convenience to the merchants, requires immediate attention . . . The principle adopted in the engraved plan, if carried into effect and *finally established in the plan now laid out upon the ground,* when aided by proper regulations as to the materials and mode of constructing wharves for vessels to lay at and discharge their cargoes on, seems well calculated to preserve the purity of the air. The other streets will here terminate in a street or key, open to the water, and admitting a free current of air. It will form a general communication between the wharves and warehouses of different merchants, and, by facilitating intercourse, render a greater service to them than they would derive from a permission to wharf as they pleased. The position of this Water Street being determined, it will ascertain the extent and situation of the building squares and streets on the made ground, from the bank of the river and bring the present as near to the published plan as now can be done. It will define the extent and privileges of water lots, and enable the owners to improve without fear of infringing on the rights of others.

. . . Along the water side of the street, the free current or stream of the river should be permitted to flow and carry with it whatever may have been brought from the city along the streets or sewers. The wharves permitted beyond this street to the channel may be stages or bridges with piers and sufficient waterways under them. And on the wharves so erected, it would seem proper to prohibit the erection of houses or anything obstructing a free circulation of air.

. . . The surveying is now so far completed that it can be done with the utmost precision, and every foot of ground within the limits of the Federal City, with its appurtenant privileges, may be so defined as to prevent litigation or doubt on the subject. If it is not done at this time the evils will increase and every year add to our difficulties. Even now, from the various decisions or neglects, alterations or amendments which have heretofore taken place, some time an investigation may be necessary in the arrangement of a system which shall combine justice with convenience. If this decision is left to a future period and our courts of law, they can only have a partial view of the subject, and any general rule they may adopt may be attended with serious disadvantages.

[Pp. 258–9, MORRIS v. UNITED STATES, UNITED STATES REPORTS, Vol. 174, October 1898, Cases adjudged in The Supreme Court.]

JEFFERSON TO LENTHALL

THE PRESIDENT TO LENTHALL

October 21, 1806

Dear Sir: The skylights in the dome of the House of Repre-

sentatives' Chamber were a part of the plan as settled and communicated to Mr. Latrobe; that the preparation for them has
not been made and the building now to be stopped for them
has been wrong; to correct that wrong now they must be immediately prepared, and that the building may be delayed as
short a time as possible as many hands as possible should be
employed in preparing them.

Accept my salutations and best wishes.

[Glenn Brown, HISTORY OF THE UNITED STATES CAPITOL, I, 42.]

JEFFERSON TO CONGRESS

THE PRESIDENT TO THE HOUSE OF REPRESENTATIVES

December 15, 1806

I lay before congress a report of the surveyor of the public
buildings, stating the progress made on them during the last
season, and what is proposed for the ensuing one.

I took every measure within my power for carrying into
effect the request of the house of representatives, of the 17th of
April last,[54] to cause the south wing of the capitol to be prepared
for their accommodation by the commencement of the present
session. With great regret I found it was not to be accomplished. The quantity of free stone necessary, with the size and
quality of many of the blocks, was represented as beyond what
could be obtained from the quarries by any exertions which
could be commanded. The other parts of the work which might
all have been completed in time, were necessarily retarded by
the insufficient progress of the stone work.

[Pp. 119–20, DOCUMENTARY HISTORY . . . OF THE CAPITOL.]

[54] On April 17 the House "Resolved that the President of the United States be requested
to take effectual measures to cause the south wing of the Capitol to be prepared for the
accommodation of the House of Representatives, by the commencement of the next
session of Congress." Four days later, on April 21, the House voted a sum of $40,000,
"to be applied under the direction of the President of the United States, towards completing the south wing of the Capitol."

Latrobe to Jefferson

TO THE PRESIDENT OF THE UNITED STATES OF AMERICA.

The Report of the Surveyor of the public Buildings of the United States at Washington.

Washington Novr 25.th 1806.

Sir,

The difficulty of procuring a sufficient supply of freestone, of a quality suitable to the construction of the interior of the House of Representatives, and of its communications, which I stated and explained to you in my report of the 22.nd day of December 1805, has rendered the completion of the South wing of the Capitol, so that it could be occupied by the House during the approaching Session, impracticable.

All the parts of the work which depended on the covering of the building, and the construction of the Stonework have therefore necessarily been retarded, or postponed. In order to prevent the disappointment thus occasioned, every encouragement was offered to the Quarriers to make extraordinary exertions. But the actual State of the Quarries, the manner in which the labourers are hired & employed in them, and the limited prospect of supply to the public Works after the present Year, appear to have offered insuperable obstacles: — and the last Load which was wanted for the South wing, and which should have arrived in August was delivered only a few days ago.

In every other branch of labour and of materials we have been in sufficient forwardness. The Carpenters work has for some time waited for the progress of the Stonework: the roof was framed last winter; the Sashes are made & glazed: the doors & shutters are in readiness to be put together: and all the work that could be fixed, is in its place. Stonecutters have been collected from distant parts of the Union who have often been set to work on parts of the building that might have been postponed to another season, for want of freestone. All the buildin

stone which will be wanted is on the spot: — and the sand &
lime required for the plaistering has been procured; and in no
other material or preparation have we been deficient.

Under circumstances so entirely beyond the controul of
those to whom you have committed the charge of the public
Works, it has not been possible, that the request of the House of
Representatives, urged by your constant attention to the means
of its accomplishment, could be complied with. And when it is
considered, that this infant establishment has none of the
means of extraordinary exertions which are to be found in
great & populous cities, — that for almost every material we
use, we are dependent upon distant places; — for our lime on
the new England States, — for our Lumber on the Delaware &
the Eastern shore of the Chesapeak, — for our iron on Pennsylvania; for many other articles for which there is no demand
here, excepting for the supply of the public buildings, on Baltimore & Philadelphia — and that even for our freestone, the
most important article in the work, the wants of the public
buildings are not sufficient to encourage the employment of
much capital and labour in the quarries, when all this is considered, it will not appear surprizing that the most reasonable
calculations as to lime, and estimates as to expense, are disappointed. Rough building stone, bricks & sand are to be procured in sufficient quantity, of excellent quality, and on reasonable notice; but of every other article provision must be made a
considerable time beforehand, and from distant Sources.

In answer to a letter from the Chairman of the Committee of
the House of Representatives to whom your message relative to
the public buildings was referred, — dated December 30th 1804
I stated that the sum required at that time for the complete
erection of the South wing was 109.100 and of the Recessed
part of the House [55] 25.200
                                    $134.300.

[55] NOTE. In my report of the 22[d] December 1805 by an error of Clerkship, for which

An appropriation was made in January 1805 for the completion of
the South wing of...................................... 110.000
and in 1806, a further appropriation of.................... 40.000

was granted.   Total............... 150.000

The Accounts of the buildings cannot be collected & made up at
present, — but from a general view of them, with which the Superintendent of the City has politely favoured me, there appears to
be still applicable to the South wing of the Capitol the sum of   11.000
To this sum must be added the amount of materials purchased for
the roof of the North wing in order to be able to finish the new roof
without delay & the necessary Glass for repairs which was bought
in consequence of the Act prohibiting the importation of Glass
from England, & the difficulty of procuring it from Germany   5.000

                    Total............... 16.000

which being deducted from the above appropriations leaves a
balance of Dollˢ 134.000 being the sum already expended on
the South wing, out of the appropriation of 150.000 dollars.

There still remains to be finished the upper part of the Recess, and its roof, the covering of the roof, all the plaistering, an
inconsiderable part of the Stonecutting, part of the Carpenters
work, the painting — and all the smaller works and fixings required in the ultimate finishing.

Independently of the difficulty of accurately estimating any
work in the progressive state in which it was in the year 1804,
the excess in the estimate is to be accounted for, from the use in
the price of many of our materials, especially freestone, — and
also of our Labor in different branches, — from the charge of
contingencies not included in the building estimate, — and
from the expensive exertions we have made in the present
Year.

To compleat the work on the South wing, I respectfully sug-

I cannot now account, the estimated expense of the Recess is set down at only 13.000,
instead of 25.200 Doˡˢ as stated in my letter of the 30ᵗʰ Decʳ 1804, from which this
item was copied: On reference to my original estimate which I have reexamined the
sum ought certainly to have been $25.200. [Note of Latrobe.]

gest, that in addition to the money in hand a further appropriation will be necessary; and as there cannot now exist a doubt
but that the House will be ready before the next Session of Congress, I also beg leave to state, that the numerous committee
rooms and offices, together with the encreased size and altered
form of the house, will require a special appropriation for furnishing the same, and supplying the necessary Stoves & fireplaces.

North Wing. In my report of December 22^d 1805, I stated
the result of a careful survey of the North wing of the Capitol.
Towards the close of the Session, a large part of the ceiling of
the central Lobby fell down. The whole of the plaistering of
that ceiling has been removed. It was found to be in a very
dangerous state, and on examination of the plaistering of the
Dome of the Staircase it was judged prudent to take down all
the ornamental part of the ceiling, and part of the ceiling itself,
& to receil it. The whole of the ceiling of the Senate chamber
has also been removed, and new lathing & plaistering put in
its place. The plaistering of the columns which were burst, has
also been secured.

The other ceilings are judged to be perfectly safe for the
present.

Many attempts have been made during the last Season to
prevent the leakage of the Gutters and of the Skyligthts [sic].
But as the lead of the gutters is coated with Tar & sand, it is not
only almost impossible to discover the place of the leaks, but
also when discovered, to cure them. To take up the gutters
without breaking up the whole roof its peculiar construction
rendered very difficult; and besides, unless at the same time its
whole form had been altered, it would have been an useless
expense.

The necessity of accommodating both Houses in the same
Wing, has therefore prevented any attempt of this kind, — for
should a heavy rain have occurred during the operation, the

destruction of the plaistering of the Walls and of the ceiling
would have been such, as to have occasioned enormous expense
in useless repairs, and perhaps have endangered the accommodation of one or both houses of congress, during the present
Session.

It being however ascertained by the present state of the
South wing of the Capitol, that it will certainly be finished before the next session of congress, I have to lay before you, agreeably to your requisition, a plan of the alterations which may be
made in the North wing so as to adapt it, not only to the ample
accommodation of the Senate and of its Committees and officers, but also of the Judiciary of the United States, without any
addition to the Body of the building.

The principle of the proposed alteration is this; to appropriate the whole of the lower, or Basement story to the use of the
Judiciary, by making the centre door of the north front, the
entrance, shutting up the communication of the centre Lobby
with the Greatstairs — and raising the floor of the Senate
chamber to the principal floor, on the level of the Bases of the
external Pilasters. The Door & vestibule in the East front, the
great stairs, and the whole of the upper part of the building, to
be for the occupancy & use of the Senate.

The Judiciary branch of Government would then have the
following accommodations:
A Court room, on the present floor of the Senate chamber
A Grand jury room,
Two Jury rooms,
The Office of the Clerk of the Supreme Court.
The Office of the Clerk of the circuit court.

The Senate of the United States would have its door of Entrance in the Recess on the East front as at present. The great
stairs would be in the great Elliptical area in which the stairs
now are.

The Senate chamber would be over the court room, — being

carried up through the upper Story now entirely unfinished and useful only for Lumber.

Three Committee rooms would occupy the North front.

The Lobby of the house to the South of the Senate chamber, &

The Secretary's Office would be on the East front.

The Library would retain its present situation with alteration of its form. Above the Committee rooms three other rooms would be on the North front which may be occupied by the Records, and over the office of the Secretary would be the Lodging of the assistant doorkeeper.

On the ground floor would be an internal court & Privies, and every apartment, and stairs would be perfectly light.

These arrangements are very fully explained by the drawings herewith submitted, in which the parts to be added or removed are distinctly pointed out. The ease with which they may be made considering their extent, and the great additional accommodation they will afford, is very evident. No Wall is proposed to be pulled down, nor even cut, but in detached parts of no consequence to its solidity. And I must here remark that the external and internal Walling has been most faithfully performed, and that the Walls are capable of resisting and bearing any stress or pressure proposed to be put upon them.

On the other hand the plaisterers work, is universally bad, & scarcely adheres even to the brick Walls, and the carpenters work is not only rotten, but injudiciously and insecurely put together.

Therefore, if no alteration of arrangement were proposed, the whole of what is proposed to be taken away by the present design, would necessarily be taken away for the sake of security, much of it immediately, and all of it in the course of a few years; — as soon as the convenience of the Legislature would permit. The expense of the proposed arrangements will therefore be comparitively [sic] small, when the necessary expense of repair is deducted.

In making these alterations & repairs there will be the advantage of working under cover of the present roof, an advantage of very great importance, both in point of expense and of expedition, and the work never being soaked by the rain, will soon be dry & the house fit for occupation: I respectfully submit to you the following plan for proceeding in the execution of this proposal.

As soon as the Session is ended, March 4th 1807, the whole of the Eastern side of the house, — including the E. Vestibule, the small & great staircase, — the central Lobby — the north Vestibule & the Senate chamber shall be taken in hand, and the alterations made with all possible speed.

The Library & all the West apartments shall remain untouched, and shall be occupied by the Senate at their next Session of 1807–1808. I have not the smallest hesitation in saying that the whole Eastern part of the House will be finished in 1808 so as to be occupied at the Session beginning in that year.

The Western apartments may then be altered & can easily be finished in one season. Each half of the roof can be separately altered, and rebuilt on a plan perfectly secure. In 1809–1810 the whole wing will be completed.

Estimate of expenditures proposed to finish the South wing for the occupancy of Congress previous to the next session independently of the money in hand.............................. [56] 25.000
furnishing the same....................................... 20.000
Towards altering the East side of the North wing............ 50.000
Contingencies.. 5.000
                                              Total   100 000

[56] I must observe that the finishing of the capitals of the columns of the house of Representatives will be the work of a few years to come, — the time of finishing them will depend on the number of artists which can be procured. [Note of Latrobe.]

President's House

At the close of the last season there remained unexpended of the funds assigned to the other public buildings the sum of $6.255.92/100.

The whole of this sum has been exhausted in completing the erection of the domestic offices of the President's house, in building a stable in addition to them, and in a great variety of small repairs and improvements which are perpetually required in and about so extensive and unfinished a building.

The inconvenience which has been hitherto suffered for want of stables, and which still arises from the want of carriage houses near the President's house is not inconsiderable. The range of offices on each wing has added something to the accommodation of the president, but they are still unfinished, and imperfect, and the balance of former appropriations was not sufficient even to construct the covered approach to them, which is intended to form the South front, not only for convenience, but for the decency of their appearance.

But independently of the addition of a carriage house, a fund will be wanted to pay the current expenses of repairs & minor improvements for the next year, and to settle the current accounts: the sum of 5.000 Dollars would be required for that purpose. Should it be agreed to add the carriage house proposed, and to dress the grounds around the house preparatory to their being planted and enclosed permanently an additional appropriation proportioned to what shall be proposed would of course be necessary.

              I am, Sir,

                    with high respect

                        Y^{rs} faithfully

                                B Henry Latrobe

[Ms., *Records of the U. S. Senate, National Archives;* pp. 120–3, DOCUMENTARY HISTORY . . . OF THE CAPITOL . . ., incompletely published.]

JEFFERSON TO CONGRESS

THE PRESIDENT TO THE HOUSE OF REPRESENTATIVES

December 23, 1806

I now lay before you accounts of the sums which have been expended by the United States on the capitol, the President's house, the public offices, the navy yard, and the marine barracks, respectively, and the amount expended on other objects of public expense within the city of Washington, as requested by your resolution of the fifteenth instant.

[P. 124, DOCUMENTARY HISTORY . . . OF THE CAPITOL.]

THOMAS MUNROE TO JEFFERSON

THOMAS MUNROE TO THE PRESIDENT

December 20, 1806

Sir, In obedience to your letter of the 16th instant, I have the honor to transmit to you herewith an account, stating the several sums received from the treasury of the United States, and expended on the capitol, the President's house, the public offices, and other objects of public expense within the city of Washington.

Your most obedient servant.

An account stating the several sums received from the treasury of the United States, and expended on the Capitol, the President's house, the Public offices, and other objects of Public expense, within the city of Washington.

The monies received for these objects from the treasury of the United States, have been under the authority of appropriations made by the following acts of congress:	Received from the treasury
Dollars Cents	*Dollars*
Act of 6th May, 1796............ 200,000	

The monies received for these objects from the treasury of the United States, have been under the authority of appropriations made by the following acts of
congress:

	Dollars	Cents	Received from the treasury
			Dollars
18th April, 1798..........	100,000		
24th April, 1800..........	10,000		310,000
3d March, 1801 (general ap-propr.).................	5,122		
3d May, 1802............	8,000		
2d March, 1803 (general ap-propr.)................	3,702	66	
3d March, 1803..........	50,000		
27th March, 1804.........	50,000		
25th January, 1805........	110,000		
Ditto....................	20,000		
1st March, 1805...........	9,000		
21st April, 1806...........	40,000		295,824 66
			605,824 66

These monies have been expended as follows:

On the Capitol

Act of 3d March, 1803. Of the 50,000 dollars, appropriated by this act, there were expended on
the capitol.

Dollars

37,342 75

27th March, 1804. Of the 50,000 dollars, appropriated by this act, there were expended on the
capitol.

36,896 04

25th January, 1805. An appropriation by this act,
was expended on south wing...... 110,000
And of the $20,000 further appropri-
ated by the same act, were expended
on the north wing.............. 1,130 89

111,130 89

25th April, 1806. Of the appropriation by this act, there have been expended on south wing........... 35,327 96

The monies received for these objects from the treasury of the United States, have been under the authority of appropriations made by the following acts of congress:	Received from the treasury
Dollars Cents	*Dollars*
Remaining to be expended........ 4,672 04	
40,000	
	225,369 68

* * *

Other Objects of Public Expense:
1796, May 6th. Of a loan of 200,000 dollars, by the state of Maryland, guaranteed by the United States, $120,000 have been paid, and $80,000 are still due (both sums exclusive of interest) paid from time to time....................... 200,000

1798, April 18th. By this act the United States loaned the city this sum, which, with the other monies borrowed under the guarantee of the United States, was expended promiscuously, amongst the monies which arose out of the funds of the city, on the public buildings, and other objects of expense. 100,000.

NOTE. It appears by a representation of the late commissioners of the city of Washington, laid before Congress in January, 1801, that, exclusive of the grounds reserved to the United States, for public purposes, which cost the city funds $37, 774, 50, property amounting to $884,819.88, estimating the unsold lots at the prices for which previous sales had been made, then remained at the disposal of the government. Since that time the chancellor of Maryland has decreed the sale of 1,000 lots, not included in the above estimates, for the payment of 80,000 dollars, purchase money due thereon, with interest from the 1st May 1800. The proceeds of these 1,000 lots, and 150 others, not included in the commissioners estimate, but since ascertained to belong to the United States, may be considered as additions to the property stated in that estimate, and will be considerably more than equal to the subsequent sales which have been made.

THOMAS MUNROE, *Superintendent*

[Pp. 124–26, DOCUMENTARY HISTORY OF . . . THE CAPITOL; INCOMPLETE.]

Robert Brent to Jefferson

City of Washington March 9ᵗʰ 1807
recᵈ Mar. 9.

Sir

The last Congress having appropriated 3000$ to be applied under your direction to the improvement of Roads Streets and Avenues I must ask the favor of you, if you do not deem it improper, to direct an application of part of that fund to the opening and improveing the Delaware and Maryland Avenues from the Capitol to their intersection with the potowmack.

The First of these Avenues will open a communication between the Capitol and Greenleafs point, the Rope Walk and Magasine; and, if improved, some arrangement will probably be made for establishing packets at its junction with the River to ply between Alexandria and this City, which, you will readily perceive, by viewing the map, will afford the nearest point of communication in that way.

The Second, Maryland Avenue, leads to a situation on the potowmack at which a Ferry is about to be established. thus while these Avenues will afford two additional communications from Alexandria, they will add much to the convenience of persons now settled, or who may settle, on the point or in the neighbourhood of either of them.

I am informed that measures will probably be taken to finish in the course of the ensuing summer, the Houses which have been so long in a ruinous state at the point, and that they will be occupied by respectable and Reputable Inhabitants. By opening the Delaware Avenue it will add to the inducement of persons wishing to settle in them: Besides the present population at that place is not inconsiderable.

I can not ask you for this application of money unless you see in it a proper discharge of the Trust which is confided in you.

But if you see no impropriety in the application as it regards this trust, I would add this observation as some inducement to the application, that no original proprietor made greater sacrifices in comfort and convenience than did the late M.ʳ Young, whose Family now represents him, by yielding up his property for the City; and none have had less of the public money laid out on the land given up by them, by which that which they retained could be brought into action.

I have the honor to be With respect & esteem Sir

Your Mo Ob.ᵗ Ser.ᵗ

ROBERT BRENT

[Ms., *Jefferson Papers*, Library of Congress.]

JEFFERSON TO ROBERT BRENT

Washington Mar. 10. 07.

Sir

I have received your letter of yesterday asking the application of a part of a late appropriation of Congress to certain avenues and roads in this place.

The only appropriation ever before made by Congress to an object of this nature was 'to the public buildings & the high ways *between* them.' this ground was deliberately taken, and I accordingly restrained the application of the money to the avenue between the Capitol and Executive buildings & the roads round the two squares.

The last appropriation was in terms much more lax, to wit, 'for avenues & roads in the district of Columbia.' this indeed would take in a large field, but besides that we cannot suppose Congress intended to tax the people of the US. at large for all the avenues in Washington & roads in Columbia, we know the fact to have been that the expression was strongly objected to, and was saved merely from a want of time to discuss (the last day of the Session) and the fear of losing the whole bill. but the sum appropriated (3000 D.) shews they did not mean it for so large a field. for by the time the Pensylvā avenue between the two houses is widened, newly gravelled, planted, brick tunnels instead of wood, the roads round the squares put in order & that in the South front of the War office dug down to it's proper level, there will be no more of the 3000 D. left than will be wanting for constant repairs. With this view of the just & probable intention of the legislature, I shall not think myself authorised to take advantage of a lax expression, forced on by circumstances to carry the execution of the law into a region of expence which would merit great consideration before they should embark in it. Accept my friendly salutations and assurances of great esteem & respect.

TH: JEFFERSON.

ROBERT BRENT ESQ.

[Pp. 33–4, Ford, WRITINGS, IX; Memorial Edition, XI, pp. 164–5.]

JEFFERSON TO LATROBE

Monticello Apr. 22. 07.

Dear Sir

Yours of the 14th came to hand on the 20th. the idea of spending 1000. D. for the temporary purpose of covering the pannel lights over the representatives chamber, merely that the room may be plaistered before the roof is closed, is totally inadmissible. but I do not see why that particular part of the plaistering should not be postponed until the pannel lights are glazed. I hope there is no danger but that the glazing may be ready so as to leave time enough to so much of the plaistering as would be injured by the want of it. It is with real pain I oppose myself to your passion for the lanthern, and that in a matter of taste, I differ from a professor in his own art. but the object of the artist is lost if he fails to please the general eye. You know my reverence for the Graecian & Roman style of architecture. I do not ~~believe~~ recollect ever to have seen in their buildings a single instance of a lanthern, Cupola, or belfry. I have ever supposed the Cupola an Italian invention, produced by the introduction of bells in the churches, and one of the ~~instances of~~ degeneracies of modern architecture. I confess they are most offensive to my eye, and a particular observation has strengthened my disgust at them. in the projet for the central part of the Capitol which you were so kind as to give me, there is something of this kind on the crown of the dome. the drawing was exhibited for the view of the members, in the president's house, and the disapprobation of that feature in the drawing was very general. on the whole I cannot be afraid of having our dome like that of the Pantheon, on which had a lanthern been placed it would never have obtained that degree of admiration in which it is now held by the world. I shall be with you in three weeks: in the mean time I salute you with esteem & respect.

Th: Jefferson

Mᴿ. LATROBE

[Ms., *Jefferson Papers*, Library of Congress.]

LATROBE TO JEFFERSON

Washington, April 29, 1807.

THE PRESIDENT OF THE UNITED STATES

Sir: At the President's house I have laid out the road on the principle of the plan extended to you. A small alteration of the outline of the inclosures to the south was necessarily made, which renders the whole ground infinitely more handsome and accommodates the public with an easier access from the Pennsylvania Avenue to the New York Avenue. In the plan submitted to and approved by you a semicircle was struck to the south from the center of the bow of the house. The semicircle carried the inclosure too far to the south. Mr. King will lay before you the new plan, which differs from the other in being of oblong figure instead of a semicircle.

By this alteration many very important objects are gained:

1. The Pennsylvania and New York avenues are by the wall and gate opposite to them at right angles.

2. A direct access is obtained from the New York to the Pennsylvania Avenue and on the shortest line.

3. The wall is straight from point to point, and thus all circular work is avoided.

4. The nature of the ground is consulted so far as to obtain the best level for the road with the least removal of earth.

5. The road runs in such a manner that the President's house is not overlooked from the *low* ground and is covered by the rising knolls as the road rises.

Having laid out the ground with the assistance of Mr. King, to whose kindness and skill I am under the greatest obligations, the next consideration was how to do the greatest quantity of business with the fund appropriated, and if possible to get at least the south half of the wall built this summer. I therefore bought a cargo of lime, made a contract for stone, and preparatory arrangements for the work itself.

The next step was to get down to the foot of the wall on the south side by cutting out the road to its proper width, leaving the internal dressing of the ground to the last. The building of the wall rendered it necessary to go to the permanent depth of the road, otherwise I should have contented myself with laying it down on its right place, removing only so much earth as would have made the declivities convenient to the carriages. But this could not be done, and I contracted to loosen the ground from the first walnut southeast of the President's house to the War Office, the width of the road, footpath, and wall.

The next consideration was to execute your directions as to the north side of the President's house, and to level the ground regularly and gradually from the level of the stones in front of the steps, which nearly agrees with the site of the offices, sloping in their direction toward the inclosure. The earth which was to effect this necessarily was removed from the site of the offices between the President's house and the War Offices.

B. H. LATROBE

[THE JOURNAL OF LATROBE, pp. 135–137.]

LATROBE TO JEFFERSON

Philadelphia, May 21, 1807.

THE PRESIDENT OF THE UNITED STATES

Sir: In arranging the papers which I brought with me from Washington I have had the mortification of finding the inclosed letter, written immediately before my departure from the city and intended to have been forwarded by the post of the evening, but which, it appears, in the hurry of packing up, had slipped into my paper case. I still beg the favor of you to read it, as it contains my reason for the measures I took previous to my departure, and will explain the manner in which I hope to accomplish your objects as respects the arrangement of the ground around the President's house.

On the 16th inst. your letter, Monticello, April 22, reached me here, being forwarded by Mrs. Lenthall. Hoping to be at Washington as soon at least as you return I did not immediately answer it. But I am waiting from day to day for the arrival of one of the Georgetown packets in order to put my things on board previous to my removal.

I am very sensible of the honor you do me in discussing with me the merits of the detail of the public building. I know well that *to you* it is my duty to obey implicitly or to resign my office: to myself it is my duty to maintain myself in a situation in which I can provide for my family by all honorable means. If in any instance my duty to you obliged me to act contrary to my judgment, I might fairly and honorably say with Shakespeare's apothecary: "My poverty, not my will consents." Such excuse, however, I have never wanted, for although in respect to the panel lights I am acting diametrically contrary to my judgment, no mercenary motive whatever has kept me at my post, but considerations very superior to money — the attachment arising from gratitude and the highest esteem. At the same time I candidly confess that the question has suggested itself to my mind: What shall I do when the condensed vapor of the hall showers down upon the heads of the members from one hundred skylights, as it now does from the skylights of our anatomical hall, as it did from the six skylights of the Round House, as it does from the lantern of the Pennsylvania Bank, and as it does from that of our university — an event I believe to be as certain as that cold air and cold glass will condense warm vapor? This question I have asked myself for many months past. I shall certainly not cut my throat as the engineer of Staines Bridge did when the battlement failed, and his beautiful bridge fell because the commissioners had ordered him to proceed contrary to his judgment. But I dare not think long enough on the subject to frame an answer to my own mind, but go blindly on, hoping that *"fata viano invenient."*

In respect to the general subject of cupolas, I do not think that they are *always*, nor even *often*, ornamental. My *principles* of good taste are rigid in Grecian architecture. I am a bigoted Greek in the condemnation of the Roman architecture of Baalbec, Palmyra, Spaletro, and of all the buildings erected subsequent to Hadrian's reign. The immense size, the bold plan and arrangements of the buildings of the Romans down almost to Constantine's arch, plundered from the triumphal arches of former emperors, I admire, however, with enthusiasm, but think their decorations and details absurd beyond tolerance from the reign of Severus downward. Wherever, therefore, the

Grecian style can be copied without impropriety, I love to be a mere, I would say a *slavish*, copyist, but the forms and the distribution of the Roman and Greek buildings which remain are in general inapplicable to the objects and uses of our public buildings. Our religion requires churches wholly different from the temples, our Government, our legislative assemblies, and our courts of justice, buildings of entirely different principles from their basilicas; and our amusements could not possibly be performed in their theaters or amphitheaters. But that which principally demands a variation in our buildings from those of the ancients is the difference of our climate. To adhere to the subject of cupolas, although the want of a belfry, which is an Eastern accession to our religious buildings, rendered them necessary appendages to the church, yet I cannot admit that because the Greeks and Romans did not place elevated cupolas upon their temples, they may not when necessary be rendered also beautiful. The Lanthorne of Demosthenes, than which nothing of the kind can be more beautiful, is mounted upon a magnificent mass of architecture harmonizing with it in character and style. The question would be as to its real or apparent utility in the place in which it appeared, for nothing in the field of good taste, which ought never to be at warfare with good sense, can be beautiful which appears useless or unmeaning.

If our climate were such as to admit of doing legislative business in open air, that is under the light of an open orifice in the crown of a dome, as at the Parthenon, I would never put a cupola on any spherical dome. It is not the *ornament*, it is the *use* that I want.

If you will be pleased to refer to Degodetz, you will see that there is a rim projecting above the arch of the Parthenon at the opening. This rim, in the dome projected for the centerpiece of the Capitol, is raised by me into a low pedestal for the purpose of covering a skylight, which could then be admitted, although

I think it inadmissible in a room of business. But I should prefer the hemisphere, I confess. As to the members of Congress, with the utmost respect for the Legislature, I should scarcely *consult*, but rather *dictate* in matters of taste.

I beg pardon for this trespass on your time. You have spoiled me by your former indulgence in hearing my opinions expressed with candor. A few days will give me the pleasure of personally assuring you of the profound respect of yours faithfully.

B. H. LATROBE

[THE JOURNAL OF LATROBE, pp. 137–141.]

KING TO JEFFERSON

27.th *May* 1807

rec.d *May* 27.

Sir

Agreeably to your request of the 25.th I have ascertained the height of the water in the branch and Spring, where Massachusetts Avenue crosses 16.th Street West; the former is 9 feet 9 inches, and the latter 8 feet 6 inches above the base of the presidents house. The highest part of the ditch in 16.th Street is about 8 feet above the base of the house; at the intersection of K Street and 16.th Street the ground is one foot, and at the crossing of L Street 2 feet 8 inches lower than that point.

If it is desireable to bring the water of this branch and spring to the presidents house along 16.th Street, it must come in pipes, as some of the ground is more than ten feet below the head of water, and also considerably lower than the place where it will be discharged. Should carrying the water along the surface in an open canal be preferred until it arrive at the ridge where the cut is now made it will have to be taken so far to the eastward as to cross K Street near Vermont Avenue, intersecting the lots and Streets in its course.

The surface of the garden at the gate, is two inches longer than the base, or freestone work, of the house.

The distance from the Presidents house to the Spring is about three thousand six hundred feet along 16.th Street.

> With great respect I am
>
> Yours Truly
>
> NICH.^S KING

[TO THE PRESIDENT]

[Ms., *Jefferson Papers*, Library of Congress.]

JEFFERSON TO THOMAS MUNROE

Th: Jefferson presents his compliments to m͞r Monroe, & on a view of the expences incurred & engaged for the Pensylvania avenue, that the funds will admit only to gravel it *where* it is wanting and *as much* only as is necessary to make it firm. the planting with oaks et. & additional arch to the bridge must be abandoned.

June 17. 07.

[*Letters of the Presidents of the U. S. to the Commissioners of Public Buildings and Grounds*, original in the Manuscripts Division, Library of Congress, photostat in the National Archives.]

JEFFERSON TO THOMAS MUNROE

While Th: Jefferson regrets the cause which obliges m͞r Munroe to be absent from this place, it is too imperative a one to admit of objection. as Th: J. will be absent himself shortly, he wishes, before m͞r Munroe's departure to give orders for whatever monies may be wanting from the different funds for July, Aug. & Sep. dating them monthly. on this subject, a previous conversation might perhaps be useful. he salutes m͞r Munroe with esteem.

July 23. 07.

[*Letters of the Presidents of the U. S. to the Commissioners of Public Buildings and Grounds*, original in the Manuscripts Division, Library of Congress, photostat in the National Archives.]

LATROBE TO JEFFERSON

Washington, August 13, 1807.

THE PRESIDENT OF THE UNITED STATES

My whole time, excepting a few hours now and then devoted to the President's house, is occupied with drawing and directions for the north wing, in the arrangements for which I am pursuing the eventual plan approved and presented by you to Congress at the last session, and in pushing on the work of the south wing. But I am again almost in despair about the roof. We had a gentle northeast storm without much wind, but with a persevering rain of thirty-six hours. It began on Wednesday evening and did not cease raining till Friday morning (yesterday). I was often under the roof and upon it during this time, and must say that the leakage was such that Congress could not have sat either on Thursday or Friday in the room. And what is as bad as the leakage, the ceiling is stained all over, and the entablature of the colonnade is in some places black with the water soaking through the ribs and receiving iron from the numerous nails. Yesterday I took off one of the strips which cover the joints, and discovered one cause of leakages.

It is now too late to make experiments. Nothing appears clearer to me than that we are in a situation in which there is no room to deliberate on the cost of any method whatsoever which to common sense and experience appears effectual. To place Congress at its next session under a leaky roof would be considered almost an insult to the Legislature after what passed at the last session. Of the total destruction of my individual reputation, of the personal disgrace I should incur after the censure implied by my reports of my predecessors, I say nothing. I dare not think of it. It would drive me, who have never yet failed in any professional attempt, to despair. But there are public considerations which seem to involve higher interests. Your administration, sir, in respect of public works, has hitherto claims of gratitude and respect from the public and from posterity. It is not flattery to say that you have planted the arts in your country. The works already erected in this city are the monuments of your judgment and of your zeal and of your taste. The first sculpture that adorns an American public building perpetuates your love and your protection of the fine arts. As for myself, I am not ashamed to say that my pride is not a little flattered and my professional ambition roused when I think that my grandchildren may at some future day read that after the turbulence of revolution and of faction which characterized the two first presidencies, their ancestor was the instrument in your hands to decorate the tranquillity, the prosperity, and the happiness of your government. Under this stimulus I have acted, and I hope, by the character of what I have executed hitherto under your orders, obtained an influence over the feelings and opinions of Congress, which, without some fatal disaster or miscarriage, would insure the progress and completion of all your objects of which you can make me the instrument. But I am now in despair. The next session is to decide not my fate only, but the whole dependence which Congress shall in future place upon anything which may be proposed by you on the subject of public works. My former representations on the certain event of the panel lights prove that I am not now attempting by flattery to obtain the prevalence of my individual opinions. How unworthy of all your kindness and confidence should I be, could I for a moment degrade myself and insult you by insincerity. If I offend it will be by too indiscreetly laying before the Chief Magistrate of the Union, the nervous, irritable, and perhaps petulant feelings of an artist. But you will forgive me for the sake of my candor.

I have strayed from my subject to represent my feelings.

I cannot add any consideration to what I have said which will not occur to you, and I beg you will have the goodness to give me as early a decision as convenient to you, that we may proceed to work. I cannot help thinking that it would be highly useful to present to Congress fair drawings of the Senate chamber, etc., as proposed to be executed. It would probably be the means of carrying the point, and perhaps progressing with the center. I am at present entirely without a clerk. Might I engage the assistance of a clerk, for my time is so wholly occupied that it is scarcely possible for me to take the necessary rest, and the most pressing engagements of the *practical* execution are such that I can only make the working drawings, and that at home and in the evenings?

[B. H. LATROBE]

[THE JOURNAL OF LATROBE, pp. 141-44.]

LATROBE TO JEFFERSON

Washington, September 1, 1807.

PRESIDENT OF THE UNITED STATES

Dear Sir: The greatest inconvenience we suffer is from the most troublesome multitudes of visitors, who crowd the house at all times, and who do infinite mischief to the plastering and the stone work, and the lower classes who carry off whatever they can lay their hands on. The building was for some time the regular play place for all the boys in the city, and nothing but great exertion has kept them in better order. It appears to me absolutely necessary, whenever the furniture shall be brought into the house, and much of it is already there, that access should be denied to everyone without exception, otherwise great offense will be given by a partial restriction, and indeed the visits of the more respectable would be very inconvenient. It has, therefore, occurred to me that after the 15th of September admittance will be prohibited, and also to put up the notice at the Capitol. In favor of strangers passing through I might make what exceptions appeared proper. It would give additional sanction and weight to this notice could I plead the direction of the President of the United States, but if you do not think it of sufficient importance to use so mighty a sanction, I have no reluctance to take upon me all the obloquy which I know it will occasion.

[B. H. LATROBE]

[THE JOURNAL OF LATROBE, pp. 144–45.]

JEFFERSON TO LENTHALL

September 2, 1807

Tho. Jefferson presents his compliments to mr. Lenthall, and sends him a letter this moment received, inclosed from mr. Latrobe; being handed him among his own, he broke it open without looking at the superscription; but seeing Mr. Lenthall's name at the head of it, he closed it instantly, and assures him on his honor that he did not read one other word of it.[57]

Sunday evening.

[*Records of the Columbia Historical Society*, Vol. XXXI, 9. Reprinted through the Courtesy of the Columbia Historical Society, Washington, D.C.]

ROBERT BRENT TO JEFFERSON

City of Washington Sepr 8th 1807

Sir

It has been made my duty, by a resolution of the Board of Trustees for the public School in this City, to communicate to you that you were, on the 4th Ins^t reappointed, unanimously, president of the Board.

With Sentiments of esteem

---

[57] Endorsement, in Jefferson's hand, on a letter from Latrobe to John Lenthall, sent by mistake to the President. Lenthall was an architect and builder, whom Latrobe appointed "Clerk of works and principal Surveyor" of Washington, D.C.

respect I have the honor to
be Sir

Your mo Ob^t Ser^t

ROBERT BRENT

[Ms., *Jefferson Papers*, Library of Congress.]

JEFFERSON TO ROBERT BRENT

TO ROBERT BRENT, ESQ.

Monticello, September 19, 1807.

Sir:

I have just received your favor of the 8th, informing me that the Board of Trustees for the public school in Washington had unanimously re-appointed me their President. I pray you to present to them my thanks for the mark of their confidence, with assurances that I shall at all times be ready to render to the Institution any services which shall be in my power. Accept yourself my salutations, and assurances of great respect and esteem.

TH: JEFFERSON.

[Pp. 196–7, WRITINGS OF JEFFERSON, Washington, V.]

JEFFERSON TO CONGRESS

TO THE SENATE AND HOUSE OF
    REPRESENTATIVES OF THE UNITED STATES:

I transmit to both Houses of Congress a report from the Surveyor of the Public Buildings of the progress made on them during the last season, of their present state, and of that of the funds appropriated to them. These have been much exceeded by the cost of the work done, a fact not known to me till the close of the season. The circumstances from which it arose are stated in the report of the Surveyor.

TH: JEFFERSON

March 25, 1808

[Pp. 2750, Appendix, Annals of Congress, 10–1; p. 131, DOCUMENTARY HISTORY . . . OF THE CAPITOL.]

LATROBE TO JEFFERSON

Report of the Surveyor of the Public Buildings of the United States at Washington, March 23, 1808.

My report on the progress and state of the public buildings of the United States in the City of Washington during the year 1807 has been delayed until all the work performed at the Capitol and President's house could be measured, and the accounts closed as nearly to the present time as possible; and also until those additions and alterations could be made in the south wing of the Capitol, which have been pointed out as necessary by the experience of the first part of the present session.

There remain now very few (and those small) accounts in any department of the public buildings which have not been ultimately settled; and the statement which I shall annex to this report may be considered as comprising all the demands against them of every kind up to the present time. Ever since the year 1803, when the work on the south wing of the Capitol was commenced, accounts of particular parts of the building have necessarily been in an open state, although partial settlements, at as short periods as possible, have always been made. But until the work had arrived at its present state, no complete admeasurement and valuation of the whole was practicable. The accumulated balances of settled accounts form a very considerable total, which has been increased by the stock of particular kinds of materials on hand, the purchase of which appeared highly prudent, if not absolutely necessary, should Congress think proper to proceed further with the public works.

I now beg leave to report on each of the public buildings, separately:

1. *South wing of the Capitol*

At the close of the year 1806, the framing of the roof of the south wing was put on, and during the winter it was covered in. The greatest exertions were then used to finish the interior; and, notwithstanding the early meeting of the Legislature in October last, the building was so far completed as to be occupied by the House of Representatives; and at the present moment this wing of the Capitol may be considered as finished, excepting in the following particulars:

1. All the wood-work and walls require to be painted. The wood-work is only primed.

2. Of the 24 Corinthian columns of the Hall of Representatives, the capitals of only two are entirely finished; eight are in a state of forwardness; and fourteen are only rough-hewn or bosted.

3. Only part of the moulding of the cornice is finished.

4. The sculpture over the entrance is incomplete.

5. The enclosure of the lobbies is not yet finished.

6. All the chimney pieces of the principal story, and two of the vestibules, ten in number, are wanting.

7. Two small capitals in the circular vestibule are still to be carved.

8. The platform on the south front giving access to the galleries, is erected upon the old scaffolding, which having been some years in use, is weak and decayed. It is required by the nature of the ground that a permanent platform on arches should be extended along this front.

In respect to these deficiencies, I beg leave to submit the following remarks:

To preserve the wood-work, the painting should be performed in the ensuing season; the walls are not yet sufficiently dry to admit it; but the painting of the ceiling of the Hall of Representatives ought not to be postponed. Its present state constitutes the only defect which remains to be corrected in that room, as I shall endeavor to explain, in speaking of the very just complaints that were made at the commencement of the session of the difficulty of hearing and speaking in it.

The sculpture, which is still deficient, can only be completed in the course of time. There are at present in the service of the United States two very skilful Italian sculptors, Messrs. Andrei and Franzoni, whose talents are evident in their works. They and their pupil, Somerville, one of our own citizens, will make very considerable progress during the next season; and much other assistance can be obtained in the less difficult parts of the work.

The chimney pieces have been ordered, and may soon be put up; and the platform on the south front is not a work of great expense.

But, besides completing the south wing in these particulars, it appears equally necessary to erect during the present year that part of the west front which is opposite to the eastern entrance of the House, and projects westward from the northwest corner of the present building. In this part of the work it is intended to provide a dwelling for the Doorkeeper of the House, in the height of the office story, and above to have committee rooms for the House of Representatives. The necessity of the work arises from two causes, which I beg leave to state to you.

1. In my former reports, and especially in a printed letter to the members of the Legislature, which I have had the honor to communicate to you, I explained the reasons which obliged me to carry up the external north wall of the House independently of those internal walls with which it is connected, and upon which it depends for the principal resistance against the lateral

pressure of the arches and roof of the House. This very bold undertaking succeeded in enabling us to get much more forward with the work than would have been otherwise possible; and, by the erection of the entrance and its communication, this wall is now firmly supported as far as they extend. But the western end of the wall still remains without any counterpoise against the pressure outwards, but what arises from its own weight. The cellars, which were formerly sunk at the northwest angle of the south wing, and which for many years have been the receptacle of rain water, will, until covered, remain a source of injury to this part of the building. Every feasible step has been taken to prevent the lodging of the water in them, but much mischief was done before this could be effected; and a gradual settlement of the northwest part of the wall has been going on from the commencement, and still increases, though very slowly. It may be observed in the lobby of the House, and, though not immediately dangerous, it ought to be stopped as soon as possible.

2. There is another consideration which is perhaps of equal importance in another point of view.

On the removal of the National Legislature to this city, an act was passed appropriating *forever* to the use of the Doorkeepers of the two Houses of Congress the buildings erected for the temporary accommodation of the workmen while employed on the Capitol. It was, perhaps, not observed that these buildings stand actually in the street which passes on the south side of the Capitol square and in the Jersey avenue, and thus destroy not only the appearance and regularity of the square and streets, but, being placed high above their level, are a dangerous obstruction to the intercourse around the Capitol. They are, besides, so badly built, and already so rotten, as scarcely to be habitable; and, from being placed on the surface of the vegetable mould, having no cellars, and having a very bad aspect, they are so unhealthy that, of the families who have inhabited them, many have died, and all have been afflicted with severe sickness. Provision will require to be made to carry the intention of the Legislature to provide dwellings for their Door-keepers into effect; and a slight observation of the necessity of a more close attention to the domestic arrangements and expenses, and the better government of the servants of the House than at present can possibly be had, would point out a powerful reason for the speedy erection of this part of the building, even if it were not necessary to the support of what is already carried up.

Before I close my account of the south wing of the Capitol, I most respectfully beg permission to notice in this report the two objections to the Hall of Congress, which were discovered immediately on the opening of the session — the difficulty of hearing and speaking in it, and the unpleasant effect of the mode adopted to warm the House upon the air of the room. These objections have been forcibly stated and permanently recorded in the speeches of the members, and the appointment of committees for the purpose of inquiry into their cause and remedy; and I crave this permission, not only for the purpose of personal exculpation, but with the hope that the explanation I shall give will prove of public utility in similar cases.

In every large room the great average distance of the speaker from the hearer is a cause of difficulty of hearing and speaking which cannot be removed; but the effect of this cause bears no proportion to that indistinctness which arises from the innumerable echoes that are reverberated from the walls and arched ceiling of such a room as the Hall of Representatives. These surfaces give back to the ear echoes, not only of the voice of the speaker, at a perceptible distance of time from the original sound, but also distinct echoes of every accidental noise and separate conversation in the House and lobbies, and renders debate very laborious to the speaker and almost useless to the hearers. This defect was foreseen; and, in furnishing the House, the curtains and draperies of the windows were made as ample as propriety would admit; draperies were hung in other proper situations, and a large curtain closed the opening of the columns behind the Speaker's chair. But all this drapery bore a small proportion to the extent of uncovered surface, though it rendered those particular situations of the hearer, thus freed from echo, superior to all others.

If the dimensions of a room, erected for the purpose of debate, were so moderate that the echoes of the voice of the speaker could reach the ear of the hearer, without the intervention of a perceptible distance of time, then the echo would strengthen and support the voice; and we find that this is actually the case in small lecture-rooms, expressly constructed to produce innumerable echoes. But there is a circumstance attending halls of debate which distinguishes them from rooms intended for the lectures of one speaker; the impossibility of preserving perfect silence, and of confining persons to their seats, so as to prevent all sound but that of the speaker's voice; for it is evident that sounds from all quarters and of all kinds will be re-echoed with perfect impartiality.

The Hall of Representatives is one hundred and ten feet long from east to west, and fifty-five feet high; therefore, before the echo of a sound, issuing from the centre of the floor, can return to its place, it must travel one hundred and ten feet, a distance very perceptible to the ear in the return of echo. The distance will be still greater if the speaker be placed at a distance from the hearer. And as the walls, in their various breaks, return each a separate echo, their confusion must necessarily render it almost impossible to understand what is spoken.

From these plain facts it is evident that the walls of every large hall of debate should be covered with tapestry, or other material which does not reverberate sound. On reference to the original drawing it will be seen that this was intended, but neither the time nor the extent of the appropriation for furniture, which proved insufficient for the indispensable articles of carpeting, tables, chairs, desks, and curtains, would admit it.

A committee being appointed by the House to inquire into the causes and remedy of the difficulty of hearing and speaking, the foregoing facts and reasonings were laid before them; and it was proposed to suspend curtains between the columns round the whole internal area of the House, and others behind the seats of the galleries, and to paint the ceiling in flock. The proposal was approved, and has been executed, as far as it could be done, by hanging all the curtains; the painting of the ceiling must be postponed until the House rises. The fullest success attended this measure; and, although the echoes of the ceiling produce in the centre of the House some confusion of sound, it is a small inconvenience, which will be removed. When the size of this room is considered, it may be safely asserted that it is now as little liable to objection as any other hall of debate in the United States; that it is in all respects superior to most others, and that, when the proposed improvements, which are of comparatively small import, are made, it will be second to none in every legislative convenience. Another inconvenience has been felt, especially by some of the members, from the effect of the stoves by which the hall is warmed upon the air of the room, especially when the House and galleries have been crowded. The mouths of these stoves are in the office story below the hall, and a cavity being contrived of from three to five feet deep, below the platforms on which the seats are placed, the flues in this cavity wind to the extent of two hundred feet before they pass into the chimney. When the session was first opened the flues and walls were damp; the fire was injudiciously forced by the servants of the House, and the heat and steam was not only unpleasant, but highly injurious to the health of many of the members; part of this inconvenience diminished as the flues became drier, and less fire was made. But, in order to renew the air of the House, the external air has been freely admitted into the cavity of the flues, and a ventilator is made in the roof. The principle on which these stoves are constructed is not new, and it has been so often and so successfully put into practice that, when every proposed improvement is made, and the building has become dry, there can be little, if any, doubt of its being productive of no inconvenience whatever to any individual member of the House.

2. *North Wing of the Capitol*

The appropriation made at the last session of Congress had, for its principal object, such repair of the House, and especially of the roof and gutters, as should keep out the weather and prevent the danger arising from the frequent falling down of the plastering of the ceilings. It was late in the season before the weather permitted any part of the roof to be stripped for examination, and, when this was done in the centre of the building, all the timbers were found in such a state of decay that no part of them could be suffered to remain in their place. The decay was not, however, confined to the timbers of the roof; the floors down to the ground-floor were discovered to be in the same state. The floors and ceiling of the Senate chamber and library being also rotten, it was judged most prudent and necessary to begin with a thorough repair of the centre from the foundation, and not to disturb these apartments, the use of which could not be dispensed with the ensuing session; for, had the roof of the Senate chamber been opened, no exertions could have completed the repairs in proper time, while the south wing called for all the workmen which by any means we could collect. Besides, the permanent repairs and alterations proposed for the centre of the House were of such a nature as to stop the leakage of every other part of the House; and it was, therefore, executed in the most permanent manner, and on the principles on which the south wing has been built. All the timber floors, and galleries of the centre lobbies, were taken up, and the work carried up by solid vaulting in brick from the foundation of the House to the top of the dome; a staircase, much wanted, was made to lead into the fuel cellars; and arched galleries constructed, giving access into the rooms in the third story, which have never been finished, but which will be highly useful apartments whenever the wing shall be completed.

In the great staircase the old wooden skylight and cove was entirely taken down, and a solid brick cupola turned over this large area of forty-five by thirty-five feet, and crowned by a lantern light. The stairs themselves remain in the same dangerous and decayed state in which they were found, but they have been properly secured for the present.

All that could be done with the rest of the roof, was to put it in the best repair that was practicable without stripping it. But it cannot be denied that all the timbers of the House, especially those parts that are inserted into the walls, are in a state of the most dangerous decay; and, as far as the ceilings and floor have been opened, the dry rot is found to have possession, and to be making progress. It appears, therefore, unavoidable that a thorough repair of the whole House, upon the permanent construction of the work of the last season, should be pursued, more especially as the accommodation of the Senate and of the Courts is very far from being convenient to the despatch of public business. On this head I beg leave to refer to my report of last year, and will now only state once more my opinion that the present chamber of the Senate cannot be considered as altogether safe, either as to the plastering, of which the columns and entablature consist, or as to its floor and ceiling.

3. Besides the work executed in the buildings themselves, a large sum has been expended in rendering them safe from injury, and accessible to the members. The quantity of earth to be removed in front of the south wing, and the ground to be raised to the southward and eastward, was considerable. A

permanent drain was required to prevent the wash of the hill on which the building stands to the south of the circular road, and the road leading to the House was to be raised and covered with gravel.

On the north the main drain was carried away by the heavy rains of the season. This drain has, for some years past, been an annual source of expense and inconvenience; it is now durably constructed. Nothing has been done which did not appear unavoidable, or done in a manner to require further alteration and expense; and, although all the work which does not properly belong to the building itself has been expensive, the objects of the expense have been permanently effected.

4. *Highways*

The sum of three thousand dollars, appropriated to the use of the roads, has been expended in widening the carriage-way of the Pennsylvania avenue, in substituting permanent for temporary drains, in general repairs and improvements, and principally in making a permanent road south of the President's square. Several of the drains on the Pennsylvania avenue still require to be more permanently built; and a large permanent sewer is required across the new road opposite to the President's house, without which that road, now the proper and permanent means of reaching the offices from the Capitol, will never be passable in winter. This road, without which the enclosure of the President's ground could not be at all undertaken, has been executed in the most economical manner that could be devised, by laying it out so as to make that part in which earth was greatly deficient out of the spoils of the hill which was to be cut through; it is still required to be covered with gravel.

President's House

The work performed at the President's house has consisted of the covered way in front of the offices on each wing; of the erection of one-half of the wall of enclosure and one of the gates; of the levelling of the greatest part of the enclosed grounds, and of minor repairs and improvements of the house itself. Neither the wall of enclosure nor the levelling of the ground could be completed by the appropriation, but as much has been done as was practicable, and the ground is now partially enclosed and ready to be planted.

The state of the south wing of the Capitol has enabled me to make a complete measurement of all the work of every kind performed, at the principal object of expenditure since the year 1803, and not only in respect to that work, but in every other department of the buildings; I have obtained settlements of accounts and measurements up to the present period, and also correct valuations of all the work lying contiguous to the buildings in a state of greater or less preparation. From hence, by favor of the Superintendent of the city, I am enabled to lay before you a statement of all the expenditures and outstanding claims up to the present time, which may be considered as correct; the unascertained and unsettled accounts being of very small amount and importance, and capable of tolerably correct estimation. From this statement it will appear that the outstanding claims are of very considerable amount in the aggregate; an amount which could only have been reduced by leaving the works in an unfinished and useless state. In respect to the south wing of the Capitol, no consideration of the risk of future appropriation operated with the workmen who have so long and so faithfully labored at the public buildings, to induce them to stop when it was known that the appropriation was exhausted, and by this means very large sums have become due to two of the principal and most respectable persons engaged in the work. Another increase of expenditure, not as yet properly chargeable to any branch of the work, has been incurred by the very evident utility, if not absolute necessity of supplying the public with particular kinds of ironmongery and glass, of which it was evident that no supply on reasonable terms would shortly be attainable. This swells the amount of the deficit very greatly, although the value of the materials on hand would be greater than is stated if sold at the market price. I have, in the first instance, charged all deficiencies not specially stated to its proper appropriation to the south wing of the Capitol, and, in the general account current, which I subjoin, I have given the proper credits for materials on hand, and moneys advanced to collateral uses.

1. South Wing of the Capitol

Appropriation for 1807		$25,000 00
Amount of all outstanding claims not specifically stated below	$40,598 19	
From which deduct this sum in hand	$2,167 00	
Due from the contingent funds of the offices of State, War, Navy, and the Post Office [58]	3,218 65	
Deficit on the south wing and on general charges	35,212 54	$35,212 54
	$40,598 19	

2. North Wing of the Capitol

Appropriation of 1807		$25,000 00
Expenditures in 1808:		
Settled accounts	$22,388 49	
Unsettled accounts	402 01	
Proportion of salaries of the surveyor of public buildings and clerk of the works, charged to the south wing heretofore	2,050 00	
	$24,840 50	
Cash in hand	159 50	
	$25,000 00	

[58] This sum was laid out in the year 1806, when, by the falling in of the old drains, and the filling of the cellars with water, the offices became unhealthy; and it was absolutely necessary to remedy the evil or desert the buildings. I have stated it below as a deficit, as it has not yet been repaid. [Note in the original.]

3. President's House

Appropriation, 1807.................................... $15,000 00

Expenditures on all objects above mentioned . . . $18,919 46

Deficit of the appropriation, 1807. . . . .   3,919 46
To this must be added the amount of the claims
    which were incurred prior to the appropriation   1,737 44

                                            $ 5,656 90

4. Public Highways

Appropriation, 1807.................................... $3,000 00
Expenditures on roads, highways, drains, and
    making the new road south of the President's
    square................................. $6,644 79
           Deficit......................... $3,644 79

5. *Furniture of the south wing of the Capitol*

In my former report, I stated the sum required to furnish the
House to be $20,000. This estimate did not include the expense
of new desks, because from the best information I could obtain,
the old desks were supposed applicable to the new House. But
the frequent removals of the platforms, and the erroneous opinions of those who had made them, led into error; and when the
session was closed and the desks removed, it was found utterly
impracticable either to place the desks on the new platforms, or
to accommodate the platforms to the desks, without destroying
all convenience within the House. New desks have therefore
been made. In other respects, the estimate was founded on very
simple data, as the numbers of tables, curtains, blinds, chairs,
and bookcases, and the quality and quantity of the carpeting,
and of the ironmongery, could not be so varied as to make any
material difference in the expense; and, on inspection, I trust it
will be found that no unnecessary furniture has been introduced
into the House or committee rooms.

The amount of appropriation was...................... $17,000 00

Expenditure on new desks...................	$2,164	66
On all the articles included in the estimate....	19,051	68
	$21,216	34
Deficit..........................	$4,216	34

Recapitulation

1. South wing of the Capitol...............	$35,212	54
2. To make good the sum loaned to the public offices................................	3,218	65
3. President's house.............. $3,919 46 Prior claims to 1807, on President's house................. 1,737 44	5,656	90
4. Public highways.......................	3,644	79
5. Furniture funds.......................	4,216	34
	$51,949	22

Estimate for the Year 1808

To make good the deficit of 1807, including the debt due from the public offices...........	$51,500	00
To execute the work deficient in the south wing	11,509	00
To carry up that part of the west front which is necessary to secure the northwest angle of the south wing.............................	15,000	00
To carry up, in solid work, the interior of the wing, comprising the Senate chamber......	25,000	00
To complete the wall of the President's house; plant the ground, so as to close this branch of expenditure; build a solid flight of steps to the principal door, and minor expenses........	15,000	00
To repair the highways and build drains......	5,000	00
Total..........................	$123,000	00

I now beg leave to add a statement of the actual expenditures on the north and south wings of the Capitol, up to the present time.

1. SOUTH WING OF THE CAPITOL

Expended from April, 1803, up to January 1, 1807, including the pulling down and rebuilding the work formerly erected..		$216,061 47½
Cash on hand, 1807......................	$11,000 00	
Appropriation, 1807......................	25,000 00	
Deficit, 1808............................	35,212 54	71,212 54
		$287,274 01½

Per contra.

Materials on hand, Crown glass.............	$1,000 00	
Plate glass and ironmongery................	2,000 00	
Sheet iron, for roofing....................	3,000 00	
Scaffolding and utensils...................	1,500 00	
Freestone................................	1,500 00	
Glass and lead used in other parts of the works, not yet charged to their account..........	1,383 00	
Proportion of salaries chargeable to the north wing..................................	2,050 00	12,433 00
Actual cost of the south wing...................		$274,841 01½

2. NORTH WING OF THE CAPITOL

Expended on the north wing of the Capitol, prior to 1803, including the foundations of the south wing and center................	$337,735 38	
From this sum deduct the full value of the above foundations......................	30,000 00	$307,735 38
Expended in 1803................................		3,301 75
Expended in 1807................................		24,840 50
Total cost of the north wing....................		$335,877 63

All which is most respectfully submitted, by your faithful humble servant,

B. HENRY LATROBE,
Surveyor Public Buildings U. S.

TO THE PRESIDENT OF THE U. S.

[Pp. 2750–2759, APPENDIX, ANNALS OF CONGRESS, 10–1; incompletely published: pp. 131–137, DOCUMENTARY HISTORY . . . OF THE CAPITOL.]

Jefferson to Latrobe

Copy of a letter to mr̄ Latrobe.[59]

Washington April 25. 1808.

Sir,

   I took a note last night of the appropriations of the Bill for the public buildings. they are as follows.

For Debts	51.400. D.	
For the wall round the President's square. ⎫	"so as to close this part of	
Planting the Grounds. ⎬	the expenditure" 14.000. D.	
Steps at the principal entrance. ⎭		
South Wing, finishing —	11.500. D. —	
North Wing . . .	25.000. D. —	

we will consider these heads singly.

   Debts.   Under this head is to be considered all work done before the date of the Act; so that all accounts should be immediately settled up to April 25. and paid out of this fund. what is done from this day forward is to be charged to the new appropriations. particularly let the further proceedings in preparing capping stones for the wall of the President's square be immediately stopped, & not resumed till all the other work chargeable to the 14.000. D. appropriation be done.

   President's house.   Let the other half of the wall be immediately begun, & be raised one foot higher than what is already done, & that which is already done be raised one foot higher, & the capping then to be put on as far as it is already prepared. no Gate or lodge to be attempted till we see the state of our funds at the finishing of the wall so far. when this is done so far, let us begin the stone steps, & when they are finished, and money enough put by for planting the grounds we will consider how best to employ what may remain on capping &

[59] Th: Jefferson with his compliments to mr̄ Munro, sends him the inclosed copy of a letter to m⁻ Latrobe, that he may be informed of the plan of proceeding on the public buildings for this summer. Apr. 27.08.

Gates. so that the order of this part of the work is to be 1st the wall completed and raised — 2. the steps — 3. planting — 4. capping, Gates, Porter's lodge, doing one thing at a time, finishing, settling & paying off one article before we begin another.

SOUTH WING.   You best know what is to be done here. but I would advise the different branches of the work to be done *successively*, paying off each before another is begun.

NORTH WING.   to be begun immediately and so pressed as to be finished this season.   1. Vault with brick the cellar story. 2. leave the present Senate Chamber exactly in it's present state.   3. lay a floor where the Gallery now is to be the floor of the future Senate Chamber. Open it above to the roof to give it elevation enough, leaving the present columns uninjured, until we see that every thing else being done & paid for there remains enough to make these columns of stone.

You see, my Dear Sir, that the object of this cautious proceeding is to prevent the possibility of a deficit of a single Dollar this year. The lesson of the last year has been a serious one, it has done you great injury, & has been much felt by myself. it was so contrary to the principles of our Government, which make the representatives of the people the sole arbitors of the public expense, and do not permit any work to be forced on them on a larger scale than their judgment deems adapted to the circumstances of the Nation. I give to m^r. Monroe a copy of this letter, that he may conform his warrants to it. matters of detail may be the subject of verbal consultation between us before I leave this which will be on the 5th of May.

I salute you with esteem and respect.

TH: JEFFERSON

P.S. on further consideration, if a contract can be made for finishing the wall of the President's square at a fixed price, we may then with safety begin the stone steps without waiting the actual execution of the wall.

Mᴿ LATROBE

[*Letters of the Presidents of the U. S. to the Commissioners of Public Buildings and Grounds*, original in the Manuscripts Division, Library of Congress, photostat in National Archives; Incompletely published in DOCUMENTARY HISTORY . . . OF THE CAPITOL, p. 145.]

THOMAS MUNROE TO JEFFERSON

T Munroe contrary to his expectations finds that the $20,000 Drawn 28 ult° will probably be out on Saturday, in consequence of some large payments which he did not expect would have been called for so soon — He therefore respectfully submits to the President whether it may not be as well to give a warrant for a further sum before his departure, $10,000.

5th May 1808

[Ms., *Jefferson Papers*, Library of Congress.]

THOMAS MUNROE TO JEFFERSON

Washington 13 *May* 1808

Sir,

Out of the $30,000 Drawn on your warrants of 2ᵈ & 5ᵗʰ Instant, on accᵗ of the Deficit in previous Appropriations, provided for by the Act of last session of Congress I have paid the following claims out

Thomas Rayner	242.87	Thomas Machem	1988.60
Ninian Magruder	154.	Cooke & Brent	390.
Sam Wetherill & Son	102.01	Carpenters & labourers Capⁱ	1303.80
John Freeman	12.	George Blagdin in part	5000.
Henry Foxall	723.39	Jnᵒ McIntire	130.
James M. Robertson	1159.74	Henry Ingle	206.78
Whelan & Connelly	1192.89	Jnᵒ Davis of Abel	327.82
Griffith Coombe	328.24		Dˢ 14.033.11
roll Carpenters, Presᵗˢ Hᵒ	770.97		

Brought up	$14033.11	Hugh Densley	74.92
George S[t] Claire	6.60	Sam Maffitt & Co	46.03
James Martin	318.22	Morin & Moore	290.15
Robert Brown	216.57	Thackara & Foxton } plaisterers	10,824.13
Alexander McCormick	19.61		28,107.74
William Knowles	115.50	Balance in hand	1,892.26
Shaw & Birth	1,825.12		
R & W Clarke	337.78		30,000.

And the following Accounts due out of the same fund are presented for Payment

Charles Pleasants for Glass & hardware................... $5,991.53
George Blagdin, Stone Cutters work — balance............ 10,165.40
Jn[o]. Lenthall — balance of Salary due him to this 25. April 1808
    at $1400 p Annum................................. 2,449.58
William Foxton..................................... 284.39
John Richards...................................... 185.90
Timothy Caldwell................................... 91.16
Walter Hellen...................................... 6.90
Ben H Latrobe Salary from 1 Jan[y] to 25 Ap[l] 1808..........
    at $2,000 p An. & $15.49 due before 1 Jan   ab[t].......... 655.
                                                   $19,829.86

Debts due prior to 25. Ap[l] 1808 said to be outstanding
H[y] Ingle .... said to be about.......... $50
L. Clephan......... } painting & glazing not finished
R & W Clarke...... } [illegible]...returned — about $500
Cooke & Brent .... not returned, said to be $600 say 1,000.
                                           D[s] 20,829.86

Statement of the Acc[t] of the Appropriation to cover the deficit
Am[t] of Appropriation....................... $51,500
Drawn by Thomas Claxton, for the furniture fund   5,403.76
                    Balance for Other Debts........ $46,096.24

Amount of claims paid...........$28,107.74 see other side
Am[t] of D[o] presented for pay[t] ...... 19,829.86   D[o]
Am[t] outstanding supposed by M[r]
    Latrobe & M[r] Lenthall to be about   1,000   D[o]
                                        $48,937.60
              The above balance bro[t] down 46,096.24
                          Deficiency $2,841.36

Am^t heretofore expended on the public Offices, and stated, in ⎫
Mr Latrobes estimate & the law to be included in and covered ⎬   3,218.65
by the Appropriation of $51,500. . . . . ⎭ $6,060.01

It gives me real concern, Sir, to state that even admitting
that the Am^t of outstanding debts does not exceed $1000 as
estimated above there will be a deficit of nearly $6000, includ-
ing the $3,218.65 for the Offices.

I have conversed with Mr Latrobe on this unpleasant subject, and he says the deficit was occasioned in part by the following circumstances V^t His estimate of debts, on which the
appropriation was intended to be predicated, was, as appears
by the printed copy

$51,949.22, and only $51,500 was appropriated, short. . $449.22
2. In his estimate, the debt of furniture fund is stated
   at. . . . .$4,216.34, and Claxton has
   Drawn, to pay acct^s presented 5,403.76 except. 1,187.42
3. His estimate was only to the 1. Jany 1808 instead of 25. Ap^l ,
   as directed by the president, being the day the Appropriation
   was made, between which periods there accrued, and is in-
   cluded in the foregoing statement. . . . .   2380.
                                                          $4,016.64

I have recommended to Mr Claxton to keep the excess drawn
by him (altho' the real debts due from the furniture fund he
says will absorb it) until your pleasure can be known, whether
he shall pay it away, or refund it — there is no other reason
why he should refund it, to be applied to the debts of the buildings, but that in strict impartiality the claimants should fare
alike, which will not be the case if the furniture debts be fully
paid — but Sir, may I be pardoned for asking whether under
the words of the appropriation, being "To make good the deficit of 1807" we might not charge all claims arising in 1808 to
the appropriations made to carry on the work in 1808, instead
of charging the amount that accrued between 1. Jan^y & 25.
April to the deficit acc^t, as you have directed.

I have the honor to inclose for your signature a warrant for the Balance of the $51,500 to be paid (unless you should otherwise direct) to the claimants as they may apply, after it comes into my hands. I also inclose a warrant for $10,000 in part of the Appropriations for the Current year, there being several sums due for lime, bricks &c purchased by Mr Latrobe for which Certified bills are now in my hands, waiting till I receive funds to discharge them. With respect to the part of the $51,500 mentioned to be appropriated to cover the sum due from the public Offices, You, Sir, can best tell whether the provision here made will prevent your sanctioning that expenditure and letting it be adjusted at the Treasury with my other Accounts; for the appropriation out of which it was paid or borrowed was $50,000 "to be applied under the direction of the President of US. in proceeding with the public buildings at the City of Washington, and in making such necessary improvements & repairs thereon as he shall deem expedient." If such sanction cannot be given will it not be necessary to take the Amount out of the $51,500, and pay away the balance only?

I have the honor to be with the highest respect Sir

Y^r m^o Ob Servt

THOMAS MUNROE

PRESIDENT U S

[Ms., *Jefferson Papers*, Library of Congress.]

JEFFERSON TO THOMAS MUNROE

Monticello May 17. 08.

Sir

Yours of the 13th was recieved last night, and really presents a painful state of things. however our object now can be only how to meet the new deficit with the least injustice. your statement is as follows.

Debts paid by mr Monroe	28,107.74
by mr Claxton	5,403.76
d° remaining unpaid	20,829.86
expenditures on the public offices	3,218.65
	57,560.01
Appropriation for the deficit of 1807	51,500.
apparent deficit	6,060.01
charge upon the funds of 1808. each it's own part of the monies expended from Jan. 1. to Apr. 25. 08	2,380.
	3,860.01

levy this sum of 3,860.01 rateably on all the outstanding debts of more than 1000. D. these will amount (according to your statement) to 18,606.51. consequently each of these large creditors must be content to recieve about 80. D. in the 100. and to wait awhile for the remaining 20. D. it will then be our duty to save the 3860.01 out of the expenditures of 1808. what part of these expenditures may be dispensed with, must be the subject of consideration when I return to Washington. as I am detaining the post for this letter, I must pray you to communicate it to mr Claxton as the answer to his letter of the 15th and also to mr Latrobe as what must govern our future expenditures. I salute you with esteem & respect

Th: Jefferson

Mr. Monroe.

P.S. I inclose the two warrants for 16,096.24 & 10,000. D.

[*Letters of the Presidents of the U.S. to the Commissioners of Public Buildings and Grounds*, original in the Manuscripts Division, Library of Congress, photostat in the National Archives.]

Latrobe to Jefferson

PRESIDENT OF THE U STATES

Washington May 23d. 1808.

Sir

Since your departure I have made every possible exertion to

forward the progress of the public Works, and will concisely state their present situation.

1. *North Wing, Capitol*

To support the Vaults of the Courtroom-cellar, it was necessary to take up & vault the floors of the stairs & north lobby, against which they abutt. This has been done, & the vaults are finished. The Cellar of the Court is also vaulted, excepting only the center part which is to be sunk. It will probably be completed this week.

All the floors of the East part of the house, from the Cellar to the roof have been taken up. The timber is much more decayed than I expected. Its state is now evident to the public: the building being now surrounded with rotten girders, plates & joists, with exception only of the *Pine* timber, which is generally sound, — altho' the Oak trusses which have been enclosed within them are rotten.

The Arcade of the former Senate chamber must also be pulled down, as anxious as I was to retain it, & for two reasons. The first because every pier stands upon two plates 14 inches broad, which are wholly decayed, thus: The piers are 3^{ft} 5^{in} deep. The plates together 2^{ft} 4^{in} broad, so that they stand upon only 1^{ft} 1^{in} of brick work. They are besides wounded by the joists in such a manner as to be unsafe as the support of any arch.

The second reason is that they are placed in so irregular a curve, partly eliptical, partly circular, that it is next to impossible to fit a center to them, or to make a regular room of the area they enclose, without a very increased expense. I have therefore begun to take them down & hope to rebuild them in a semi-circular form before the end of next week.

Independently of rotten Timber we have found other dangerous circumstances in the state of the building. The East Wall of the North lobby, has been cut away 40 feet high to the thickness of 9^{in} & the remaining part is so shattered & weak as to require great care in managing this part of the work. This 9^{in} shattered wall carries 15 feet of 3 brick Wall at the top of the house, filled with rotten timber. In a few Years it is very probable that this trencendant weight held up only by decayed girders would have suddenly fallen into the Senate chambers, whenever the timber was so far decayed as to be too weak to resist its pressure.

South Wing, Capitol

The Scaffolding for painting the cieling & carving the Capitals is erected. It was finished yesterday. Mr Bridport has gone to Philadelphia to procure his materials & will begin painting next week. The necessary preparations are making.

President's house & square

I have made all the drawings necessary for the North steps of the house. The scheme of a Quadrant Arch I have necessarily abandoned. From the bottom of the Area to the level of the Ground floor is only 13 feet, while the area is more than 20 feet wide at the bottom & more than 30 feet at the top. Therefore, if a Quadrant Arch of 10 feet radius (3 feet being necessary for the thickness of the arch, the paving, & a step at the door) were employ[ed], half the area at bottom & 20 feet & upwards at the top would be filled up with useless work & materials, & render much light lost to the kitchen. I have therefore thrown a flat segment arch across the Area of 20 feet span, & thus saved all the unnecessary materials, making the whole work as little expensive & light in appearance as possible.

The freshet has prevented a supply of stone for the Wall, but Lime is purchased & on the spot. I have entered in no contracts whatever, for reasons which I must beg to lay before you at large, presently; — & therefore it is yet uncertain who will build the Wall & at what price it will be erected. In this state

of things, however, I beg to lay before you an estimate by
which your opinion of the expense may be formed. It is the
estimate on which I founded my requisition of 15.000$ & on
reviewing it, I find nothing to correct.

The whole wall, including 27 feet across the Wing (equal to
the width of the Treasury fireproof) is 3.461. 4 long — Half of
this may be said to be finished (excepting the coping & the
raising one foot).

The other half will require at an average a foundation 2^{ft} 6^{in}
deep. Wall 6^{ft} 6^{in} The result will be as follows

foundations 349½ perch. @ 4$............................	1398.$ —
Wall, West side 832 ¾ d°.............................	3.331. —
Topping East d° 1154¼ d°..............................	461. —
Coping, Stone 404 Tons at 7$........................	2828. —
to the whole Wall.	
d° Labor & setting 11.537^{ft} @ 30..................	3.461.10
Digging, — 577 Yds @ 18^{cts}...........................	103.86
	$11.582.96

Out of this may, I think, be saved
The raising of the Wall on the North side which when coped,
& the path laid at its proper level will be 6^{ft} 6^{i} high. As the
estimate is full, it may stand at $11.000.

The Coping of the Wall is absolutely necessary to its preservation even for a few Years. The Want of coping has last
Winter done injury.

This would then remain 2500$ for the steps & minor im-
provements, — & no more. In my report copied into the Law,
I have expressly stated that 15.000 would enable us to close the
expenditure of enclosing & planting of the ground, & to make
other improvements; and altho' Congress have thought proper
on this, as on other occasions to curtail my estimate, & yet by
the words of the law to require the object to which it related to
be accomplished, I respectfully submit to you whether the object of enclosure & planting ought not to take precedence of all
others. I have made no estimate on which I can rely, as to the

steps, but suppose they will cost from 800 to 1000 Dollars. The work is not a small one. It covers near 6 squares. I have already ordered the West piazza to be plaistered for the sake of light in the lower Coridor of the Offices as well as appearance, — & all the wooden Cornice to be painted. These expenses may be about 150 to 200 Dollars. They seem to me to be unavoidable. Nothing else is going on.

I now beg leave to lay before you, with that candor which your kindness has always encouraged in me, & which my high respect for you, as well as my situation demands, difficulties that induce me at this very moment to hesitate as to the propriety of my continuing any longer in the public service, and even as to the *certainty*, whether you can possibly wish me to do so. In reports, without acknowledged authors, as to the unfavorable impressions which you have received of me, I do not for a moment attend. If I did, I should not now be in the Office you have bestowed upon me. During the session of Congress I was overwhelmed with that sort of information; but believing it to have been intended to draw me into the party opposed to your administration I placed no confidence whatever in what I heard, & dismissed it from my mind.

But when I consider the *undeniable facts* which have passed before my eyes, I cannot help thinking that I ought long ago to have resigned.

In the first place, the whole blame of the deficiency has been thrown upon my shoulders by the very words of the Message accompanying my report; & Mr Eppes, even after I had spoken to him & apparently satisfied him as to my not being the party to blame, he spoke at the close of the Session more harshly than any other [illegible], and by his means the appropriation for the N.W. corner of the building fell through which would otherwise have passed.

How little I deserved all this is evident from the facts preceding the Session, & my conduct during the discussion. The whole deficiency 52.000 of which (with the materials on hand, all bought for the South Wing) 35.000$ arose from the work on that wing 3.200 was by your express order expended on the removal of Earth from the Public Offices: — making nearly 3/4th of the whole deficiency. Now by your letter of the 30th of July I was expressly ordered to hire more workmen & not on any account whatever to neglect to get the house ready by the Session. Add to this that from July to Septr 17 Mr Munroe was at Baltstown springs, & if, in the nature of things it had been possible (which it was not) to form an opinion of the state of the funds from his books, — it was utterly impossible to do so, during his absence. had I therefore been willing to exonerate myself at all hazards from the censure so copiously & coarsely heaped upon me by the friends of the administration in the house as well as by the federalists & the third party, I had the means in my hands. I might have produced my orders, & quitting the ground I took, that of *the propriety & necessity of the expenditures*, have earned the plaudits of all the federalists, who being many of them, my personal acquaintances, were not behindhand in their endeavors to draw me into every different mode of defence. But as a man of honor, & grateful for the favors I have received, and firmly fixed in my political principles, I suffered myself to be abused as if I had deserved it, & by perseverance in explanation & application to individual members, the event was favorable to me & the public, & involved no character but my own.

Willing however as I was, and still am to go all honest & reasonably lengths to prove the sincerity of my professions the late occurrences ought at least to warn me to discretion for the future. that you Yourself consider me as the only responsible agent is evident from the confidence with which you have honored me & from the express words of your most friendly letter of the 26th of April in which you warn me against *similar* error & state the injury I have suffered already. *That I ought to be re-*

sponsible is certain. But how can I consent to be so, while I am a mere shadow as to power of acting, *inherent in my office*, & am not even allowed those means of knowing what I am about, & on what I have to depend, without which it is the extreme of madness in me to proceed. My respect for M.ʳ Munroe & his excellent disposition & temper, has alone enabled me to act hitherto. The subject is delicate, & I have hitherto avoided it, but it has become necessary for me to touch it.

It appears then, that I have not a right to make a single contract, to engage a single workman, to purchase materials of any kind, but thro' him & by his consent: and he has permitted me to do all this, & sanctioned my proceedings, — the comptroller of the Treasury claims a right to decide whether I have given too much for bricks, stone or plaistering & to reject every [contract] which to him shall seem improper, and even (to use his expression) to appoint agents to see that every workman does his duty in the manner charged in his account.

To the power of M.ʳ Munroe I most cheerfully agree to submit *in practice*, though *in principle*, I could never for one moment conduct business on such terms. To originate all measures of operation out of which accounts grow, & then when the work is done, to have the whole proceeding liable to be questioned, is to forbid the smallest movement towards a purchase a contract, or a direction of any kind: — and if the absurdity & impracticability of the pretension did not necessarily defeat it, nothing under heaven would prevent my sending every laborer to be hired at the Treasury. Since this pretension has been declared, I have ceased to make new contracts.

But there is another point in which M.ʳ Munroe & myself differ entirely in opinion, and hitherto I have, though always reluctantly given way. I consider it absolutely necessary that I should keep a set of books & have a clerk for this purpose. I have always done so at every public Work, & the Clerk, or more than one, has never been refused me. Here I have made [illegible] without such books, tho' I have annually stated to You & him, the absolute necessity of the thing. The consequence of my having no books, & of course no knowledge whatever of the state of the expenses, has been the enormous deficit of last Year. How could I possibly suppose that Lenthall, for instance, had suffered his Salary to be in arrears for more than 3 Years & that 2.500 (the 20th part of the whole deficit) was due to him? It never would have happened could I have known it. To carry on a large Work regularly, books, & very voluminous calculations are necessary. I have sat up every night till one o'clock for three weeks after measuring the plaistering & stone work to make the calculations which any clerk could have done. Why should I say that one is necessary if it were false? What interest have I in deceiving you? After the experience of last Session I cannot move without books. Lenthall cannot keep them. His business is out of doors, & there too he wants assistance; for we have to do more work in the next six months than I can ever remember to have been done, in the same space, in twelve.

All this I took the liberty to represent to you while here, & thought that I had your consent to engage at a small salary such an assistant. But with the most friendly manners M.r Munroe refuses his consent. In the meantime I am already in utter confusion as to our transactions with a view to their expense.

I have already, unwarily trespassed too much on your time. If I have your sanction, I can get an assistant in the office at 1$25 p day who is capable of taking great part of the outdoor business on him. If not: I know not how I shall again encounter the responsible [sic] thrown upon me from all quarters, & especially by the public, who see at once that all expense arises out of my operations, & *nowhere else*.

I am with the highest respect

Y.rs

B. HENRY LATROBE

[Ms., *Jefferson Papers*, Library of Congress.]

Latrobe to Jefferson

THE PRESIDENT OF THE U STATES

Washington May 25th 1808

Sir,

I herein enclose the strongest specimen of the plant which under the name of *Dryrot* commits such ravages upon the timber of buildings, — which I had ever met with. It was taken from the timber upon which the principal piers of the Senate chamber were built. The timber itself is reduced almost to powder, being more decayed than any other part of the work. We have now pulled them all down, & I hope to have them up again in a fortnight at most, & the Center of the Vault set. — Nothing is now more evident than that in two or three Years the Senate chamber would have fallen in. I have every reason to believe that the Presidents house is in the same state. I observe a crush of the plaistering even the Columns in the Hall which deserves examination — in the situation marked A.

I am with high

respect Y^r faith^y

B H Latrobe

[Ms., *Jefferson Papers*, Library of Congress.]

Robert Brent to Jefferson

(To President Jefferson)

City of Washington, May 31st, 1808.

Dear Sir:

The Commission with which I have been honored, as Mayor of this city expires this day, it will therefore be proper that a new Commission be made out and forwarded as early as possible.

Presuming that the situation of paymaster, to which Genl. Dearborn has intimated you desire to appoint me, will occupy my whole time, it will be proper that some other person should be commissioned as Mayor of this City and I could wish the new Commission may be so made out. If, however, you should not have made up your mind as to a successor — at this moment — when it is essential the office should not be vacant — you may again fill up the Commission to me, with an understanding that on the first of July some other person be selected to fill that office at which time I shall resign in his favor. I have the honor to be with sincere respect and esteem, Dear Sir,

Your Mo. Obt. Ser.

ROBERT BRENT.

[RECORDS OF THE COLUMBIA HISTORICAL SOCIETY, Vol. 2, pp. 242–43.]

JEFFERSON TO LATROBE

Monticello June 2. 08.

Sir

Your favor of May 23. is duly recieved, and reserving fuller explanations to my return, which will be during the next week, I shall enter into some brief explanations at present. on the dissolution of the board of Directors of the public buildings, and substituting by law a Superintendant to exercise all their functions, the numerous litigations in which the city rights were involved, and m͞r Monroe's perfect intimacy with them, pointed him out as the proper successor to the board. when some years afterwards, Congress proceeded to the erection of the S. wing, m͞r Monroe being no architect, it became necessary to revive the former office of m͞r Hoben and you were invited to accept it. the board had exercised a minute direction over m͞r Hoben, but m͞r Munroe understood that the whole direction in the constructions of the public buildings was to be with you, altho' his name was, by the law, still necessary as a sanction.

when a given appropriation was made for a particular building, the execution of the building and the application of the money was with you, and the appropriation was made on estimates formed by yourself, & neither by him or me. when the great deficit therefore happened the last year, it was impossible not to consider it as proceeding from a defect in your estimates, and continuing the work after the funds were exhausted. for the 3200. D. expended at the War office, nobody ever attached blame to you. that was deliberately sanctioned by the heads of departments & myself. but it is impossible to ascribe to me any agency in any other portion of the deficit, because I certainly did not know of that until my return in autumn when it was already incurred. it is true, as you observe, that I had urged you to employ a greater number of workmen, to ensure the completion of the S. wing for the ensuing session. but I did it on the ground, always expressed, that, the money being fixed & in hand, it would cost no more to employ 100. hands 50. days, than 50. hands 100. days. there never was a hint expressed, or a thought entertained, of going beyond the appropriation. still I will say candidly that had it been suggested to me that the appropriation was inadequate, I should in the first place have advised the doing only those things substantially necessary for the comfort of Congress, and if a moderate sum beyond even this were necessary (omitting every thing of mere ornament) I should probably have advised the going on to make the room capable of recieving them, and would in that case have taken on myself a candid explanation of the motives to Congress, and thrown ourselves on their indulgence. but as I never apprehended a deficit, & indeed expressed continual cautions against going beyond the funds, whenever I was called on for a warrant, it was impossible I could take to myself any part of the agency in producing it. and when I was obliged to state it to Congress, I never was more embarrassed than to select expressions, which, while they should not charge it on myself, should commit you as little as possible. as short as that message was, it was the subject of repeated consultations with the heads of departments separately, to help me to find expressions which should neither hurt your feelings or do you any injury. and in my conversations afterwards with individual members, I always observed that their own experience probably had taught them that in executing a building, if it did not in the end cost more than 1/5 or 1/6 beyond their calculation they were well off. whatever stories you may have heard imputing to me a different spirit or conduct, are not true. the inferences you draw from mr̄ Eppes's expressions are not just, altho' it has been very common to suppose that whatever came from either him or mr̄ T. M. Randolph, was in unison with my opinions. they respected too much their own indepen[den]ce to take opinions from me, and I respected them too much to wish to influence them. the consequence was we observed an entire silence & reserve as to what was doing in Congress, and no republican members voted oftener or more freely than they did, differently from what I should have done. — to relieve us from future dangers of similar errors, which you say can only be done by your having a clerk to keep accounts, you know I mentioned to you my unwillingness to create a new office, and that I thought it better you should employ one of your capable workmen in these accounts: but if it be necessary that he be called a clerk, I will consent to it. with the settlement of the accounts at the Treasury I have no right to interfere in the least. the Comptroller is a law officer. he is the sole & supreme judge in all claims for money against the US. and would no more recieve a direction from me as to his rules of evidence than one of the judges of the supreme court.

As to the work to be done at the president's house this summer, let us compleat the wall, & the steps, because they are definite objects named in the law. if any money is left, we will plant, and omit till then the digging & gates.

I thank you for the opportunity given of making this explanation. if all, to whom falsehoods are carried for purposes of embroiling, had been equally just, I should have saved to them as well as myself the uneasinesses of a silent separation for causes never made known. I salute you with esteem & respect.

TH: JEFFERSON

LATROBE B. H.

[Ms., *Jefferson Papers*, Library of Congress.]

ROBERT BRENT TO JEFFERSON

(To President Jefferson)

D Sir:

The foregoing is a copy of a letter which I wrote you, and was about delivering it at the post office when you were in Virginia, but which I was prevented from doing by an intimation from Mr. Munroe that you had directed the letters addressed to you to remain at the post office here on and after that day. I have thought it proper imm-ly on your arrival to repeat my desire that some other other person may be selected as Mayor in my place, believing as I do that the situation to which I am about to be called will require all my attention.

With sentiments of much respect

I have the honor to be Sir,

Your Obt. Ser.

ROBERT BRENT.

Washn, Saty. June 11th, 1808.

[RECORDS OF THE COLUMBIA HISTORICAL SOCIETY, Vol. 2, p. 243.]

LATROBE TO JEFFERSON

THE PRESIDENT U STATES

Washington, July 6th 1808

Sir,

The stone for the steps of the President's house is, in part arrived, & I am in hopes that the remainder will come up this week. It is now to be decided where it shall be wrought. If it could be prepared immediately on the spot marked ☉ not less than 250 Dollars would be saved out of the expense of hauling & time which would be necessary if wrought out of the enclosure: — and I suppose a fortnight in time; — besides the advantage of avoiding the risk of losing some of the stones by injury in removal. As You will be absent a very considerable part of the time while it is in hand the annoyance will be inconsiderable. — I beg to submit this to your consideration.

I have been confined to my bed & room from the 26th June to the 4th July, & propose to go to Phil^a as much for the benefit of my health as on business. Mr Lenthall waits upon you for your determination on the question submitted.

Believing the Cistern & every thing relating to the Water closet to be in perfect order I have not again sent the plumber to the house. If there is a deficiency, it shall be immediately removed.

With the highest respect I am Yours faithfully

B HENRY LATROBE

[Ms., *Jefferson Papers*, Library of Congress.]

JEFFERSON TO LATROBE

July 25, 1808.

. . . . . .

Lay the floors [of the Senate Chamber] where the gallery floor now is to be the floor of the future Senate Chamber, open it above to the roof to give it elevation enough, leaving the present columns uninjured until we see that, everything else being done and paid for, there remains enough to make these columns of stone.

. . . . . .

[TH: JEFFERSON]

[P. 25, HISTORY OF THE UNITED STATES CAPITOL, Glenn Brown, I.]

LATROBE TO JEFFERSON

B. HENRY LATROBE TO THOMAS JEFFERSON

Washington, September 11, 1808

South Wing

Franzoni [60] has completed his sculpture both on the frieze over the entrance and the Speaker's chair. The figure of Commerce which is entirely new, is not. I think equal to the other three (Agriculture, Art and Science), though remarkably well finished. The eagle has also acquired more repose and correctness.

Mr. Bridport's [61] ceiling will do him great honor. I fear the members will think it too fine, and I doubt not but that Mr. Randolph will abuse it. The contract is for $3,500 all expense included.[62] The columns proceed slowly in the completion of the capitals. We shall add only three to the number that are finished, but the capitals of all the pilasters are done. All the dentils of the cornice are cut, and much progress made in the enrichment of these members below the modillions. All the rosettes on the heads of the modillions are also finished.

[60] Giuseppe Franzoni, son of the president of the Academy of Fine Arts at Carrara, who was selected as a sculptor for the Capitol by Jefferson's friend, Philip Mazzei. After his arrival in Washington, Franzoni made a call upon President Jefferson and left him some "articles of marble." Jefferson wrote him on March 2, 1806: "I did not understand until told so by the servant at the door, that the articles of marble which you had left here, had been intended as presents to me. Be assured that I receive this mark of your good will as thankfully as if I could accept of it, but I have laid it down as a law to myself to accept no presents of value while I am in public office, and adherence to this rule is necessary for the tranquility of my own mind and it is necessary for the public good. These motives cannot fail to meet your approbation and to justify my request that you receive the objects back again, and with them the same thanks for the offer as if I had retained them. Be assured that I shall avail myself of every occasion of being useful to you, and accept my salutations. Th: Jefferson."

[61] George Bridport, of Philadelphia.

[62] The reference is to the ceiling of the House of Representatives (it was destroyed by fire in August, 1814).

All this work though it adds exceedingly to the general effect does not tell so well in detail and I have preferred executing it this year and leaving nothing but the capitals of the columns unfinished, because the necessity of the latter work is much more evident to the untrained eye, than of the former.

The workmen are also now engaged in moving the situation of the fireplaces from the back of the Speaker's chair to the 2d intercolumination of the right and left.

This improvement was distinctly pointed out by the experience of the last session. The crowding of the members behind the chair where they could not be seen was highly inconvenient. I shall also move the chair three feet further back . . .

[Charles E. Fairman, Art and Artists of the Capitol of the United States of America, 16.]

JEFFERSON TO LATROBE

Monticello Sep. 20. 08

Sir

Yours of the 11th was recieved on the 15th but too much other business having made it impossible to answer by the return of that post, I avail myself of the first afterwards to say that as I propose to set out for Washington in a week I will defer concluding about fixing up the court room for the Senate till I see you in Washington. This will not occasion more than a week's delay, and you will still have 5. weeks to do it. would it not be easy to prepare their former room for them, the walls of which are of course dry? & the room would probably be more pleasing to them. if this will do, there will be no occasion to write to the Vice President, as no change of their position will be made. — the enclosure round the President's house being compleated, let us see the North steps finished, & the then state of the funds, before we undertake any thing else, as that will enable us to decide what we may undertake.

I salute you with esteem & respect.

TH: JEFFERSON

MR. LATROBE

[Ms., *Jefferson Papers*, Library of Congress.]

LATROBE TO JEFFERSON

THE PRESIDENT OF THE U. STATES

Washington Sept. 23ᵈ 1808

Sir,

The fall of the arch or Vault of the Court room in the North Wing of the Capitol on Monday last, & the death of Mʳ Lenthall who was buried in its ruins, must be known to you through the medium of the National Intelligencer & the Monitor in all its circumstances. Among the multitude of vexations, regrets, & business which this unfortunate event has thrown upon me, I feel extremely mortified that I have not been able untill this day, to command the time to write to you, with a perfect knowledge of all the circumstances. The account which appeared in the Monitor of yesterday is minutely correct, & contains all that can be said on the subject. I had drawn it up as the Substance of a letter to you, but Mʳ Cobien was so pressing in his wish to lay before the public a correct statement of the facts, and such improbable & malicious reports were already getting into circulation, that I was prevailed on to give him the manuscript and I hope to be pardoned by you, when I take the liberty to refer to it. — The truth is; that altho' delicacy to the memory, & to the talents of Mʳ Lenthall forbid me to excuse myself publicly by laying the blame upon him, his anxiety to save expense, & afterwards, his fears of the failure of his project were the real causes of the fall of the Vault.

The account given in the Monitor of the causes of failure will be immediately understood by the annexed drawing.

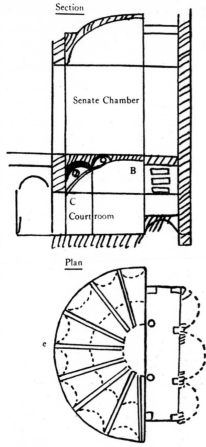

Section

Senate Chamber

B

C

Court room

Plan

e

O

O

My directions were to carry over the back of the Vault-walls, the bricks laid arch wise, as at a b c d e f g and to turn a conical arch over each of the spaces between, in order to obtain a level floor for the Senate Chamber. It is true that this method would have consumed twelve times the labor in making centers & that all the Centers would have been lost; but then, it would have been utterly impossible for the Vault to have fallen without throwing down the Butments all round, — which never could have happened. During my absence however Mr. Lenthall hit upon the scheme represented in the Section. He made 2 centers on a circular plan 10 feet long, & having turned so much of the arch O O on the back of the Dome, he then lowered them a little & drew them forward and turned ten feet more, & thus successively till he got round. He then got them out over the back of the cylindrical Arch at the end & thus saved perhaps 500$ in labor & materials. But it is evident that he loaded a part of the dome 1'.1" wide at A with half the Materials of these Floor arches, weighing about 60 Tons, chiefly stone chips & Brickbats. And yet such was the soundness & strength of the Vault that I believe it would have stood even thus injudiciously constructed had he not become alarmed, & lowered the props of

the center at B & C, leaving those at A standing. The consequence was that the Arch settled at those points & of course
opened & cracked at A all round, & when at last he attempted
to take away the posts at A the common foot of the two Arches
at A broke thru the Vault, broke all the Ribs of the Center at
that place (for thus we have formed them) & acting upwards
against the cylindrical Arch at B, which had stood firm for two
months forced it down with it. — The Vault of the Senate
Chamber, especially the great Cylindrical Arch, which is 54$^{ft.}$
spans & which is quite naked at the higth of 50 feet from the
present floor is as firm as a rock, & has a most extraordinary &
beautiful appearance. Every other Wall & Arch in the Building
is as sound as at the moment it was built.

On the 15th Septr Mr Munroe stated to me the balances remaining; — for the North wing 3,049$. My intention was to
strike the Centers of the Courtroom hoping, yet doubting, that
the Vault was safe, & if necessary to rebuild it, which would
have cost 600 Dollars, & to finish the stairs, & no more, — for
which this fund would have been sufficient. But this unfortunate accident has rendered this impossible with so small a fund.
— All our Workmen have however offered a *Weeks work* as a
subscription, & many gentlemen have proposed subscribing to
an amount amply sufficient to repair & render the Mischief
invisible by the meeting of congress. We have no materials to
buy, & propose to proceed upon a different plan, and instead
of one great arch on the east side to have 3 arches, resting on
the Columns and Pilasters as shown in the plan, and to Rib the
Dome in stone, of which we have plenty on the spot, so as to
make an Arch requiring no backing; as in the Octagon Vestibule of the house of Representatives. All this can be done in a
Month. I have consulted Mr Munroe, — but without your
approbation we are not willing to step forward & *lead* the
thing. To the interests of the city it appears so essential that
something of the sort should be done, that the impatience of

many of the citizens can hardly be restrained. — If therefore You would be pleased to express your opinion on the subject as early as possible, — if it does not amount to an absolute disapprobation, the subscription may be immediately carried into effect. In the meantime I am clearing off the rubbish & making preparations, keeping the fund always in View. —

The Walls of the Buildings are now as sound as in 1803 when I first undertook the direction of the Works.

With the highest Respect I am

Yours faithfully

B. Henry Latrobe

[Ms., *Jefferson Papers*, Library of Congress.]

Thomas Munroe to Jefferson

Oct 3 1808 (received)

Appropriated for South wing Capitol $11,500

Expended, Charged 26th May —		$1,237.55	
Dº	17	June —	1,793.87
Dº	30	. . . .	135.49
Dº	12	July —	583.61
Dº	31	Augᵗ —	669.18
Dº	24	Sep —	524.90
Painting ceiling —	.	3,500	
Proportion of Latrobe			
& Lenthall's salaries		750	
Italians House, Lenthall		200	
Clarke — painter &ᶜ		500	
		——————	
		4,950	9,894.58

Appropriated for the Presidents house $14,000

Expended, Ch^d 26th May — $1,766.80
            17   June   169.27
            30   D°   31.78
            12   July   172.41
            31   Aug^t   495.14
            24   Sep   653.00

Due for wall, estimated at $5,000
Steps estimated at about   3,000
rolls   Septem   say —   300
                           8,300   11,588 [Sic]
                                   2,500 [Sic]

Appropriation of Latrobe & Lenthalls Salaries about $500

[Ms., *Jefferson Papers*, Library of Congress.]

THOMAS MUNROE TO JEFFERSON

Tuesday Even^g 25th Oct° 1808

Sir,

On the receipt of the enclosed, I went down to the road to
see what Mr King meant, when I found that a foot way round
the wall similar to that at the north west fronts of the Presidents
square; & some other work on the road, was in hand and
nearly half done by order of Mr Latrobe —. Although what is
doing and what I was informed is ordered to be done by Mr L.,
will be a convenience, as well as to the Members of Congress &
persons attached to the public offices, as to all others who may
have occasion to pass that way, yet as neither the words of the
Act of Appropriation of last session, nor your sentiments on the
subject, as well as I recollect them, authorise any expenditures
on these roads or ways between the buildings, I considered it
my duty to stop the Laborers employed on that work until your
pleasure can be known, which I respectfully solicit an expression of in the morning, if it should be convenient —. The work
is necessary both for the preservation of the wall & to prevent

a large wash or gully in the road; and also to facilitate & render convenient the travel between the public buildings; but without your Approbation, Sir, I do not feel authorised to incur the expense tho' I do not believe it will exceed $50; a sum which I think will be well laid out, if it can be charged, with propriety, to the App^n for the Presidents house & lot, the only fund out of which it can be paid — .

I have the honor to be with the greatest respect
    Yr mo Ob Servt

THOMAS MUNROE

[Ms., *Jefferson Papers*, Library of Congress.]

JEFFERSON TO THOMAS MUNROE

TH: J. TO M$\overline{R}$ MONROE

As the work you mention will cost, as is supposed not more than 50. D. & is so necessary for the preservation of the wall, I think it may be so far considered as appurtenant to the wall & necessary to it's duration, that it may be placed to that account.

Oct. 26. 08.

[*Letters of the Presidents of the United States to the Commissioners of Public Buildings and Grounds*, original in the Manuscripts Division, Library of Congress, photostat in the National Archives.]

THOMAS MUNROE TO JEFFERSON

Office of the Superintendent of the City of Washington, 15th *Nov.* 1808

Sir.

In the year 1794, the then Commissioners of this City convey'd to James Greenleaf one thousand Standard Lots on the personal responsibility of himself Robert Morris and John Nicholson, whose Bond was taken for the purchase money,

amounting to Eighty thousand dollars. This money not having
been paid, a Bill was filed in the Chancery Court of the State of
Maryland, before the Jurisdiction of the District of Columbia
was assumed by Congress, and, under a Decree of that Court,
obtained in the last year, these lots are advertised for sale on
the 28th of the present month, to raise, in the first instance the
above sum of 80,000 dollars and interest from the 1st of May
1800, due thereon to the United States, and the surpluss, if any,
to be paid to certain persons claiming under Mr. Greenleaf.

Judging from the result of a public sale of a large number of
City Lots, made a few years since, in pursuance of an Act of
Congress which was imperative in its direction, and contained
no discretionary or conditional power to the Agent, — indeed
from the almost certain consequence of forced sales of all articles in greater quantities than there is demand for, the expectation may reasonably be entertained, that at the approaching
sale great sacrifices of the property will be made, and a considerable part of the claim of the United States be lost, if some
measure be not adopted to prevent it. The injurious effects now
apprehended were experienced in the sale above mentioned, to
such extent, that many lots then purchased have since been sold
for upwards of a thousand p^rcent advance: for, as the public
Agent had neither the power to decline selling, or to authorise a
competition in behalf of the United States, few of the persons
who attended to purchase would bid against each other, and
thus they bought, by an understanding and accommodation
amongst themselves, for comparatively nothing, or at such
prices only as they chose to offer.

I beg leave therefore, respectfully to submit to your consideration, Sir, whether it may not be promotive of the public interest for the government to give authority to an agent under
the direction of the President to attend the sale about to be
made, and to bid in behalf of the United States, to such amount
as may be prescribed, to prevent an unwarrantable sacrifice of

the lots and to counteract the speculations, which without some interposition there are strong reasons to believe will take place.

The Decree under which this sale is ordered, requires that the purchase money shall be paid into the Chancery Court. That requisition, however, would, it is supposed, be dispensed with in case of purchasers on public account, except as to the costs, expenses and the Trustees Commissions for selling &c. — but for the amount of these and some other claims against the *City funds* (to the payment of which the monies arising from this sale are in the first instance applicable) it may probably be expedient to obtain provisional Authority for a temporary advance from the Treasury, to be used if necessary in the opinion of the President. And, when it is considered, that these lots and the other unsold property of the United States in the City, estimated even at one half the average price of sales heretofore made, will amount to nearly half a million of Dollars, it is, with deference, presumed that such an advance will not be deemed objectionable under the circumstances above stated.

I have the honor to be, with the highest respect, Sir,

Y^r most obed^t Servt

THOMAS MUNROE

PRESIDENT OF THE UNITED STATES.

[Ms., *Jefferson Papers*, Library of Congress.]

JEFFERSON TO GALLATIN

TH: J. TO M$\overline{R}$ GALLATIN

I am really at a loss what to do in the inclosed case. the President as trustee for the city by it's constitution, is nominally the plaintiff. but the US. as creditors to more than the whole amount of the proceeds of the sale, being really the cestui que trust, I believe it will be more correct for the trustee to abandon the management of the case to the creditor. if so, it will fall under your direction, aided by the advice & agency of the Attorney General. if I rightly recollect my law, a plaintiff may, in any case of execution, give what indulgences he pleases as to pressing or not pressing the sales; and consequently there would be no necessity for the US. becoming the purchasers merely to prevent loss by forced sales. I will govern myself however in the case by your advice & that of the Attorney general. it seems to be urgent. Affect.^{te} salut^{ns}

Nov. 17. 08.

[*Letters of the President of the U.S. to the Commissioners of Public Buildings and Grounds,* original in the Manuscripts Division, Library of Congress, photostat in the National Archives.]

JEFFERSON TO THOMAS MUNROE

Th: Jefferson incloses to m͞r Monroe m͞r Duval's opinion on the sale of the city lots under the decree in Chancery. considering that there are three parties in this case, 1. the Debtor, 2. the US. as privileged creditor, 3. the residuary creditors, the only chance to avoid sacrificing all three of the parties is to obtain the consent of all three to have the sales opened and adjourned from time to time so as best to consult the interests of all. care must be used however to obtain effectively the consent of the residuary creditors, that we may run no risk of making ourselves liable to them by acting without their consent. at the first session of the court, or the earliest moment practicable, this proceeding should be placed under the sanction & government of the court.

Nov. 24. 08.

[*Letters of the President of the U.S. to the Commissioners of Public Buildings and Grounds,* original in the Manuscripts Division, Library of Congress, photostat in the National Archives.]

LATROBE TO JEFFERSON

Wednesday Nov. 30.th 1808

Sir

The impossibility in the present hurry of the Post Office of

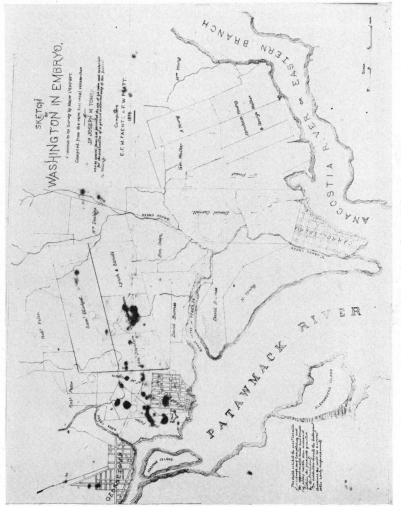

Location of land of the Original Proprietors.

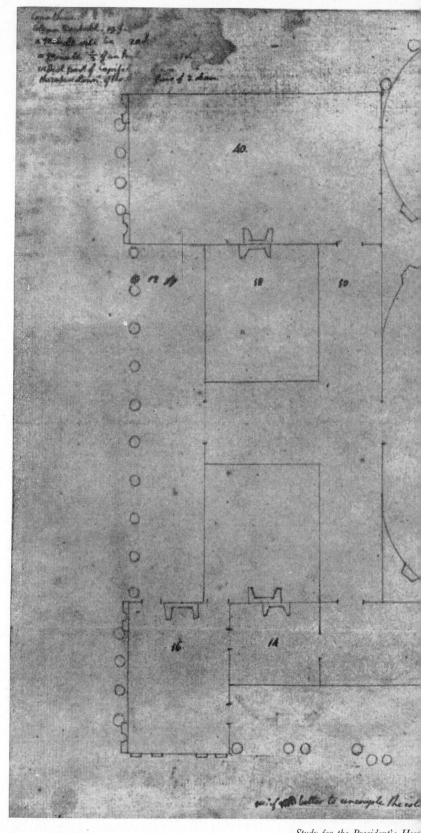

Study for the President's Hou

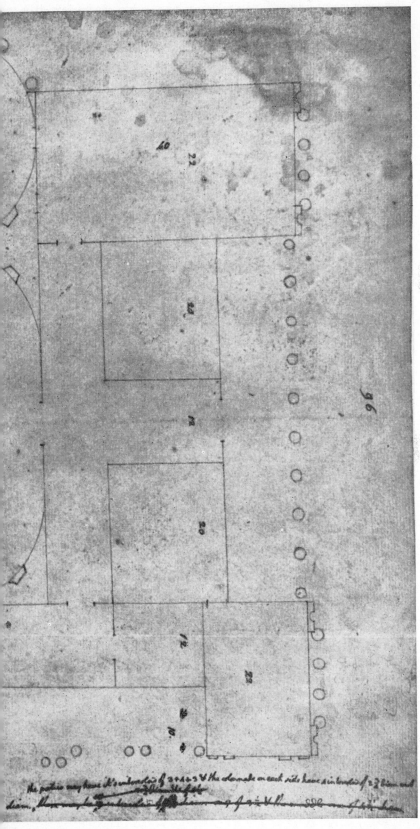

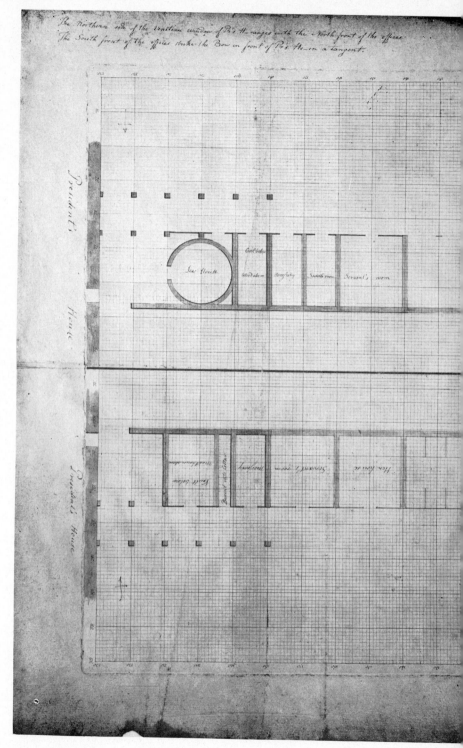

Study for section of President's House—Drawn by Jefferson a

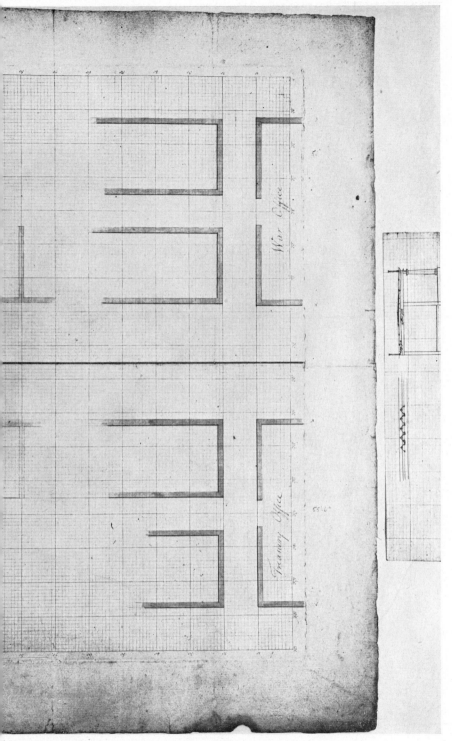

War Office

Treasury Office

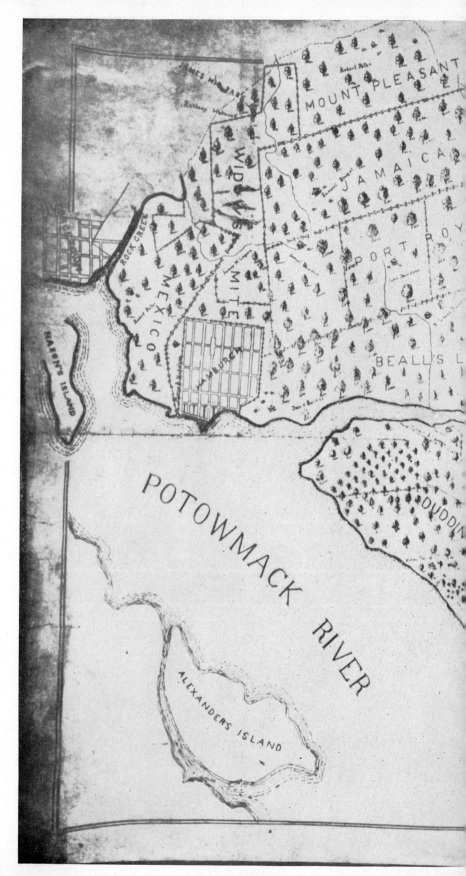

VIEW

OF THE

CITY OF WASHINGTON

IN

1792.

SHERWOOD

ABBY MANOR

HOP YARD

ANACOSTIA RIVER OR EASTERN BRANCH

anorial Estates.

TERMS and CONDITIONS declared by the PRESIDENT of the UNITED STATES, this seventeenth day of October, seventeen hundred and ninety-one, for regulating the Materials and Manner of the Buildings and Improvements on the LOTS in the CITY of WASHINGTON.

1st. THAT the outer and party walls of all houses within the said City shall be built of brick or stone.

2d. That all buildings on the streets shall be parallel thereto, and may be advanced to the line of the street, or withdrawn therefrom, at the pleasure of the improver, but where any such building is about to be erected, neither the foundation or party-wall shall be begun without first applying to the person or persons appointed by the Commissioners to superintend the buildings within the city, who will ascertain the lines of the walls to correspond with these regulations.

3d. The wall of no house to be higher than forty feet to the roof, in any part of the city ; nor shall any be lower than thirty-five feet on any of the avenues.

4th. That the person or persons appointed by the Commissioners to superintend the buildings may enter on the land of any person to set out the foundation and regulate the walls to be built between party and party, as to the breadth and thickness thereof: Which foundations shall be laid equally upon the lands of the persons between whom such party-wall are to be built, and shall be of the breadth and thickness determined by such person proper; and where any building be reimbursed one moiety of the party-wall, or so much thereof as the shall have occasion to make use of, next builder shall any want use or break wall—The charge or value thereof to be set by the person or persons so appointed by the Commissioners.

5th. Temporary conveniencies will be proper for lodging workmen and securing materials for building, and is to be understood that such may be erected with the approbation of the Commissioners: But they may be removed or discontinued by the special order of the Commissioners.

6th. The way into the squares being designed in a special manner for the common use and convenience of the occupiers of the respective squares—The property in the same is reserved to the public, so that there may be an immediate interference on any abuse of the use thereof by any individual, to the nuisance or obstruction of others. The proprietors of the Lots adjoining the entrance into the squares, on arching over the entrance, and fixing gates in the manner the Commissioners shall approve, shall be intitled to divide the space over the arching and build it up with the range of that line of the square.

7th. No vaults shall be permitted under the streets, nor any encroachments on the foot-way above by steps, stoops, porches, cellar doors, windows, ditches or leaning walls ; nor shall there be any projection over the street, other than the eves of the house, without the consent of the Commissioners.

8th. These regulations are the terms and conditions under and upon which conveyances are to be made, according to the deeds in trust of the lands within the city.

George Washington.

TERMS of SALE of LOTS in the CITY of WASHINGTON, the Eighth Day of October, 1792.

ALL Lands purchased at this Sale, are to be subject to the Terms and Conditions declared by the President, pursuant to the Deeds in Trust.

The purchaser is immediately to pay one fourth part of the purchase money; the residue is to be paid in three equal annual payments, with yearly interest of six per cent. on the whole principal unpaid: If any payment is not made at the day, the payments made are to be forfeited, or the whole principal and interest unpaid may be recovered on one suit and execution, in the option of the Commissioners.

The purchaser is to be entitled to a conveyance, on the whole purchase money and interest being paid, and not before. No bid under Three Dollars to be received.

Building Regulations issued by President Washington.

ascertaining correctly the balances of the appropriations & indeed the variation hourly taking place in them by the payment of accounts, induced me to alter in the Report the passage relating to them, & to state merely that *they were so nearly exhausted that the Work must soon close and Workmen be discharged unless the legislature should proceed further towards the completion of the public Works.* Mr. Munroe has 3.700 still in hand.

Yours

B H LATROBE

THE PRESIDENT OF THE UNITED STATES

[Ms., *Jefferson Papers*, Library of Congress.]

JEFFERSON TO CONGRESS

THE PRESIDENT TO THE SENATE AND HOUSE OF REPRESENTATIVES

December 1, 1808

I transmit to both house of congress, a report from the surveyor of the public buildings, of the progress made in them during the last season, of their present state, of the expenditures incurred, and of those which may be requisite for their further prosecution.

[P. 146, DOCUMENTARY HISTORY . . . OF THE CAPITOL.]

LATROBE TO JEFFERSON

TO THE PRESIDENT OF THE UNITED STATES

The report of the surveyor of the Public Buildings of the United States in the City of Washington   November 18.th 1808

Sir,

The several appropriations made at the last session of Congress for the progress of the work on the Public Buildings, have, during the late recess of the Legislature been applied to their specific objects in the manner which I now beg leave to report to You.

I. *South Wing of the Capitol*

In this wing all the wood work & the covering of the Roof have been painted, — the Iron railing of the Vestibule & stairs has been provided, — the Sculptors have been diligently employed in the interior of the Hall upon the figures of the frieze on the cornice and the Capitals of the columns. The cieling has been painted in a masterly manner by Mr Geo. Bridport of Philadelphia, the lobbies of the House have been finished, and the inconveniences experienced during the last session have been obviated by a great variety of improvements in detail.

II. *North Wing of the Capitol*

The appropriation for this wing has been specifically applied, agreeably to the words of the Act, — *to carry up in solid work the interior of the North Wing, comprizing the Senate Chamber*, according to the design submitted to congress in the year 1806, & partly executed in 1807.

This design, presuming that the brickwork of the building could be depended upon, did not contemplate the removal of the brick Arcade surrounding the Senate Chamber. But on opening the floors every part of the woodwork was found to be much more decayed than was ever apprehended; so that no one floor in the whole building could be considered as safe. Scarcely a single principal girder or beam was entirely sound, the tenants of the Oak joists were generally rotten, — and the only Species of timber, which had at all withstood decay, was the pine & poplar of which the beams & the Pillars were made. All the White Oak was siezed by the dry rot, and even the trusses of oak, let into sound beams of pine were far advanced in decay.[63] Almost all the plates & bond Timber, which were partly

---

[63] The state of the timber generally may be observed as it lies near the building in a situation open to inspection. [Note in the original.]

buried in the walls, were in the interior reduced to powder; and even many of the pine posts, over which the lathed & plaistered columns of the Senate Chamber were formed, were rotten.

Upon the most decayed part of such timber the brickpiers of the senate chamber stood; — they were admirably constructed; but of seven superficial feet, which each of them occupied, 5 feet had no other foundation to rest upon. Independently of this general rottenness of the timber, the Frequent alterations which the design had undergone during its original progress had weakened the work, and one of the most heavy walls had been so cut down in its lower part that whenever the timber had given way, the top must have fallen into the senate chamber.

It became therefore necessary to go down to the very foundation, to take down & rebuild the Arcade, now a part of the court room, and to carry up the whole work solidly from the bottom of the cellar. All this was accomplished about the middle of Sept.: but on the 19th of that month the floor of the senate chamber, with the Vault of the court room which supported it, fell in; and tho' no other part of the work, except the cellar arches below was thereby damaged; — and the value of the loss suffered in labour & materials did not exceed 800$ yet the death of M.r Lenthall, Clerk of the works, who was buried in the ruins, renders this accident a most serious misfortune to the public: for to his consumate skill as a mechanic & to his unimpeachable integrity the public are indebted in a great measure for the perfect execution which characterizes the works erected since the year 1803. The cause of this accident is to be found in the manner in which the level floor of the senate chamber was raised upon the back of the vault; in the construction of which, my better judgement yielded to arguments of economy.

Since this accident progress has been made in rebuilding this vault in a safe, though less expeditious manner, and in a few weeks of the next season all may be restored. In addition to the apartments of the senate a stone stairs has been executed by M.̠ Geo. Blagden in a style of very superior workmanship.

III. *Presidents House*

Agreeably to the provisions of the law, the wall of inclosure round the Presidents Ground has been completed & the workmen are now setting the coping. A flight of stone steps, a bridge, & platform, over the area of the North front are nearly completed.

The appropriated [sic] being now nearly exhausted the work must soon be closed, & the workmen discharged unless it should please the legislature to proceed further towards the completion of the public buildings. I therefore beg leave to submit the following:

STATEMENT & ESTIMATE OF WORK PROPOSED FOR THE
NEXT SEASON

1. *South Wing of the Capitol.*

To continue the work on the capitals of the columns of the house of representatives, to defray expense of repairs, of glass, & minor repairs; to procure strong american glass for the large Windows of the hall, which have been hitherto imperfectly glazed, & independantly of the inconvenience, are liable to frequent breakage; & to put up 10 deficient chimney pieces will be required $6000.

I beg leave to remark that this sum includes the salaries of the Italian sculptors engaged by contract in the service of the united states, & who when no longer employed are to be sent home at the public expense. The future annual expense of this Wing until completed will not exceed $5.000.

2. *North Wing of Capitol apartments of the senate.*

The Apartments of the Senate consist of
1. The senate chamber.

2. The Vestibule in the center of the House.

3. The Lobby or Withdrawing room.

4, 5. The Secretary's Office, 2 Rooms, — one for the records;

6, 9. Four committee rooms; two on a level with the floor of the Senate, two above stairs.

10, 11. The Gallery stairs, & committee room stair case.

12. The Passage to the Lobby & cloak room &c. —

13, 16. Three storerooms above stairs.

18, 19. The lower entrance and principal stairs.

All these apartments may be completely finished by the middle of August next. All the rooms are ready for the plaisterer excepting the Senate Chamber & the rooms in the recess which are to be rebuilt from the foundation being the most rotten part of the remaining building, excepting the library.

These works will require independently of furniture $20.000.

3. *Library & Offices of Judiciary on the West side of the North Wing.*

The room now containing the library is much too small for the books already purchased, which are obliged to be piled up in heaps; and unless immediate steps be taken to compleat the permanent accomodations for the library, the utmost embarrassment will ensue. This and the rotten state of the west side of the North Wing which remains untouched, induces me to propose immediate measures to this Effect. An appropriation of 25000$ will carry up the whole of this side of the house solidly complete the staircase & after the next session, the library may be fitted up & recieve the books before the session of 1810–11.

The Library will consist of, besides a private reading room, for the members of the legislature, the great library, which is calculated to contain not less than 40,000 books against its walls in three stages or galleries; & two store rooms for unbound books pamphlets & deposited copies of the laws.

The Apartments of the Judiciary will be

1. The Court Room.

2. The Judges chamber for consultation & library.

3. The Office of the Marshall.

4. — do. — of the Clerk of the supreme court.

5. — do. — of the Clerk of the circuit Co.ᵗ.

6. 7. Two petit jury rooms.

8. Grand Jury room.

9. 10. rooms for records.

11. 13. Lobbies, passages & stairs.

I beg leave in one view to exhibit the advantages gained by this alteration of the North Wing. The senatorial apartments formerly consisted of

1. The senate chamber.

2. The secretary's office.

3. 6. Two committee rooms one above one below & two detached rooms over the entrance.

7. 9. Two large lumber rooms above.

10. 16. Four lobbies & two stair cases   14

The court occupied one room   1
                                                                         ──
                                                                         15

There are three rooms & a staircase in the brick part of the wing which are not proposed at present to be changed.

By the alterations is gained

1. Senatorial apartments   19

2. Judiciary   13

3. Library   4
                                                                            ──
                                                                            36

Besides the whole range of cellars formerly useless neither light nor air being admitted to them.

4. *Addition to the North West corner of the south Wing.*

I again beg to point out the necessity of building the North West part of the apartments of the House of Representatives in the South Wing and to refer to my report of last session. The accumulation of Water in the Cellars formerly dug on this spot which cannot be prevented continues to injure the foundation & a perceptible tho' small settlement of this corner has taken place during the present year. The temporary Water closets are at present a great nuisance which can only be removed by compleating this part of the design, which will contain additional committee rooms one for the standing committee of the district of columbia & 2 others for special committees for whom no accomodation whatever now exists.

This work will require an appropriation of $18000.

IV. *Presidents House*

The wall of enclosure being now nearly finished the following additions are necessary toward the completion of this building. 1. Carriage house which is now entirely deficient. 2. The Gate of the North front, 3. The platform on the south front now of wood & entirely rotten. 4. The regulation of the ground west of the House struck out of the appropriation of last year & the current repairs & improvements of the House. — to perform this work will be required $12.000.

RECAPITULATION

1.	South Wing...............................	6.000
2.	North Wing, Senate........................	20.000
3.	do. Library & Judiciary.............	25.000
4.	N W. corner of South Wing................	18.000
5.	Presidents House..........................	12.000
		$81.000

I also beg leave to suggest whether it will not be necessary at the public expense to make the road on the south side of the Presidents square, which for want of gravel & the necessary sewers will in a short time be impassable. An annual appropriation for the roads between the public buildings has been made untill the last year. If this object is to be provided for, the sum of 3000$ would be required to secure the work already done &

provided for general repairs. All which is most respectfully submitted.

B. HENRY LATROBE
Surveyor public Bldgs U States

[Original ms. in Senate Archives, accompanying message from the President, dated December 1, 1808. Also printed in part in DOCUMENTARY HISTORY . . . OF THE CAPITAL, pp. 146–9.]

JEFFERSON TO THOMAS MUNROE

December 4, 1808.

JEFFERSON TO THOMAS MONROE

The case of the sale of city lots under a decree of the Chancellor of Maryland.

The deed of the original owners of the site of the city of Washington to certain trustees, after making provisions for streets, public squares, &c., declares that the residue of the ground, laid off in building lots, shall one moiety belong to the original proprietors, and the other moiety shall be sold on such terms and conditions as the President of the United States shall direct, the proceeds, after certain specified payments, to be paid to the President as a grant of money, and to be applied for the purposes, and according to the Act of Congress; which Act of Congress (1790, c. 28) had authorized the President to accept grants of money, to purchase or to accept land for the use of the United States, to provide suitable buildings, &c. Of these residuary building lots, one thousand were sold by the Commissioner to Greenleaf for $80,000, who transferred them to Morris and Nicholson, with an express lien on them for the purchase money due to the city. Under this lien the Chancellor of Maryland has decreed that they shall be sold immediately for whatever they will bring; that the proceeds shall be applied first to the costs of suit and sale, and the balance towards paying the original purchase money. The sale has now proceeded, for some days, at very low prices, and must proceed till the costs of suit and sale are raised. It is well understood that under no circumstances of sale, however favorable, can they pay five in the pound of the original debt; and that if the whole are now forced into sale, at what they will bring, they will not pay one in the pound; and being the only fund from which a single dollar of the debt can ever be recovered, (on account of the bankruptcy of all the purchasers,) of $25,000 which the lots may bring if offered for sale from time to time pari-passu with the growing demand, $20,000 will be lost by a forced sale. To save this sum is desirable. And the interest in it being ultimately that of the United States, I have consulted with the Secretary of the Treasury and Comptroller, and after due consideration, I am of opinion it is for the public interest, and within the powers of the President, under the deed of trust and laws, to repurchase under the decree, at the lowest prices obtainable, such of these lots as no other purchaser shall offer to take at what the Superintendent shall deem their real value, that is to say, what they will in his judgment sell for hereafter, if only offered from time to time as purchasers shall want them. The sums so to be allowed for them by the Superintendent to be passed to the credit of Greenleaf, and retaining a right to the unsatisfied balance as damages due for non-compliance with his contract; a matter of form only, as not a cent of it is expected ever to be obtained. I consider the reconveyance of these lots at the price which the Superintendent shall nominally allow for them, as replacing them in our hands, in statu quo prices, as if the title had never been passed out of us; and that thereafter they will be in the condition of all other lots, sold, but neither conveyed nor paid for; that is to say, liable to be resold for the benefit of the city; as has been invariably practiced in all other cases. The Superintendent is instructed to proceed accordingly.

[Pp. 395–6, WRITINGS OF JEFFERSON, Washington, Vol. V, Memorial Edition, XII, pp. 206–8.]

LATROBE TO JEFFERSON

THE PRESIDENT OF THE U STATES

Washington, January 31st 09

Sir,

Your letter of the 29th [64] relative to the Glass supplied to you from the public Stock, was received on Sunday and I have since then searched all the papers belonging to the office for an account of it, an employment which took up the whole of yesterday, & part of this morning before I succeeded. I hope this will plead my apology for the late answer to your note. It was Mr Lenthall's habit to make all his entries on loose slips of paper, & never to throw away a memorandum even after it had ceased to be useful. Immediately after his death the order in which all these slips were kept was disturbed by the family in examining his papers: & prior to the first date of the book I now keep it is difficult to find any thing relating to the public acc^{ts} without a thorough search.

In the account stated the prices are put down agreeably to the rate at which we have sold the glass which was too small for the windows of the public buildings, and at which Mr Clephan the glazier has himself bought it to sell again. But when it is considered that the Glass which you have received has been cut out of useless pieces, I think it ought not be charged higher that the small Glass can be bought by the box in common times, to wit from 12 to 13 $ p box containing 100 feet superf! and at this price, namely 12 ½ Cents p foot Mr Barry the painter paid for his Glass, if I am not very much mistaken.

The account rendered by Mr Lenox, was directed by me to be charged at 10^{cts} being the actual cost to the public by the Crate, & making no allowance for breakage. In the annexed account I have put down every thing at this price. At the same time I copy the account for you from Mr Lenthall's statement,

---

[64] Unable to locate this letter. — S.K.P.

which I always till now supposed to have been rendered long ago to the Superintendant to whom it is directed & for whom it is made out.

> I am with the highest respect
>
> Y^{rs}
>
> B HENRY LATROBE

[Ms., *Jefferson Papers*, Library of Congress.]
Copy).

> *The President of the United States D^r*
> *From the Capitol*

1808

March 15th

To 200 panes of Glass cut 12 $\times$ 12 — @ 22^{cts} —	44\$ —			
300 d°	12 $\times$ 18	40	120 —	
50 d°	14 $\times$ 18	50	25 —	
N°. 8 boxes for package of d°			5.04	
averaging 25 6/10 p^r foot [65]			\$194.04	

from the Presidents house

422^{ft} 9^{in} d°   12   50.73

averaging 12. cents p^r foot [65]   224.77

[Ms., *Jefferson Papers*, Library of Congress.]

THO^s. JEFFERSON, *Presid^t.* US. D^r.

> *To Thos. Munroe Sup^t. city of Wash^n.*
> *For Glass cut from the public Stock.*
> *North Wing, Capitol —*

1808

March

200 squares	12 $\times$ 12	@ 10^{cts} =	\$20.
300 d°	12 $\times$ 18	15 =	45
50 d°	14 $\times$ 18	$17\frac{1}{2}$ =	8.75
N°. 8 packing boxes			5.04
			78.79

Presidents' house

422^{ft} 9^{in} superf^l.   @ 10^{cts} 42.27

121.06

[65] Comment by Jefferson.

The above squares of Glass, being cut from the parts of Tables which were useless for glazing the large Windows of the public Bldgs, are charged at the price at which the public bought them by the Crate.

B HENRY LATROBE

January 31ˢᵗ 1809.   *Surv. Pblic Bldgs U.S.*

[Ms., *Jefferson Papers*, Library of Congress.]

JEFFERSON TO THOMAS MUNROE

Washington Feb. 6. 09.

Sir,

I inclose you mr̄ Latrobe's account [66] for the glass I purchased at the Capitol & President's house. he has charged it at what it cost the public, 10. cents the square foot. but on the back I have calculated it at $12\frac{1}{2}$ cents, for which he says I might have bought it, by the box, from the merchants. the amount at this last price is 150 7/100 D. for which I inclose you a check on the bank US. will you be so good as to give me a reciept on the back of the inclosed account & return it. accept my friendly salutations.

TH: JEFFERSON

Mʳ. THOMAS MUNROE

[*Letters of the President of the U. S. to the Commissioners of Public Buildings and Grounds*, original in the Manuscripts Division, Library of Congress, photostat in the National Archives.]

MUNRO THOˢ.

I   I

200. panes 12. by 12 = 200. square feet
300. dᵒ   12. by 18 = 450.
 50. dᵒ   14. by 18 = $87\frac{1}{2}$ 737.5
422.75   12. by 12 =   422.75

                                                        cents
                                        1160.25 @ $12\frac{1}{2}$ 145.03
       packing boxes.............................   5.04
                                                     $150.07 [67]

[66] See enclosure, Latrobe to Jefferson, January 31, 1809.
[67] These figures in Jefferson's handwriting.

6th February 1809   Received of the President of US. the sum of One hundred and fifty Dollars, seven cents for the Glass within mentioned note. The price or Am.^t paid in addition to that certified by the Surveyor of the public buildings is explained in the Presidents letter of this day, on file; vizt that the common selling price by merchants is about 12½ cents p foot, and that he therefore would not take it of the public at a less price.

THOMAS MUNROE Sup.^t

737.5 sq. f. from capitol	92.1875
422.75 d.^o from Pr's H	52.84375
1160.25 sq. f. @ 12 1/2 cents..........................	145.03
packing boxes	5.04
	150.07

Clephan bought to sell again @ 10. cents
but 12½ cents is what such glass can be bought at by the box.[68]

[Ms., *Jefferson Papers*, Library of Congress.]

LATROBE TO JEFFERSON

Sir

   Mr Le Mair has no inventory of the furniture of the President's house, but he informs me that Mr Claxton's is perfect excepting as to some articles of Plate made at Richmond. Under the circumstances of the case, if Mr Madison does me the honor to confide the future expenditure to me, it would be necessary for me to possess the inventory as soon as possible, or otherwise to refer the Member of the Senate who applied to me for information, to Mr. Claxton. — I am very unwilling to intrude into his province, especially as it obliges me to become troublesome to you at the present moment.

   With high respect I am

   Yours,   B H LATROBE

Feby 16th 09

[Ms., *Jefferson Papers*, Library of Congress.]

[68] These computations and comments are in Jefferson's handwriting.

LATROBE TO JEFFERSON

[*Feb.* 19. 1809]

Mr Latrobe presents his most respectful Compliments to the President U. S. — & thanks him for the Inventory [69] sent him. Mr Latrobe's object in going to Philadelphia is to take some measures necessary for the supply of sundry materials for the Pblic Bldgs, & articles of furniture for the Presid^s house. He intends to return without fail on the 2^d of March. Before the President's journey to Monticello he will have the pleasure to acquit himself of the engagements of respect to him which are yet unperformed, particularly in respect to the book of plans, & the *red stone* in possession of the Italians. His address at Ph^a is, — at Isaac Hazlehurst's Esqr

[Ms., *Jefferson Papers*, Library of Congress.]

WASHINGTON CITIZENS TO JEFFERSON

COMMITTEE OF WASHINGTON CITIZENS TO PRESIDENT JEFFERSON

March 4, 1809

Sir,

The Citizens of Washington cannot forego the last opportunity which may, perhaps, ever occur, to bid you a respectful and affectionate farewell. As members of the great and flourishing nation, over which you have so illustriously presided, your virtues, talents and services command their esteem, admiration, and gratitude. Embarked in the fate of this solitary republic of the world, they have in common with their fellow citizens, rejoiced in its prosperous and sympathised in its adverse fortunes, as involving everything dear to freemen. They have marked with exultation, the firm column of its glory, laid on imperishable foundations, using as a monument of the reign of principle

[69] Unable to locate this paper. — S.K.P.

in this quarter of the globe. To you they have been instructed to ascribe the memorable act, which, by declaring a gallant people free and independent, in a tone that appalled tyranny, instilled those sentiments and principles, which, inspiring every virtue, and urging every sacrifice, led them to triumph and empire.

We have since beheld you with parental solicitude, and with a vigilance that never sleeps, watching over the fairest offspring of liberty, and by your unremitted labors, in upholding, explaining and vindicating our system of government, rendering it the object of love at home and respect abroad.

It would be a pleasing task for us, as citizens of the United States, to fill up and extend the outlines we have sketched. But, it is, as citizens of the national metropolis, that we now appear before you. In addition to every patriotic feeling that can warm our breasts, we have still further inducements to open our hearts to you on this proud, yet painful occasion.

The world knows you as a philosopher and philanthropist; the American people know you as a patriot and statesman — we know you in addition to all this, as a *man*. And, however, your talents have extorted our respect, there is not one among us, whose predominant feeling at this moment is not that of affection for the mild and endearing virtues that have made every one here your friend, and you his. We should be lost to gratitude, did we not acknowledge that it is to you we owe much, very much of that harmony of intercourse and tolerance of opinion, which characterize our state of society — of that improvement, which, amidst unpropitious circumstances, has progressed with sure and steady steps, and above all, of that spirit of enterprise, which your beneficence and liberality have invariably aided, and which promises in a few years to render this place the fairest seat of wealth and science.

Deeply as we feel your retirement, we approve, nay applaud it. Personal considerations aside, it was to be expected from the friend and protector of republican institutions, that he would follow, and by his co-operation strengthen, the example of the illustrious hero of the revolution.

May you, in the retirement to which you go, be happy! As your fellow citizens will still look towards you with interest, and pray for your felicity, so will you find it impossible to lose sight of the arduous scenes through which we have passed, as well as those in store for our country. Your heart will still beat with patriotism, and the energies of your mind continue to be engaged on rational objects. In your retreat may every anxious thought be softened by the mild and tender occupations of private life! Happy, thrice happy retreat! Where patriotism and philosophy, friendship and affection, will animate, direct and soften the purest feelings of the heart! With a grateful nation we pray that you may be happy, and if the just Being, that presides over the universe, insure to you but a portion of that felicity you have conferred on others, our prayers will be fulfilled!

ROBERT BRENT, *Chairman.*

NICHOLAS KING, *Secretary.*

[COLUMBIA HISTORICAL SOCIETY, Vol. XXIV, 153–4. Reprinted through the courtesy of the Columbia Historical Society, Washington, D.C.]

JEFFERSON TO WASHINGTON CITIZENS

JEFFERSON TO THE CITIZENS OF WASHINGTON

March 4, 1809

I receive with peculiar gratification the affectionate address of the citizens of Washington and in the patriotic sentiments it expresses, I see the true character of the national metropolis. The station we occupy among the nations of the earth is honorable, but awful. Trusted with the destinies of this solitary republic of the world, the only monument of human rights, and the sole repository of the sacred fire of freedom and self-government, from hence, it is to be lighted up in other regions of the earth, if other regions of the earth ever become susceptible of its genial influence. All mankind ought, then, with us, to rejoice in its prosperous, and sympathize in its adverse fortunes, as involving everything dear to man. And to what sacrifices of interest or convenience, ought not these considerations to animate us! To what compromises of opinion and inclination, to maintain harmony and union among ourselves, and to preserve from all danger this hallowed ark of human hope and happiness! That differences of opinion should arise among men, on politics, on religion, and on every topic of human inquiry, and that these should be freely expressed in a country where all our facilities are free, is to be expected. But these valuable privileges are much perverted when permitted to disturb the harmony of social intercourse, and to lessen the tolerance of opinion. To the honor of society here, it has been characterized by a just and generous liberality, and an indulgence of those affections which, without regard to political creeds, constitute the happiness of life. That the improvements of this city must proceed with sure and steady steps, follows from its many obvious advantages, and from the enterprizing spirit of its inhabitants, which promises to render it the fairest seat of wealth and science.

It is very gratifying to me that the general course of my administration is approved by fellow-citizens, and particularly that the motives of my retirement are satisfactory. I part with the powers entrusted to me by my country, as with a burthen of heavy bearing; but it is with sincere regret that I part with the society in which I have lived here. It has been the source of much happiness to me during my residence at the seat of government, and I owe it much for its kind dispositions. I shall ever feel a high interest in the prosperity of the city, and an affectionate attachment to its inhabitants.

[RECORDS OF THE COLUMBIA HISTORICAL SOCIETY, Vol. XXIV, 154–55. Reprinted through the courtesy of the Columbia Historical Society, Washington, D.C.]

Latrobe to Jefferson

BENJAMIN H. LATROBE TO JEFFERSON

August 28, 1809

Dear Sir: I have packed up and sent to Richmond to be forwarded to Monticello a box containing the model of the capital of the columns of the lower vestibule of the Senatorial department of the north wing of the Capitol, which is composed of maize, on a short frustum running about 4 feet from the ground. It may serve for a dial stand, and should you appropriate it for that use I will forward to you a horizontal dial in Pennsylvania marble of the proper size. These capitals during the summer session obtained me more applause from members of Congress than all the works of magnitude or difficulty that surrounded them. They christened them the 'Corn-cob capitals,' whether for the sake of alliteration I can not tell, but certainly not very appropriately.

[Glenn Brown, HISTORY OF THE UNITED STATES CAPITOL, I, 45.]

Jefferson to Latrobe

Monticello Oct. 10. 09

Dear Sir

Your favor of Aug. 28. came duly to hand, and I congratulate you on the successful completion of your great arch of the Senate chamber as well as that of the Hall of Justice. I have no doubt you will finish those rooms so as to be worthy counterparts of that of the Representatives. it would give me pleasure to learn that Congress will consent to proceed on the middle building. I think that the work when finished will be a durable and honorable monument of our infant republic, and will bear favorable comparison with the remains of the same kind of the antient republics of Greece & Rome. I have no doubt that your

Cerealian capitel will be handsome: and shall be happy to recieve the model of it. the stone which Andrei and Franzoni are
preparing for me, need only be sculptured on one side. I propose to set it into the middle of the frieze of a chimney piece.

Your promised visit to Monticello, whenever it can be
effected, will give me real pleasure, and I think could not fail
of giving some to you. my essay in Architecture has been so
much subordinated to the law of convenience, & affected also
by the circumstance of change in the original design, that it is
liable to some unfavorable & just criticisms. but what nature
has done for us is sublime & beautiful and unique. you could
not fail to take out your pencil & to add another specimen of
it's excellence in landscape to your drawing of the Capitol &
Capitol hill. the difficulty would be in the choice between the
different scenes, where a panorama alone could fully satisfy. I
salute you with great esteem & respect.

TH: JEFFERSON

MR. LATROBE

[Ms., *Jefferson Papers*, Library of Congress.]

LATROBE TO JEFFERSON

THO.ˢ JEFFERSON ESQ.ᴿ

Washington, April 5th 1811

Sir

The high respect & attachment which I have always pro-
fessed and very sincerely felt for you has not been proved by the
frequency of my letters to you. But knowing how much your
time & mind are occupied by correspondence of infinitely
more importance, I have never had the vanity to believe that I
am entitled to intrude upon you with.ᵗ special occasion. — Another reason, — the reason indeed which now induces me to
write to you, has kept me silent hitherto. I have been per-

suaded, at last, after resisting all that has been said to me for several Years past, to believe that you have long ago changed the favorable sentiments respecting me which induced you to commit to my charge the direction of the public buildings of the U States.

It is always *useless* to argue against sentiment & feeling, and ambitious as I am that your personal *feelings* towards me should be favorable, it would be very impertinent in me to take up your time with professions the opportunity to prove which, by actions, is past; — or to attempt to wear out the impressions made upon your mind ever since the Year 1808 at least, by the written words of a single letter. But it is never too late to re-move wrong impressions as to facts, by documents, and to do this I now write to you, and solicit you to give me as a matter of justice, your attention. —

There has been current for at least four years, an opinion in this city that I had erected, in the North wing of the Capitol the Court-room & the offices attached to it, and had removed the Senate Chamber and its Offices & committee rooms upstairs not only without your knowledge of what I was about to do, but absolutely contrary to your wishes and orders. — This opinion was originally published in an anonymous piece in the Washington Federalist in 1807. Early in 1808 Dr Thornton in the most gross libels which, under his own name, he published in the same paper made the charge without any modification. When the Federalist was bought by Mr Patterson in 1809 & the title changed to that of the Independent american, — he opened his career by a series of papers so gross & calumnious, that the end of making an impression was defeated by his prov-ing too much. One of his principal charges against me was the alteration of the North wing contrary to your intentions & orders. —

Knowing as I supposed better than any one else in how far such a charge could be founded, it gave me no uneasiness. —

With congress it could not injure me because those members who would enquire of you would be undeceived, and the public could not feel much interest on the subject. I therefore took no trouble to contradict the assertion publicly, altho' it was made from all quarters. — I considered Dr Thornton to be its author.

But I have lately heard from a gentleman who resides near you, that the impression on your mind respecting my conduct in altering the capitol is this, "that I had pushed the work without your knowledge to a point from which it was impossible to recede, & that I had then been permitted to go on by you; because it was impossible for your to prevent it." — On hearing this I immediately called upon Mr Munroe, who told me that on your return to Washington in 1806 or 1807, (it must have been in 1808) you had, on hearing or seeing the demolition of the piers & Columns in the Senate chamber, expressed the utmost dissatisfaction with my proceedings — that however after having visited the works with me, you appeared, on his next interview, quite satisfied with the explanation I had given you. — On conversing however since then with the president U. S. I have again been induced to believe that there has always been more foundation in your own mind for the report that has been so injurious to me than I at first supposed, and that altho' I knew *myself* that I did nothing in the erection of the North wing of the capitol that had not had your sanction, and which you had not submitted to congress, yet that you were not entirely satisfied on that head, and may probably have so expressed yourself, not recollecting the details of the plans which had been submitted by you. —

It is of great importance however to my peace of mind that this impression should be removed, and that my conduct during your administration should be exhibited to you in its true light. I am not satisfied, that by a submission of all my reports & correspondence I could convinced [sic] any third person or persons that I have not devoted the 8 best years of my life to the mean & dirty employment of establishing a professional reputation by destroying the labors of my predecessors uselessly, in order to make room for my own, — and in disobeying the orders of the president to whom I owed the means of acquiring that reputation. —

The first document to which I refer is the original book of drawings submitted with my report of the 25th of Novr 1806 to Congress. This paper I have borrowed on my receipt & promise to return it, of Mr. McGruder Clerk of the House of Representatives. — It is very evident that this plan (in reference to which all the appropriations for the North wing have been made, & to which in all my subsequent reports I have referred), could not possibly have been executed without removing all those parts which are colored as being required to be removed, & making all those additions which the color points out as necessary. Nothing is so easy as to deceive by means of drawings. To compare drawings with work actually executed requires professional knowledge as well as strict examination & measurement of the work itself. Besides, drawings, unless in great detail do not exhibit more than the governing features of a design, the subordinate parts of which may be infinitely varied, & still be justified by reference to the plan. — Aware of this I have given two plans of each floor, so as to exhibit not only the ultimate effect of my proposed alteration but the means by which I meant to accomplish it. —

Of these drawings I have always possessed a correct copy in my office. But lest any doubt should arise in your mind I have thought it best to send the original, in which the parts covered with letter paper were covered by yourself as being part of the center, my plan of which you did not approve. —

I have, on this document only to add, that there is not the slightest alteration in the execution of the work from these drawings excepting only that in the North Vestibule two rooms (as marked in pencil) are taken off, the one (East room) being the office of the Clerk of the supreme court, the west the shop, — for the present, — of Mr Frazoni, — but intended to be the Office of the Marshall of the district. The West side of the house remains at present in the state in which it originally was, the new works having been carried up only so far as to include the central Lobby. 2. I will next refer to my letter of the 13th of Augt 1807 in which are these words "*Capitol*. My whole time excepting a few hours now & then devoted to the president's house is occupied in the drawings & directions for the N. Wing in the arrangement of which I am pursuing the eventual plan *approved* & presented by You to congress at the last Session."

3. In my letter of the 10th of Novr 1807, I thanked you for the "liberal manner in which you had been pleased to enable me to get thro' the business of the public works by your approbation of all I had done." It is not possible that I could have been so insolent as to thank you to your face for an approbation I had never received: & had I been guilty of such insolence, surely you would have dismissed me from my Office. — During your absence at Monticello I had communicated to you on the 2d & 17th of Septr the course of our proceedings all calculated to execute the plan now actually compleated.

4. In the year 1808 the work in the North wing again proceeded after the rising of congress which took place on the 29th of April. On the 23d of May I sent to you a voluminous report, the first part of which relates to my works in the North wing. I cannot refer to my directions in writing for the authority on which I proceeded, but from the confident manner of my report, & your not having objected to it in any letters I ever received, I cannot but conclude that it was conformable to the general plan of proceeding, which you expected. The report is so long that I beg you to turn to my letter in your possession, which even now proves the necessity of what I was doing. —

I have already so far exceeded the bounds I had prescribed to myself that I will not adduce the rest of my testimony as to my having acted, — as I supposed, in strict conformity to my communications to you. — I beg that you will have the goodness to communicate to me your own conviction on this head. — I do not expect the public buildings to be finished under my direction. As far as I have conducted them they will not disgrace your presidency. It is my intention to publish the designs & history of the work while the facts can be verified, as soon as I can make the necessary arrangements. — With the highest respect

I am & shall always be, Your Obliged & not ungrateful

B H LATROBE

[Ms., *Jefferson Papers*, Library of Congress.]

JEFFERSON TO LATROBE

Monticello, April 14, 1811.

Dear Sir, — I feel much concern that suggestions stated in your letter of the 5th instant, should at this distance of time be the subject of uneasiness to you, and I regret it the more as they make appeals to memory, a faculty never strong in me, and now too sensibly impaired to be relied on. It retains no trace of the particular conversations alluded to, nor enables me to say that they are or are not correct. The only safe appeal for me is to the general impressions received at the time, and still retained with sufficient distinctness. These were that you discharged the duties of your appointment with ability, diligence and zeal, but that in the article of expense you were not sufficiently guarded. You must remember my frequent cautions to you on this head, the measures I took, by calling for frequent accounts of expenditures and contracts, to mark to you, as well as to myself, when they were getting beyond the limits of the appropriations, and the afflicting embarrassments on a particular occasion where these limits had been unguardedly and greatly transcended. These sentiments I communicated to you freely at the time, as it was my duty to do. Another principle of conduct with me was to admit no innovations on the established plans, but on the strongest grounds. When, therefore, I thought first of placing the floor of the Representative chamber on the level of the basement of the building, and of throwing into its height the cavity of the dome, in the manner of the Halle aux Bleds at Paris, I deemed it due to Dr. Thornton, author of the plan of the Capitol, to consult him on the change. He not only consented, but appeared heartily to approve of the alteration. For the same reason, as well as on motives of economy, I was anxious, in converting the Senate chamber into a Judiciary room, to preserve its original form, and to leave the same arches and columns standing. On your representation, however, that the columns were decayed and incompetent to support the incumbent weight, I acquiesced in the change you proposed, only striking out the addition which would have made part of the middle building, and would involve a radical change in that which had not been sanctioned. I have no reason to doubt but that in the execution of the Senate and Court rooms, you have adhered to the plan communicated to me and approved; but never having seen them since their completion, I am not able to say so expressly. On the whole, I do not believe any one has ever done more justice to your professional abilities than myself. Besides constant commendations of your taste in architecture, and science in execution, I declared on many and all occasions that I considered you as the only person in the United States who could have executed the Representative chamber, or who could execute the middle buildings on any of the plans proposed. There have been too many witnesses of these declarations to leave any doubt as to my opinion on this subject. Of the value I set on your society, our intercourse before as well as during my office, can have left no doubt with you; and I should be happy in giving further proofs to you personally at Monticello, of which you have sometimes flattered me with the hope of an opportunity.

I have thus, Sir, stated general truths without going into the detail of particular facts or expressions, to which my memory does not enable me to say yea or nay. But a consciousness of my consistency in private as well as public, supports me in affirming that nothing ever passed from me contradictory to these general truths, and that I have been misapprehended if it has ever been so supposed. I return you the plans received with your letter, and pray you to accept assurances of my continued esteem and respect.

[Pp. 578–80, WRITINGS OF JEFFERSON, Washington, V.]

JEFFERSON TO LATROBE

Monticello, July 12, 1812

Dear Sir,

Of all the faculties of the human mind that of memory is the first which suffers decay from age. Of the commencement of this decay, I was fully sensible while I lived in Washington, and it was my earliest monitor to retire from public business. It has often since been the source of great regret when applied to by others to attest transactions in which I had been agent, to find that they had entirely vanished from my memory. In no case has it given me more concern than in that which is the subject of your letter of the 2d instant: the supper given in 1807 to the workmen on the Capitol. Of this supper I have not the smallest recollection. If it ever was mentioned to me, not a vestige of it now remains in my mind. This failure of my memory is no proof the thing did not happen, but only takes from it the support of my testimony, which cannot be given for what is obliterated from it. I have looked among my papers to see if they furnish any trace of the matter, but I find none, and must therefore acquiesce in my incompetence to administer to truth on this occasion. I am sorry to learn that Congress has relinquished the benefit of the engagements of Andrei & Franzoni, on the sculpture of the Capitol. They are artists of a grade far above what we can expect to get again. I still hope they will continue to work on the basis of the appropriation made, and as far as that will go; so that what is done will be well done; and perhaps a more favorable moment may still preserve them to us. With respect to yourself, the little disquietudes from individuals not chosen for their taste in works of art, will be sunk into oblivion, while the Representatives' chamber will remain a durable monument of your talents as an architect. I say nothing of the Senate room, because I have never seen it. I shall live in the hope that the day will come when an opportunity will be given you of finishing the middle building in a style worthy of the two wings, and worthy of the first temple dedicated to the sovereignty of the people, embellishing with Athenian taste the course of a nation looking far beyond the range of Athenian destinies. In every situation, public or private, be assured of my sincere wishes for your prosperity and happiness, and of the continuance of my esteem and respect.

[TH: JEFFERSON]

[Pp. 178–9, WRITINGS, Memorial Edition, Vol. XIII.]

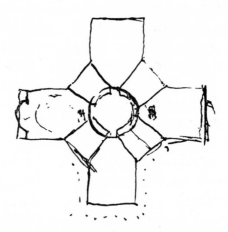

Jefferson's Sketch of the Capitol, 1792 (exterior)   (Thomas Jefferson Coolidge Collection) — Courtesy Fine Arts Division, Library of Congress

LATROBE TO JEFFERSON

[after August 1814]

LATROBE TO JEFFERSON

Permit me now to assure you that the confidence you are pleased to express in me, as to the future conduct of the public works, from your experience of my former services, is to me, by far a more gratifying reward than I could possibly have received from any emolument or any other commendation. It is not only because you are certainly the best judge of the merits of an artist, in the United States, but because you certainly know me better as an artist, and as a man, than any other, that your good opinion is valuable to me. And why should I say so to you, who have forever retired from the seat from which honours are to be dispensed, and to whom adulation would be an insult, if I were not most sincere in what I express on the subject. You will remember, that if I committed an error in executing the trust you reposed in me; it was not by blindly yielding my professional opinions to yours, or in executing, without even remonstrance sometimes, what was suggested, in order to win your favour. My thanks therefore for the kindness with which you express your approbation of what I have formerly done, are offered with sentiments of the sincerest attachment.

Some details respecting the state of the ruins of the buildings may perhaps be new, and not unpleasant to be received by you; and may perhaps find you at leisure to read them, as your library is no longer around you.

The south wing of the capitol was set on fire with great difficulty. Of the lower story nothing could be burned but the sashes and frames, and the shutters and dressings, and the doors and door cases. As all these were detached from one another, some time and labour were necessary to get through the work. The first thing done was to empty into buckets a quantity of the composition used in the rockets. A man with an axe chopped the wood work, another followed, and brushed on some of the composition, and on retiring from each room, the third put fire to it. Many of the rooms, however, were thus only partially burned, and there is not one in which some wood does not remain. In the clerk's office, the desks and furniture, and the records supplied a more considerable mass of combustible materials than there was elsewhere, and the fire burned so fiercely that they were obliged to retreat and leave all the rooms on the west side entirely untouched, and they are now as clean and perfect as ever. Two other committee rooms have escaped, and the gallery stairs have none of their wooden dressings injured. Above stairs, the committee room of Ways and Means, and accounts, is uninjured, and the whole of the entrance, with all the sculptured capitals of the columns, has fortunately suffered no injury but in the plastering, and that from the wet and frost of the winter. In the House of Representatives the devastation has been dreadful. There was here no want of materials for conflagration, for when the number of members of Congress was increased, the old platform was left in its place, and another raised over it, giving an additional quantity of dry and loose timber. All the stages and seats of the galleries were of timber and yellow pine. The mahogany furniture, desks, tables and chairs, were in their places. At first they fired rockets through the roof, but they did not set fire to it. They sent men on to it, but it was covered with sheet iron. At last they made a great pile in the centre of the room of the furniture, and retiring set fire to a great quantity of rocket-stuff in the middle. The whole was soon in a blaze, and so intense was the flame, that the glass of the lights was melted, and I have now lumps, weighing many pounds of glass, run into mass. The stone is, like most free stone, unable to resist the force of flame, but I believe no known material would have been able to resist the effects of so sudden and intense a heat. The exterior of the columns and entablature, therefore, expanded far beyond the dimensions of the interior, scaled off, and not a vestige of fluting or sculpture remained around. The appearance of the ruin was awfully grand when I first saw it, and indeed it was terrific, for it threatened immediately to fall, so slender were the remains of the columns that carried the massy entablature. If the colonnade had fallen, the vaulting of the room below might have been beaten down, but fortunately there is not a single arch in the whole building which requires to be taken down. In the north wing, the beautiful doric columns which surrounded the Supreme Court room, have shared the fate of the Corinthian columns of the Hall of Representatives, and in the Senate Chamber, the marble polished columns of fourteen feet shaft, in one block, are burnt to lime, and have fallen down. All but the vault is destroyed. They stand a most magnificent ruin. The west end containing the library, which was never vaulted, burned very fiercely, and by the fall of its heavy timbers, great injury has been done to the adjoining walls and arches, and I fear that the free stone is so much injured on the outside, that part of the outer wall must be taken down; otherwise the exterior stands firm and sound, especially of the south wing; but of about twenty windows and doors, through which the flames found vent, the architraves, and other dressings are so injured, that they must be replaced. All the parapet is gone.

The most difficult work to be performed was to take down the ruins of the Hall of Representatives. Our workmen all hesitated to touch it; to have erected a scaffold, and to have risked striking the ruins with the heavy poles necessary to be used, was not to be thought of; an unlucky blow against one of the columns might have brought down one hundred ton of the entablature, and of the heavy brick vault which rested upon it. It therefore occurred to me, to fill up the whole with fascines to the soffit of the architraves: if any thing gave way then, it would not fall down; the columns would be confined to their places, and the fascines would furnish the scaffold. The commissioners approved the scheme, but as time would be required to cut the fascines from the commons, Mr. Ringold most fortunately recommended the use of cord wood, which has been adopted, and most successfully. Four fifths of the work is done, and the remainder is supported, and will be all down in ten days. The cord wood will sell for its cost. It required five hundred cord to go half round; it was then shifted to the other side. I have already nearly completed the vaults of two stories, on the west side of the north wing, according to the plan submitted by you, with the report to Congress in 1807. I need not, I hope, apologize to you for this long detail. An alteration is proposed and adopted by the president, in the Hall of Representatives. I will send you a copy of my report, as soon as time will permit.

[B. H. LATROBE]

[Wm Dunlap, HISTORY OF THE RISE AND PROGRESS OF THE ARTS OF DESIGN IN THE UNITED STATES, II, 474-75.]

JEFFERSON TO SAMUEL H. SMITH

JEFFERSON TO SAMUEL H. SMITH, ESQ.

Monticello, September 21, 1814.
Dear Sir, —

I learn from the newspapers that the Vandalism of our enemy has triumphed at Washington over science as well as the arts, by the destruction of the public library with the noble edifice in which it was deposited. Of this transaction, as of that of Copenhagen, the world will entertain but one sentiment. They will see a nation suddenly withdrawn from a great war, full armed and full handed, taking advantage of another whom they had recently forced into it, unarmed, and unprepared, to indulge themselves in acts of barbarism which do not belong to a civilized age. When Van Ghent destroyed their shipping at Chatham, and De Ruyter rode triumphantly up the Thames, he might in like manner, by the acknowledgment of their own historians, have forced all their ships up to London bridge, and there have burnt them, the tower, and city, had these examples been then set. London, when thus menaced, was near a thousand years old, Washington is but in its teens.

I presume it will be among the early objects of Congress to re-commence their collection. This will be difficult while the war continues, and intercourse with Europe is attended with so much risk. You know my collection, its condition and extent. I have been fifty years making it, and have spared no pains, opportunity or expense, to make it what it is. While residing in Paris, I devoted every afternoon I was disengaged, for a summer or two, in examining all the principal bookstores, turning over every book with my own hand, and putting by everything which related to America, and indeed whatever was rare and valuable in every science. Besides this, I had standing orders during the whole time I was in Europe, on its principal bookmarts, particularly Amsterdam, Frankfort, Madrid and London, for such works relating to America as could not be found in Paris. So that in that department particularly, such a collection was made as probably can never again be effected, because it is hardly probable that the same opportunities, the same time, industry, perseverance and expense, with some knowledge of the bibliography of the subject, would again happen to be in concurrence. During the same period, and after my return to America, I was led to procure, also, whatever related to the duties of those in the high concerns of the nation. So that the collection, which I suppose is of between nine and ten thousand volumes, while it includes what is chiefly valuable in science and literature generally, extends more particularly to whatever belongs to the American statesman. In the diplomatic and parliamentary branches, it is particularly full. It is long since I have been sensible it ought not to continue private property, and had provided that at my death, Congress should have the

refusal of it at their own price. But the loss they have now incurred, makes the present the proper moment for their accommodation, without regard to the small remnant of time and the
barren use of my enjoying it. I ask of your friendship, therefore,
to make for me the tender of it to the library committee of Congress, not knowing myself of whom the committee consists. I
enclose you the catalogue, which will enable them to judge of
its contents. Nearly the whole are well bound, abundance of
them elegantly, and of the choicest editions existing. They may
be valued by persons named by themselves, and the payment
made convenient to the public. It may be, for instance, in such
annual instalments as the law of Congress has left at their disposal, or in stock of any of their late loans, or of any loan they
may institute at this session, so as to spare the present calls of
our country, and await its days of peace and prosperity. They
may enter, nevertheless, into immediate use of it, as eighteen or
twenty wagons would place it in Washington in a single trip of
a fortnight. I should be willing indeed, to retain a few of the
books, to amuse the time I have yet to pass, which might be
valued with the rest, but not included in the sum of valuation
until they should be restored at my death, which I would carefully provide for, so that the whole library as it stands in the
catalogue at this moment should be theirs without any gar
bling. Those I should like to retain would be chiefly classical and
mathematical. Some few in other branches, and particularly
one of the five encyclopedias in the catalogue. But this, if not
acceptable, would not be urged. I must add, that I have not
revised the library since I came home to live, so that it is probable some of the books may be missing, except in the chapters of
Law and Divinity, which have been revised and stand exactly
as in the catalogue. The return of the catalogue will of course
be needed, whether the tender be accepted or not. I do not
know that it contains any branch of science which Congress
would wish to exclude from their collection; there is, in fact, no

subject to which a member of Congress may not have occasion to refer. But such a wish would not correspond with my views of preventing its dismemberment. My desire is either to place it in their hands entire, or to preserve it so here. I am engaged in making an alphabetical index of the author's names, to be annexed to the catalogue, which I will forward to you as soon as completed. Any agreement you shall be so good as to take the trouble of entering into with the Committee, I hereby confirm. Accept the assurance of my great esteem and respect.

[Pp. 383–385, WRITINGS OF JEFFERSON, Washington, Vol. VI.]

LATROBE TO JEFFERSON

B. HENRY LATROBE TO THOMAS JEFFERSON

Washington, November 5, 1816

Dear Sir: Your letter of the 27th of August received. I was confined to my bed by a bilious fever . . . You have done my capital much honor in making it the support of your dial. The columns and capitals as executed and standing in the north wing of the Capitol on the ground floor were not much injured by the British, so little indeed that I wish some part of the building to remain as they left it. I do not propose to repair them unless the president shall order it to be done.

By the suggestion of the Senate I devised a very material alteration of their accommodations especially a great enlargement of the Chamber itself.

The great staircase must give way to the improvements. You probably recollect that, as a curious and difficult combination of admirably executed stone work, it was one of the most remarkable parts of the Capitol, but it was much injured by the Lanthorn, which being of wood, fell burning through the dome, and resting on the stairs, burnt many of the principal stones.

The staircase has now another situation. It will be less curious but have I think some beauty. The area of the stairs will be occupied by a vestibule, in the center of which a circular colonade will support a dome for the purpose of admitting light. The columns of the rotunda, 16 in number, must be more slender than the Ionic order will admit, and ought not to be of the Corinthian because the chamber itself is of the Ionic order. I have therefore composed a capital of leaves and flowers of the tobacco plant which has an intermediate effect approaching the Corinthian order and retaining the simplicity of the Clepsydra or Temple of the Winds. Below is a very hasty, and imperfect sketch of the capital.

Iardella [70] a sculptor who has just arrived, has made an admirable model for execution in which he has well preserved the botanical character of the plant, although it has been necessary to enlarge the proportion of the flowers to the leaves, and to arrange them in clusters of three. When we have done with the model I will take the liberty of forwarding it to you. I have neglected so long to answer your very kind letter, that I must intreat you to attribute my silence to anything but a diminution of my respect and attachment. Believe me, that it never can cease.

Yours very respectfully,

B. HENRY LATROBE.

[Charles E. Fairman, ART AND ARTISTS OF THE CAPITOL OF THE UNITED STATES OF AMERICA, 29.]

LATROBE TO JEFFERSON

Washington, June 28th 1817

THO^S JEFFERSON ESQ^R

Monticello

Dear Sir,

I have found so much pleasure in studying the plan of your

[70] Francisco Iardella.

College, that the drawings have grown into a larger bulk than can be conveniently sent by the Mail. If you can point out to me any convenient mode of conveyance within a few days, I should gladly avail myself of it. I have put the whole upon one very large sheet, which I am very unwilling to double; and to roll it on a stick will make it inconvenient for the Mail bag. Colonels McCrae & McCraw of Richmond are now here, & in a week will return. If the conveyance from Richmond is more convenient, they will cheerfully take it thither.

The Capitol is growing into a more intelligible form & arrangement, than it had since its destruction by the British. — If the permanence of the seat of the Government at Washington would not have been endangered by it, — it would have been better in every point of view that the wish of Adm. Cockburn had prevailed over the humanity of Gen! Ross, & the whole building had been destroyed by Gunpowder. At a less expense to the U States, a much more convenient, & magnificent building could have been erected, than will be made of the ruins of the former. Many alterations have been made in the interior. The form of the house of Representatives is changed so as to admit the members to the South windows, & the Gallery is of course on the E. N. & West sides. — The Senate Chamber is enlarged to the utmost possible extent which the walls would permit. The staircase the construction of which you may remember to have been rather singular & the execution uncommonly excellent, is now converted into a large Vestibule with a rotunda to admit light into the lower story, and a more easy ascent is made by a new Staircase on the S. E. side where a Court was intended by the plan of 1806–7. The President has taken a very strong interest in the completion of the Capitol, & the work is going on as rapidly as Men & money can execute it.

In the National Intelligencer of January 18th 1817 I gave some account of the beautiful Marble of which most of the Columns of the Capital are to be made. — There are now 9 blocks here, from 6 to 8 feet long each. Three of them make one Column. They are rounded, but not yet polished. — Nothing can exceed the beauty of the Stone when polished, & as the Cement which unites the pebbles does not receive quite so high a polish as the pebbles themselves, the Mass acquires a spangled appearance, which adds greatly to the brilliancy of its effect.

The remark I have made on the difficulty of introducing this marble is not one of those tirades, in which disappointed men are apt to indulge. The opposition of so respectable a Man as Mr Blagden was to be encountered, & of many others. He reported in writing, that the stone would not bear its own weight, when *lewis'ed*. I immediately suspended by a small Lewis, a block of 2 Ton weight in the Capitol. He then doubted whether it could be wrought, — & to try the experiment, a small Column 3 inches in diameter *which had been wrought & polished*, & had been placed in the temporary house of Representatives the whole Session, was knocked to pieces by the Sand stone cutters, & the fragments produced to prove that it could *not be wrought or polished*. But the President soon decided the contest & there are now 100 men, laborers & Stone cutters at work in the Quarry. — I presumed, that below Your mountain the same stone must be found. It crosses the Reppahannoc in Orange County, in very large Masses. —

I need not assure you, that any opportunity which may occur, to prove to you how sincere is the respect & attachment, which as an individual and as a citizen I feel towards you, will be eagerly seized by me & improved.

Most respectfully Y^{rs}

B Henry Latrobe

P.S. I have a rough Stone Model of the Capital of a Column composed of Tobacco leaves & flowers which I wish to send to you. I can easily get it to Richmond by a coal Vessel returning this. If you will please to let me know to whom I shall direct it,

I shall be obliged to You. I will enclose in the box some specimens of the Pebble Marble. — The Capital has too weak an
effect, & I intend to cut the relief of the leaves deeper. But it
never will equal the Corn capital.

In the printed account of the Marble there are many typo-
graphical Errors. — *Bedding stone* is printed for Pudding stone
&c.

I write still with Peale's or rather Hawkin's, polygraph. —
the same which I have had since 1803. — It is a little crazy, &
has lost its spring which I have not been able to replace so that
I write a somewhat different hand with the polygraph, from
that which I write without it. You had adopted Bolton's mani-
fold Writer when I last saw You, but as your letter is written
with common ink I presume you have returned to the Polygraph.

> [has taken too much trouble with
> drawings
>   send by mail
> the new marble
>   send capital to G. & J. Richm^d
>   Polygraph] — (marginal comment in
> Jefferson's hand — S.K.P.)

[Ms., *Jefferson Papers*, Library of Congress.]

LATROBE TO JEFFERSON

THO^S JEFFERSON ESQ^R.
Monticello.

                               Washington July 20th 1817

Dr Sir

    Since my last of the 24th [71] I have engaged a young man of the

[71] Unable to locate this letter. — S. K. P.

name of Johnson, to undertake your Stone cutting, should the terms be approved. He is not only capable to cut a Doric Capital, or a Base, but to execute the common Architectural decorations, as foliage & Rosettes, with great neatness & dispatch, for, in the scarcity of Carvers, I have, for some time past, put him under Andrei, & have lately employed him to carve the rosettes in the Caissons of the cornice of the H. of Rep. which he has done quite to my Satisfaction. He also possesses that quality, so essential to the workmen, *you* employ, *good temper*, & is besides (which is not always compatible with good temper) quite sober. — His terms are 2$.50 p day, finding himself. This is what our journeymen earn here, in Summer. If he is to have the charge of more men, he will expect his wages to be encreased, and he expects constant employment while *engaged* & *well*, & that his actual expenses to the spot, & back again (should he return to Washington) shall be paid. — He is ready to depart at a few days notice.

I observe in the newspaper a letter from a Gentleman in Virginia dated July 20th, mentioning his visit to Monticello, & that you were then at Your Bedford Estate. If so I cannot expect an early answer to this letter or to my last, but I shall keep Johnson ready for You whenever I do hear from You. —

Notwithstanding the convenience, & great utility to many of my most important interests which I find from the Polygraph, it is a fact, that Peale never could dispose of more than 60, 40 of which about, as his Son tells me, were sold by my recommendation. In each of the public offices here, one was procured, but never used, & I found them in 1812, almost destroyed. For knowing them to be useless where they were, I endeavored to borrow one for a Member of Congress, & found them in a very neglected state. — I have often recommended them to Merchants, but they object "that their Clerks are always sufficient for the copying of their letters, & would otherwise be unemployed, & moreover never write a good hand for want of practice; & that they must copy their letters into books, for safe keeping, & for production in courts of justice." — In all this there is certainly something substantial, enough to prevent innovation in a system, in which *form*, & *uniform practice* is assuredly very essential; for merchants, are generally a sort of Machinery & govern themselves as much by the *practice* of their business, as Lawyers do. Thus in the most *writing* class of men, the Polygraph has had no introduction, & is used only by a few litterary men, who will take the pains to save themselves trouble.

With the Tobacco Capital, I shall send you some polished specimens of the Potomac Marble.

I am as ever with the highest esteem

Y^{rs}

B H LATROBE.

[Ms., *Jefferson Papers*, Library of Congress.]

LATROBE TO JEFFERSON

Washington July 24th 1817

THO^S JEFFERSON, ESQ^R

Monticello

Dear Sir,

Yesterday I had the pleasure to receive your letter d. July 16th (p. mark 19th). I had presumed that you were from home, and also that as your institution has been so lately organized, some time could be given to the preparation of a design for the buildings. — But by your letter I find not only that I have been designing under a great misconception of your *local* but also have presumed upon more time for deliberation than you can give me. — I supposed from your letter, & the sketch it contains, that your ground would be tolerably level along the *long*

& *closed* side of your open quadrangle, which side, I suppose would be the North side, was to make the continued portico face to the South. But in your last letter occur these words: "The levelling the ground into Terraces will take time & labor." *We propose a distinct terras for every 2 pavilions, & their dormitories, that is a pavilion at each end of each terrace.*

Thus it appears to me, that instead of a continuous line of building, you want a series of detached masses, on different levels. I write in great haste this morning, & surrounded by interruptions, or I would send you better sketches than are below. They will explain the ideas I had. — Not having a copy of my great Sheet I will retain it, till I have again the pleasure of hearing from you when I may perhaps add something useful. — A week will thus be lost, which I regret, but it may not be in vain. —

The locks of the Potowmac lower Canal having fallen in, beyond the power of Art to restore them, we suffer difficulty in getting down our *Columbian* Marble; but a great effort will be made to bring them thence by Land. Your opinion on the suggestions which I ventured to make as to the origin of this Marble, in my paper in the Nat. Intelligencer of the 18th of Jan.ʸ, would be particularly acceptable to me. If they apply to the range with which you are acquainted, my opinion that these pebbles are the beach of the ancient Gulph stream, & are probably the ruins of Southern Marbles once occupying the excavation of the Gulphs of Darien & Mexico may receive more plausibility. The Abbe Roxas told me, & pointed out in the Block which I had polished, that many of the pieces were Mexican Marbles well known to him.

I am with the sincerest respect

Yʳˢ

B HENRY LATROBE

[Ms., *Jefferson Papers*, Library of Congress.]

LATROBE TO JEFFERSON

*Washington Aug.! 12.*th *1817.*

THO.^S JEFFERSON ESQ.^R }
near Lynchburg V.^a }

Dear Sir

A slight indisposition having prevented my attendance at my office, I did not receive your favor of the 2.^d (postmark 4.th) till the 9.th when you would have left Monticello, and I therefore did not immediately answer it, and now direct this letter where I hope it will soon reach You. I now offer to you, with the utmost freedom, a freedom which your request, as well as your long friendship to me authorizes and invites, such remarks as occur to me on the general plan of your Academy; — and as I write without preparation, you must extend your indulgence to the desultory manner, as well as to the freedom of my observations.

The drawings I have made are still by me, & I now beg you to inform me whether, as you remain so long near Lynch burg, I shall not send them to you there. My letter of the 25.th July you do not appear to have received on the 2.^d of Aug.! If you have since then obtained it, I beg the favor of you to inform me, whether you will engage the stone cutter whose terms I mentioned, & whom I can throughly [sic] recommend, — as he remains in suspense at present. I employ him now at the Capitol.

The plan and description which your letter contains perfectly explains the situation, on which your Academy must be located, — and I cannot help beginning my remarks, by calling it a most unfortunate one. — For if the general design contained in your letter be carried into execution, — and at the first view, it is *that*, which appears to be unavoidably imposed upon you, — it necessarily follows that all your apartments must face *East* & *West.* — Every one who has had the misfortune to reside in a house, — especially if it constitutes part of a range of houses, facing East & West, has experienced, both in Summer and Winter the evils of such an Aspect. In Winter the accumulation of snow on the East, & the severity of the cold on the West, together with the absence of the Sun during $3/4^{th}$ of the day, and in Summer, the horizontal Rays of the morning Sun heating the East, & of the evening Sun burning the West side of the house, — render such a position highly exceptionable. — In a large Country house, surrounded with Trees, and in which the number of Apartments enables the Inhabitants to emigrate from one side of the house to the other, as the Abyssinian Shepherds, from the forests to the deserts, — in such a house the aspect is of less importance, and the house may be located with a regard to the *View*, to the range of a hill, or of the road leading to it. But where no recourse can be had to opposite apartments, and especially where a long extent of portico on one side only creates an eddy, for the wind to accumulate Snow, & for the Sun the heat the air confined under it, — I cannot help being of opinion that the utmost power of art ought to be employed to force the aspect of the houses into a North & South position. — And from long experience in my profession, and from having witnessed the uniform regret of those whom I have been unable to persuade into my opinion on this head in the position of their houses, — I have learned to consider, the easy access to water to be the *first*, and the North & South position to the *second absolutely indispensible* principle, on which a *good* position of a building depends. I could enumerate so many instances of these regrets, & on the other hand, so many proofs of advantage (especially in the position of new Streets recommended by me in Philadelphia) that they would fill my letter. But to you they are unnecessary & I will at present only ask, whether you are so far committed, as to render the adoption of the plan of arrangement irrevocable, and to make any respectful project which I might take the liberty to submit to You useless.

On the receipt of your letter of the ⁷² I suspended my drawing. It contained a plan of the principal range of building (as I then supposed it) and seven or eight Elevations of pavilions, with a general Elevation of the long range of Pavilions & portico. In this State I will send it to you. If there is any thing in it which you think usefull, it is yours & I particularly beg the favor of you to give me further opportunity of being useful to your establishment, & of testifying my respect for yourself. — I draw with great rapidity, & ease & pleasure to myself, & you must not be deterred by any idea that you give me trouble. — If therefore what I have said seems to you worthy of consideration, it will be a pleasure to me to suggest such a plan, as the principles I think so essential, may dictate.

I have now at the Capitol Nine blocks of the Columbian Marble nearly finished for the Columns of the Hall of Representatives. I have never seen anything so beautifully magnificent. Even the most clamorous opposers of their introduction are now silenced. When the columns are in their places, they will be a lasting proof of the firmness of the character of the present President of the U. States; who in order to decide on the merits of the opposition of the introduction of this Marble, went himself, in the worst weather, to the quarry, and in person gave those orders, which, altho' they did not quell such opposition as could still be made, will ultimately be effectual, & not only render our public buildings rich in nature's magnificence, but make these useless rocks an article of considerable external commerce.

* * * * * * * * * *

I dare add no more than that I am very sincerely & truly Yʳˢ

B Henry Latrobe.

* * * * * * * * * *

[Ms., *Jefferson Papers*, Library of Congress. An excerpt of this letter appears in Fiske Kimball, THOMAS JEFFERSON, ARCHITECT.]

⁷² Blank space in original ms.

LATROBE TO JEFFERSON

Washington, Octr 28th 1817

rec^d Nov. 4

THO^S JEFFERSON ESQ^R

Monticello

Dear Sir

I thank you for your letter of the [73], & am much gratified by the approbation you express of my drawings. I hope you will do me the favor to let me know which of the pavilions you approve for your first work of next spring; with a sketch of its dimensions and its plan, that I may send you the working drawings & the details at large.

Some months ago, I sent to Jefferson & Gibson of Richmond a box for you, containing a Capital composed of Tobacco leaves & flowers. It is a cheap one, & of course cannot be expected to have great effect. If you can find a place for it, I would recommend that it be painted, & that the leaves of the upper tier, be colored in the lower part with a faint brown (umber), as I shall do in the rotunda of 16 Columns in the North wing of the Capitol, in which I have applied them. Otherwise they do not sufficiently distinguish themselves.

We are getting on with the Capitol, as well as we can under a system not calculated for dispatch. Nothing but want of time has prevented my making for you a set of plans showing all the changes which the interior of the Capitol has undergone, much, I think, for the better accomodation of both houses of Congress.

Believe me with sincere attachment & respect

Y^{rs}

B HENRY LATROBE

[Ms., *Jefferson Papers*, Library of Congress.]

[73] Blank space in original ms.

LATROBE TO JEFFERSON

Washington Nov. 20th 1817

THO^S JEFFERSON ESQ^{R.}

Dear Sir,

Your letter has remained a week unanswered in consequence
of my absence, but immediately on my return I wrote yesterday
to Philadelphia, desired one of the Carpenter's pricebooks to be
sent to You, which I have no doubt will be done without loss of
time. —

I am under the necessity of resigning my situation at the
Capitol. The present Commissioner, Colonel Lane, has from
the first week, treated me as his Clerk, & certainly not with the
delicacy with which I treat my mechanics. The public have
suffered beyond calculation by the effects of the system, & more
by its administration. I will not trespass upon your time to explain, but perhaps some enquiry made by made [sic] in Congress on the subject. I have had no access to the President since
the first days of his Administration, during which he acted in
regard to the public Works with a justice & decision, which in
spite of the Commissioner, has given us this incomparable
marble. I shall ever revere his character, as then exhibited. —

I shall probably reside in Baltimore where I am building the
Exchange, unless I could succeed Mrs Baldwin in Virginia.

Most truly Y^{rs}

B H LATROBE

[Ms., *Jefferson Papers*, Library of Congress.]

LATROBE TO JEFFERSON

Washington, Decr 6th 1817

THOMAS JEFFERSON ESQ^R

Monticello

Dear Sir,

The enclosed letter will prove to you that I have not been

unmindful of your wish to have the rate of Carpenter's prices at Philadelphia, as your rule of valuation for the work of the new College. Mr Thackara is one of the most respectable citizens & mechanics in Philadelphia. He did the Plaisterer's work, so much & deservedly admired, of the Capitol, & was sent for again, but did not agree with the Commissioner, in which he is not singular. — I also wrote to two Carpenters but received immediately an answer to the same effect, an answer which I have indeed expected.

But in order to give you the best assistance I can, I will, in 10 days from hence (when I shall be in Baltimore) send you the Pittsburg price book, compiled from that of Philadelphia, by carpenters established there from Philadelphia, and printed under their Sanction, & in the mean time I will also compile from a great number of accounts settled by me with the mechanics here, a partial list of prices which may be useful to You.

I am with the truest esteem

Y^{rs} B H Latrobe

[Ms., *Jefferson Papers*, Library of Congress.]

LATROBE TO JEFFERSON

Baltimore, March 7.th 1818.

THO^{S} JEFFERSON ESQ^{R}
Monticello

Dear Sir,

I arrived here with my family on the 12.th of Jany and a few days afterwards was taken ill of my old complaint, the Hemicrania, a complaint in which no one, I believe, can more heartily sympathise with me than yourself, as I believe you are often severely afflicted with it. I was confined to my room for three weeks. Immediately on my recovery I was called to Annapolis to examine the bar at the mouth of the harbor with a view to a proposition to Government for the Establishment of the Naval

Depot at that place. The bar is composed entirely of *blue mud*, a stratum which occurs constantly & in regular succession in the geological formation of the country. If it is this stratum, which not easily yielding to the attrition of water has remained higher than the sandy strata above & below it, or if it is, — what all blue clay, ooze, or marsh mud is, — the product of marine water acting upon vegetable matter, and has been thrown in by the Chesapeake, (as its form indicates); in either case it is easily removed, & will not be redeposited, or at all events, many centuries must elapse before it will be again produced. My report, will, I presume, be printed in which case, I will immediately transmitt to you a copy of it.

I did not remove into the house which I have taken here untill my return from Annapolis, and could not get it so arranged as to enable me to unpack my books untill 2 days ago, when I found the enclosed book of prices. — I have added to it, the prices allowed by myself & paid within the last six months. Any good workman can make a good profit upon them. — Here in Baltimore the same secrecy is observed, by the measurer's, that obtains in Philadelphia. The price book, as there, exists only in manuscript. This combination cannot last many Years. It will bring in a competition from New England, which will break it up. In Philadelphia it will be more durable, being supported by a rich & numerous Guild, the Carpenters company, into which it is the interest of every young workman to be enrolled.

I much fear that I shall be under the necessity of appealing to Congress, or the public on the business of the Capitol. Mr. Lane being an inmate of the Presidents family, has had influence enough to prevent my being even heard: — and I feel every day the effect of the situation in which I am relatively to the President. And yet out of the President's house no man is less respected that [sic] the Commissioner. For the President personally no one has more respect than myself. I suffer from the regular course of so bad a system as that of the public buildings. But I will not trespass upon the time or patience, which you have so many more agreeable & useful means of employing, than to hear my complaints, further, than by extracting from public documents, the following facts which show the effect of the system formerly established by you, *virtually*, in which the architect could controul the expenses, by controuling the contracts, & the manner of working, compared with the management of Commissioners, who had no professional knowledge.

1795 to 1801	Cost of the N. Wing of Lath & plaister internally, half finished, & in decay, under the first Commissioners. — Stone 6$ p Ton, bricks 4.50 to 6$ p M	$307.735.38
1804 to 1807	[74] Cost of the South wing, magnificently executed, finished in all its parts, vaulted & filled with Sculpture Stone 8 — 12$ p Ton, bricks 8$ p M.	274.841.01½
	Repairs & finishing of the West side of the North wing in the stile of the South wing 1806 & 1807	28.142.25
		610.718.64½

Expenses of repairs 1815–1818

Appropriation		
	1815	500,000
	1816	125,000
	1817	200,000
		825,000

If of this sum of 825,000, $225,000 be allowed for the president's house, there will have been expended on the repairs of the Capitol alone, which are not half finished, 600,000. Now there remained after the conflagration: All the external walls of the Capitol uninjured, excepting in the Architraves of some of the windows, — all the vaulting of every kind internally, — many rooms wholly uninjured, — in fact work which, on reference to my books, had cost 190,000 in the South wing, & I pre-

[74] In 1803 very little was done. Congress sat in the *Oven* 1804–1805 even. [Note of Latrobe in the original text.]

sume 200,000 in the North wing!!! — and yet I must bear the blame of all this, — *even a hearing being refused me!*

I hope you will forgive my intruding this statement upon you. I know it to be useless at present to attempt to swim against the current. It will turn of itself in time.

I enclose a pamphlet which I printed some time ago. Please to receive it as a mark of the unalterable respect & attachment with which I am

Y^{rs}

B H LATROBE

[Ms., *Jefferson Papers*, Library of Congress.]

THO^S JEFFERSON ESQ^R

Washington, March 30th, 1818.

Sir,

In resigning my office as Surveyor of the Capitol, I publickly assigned those reasons which were personal. It was my intention to lay those that regarded the public interests, before the proper authorities: but a severe illness, which confined me immediately after my removal from the city, and especially the consideration of the thanklessness, and general uselessness of every attempt of an individual to correct what he may think improper in the administration of a public concern, in which he has had a share, have prevented my taking the steps proposed.

On my present visit to Washington, I have, however, found that the old charge against me, of extravagance, in the expenditure on the public buildings is still alive: and the authority on which it is asserted is so respectable, that I owe it to my interests and character to refute it.

This I can most effectually do, by comparing the cost of the capitol, during the period from 1803, to 1811, while I had a controul over the expenditures, with the expenditure on the same objects, during the time before and after that period.

For, since the period of the restoration of the public buildings, from the year 1814, I have not only had no controul over the expenditures, in the remotest degree, but not even a knowledge of their nature and amount. And I must also remark, that the restoration of the capitol ought not to have cost $50,000 more than the parts restored had originally cost, notwithstanding all improvements and alterations. It would be a waste of time and paper to enter here into the details producing this sum, but whenever required I shall be ready to explain them.

NORTH WING OF THE CAPITOL

1. The north wing of the capitol, left unfinished by the first commissioners,[75] stands charged with................ $337,735 38
   To this must be added a portion of the general expenses of the commissioners' office,[76].... 63,005 38
Of temporary buildings...................... 1,890 32
Of the cost of the freestone — island of Acquia.. 6,000 00

73,895 70

Or somewhat less than one-fourth of the sum expended in 1808, on all the public buildings, in contingencies....... 18,000

355,735 38

I omit any proportion of the article for commissions of agents, &c. of $59,033 52, in order to avoid overcharge. As this includes the cost of all the foundations of the south wing and centre, &c. deduct a most ample allowance therefor[77]... 30,000

Actual cost of the unfinished north wing................ $325,735 38

SOUTH WING OF THE CAPITOL

In 1803, the situation of Congress, in the north wing of the capitol, and in the temporary building on the foundations of the south wing, was so inconvenient, that it was resolved to

[75] See the commissioner's books, and the President's message, March 25, 1808. [Footnote in the original text.]

[76] Report to the Senate by the superintendent, December 16, 1808. [Footnote in the original text.]

[77] President's Message, March 25, 1808, and report. [Footnote in the original text.]

build the south wing, and I was appointed surveyor of the public buildings. From that time, 1803 to 1811, I became, and hold
myself principally responsible for the economy of the work.
50,000 dollars were then appropriated to the public buildings
generally, and to the highways. The series of state papers, in
the Library of Congress, having been destroyed by the British,
they have been restored to the year 1809; between which years,
and 1814, there is a chasm. Not having been able to refer here
to any other collection, I cannot give a detailed synopsis of the
expenditures on each object of appropriation from the year
1810 to 1811. But my object in this statement will be attained,
by an appeal to the letter of the superintendent of the city, of
December 16, 1808, and the President's message of March
25th, 1808, enclosing my annual report.

From the former it appears, that the south wing, which was
    then finished, and had been occupied for a year, was
    charged with.. 323,234 26
From which deduct the items in my report, of
    March 25, 1808...................... 12,433 00
Furniture. (See ditto.)................... 21,216 34
Pulling down condemned walls, clearing the
    ground, removing earth, making the road
    east of the capital, (as per the books in my
    possession)........................... 2,318 00
Repairs of temporary buildings, 1803....... 555 $13\frac{1}{2}$
Fitting up the temporary Representatives'
    Chamber, in the north wing............ 689 23
                                                                37,211 $70\frac{1}{2}$
Total cost of the south wing......................... 286,022 $55\frac{1}{2}$

The north wing, from 1807 to 1810, was en-
    tirely changed in its interior, and built up
    up solidly, excepting on the west side which
    remained in a ruinous state at the invasion
    in 1814.

From 1803 to 1807, was expended in re-
    pairs.............................. 3,301 75
          In 1807...................... 24,840 50
Appropriation 1808, April 5,............. 25,000
           1809, March 3,.......... 20,000
Balance of accounts, 1812................ 6,857 75
    Sculpture appropriation,............. 4,000 00

                             84,000 00

To which add the sum amply sufficient to have completed
    the west side.................................... 26,000 00
                             110,000

If this sum be added to the cost of the north wing, as left by
    the commissioners,................................. 325,735 38
It will produce a total of............................ $435,735 38

    I now appeal to the recollection of every one who has seen
the capitol, prior to 1814, whether, after the completion of
the works on both wings, prior to 1812, there was not ocular
evidence of the vast superiority of workmanship, in its quality and expense in the south, to that in the north wing. If
the work had been measured that superiority would be un-
deniably proved; and yet the north wing cost........... $435,735 38
And the south wing, under my direction............... 286,022 55½

                             $149,712 83

    And if the enormous sum of near 50,000 dollars be allowed
for the slight work in timber, lath and plaster which was pulled
down to make room for solid vaulting, marble and sculpture,
there will still remain a balance in favor of the south wing of
$100,000.

    If I now compare the works executed under my directions,
and controul of expenditure, with those that have since been
constructed, the account will stand thus:

        Appropriation,....................1815 — $500,000
                        1817 —   100,000
                        1818 —   200,000
                             800,000

Expenditures by the three commissioners,[78]

[78] See the commissioner's report, February 16, 1818. [Footnote in the original text.]

1815 — 1816, on the capitol,.......... 79,211 64
A proportion of contingent expenses,....... 3,800
1817, By the one commissioner,........... 76,112 17
    Contingent expences................ 1,000
1818, By   Do...................... 159,655 11
Estimate to compleat the same,[79].......... 177,303 46
                                     497,082 38

I have taken great pains, by examination of my books of
measurement and estimate, to ascertain what was the
actual cost of those parts of the south wing of the capitol
which remained entirely uninjured; and have excluded
every thing which may require reinstatement, as plastering, glass, and the whole of the wood work of every kind;
as well as the sculpture and every part of the hall of
Representatives, and find it amounts of 213,450 dollars.
But least I should overrate its value, say............ 200,000
The north wing was more injured than the south, but a
value (if the cost be considered as the value) remains,
equal to that of the south wing: but to avoid overcharge,
I will rate it only at............................. 150,000
Total expense of restoring the wings of the capitol, includ-
ing the value of the existing parts.................. $847,082 38

I have proved above, that the south wing executed under
my control, cost only............................. 286,022 55½
And I have an undoubted right to claim, that if I had been
in Washington and allowed the same control from the
commencement, over the expenses of the north wing,
which the superintendent allowed me over those of the
south, it would not have exceeded it in cost, say....... 286,022 56
                                    572,045 11

But to avoid all cavil, and in order to allow amply for the
marble columns; without remarking on the management
of that business, I will add the sum of.............. 75,037 27
                                    647,082 38
Balance in favor of my extravagance,................ 200,000
                                    $847,082 38

[79] I suppose the estimate to be sufficient. [Footnote in the original text.]

My object in these statements has been no other than a defence of my own conduct. They are supported by documents which may always be referred to. That part of them which depends upon calculation, speaks for itself. The amounts taken from my own books, are comparatively small, and make no difference in the general result. Had I entered further into details, a result much more favorable to me, would have appeared. But I content myself with resting my character on the proofs already adduced.

   With great respect,

    I am, &c.

       B. HENRY LATROBE,

    Late surveyor of the public buildings, U. S.

P.S. I will add, that independently of the value of the labor of my pupils, whom the public did not pay, except once, during a short term, the annual salaries, from 1803 to 1811, were $3,800, and that the amount paid for the same services since 1814, agreeably to a statement of salaries, commissions and agencies, now before me, of which I have proof, but no official documents, exceeds, annually, $16,000.

[Printed statement, *Jefferson Papers*, Library of Congress. In the upper left hand corner of the first page, "Tho? Jefferson Esq!" is inscribed in Latrobe's hand.]

LATROBE TO JEFFERSON

Baltimore April 14.th 1818

THO.^S JEFFERSON ESQ.^R

Dear Sir,

 Since my retirement from the public service I no longer hear from You, in answer to the letters I have written transmitting the information you requested, ~~and~~ in the only manner in which I could, myself, obtain it. This is the only bad consequence which has resulted to me from my resignation, and the displeasure of the President US.

I enclose you, I hope without offence, a statement which was rendered necessary in consequence of my losing a very honorable & lucrative employment on the plea of my extravagance; the President's authority having been used as the ground of the charge. — For the President, I shall always retain the highest respect, well aware of the course of intrigue that suddenly induced him to forbid me all approach to him personally & by letter. He will be undeceived, tho' perhaps too late. — I have here more employ than ever, and such as produces for me respect & independence. I shall always be very truly & gratefully Yours

                                                    B H LATROBE

[Ms., *Jefferson Papers*, Library of Congress.]

BIBLIOGRAPHY

The list of references given below has been compiled from Dr. S. K. Padover's notes, during his absence abroad, to indicate the sources of the materials used in the preparation of this publication.

MANUSCRIPTS

Jefferson Papers in the Library of Congress, Washington, D. C.

"American Letters," Vol. IV, October 1788 to December 1792, in the Division of State Department Archives in the National Archives, Washington, D. C.

"Miscellaneous Letters," June 1790 to Aug. 1793, Records of the Department of State in the National Archives.

"Letters Received by Commissioners of Public Buildings and Grounds, Washington, D. C.," in the National Archives, Washington, D. C. These are original letters bound in 28 volumes, covering the period March 1791 to January 1838. Material after 1838 is unbound.

"Letters of the Commissioners of Public Buildings and Grounds of the City of Washington and District of Columbia," in the National Archives, Washington, D. C. Contemporary letter-book copies of incoming and outgoing letters. Vols. 1 to 6 cover the period 1791–1802, while Vol. 7 covers the years 1815–1833.

"Proceedings of the Commissioner" (City of Washington), 6 volumes, 1791–1802, in the National Archives, Washington, D. C.

Letters of the Presidents of the United States to the Commissioners of Public Buildings and Grounds (originals in the Library of Congress; photostat copies in the National Archives).

RARE PRINTED SOURCES (COURT TESTIMONY)

United States v. *Thomas W. Smith et al.* In the Supreme Court of the District of Columbia. In Equity, No. 31138. Testimony in chief for the plaintiff, filed July 26, 1916. J. R. Young, Clerk. Government Printing Office, Washington, 1918.

United States v. *Martin F. Morris et al.* Record in the Supreme Court of the District of Columbia (The Potomac Flats Case). 7 volumes, Washington, 1898.

PUBLISHED WORKS, GOVERNMENT PUBLICATIONS, ETC.

American State Papers: Documents, Legislative and Executive, of the Congress of the United States, 1789–1809, edited by Walter Lowrie *et al.*, 38 volumes, Gales and Seaton, Washington, 1834–1861.

Annals of the Congress of the United States, 1789–1825. Gales and Seaton, Washington, 1834–1856.

At Lee, Samuel Yorke, *History of the Public Schools of Washington City, District of Columbia, 1805–1875.* Published by order of the Board of Trustees of Public Schools, for the national centennial year, 1876.

Brown, Glenn, *History of the United States Capitol.* U. S. Senate Document 60, 56th Congress, 1st Session. 2 vols., Government Printing Office, Washington, 1902.

Bryan, Wilhelmus B., *A History of the National Capital.* 2 vols., The Macmillan Company, New York, 1914.

Cases Adjudged in the Supreme Court at October Term, 1898, United States Reports, Vol. 174. The Banks Law Publishing Co., New York, 1899. (Morris v. United States, Opinion, pp. 196–359).

Columbia Historical Society, *Records of the Columbia Historical Society,* Washington, D. C. 41 vols., published by the Society, 1897– .

Documentary History of the Construction and Development of the United States Capitol Building and Grounds. House Report 646, 58th Congress, 2d Session. Government Printing Office, Washington, 1904.

Dunlap, William, *History of the Rise and Progress of the Art of Design in the United States.* 2 vols., George P. Scott & Co., Printers, New York, 1834.

Fairman, Charles E., *Art and Artists of the Capitol of the United States of America.* Government Printing Office, Washington, 1927.

Fitzpatrick, John C., Editor, *The Writings of George Washington.* Prepared under the direction of the United States George Washington Bicentennial Commission and published by authority of Congress. 37 vols., Government Printing Office, Washington, 1931–40.

Ford, Paul L., Editor, *The Writings of Thomas Jefferson.* 10 vols., New York, 1892–99.

Greely, A. W., Editor, *Public Documents of the First Fourteen Congresses, 1789–1817.* Senate Document 428, 56th Congress, 1st Session. Government Printing Office, Washington, 1900.

Journal of the Executive Proceedings of the Senate of the United States of America, Vol. 1, 1789–1805. Printed by Duff Green, Washington, 1828.

Kite, Elizabeth S., *L'Enfant and Washington, 1791–1792*. Historical Documents, Institut Français de Washington, Cahier III. The Johns Hopkins Press, Baltimore, 1929.

Latrobe, Benjamin H., *The Journal of Latrobe, Being the Notes and Sketches of an Architect, Naturalist and Traveler in the U. S. from 1796 to 1820*. D. Appleton and Company, New York, 1905.

Lipscomb, A. A. and Bergh, A. E., Editors, *The Writings of Thomas Jefferson*. 20 vols., published by the Thomas Jefferson Memorial Association, Washington, 1903–04.

Tindall, William, *Standard History of the City of Washington*. H. W. Crew and Co., Knoxville, 1914.

Washington, H. A., Editor, *The Writings of Thomas Jefferson*. 9 vols., Washington, 1853–54.

(For more complete bibliographical data, the reader is referred to the bibliography by R. H. Johnson in the Lipscomb and Bergh edition of *The Writings of Thomas Jefferson*, Vol. XX, and to Saul K. Padover's *Jefferson* (1942), pp. 435–47).

APPENDIX

BIOGRAPHICAL AND PLACE-NAME DATA

(Compiled from Dr. Padover's Notes during His Absence Abroad)

ANDREI, GIOVANNI. An Italian sculptor who worked on the Capitol building carving the capitals of the columns and adorning the frieze. He died about 1816.

BEALL, GEORGE. A property holder in Georgetown and one of the signers of an offer to President Washington, dated October 13, 1790, to sell on such terms as the President might determine to be reasonable.

BEALL, THOMAS "of George." Mayor of Georgetown in 1791 and one of the signers of the agreement between the proprietors (Georgetown) and the Commissioners, March 30, 1791, conveying their lands in trust to the Government.

BEATTY, CHARLES. One of the signers of the agreement between the proprietors (Georgetown) and the Commissioners, March 30, 1791, conveying their lands in trust to the Government.

BLAGDEN, GEORGE. He was an immigrant who came to the United States some time before 1794 and was employed in work on the Capitol as superintendent of stonework and quarries from about 1794 until killed by the caving-in of an embankment at the Capitol, June 4, 1826.

BLODGETT, SAMUEL, JR. (of Boston). He submitted a design of a plan for the Capitol in 1792 and engaged the attention of a number of wealthy men of Boston, New York, and Philadelphia in real estate investments in Washington. On January 5, 1793, he was appointed by the Commissioners as "supervisor of the buildings and in general of the affairs committed to our care." He was relieved of this post in the latter part of 1794, his dismissal being expressed in terms which indicated appreciation of the value of his services. During 1805–6, we find him soliciting funds for the national university. He died in Baltimore in 1814.

BOYD, WASHINGTON. Appointed a member of the surveyor board of the District, 1797. He succeeded Daniel Carroll Brent, in 1808, as United States Marshal, after serving as treasurer of the city.

BRENT, DANIEL CARROLL. He was a nephew of Commissioner Daniel Carroll and was interested in the stone quarries at Acquia, Virginia, which the Commissioners leased from his uncle, George Brent, part owner of the property. These business interests identified him with District affairs at an early date.

BRENT, ROBERT. He was appointed Mayor of the City by President Jefferson on June 4, 1802, and continued in this office by annual Presidential appointments seven times under Jefferson and three times under Madison, until Congress made the office elective in the city council by the charter of 1812.

BRENT, WILLIAM. Member of the first board of trustees of public schools in Washington City, August 5, 1805.

BRIDGPORT, GEORGE. Decorative painter. Decorated the ceiling of the House of Representatives.

BRIGGS, ISAAC. One of the assistants to Andrew Ellicott in the surveying department.

BROAD CREEK. See Tiber Creek.

BROMLEY, JOSEPH. Chosen by the two chambers of the city council as a member of the 13 trustees of the public schools, July 22, 1805.

BURNES, DAVID. He signed an agreement between the proprietors (Georgetown) and the Commissioners, March 30, 1791, to convey his lands in trust to the Government.

CARR, OVERTON. One of the signers of the agreement between the proprietors (Georgetown) and the Commissioners, March 30, 1791, conveying their lands in trust to the Government.

CARROLL, CHARLES (of Duddington). About 1770, he laid off a town site known as "Carrollsburg" on a portion of his property to the east of Greenleaf's Point.

CARROLL, DANIEL (of Duddington). His house was demolished by L'Enfant (in November 1791) because L'Enfant thought it protruded into the street.

CARROLL, DANIEL (of Rock Creek). On January 24, 1791, the President appointed him one of the first commissioners of the City of Washington. He owned land in the northern portion of the District of Columbia and was an uncle of Daniel Carroll of Duddington.

CARROLL, JOHN (Bishop Carroll). The first Roman Catholic bishop in the United States. He was a brother of Daniel Carroll of Rock Creek.

CARROLLSBURG. A town site east of Greenleaf's Point laid out by Charles Carroll of Duddington.

CARSTAIRS, ——. He was a builder from Philadelphia and submitted a plan of a Capitol in 1792.

COOKE, THOMAS. He was appointed clerk and bookkeeper to the Commissioners, October 22, 1791.

CRANCH, WILLIAM. President Adams appointed him a Commissioner on January 8, 1801, to fill the vacancy caused by the death of Gustavus Scott. He resigned on March 3, 1801. He was a brother-in-law of Greenleaf and a nephew of Mrs. John Adams, and served as the Washington representative of the realty syndicate of Morris, Nicholson & Greenleaf.

DALTON, TRISTRAM. He succeeded William Cranch as Commissioner on March 10, 1801, and was a Senator from Massachusetts in the first United States Congress. He died in 1817.

DEAKINS, WILL, JR. He was appointed treasurer at the Commissioners' meeting of June 30, 1791. A property holder in Georgetown, he was one of the signers of an offer to George Washington, dated October 13, 1790, to sell on such terms as the President might determine to be reasonable.

DEMPSIE, JOHN. He was chosen by the two chambers of the city council as one of the 13 members of the first board of trustees of the public schools, July 22, 1805.

DERMOTT, JAMES R. He was an employee in the surveying department from March 4, 1792, to January 3, 1798. At one time, he was in exclusive charge of dividing the city squares into lots. He was the author of the city plan later known as the "Tin Case Map," which President Adams sent to Congress.

DOUGLAS, ELIPHAS. One of the signers of the agreement between the proprietors (Georgetown) and the Commissioners, March 30, 1791, conveying his lands in trust to the Government.

DUVALL, GABRIEL. A member of the first board of trustees of public schools in Washington City, August 5, 1805.

ELLICOTT, MAJOR ANDREW. He was born in Bucks County, Pennsylvania, of English stock, and had been employed in 1784 by the State of Virginia in survey work on the Mason and Dixon Line. President Washington engaged him to mark the boundaries of the District of Columbia in 1791, and Thomas Jefferson instructed him by letter, dated February 2, 1791, to make the survey. After Major L'Enfant's resignation, the Commissioners placed Ellicott in charge of the surveying department, and in the summer and fall of 1792 he and his force were not only engaged in the survey of a boundary of the Federal territory, but were set to work laying out and dividing squares in the city of Washington. Ellicott and his corps of assistants, including Isaac Briggs, Benjamin Ellicott, and George Fenwick, were discharged on March 12, 1793. Although President Washington subsequently restored him and his assistants to their jobs, Ellicott accepted an appointment from the Governor of Pennsylvania to survey a road from Reading to Waterford, April 15, 1793, and took no further part in the planning of the city of Washington.

ELLICOTT, BENJAMIN. He was Andrew Ellicott's brother and worked as one of his assistants in the surveying department. He continued in the service of the city after his brother left it. He and Isaac Roberdeau pulled down Daniel Carroll's house, November 17, 1791.

EPPES, FRANCIS (of Virginia). A relative of Thomas Jefferson. Francis Eppes, of "Eppington," married Elizabeth Wayles, half-sister of Martha Wayles, wife of Thomas Jefferson. Francis' son, John Wayles Eppes, married Jefferson's daughter, Mary or Maria Jefferson in 1797.

FENWICK, GEORGE. One of Andrew Ellicott's assistants in the surveying department.

FORREST, URIAH (of St. Mary's County, Maryland). He had been a general in the Revolutionary War and was one of the close advisers of General Washington in the latter's negotiations to have the banks of the Potomac selected as the site of the Capital City. He became Mayor of Georgetown in 1792.

FRANZONI, GUISEPPE. A son of the president of the Academy of Fine Arts at Carrara, Italy; selected as a sculptor for the Capitol by Jefferson's friend, Philip Mazzei. He arrived in this country on March 3, 1806, and died in 1816.

FUNKSTOWN. See Hamburg.

GALLATIN, ALBERT (1761–1849). A Swiss gentleman, who came to this country in 1780 and settled in Pennsylvania about 1784. He represented Pennsylvania in Congress, 1795–1801, and was Secretary of the United States Treasury, 1801–1814.

GANTT, JOHN M. He was one of the trustees of the lands signed over to the Government by the proprietors. At the Commissioners' first meeting on April 12, 1791, he was appointed secretary.

GOOSE CREEK. See Tiber Creek.

GREENLEAF, JAMES. A native of Boston, who had resided in Amsterdam. He was a prominent real estate speculator associated with Robert Morris and John Nicholson in a plan to stimulate building in Washington. The efforts to float a loan of $1,200,000 in Holland resulted only in securing about one-tenth, or $120,000, all of which was absorbed by the necessities of the operators. By October [1797] Greenleaf was in a debtor's prison in Philadelphia. Later Morris and Nicholson joined him. Greenleaf, through bankruptcy proceedings, got a release from prison, but Nicholson died in prison and Morris was freed in August 1801.

HADFIELD, GEORGE. He was born in England, educated in London, and won the first prize for excellence in architecture at the British Royal Academy of Art. In 1795, he was appointed as architect to superintend the building of the Capitol. He received his appointment October 15, 1795, and immediately recommended numerous alterations and additions. He resigned when Washington, Thornton, and Hoban objected, but he was reappointed with the stipulation not to alter the plans. He served in this capacity until June 1798.

HALLET, STEPHEN (Etienne Sulpice Hallette, fl. 1789–1796). He came to this country from France just previous to the French Revolution and established himself in Philadelphia. He became architect of the Capitol in 1792 and continued in this office until 1794.

"There has been in recent years a persistent reiteration of the statement that Hallet, and not Thornton, was architect of the old Capitol. This statement can be traced to G. A. Townsend's book, *Washington Inside and Out* . . . [The records show:] First, that Hallet after exceptional opportunities could not produce a satisfactory design; that the alterations he was allowed to make in Thornton's work consisted in reducing the scale; that he was employed only as an assistant superintendent and draftsman, and because he attempted to overstep these bounds he was discharged. Thornton, in a letter, gives Hallet the credit of offering some 'judicious suggestions,' which is more than the records show, 'but in most of his attempts he did an injury.' 'He diminished the Senate Chamber, which is now too small. He laid square the foundation of the center building excluding the Dome, and when General Washington saw the extent of the alterations he expressed his disapproval in a style of such warmth as his dignity seldom permitted.' " (Glenn Brown, *History of the U. S. Capitol.* (2 vols., 1900–02), Vol. I, 18.)

HAMBURG. This was a tract of land which fell within the limits of the city of Washington. In the year 1768, the owner, Jacob Funk, had divided the property into town lots for a town site called Hamburg. It was also sometimes referred to as Funkstown. W. B. Bryan in his *A History of the National Capital* (2 vols., New York, 1914) I, 59, locates the property as being a short distance west of what is now 19th Street NW., to west of 23d Street, and from H Street S, to the river.

HARBAUGH, LEONARD. A Baltimore contractor with whom the Commissioners, in 1792, made a contract for the erection of a stone bridge across Rock Creek on a line with K Street. This bridge fell down because of defects in the plan of building the arches. Later, in 1800, he was employed to build the Rock Creek Bridge. A contract was made with him to erect the first executive building, the Treasury, for the sum of $39,511, with the stipulation that it be completed by July 1, 1800.

HARRISON, BENJAMIN (1726?–1791). A signer of the Declaration of Independence; member of the Continental Congress from Virginia; Speaker of the Virginia House of Delegates, 1778–81; and Governor of Virginia, 1781–1784.

HOBAN, JAMES. He was born in Dublin, Ireland, about 1762, and was educated there. In 1781, he won the medal offered art students by the Society of Arts. Shortly afterwards, he came to America and settled in Charleston, S. C., where he designed the State House Building which, in later years, was destroyed by fire. He also designed a number of private residences in that city. For 30 years, and until his death in 1832, he was employed by the Government in the city of Washington. His principal work was designing and constructing the President's Mansion.

HOLMEAD, ANTHONY. A property holder in Georgetown and one of the signers of an offer to George Washington, dated October 13, 1790, to sell on such terms as the President might determine to be reasonable. He was also one of the signers of the agreement between the proprietors (Georgetown) and the Commissioners (March 30, 1791), conveying their lands in trust to the Government.

JEFFERSON, THOMAS (April 2/13, 1743–July 4, 1826). He was County Lieutenant of Albemarle County, Virginia, 1770; County Surveyor, 1773; member of the Virginia House of Burgesses, 1769–1775; member of the Continental Congress, 1775–76; author of the Declaration of Independence; member of the Virginia House of Delegates, September 1776–June 1779; Governor of Virginia, 1779–81; delegate to Congress, 1783–84; Minister Plenipotentiary to negotiate commercial treaties in Europe, 1784; Minister to France, 1785–89; Secretary of State, 1789–94 (as such, the Commissioners of the District of Columbia were responsible to him); Vice President, 1797–1801; President of the United States, 1801–1809.

JOHNSON, THOMAS. A member of the first Board of Commissioners for the city of Washington, having been appointed by President Washington on January 22, 1791. His home was in Frederick, Md., and he has been described as one of the most distinguished public men of his day in Maryland. He served as Commissioner until August 1794.

JOHNSON, THOMAS, JR. He was clerk of the Board of Commissioners after November 1, 1793, and later called secretary of the board. It is not certain that he was the son of Thomas Johnson, the Commissioner.

KING, NICHOLAS. He emigrated from England to the United States in the spring of 1796, and was employed in the surveyor's office from September 24, 1796, to September 12, 1797, when he resigned. After the creation of the office of Surveyor of the City, he served in this post from June 1, 1803, to May 1812. It was not until January 12, 1809, that his duties were clearly defined. He was then given charge of the subdivision of lots and authority to fix the building lines.

KING, ROBERT, SR. He was employed in the surveying department of the city, September 12, 1797, to August 13, 1802.

KING, ROBERT, JR. He had charge of the surveying of lots and the certifying of levels to those about to engage in building construction. He appears to have been the son of Robert King, a surveyor employed by the Commissioners.

KING, WILLIAM. One of the signers of the agreement between the proprietors (Georgetown) and the Commissioners, March 30, 1791, conveying his lands in trust to the Government.

LATROBE, BENJAMIN HENRY (1764–1820). He was born in Yorkshire, England, May 1, 1764, his father being of French Huguenot ancestry while his mother was related to the Rittenhouse family of Philadelphia, Pa. He left England in spite of the offer of the surveyorship of the Crown with a salary of £1,000 per year, and landed in Norfolk, Va., March 20, 1796. Soon after landing he met Col. Bushrod Washington who introduced him to President Washington. He improved the navigation of the James River, directed the installation of a new water supply at Philadelphia, and did many pieces of engineering work elsewhere. On March 6, 1803, President Jefferson appointed him surveyor of the public buildings, with a salary of $1,700 per annum, his immediate problem being the erection of the south wing of the Capitol or old Hall of Representatives. Jefferson had a high regard for his ability and in July 1812 complimented him in the words: "The Representative Chamber will remain a durable monument to your talents as an architect." (Glenn Brown, *History of the United States Capitol*, I, 39.) While in Washington he designed St. John's Church, which stands on the corner of Sixteenth and H Streets, opposite Lafayette Square. He also designed Brentwood, a mansion in the suburbs, and the residence of Commodore Decatur on Lafayette Square in 1818.

LAW, THOMAS. He arrived in this country from England in 1794, after having spent more than half of his 37 years in the Indian service. In December 1794 he bought from Mr. Greenleaf $133,000 worth of lots. He paid $266 each for 500 lots which had been $80 per lot the year before.

LEAR, TOBIAS. Washington's private secretary until 1793.

L'ENFANT, PIERRE CHARLES (1754–1825). He was born in Paris and came to this country in 1777. He served in the American Army, first as a lieutenant of engineers and later as captain and major, the last promotion being accorded him by special resolution of Congress, May 2, 1783. President Washington employed him to survey the site of Washington and make a plan for the Federal city, 1791–92. He was a man of imagination and genius, but could not be persuaded to submit to due subordination, hence his resignation from office in February 1792. Afterwards, Robert Morris and John Nicholson employed him in private work. The Federal Government subsequently employed him in 1794 at Fort Mifflin and again at Fort Washington, one of the defenses of the Capital, during the War of 1812. The McMillan Park Commission of 1901 recognized the merits of L'Enfant's design of the city of Washington and recommended the restoration and extension of it. He died June 14, 1825. His remains were removed in 1909 from their original resting place to a grave in front of the Arlington Mansion in Arlington National Cemetery, overlooking the city which he designed.

LENTHAL, JOHN. He was born in England in 1762 and was appointed "Clerk of the Works" by Latrobe on April 7, 1803. It was his duty to represent the architect during his absence, to act as judge on all materials and workmanship, employ and discharge workmen, and, under the direction of the architect, to make detailed drawings. He was killed by falling brick in an accident at the Capitol, September 1808. Latrobe thought highly of his ability, skill, and integrity.

LINGAN, JAMES M. A property holder in Georgetown and one of the signers of an offer to George Washington dated October 13, 1790, to sell on such terms as the President might determine to be reasonable. He signed the agreement between the proprietors (Georgetown) and the Commissioners (March 30, 1791) to convey his lands in trust to the Government.

MADISON, JAMES (1750/51–1836). He represented Virginia in the Continental Congress, 1780–83, and was a member of the Virginia House of Delegates, 1784–86. In the Constitutional Convention of 1787 he played a leading role as one of the chief framers of the Constitution. During Jefferson's administration, he was Secretary of State and Jefferson's principal adviser. He became the fourth President of the United States, 1809–1817.

MASON, GEORGE (1725–1792). He was the author of Virginia's famous "Declaration of Rights," and played a prominent role in the framing of both the Virginia Constitution and the Constitution of the United States. He was a trustee of Alexandria, Va., from 1754 until 1779 and one of the leading gentlemen of Fairfax County until his death in 1792.

MASON, JOHN (of Georgetown). He was named brigadier general of the militia by Jefferson in 1802.

MAZZEI, PHILIP (1730–1816). An Italian physician, merchant, and horticulturist who for some years carried on agricultural experiments near "Monticello," Jefferson's home. During the American Revolution, he served abroad as an agent for the State of Virginia. Although he returned to Europe to live in 1785, he continued to carry on an active correspondence with Jefferson and other Virginia leaders.

MILLS, ROBERT. He was born in Charleston, S. C., August 12, 1781, and was appointed architect of Government buildings in 1836. He superintended repairs and additions to the Capitol until 1851. He contributed to the design of the old Post Office Building, the Patent Office, and the Treasury Building, but is best known as the original designer of the Washington Monument.

MONROE, JAMES (1758–1831). He was a Virginia delegate to the Continental Congress, 1783–86, and a member of the Virginia Constitutional Convention called to ratify the Federal Constitution, 1788; United States Senator, 1790–94; Minister to France, 1794–96; Governor of Virginia, 1799–1802; Envoy to France and participant in the Louisiana Purchase negotiations, 1803; Secretary of State, 1811–1817; and President of the United States, 1817–1825.

MONROE, THOMAS (MUNROE). On June 4, 1802, he was appointed Superintendent of the City, a position which he held for many years.

MORRIS, GOUVERNEUR (1752–1816). A member of the Pennsylvania delegation to the Constitutional Convention of 1787, and Minister to France, 1792–94.

MORRIS, ROBERT. A silent partner in the agreement for land purchases made by Greenleaf with the Commissioners in 1795.

PEIRCE, EDWARD. One of the signers of the agreement between the proprietors (Georgetown) and the Commissioners, March 30, 1791, conveying their lands in trust to the Government.

PIERCE, JAMES. One of the signers of the agreement between the proprietors (Georgetown) and the Commissioners, March 30, 1791, conveying their lands in trust to the Government.

PETER, ROBERT (PETERS). He came from Scotland and opened a store in Georgetown about 1752. He was chosen Mayor of Georgetown on December 25, 1789.

PROUT, WILLIAM. One of the signers of the agreement between the proprietors (Georgetown) and the Commissioners, March 30, 1791, conveying their lands in trust to the Government.

RANDOLPH, THOMAS MANN (1768–1828). He was a kinsman of Jefferson and married Jefferson's daughter Martha on February 23, 1790. He had many of Jefferson's scholarly interests and was prominent in Virginia politics, being a member of the Virginia Senate, 1793–94, member of Congress from Virginia, 1803–1807, and Governor of Virginia, 1819–22.

ROBERDEAU, ISAAC. An engineer employed by L'Enfant to oversee the work in the Capital while the latter was on trips up and down the country buying different kinds of building material. He and Benjamin Ellicott pulled down the house of Daniel Carroll of Dudington.

RUTLEDGE, EDWARD (1749–1800). Signer of the Declaration of Independence and leader of the South Carolina delegation in the Continental Congress. He represented Charleston in the South Carolina House of Representatives, 1782–96, and in the State Conventions of 1788 and 1790, and was Governor of South Carolina in 1798.

SCOTT, GUSTAVUS. A native of Prince William County, Virginia, educated in Aberdeen, Scotland. He became one of the city commissioners of Washington on August 23, 1794. He was an organizer of the Potomac Canal Company and had important Maryland interests, having been a member of the convention that framed the Constitution of Maryland in 1776.

SHORT, WILLIAM (1759–1849). Companion and private secretary to Jefferson while Jefferson was Minister to France, and Chargé d'Affaires, Paris, after Jefferson's return to the United States in 1789. He became minister at the Hague in 1792 and served in various diplomatic posts until 1795.

SMITH, SAMUEL H. Publisher of the Philadelphia *Universal Gazette*, 1797–1800. As a result of Jefferson's advice and encouragement, he decided in 1800 to transfer his printing equipment from Philadelphia to the city of Washington where he continued to publish the *Universal Gazette*. He also published the *Washington Intelligencer*, the official organ of the Jefferson administration.

STODDARD, JOHN. A property holder in Georgetown. One of the signers of an offer to George Washington, dated October 13, 1790, to sell on such terms as the President might determine to be reasonable.

STODDERT, BENJAMIN. He was a merchant of Georgetown and first Secretary of the Navy, 1798–1802.

STUART, DR. DAVID (of Virginia). President Washington appointed him one of the first commissioners of the city of Washington on January 22, 1790. He was a personal friend of Washington and a practicing physician. His home was a few miles from Fairfax Court House, Va. He had married the widow of John Park Custis, the son of Mrs. George Washington.

TAYLOE, JOHN. Chosen by the Washington city council as one of 13 trustees of the first board of trustees of the public schools, July 22, 1805.

THORNTON, DR. WILLIAM (1759–1828). He was born in Tortola in the British West Indies and educated in Great Britain where he obtained an M.D. degree (Aberdeen University, 1784). About 1787, he came to the United States. After living in New York and Delaware, he settled in Philadelphia. He participated in the competition for building designs for the Federal city, and President Washington accepted his plan for the Capitol. Since Thornton was not a practicing architect, the execution of the design was confided to professional architects and contractors, notably Hallet, Hoban, Hadfield, and Latrobe. Dr. Thornton was appointed one of the commissioners of the city of Washington on September 12, 1794. While residing in Washington, he designed for John Tayloe the Octagon House, which still stands. He was also the designer of Tudor Place in Georgetown. At the end of his service as a Commissioner in May 1802, he was placed in charge of patents and was in charge of the Patent Office until his death on March 28, 1828.

TIBER CREEK. This creek had a succession of names. It was first Tiber Creek; then Goose Creek; then Tiber Creek again. It was at one time also called Broad Creek.

TINGEY, THOMAS. Elected a member of the first board of trustees of the public schools by the subscribers to the public school fund, July 17, 1805.

TURNER, JUDGE. He submitted a design of a plan for a Capitol, 1792.

VALAPERTI. An Italian sculptor who worked on the Capitol and took Andrei's place when the latter died in 1816. He designed the stone eagle in the House of Representatives — present Statuary Hall.

WALKER, GEORGE (of Georgetown). He was a property holder in the eastern section of Washington and carried on a newspaper controversy with the commissioners in 1796 over the triangular pieces of land which were formed by the transverse avenues across the rectangular system of the streets.

WARING, JOHN. One of the signers of the agreement between the proprietors (Georgetown) and the Commissioners in 1791, conveying his lands in trust to the Government.

WHITE, ALEXANDER. He was born in Rappahannock County, Virginia, and was a member of Congress from Virginia. He became a commissioner of the District in 1795. He cast his vote for the funding bill "with a revulsion of stomach," according to Jefferson. Yet, his was one of the two votes that carried the measure and insured the enactment of the residence bill.

WILLIAMSON, COLLEN. He was a master mason and builder and submitted a design of a plan for a Capitol in 1792. In the conference which discussed the merits of Thornton's plan of the Capitol as compared with Hallet's plan, Williamson was called in as an expert. For a time, he was superintendent of stone cutters.

YOUNG, ABRAHAM. One of the signers of the agreement between the proprietors (Georgetown) and the Commissioners, March 30, 1791, conveying his lands in trust to the Government.

YOUNG, NOTLEY. One of the signers of the agreement between the proprietors (Georgetown) and the Commissioners (March 30, 1791) conveying his lands in trust to the Government.

YOUNG, WILLIAM. One of the signers of the agreement between the proprietors (Georgetown) and the Commissioners, March 30, 1791, conveying his lands in trust to the Government.

Names, salaries, and duties of the principal men in charge of the Capitol from 1793 to 1850

	Name	Years	Salary	Duties
Commissioners, District of Columbia	Thos. Johnson	1791–94	$1600 per annum	To put into operation the plans for the new city; laying out streets, parks, and sewers; selecting plans for buildings, architects, contractors, mechanics, and materials; their action subject to the approval of the President.
	David Stuart	1791–94	1600	
	Daniel Carroll	1791–95	1600	
	Wm. Thornton	1794–1802	1600	
	Gustavus Scott	1794–1800	1600	
	Alex. White	1795–1802	1600	
	Wm. Cranch	1801–02	1600	
	T. Dalton	1801	1600	
Superintendent of public buildings	Thos. Monroe	1802–15	1200	Given powers in relation to Government buildings held by the commissioners.
Commissioners of public buildings [1]	J. P. Van Ness	1815–16	1600	"A general supervision of both buildings (Capitol and President's House); to procure such materials as may be called for; to invite proposals for contracts; to disburse moneys and settle accounts monthly."
	T. Ringgold	1815–16	1600	
	R. Bland Lee	1815–16	1600	
	Samuel Lane	1816–22	2000	
	James Elgar	1822–1829	1500 [2]	
	Wm. Noland	1829–46	2000	
	And. Beaumont	1846	2000	
	Chas. Douglas	1847	2000	
	Ignatius Mudd	1847–51	2000	
	Wm. Easby	1851	2000	

[1] The first three served jointly. From 1816 to 1851 there was only 1 commr. In 1838 commissioner put under Secretaries of State, Treasury, and War.

[2] Received a similar amount from another office.

		Salary as Commr	
Architects	Dr. Wm. Thornton	1793–1802	1700	"It is the duty of the Architect to make out full sets of plans and sections for the workmen and such additional drawings during construction of the work as may be necessary; to make estimates of all the materials that may be required, and to see that the plans are faithfully executed."
	B. H. Latrobe	1803–17	2000 / 2500	
	Chas. Bulfinch	1818–29	2500 / 1800	
	Robert Mills	1836–51	2300 / 2500	
Draftsmen and superintendents	Stephen Hallet	1793–94	1066	Instructed to make detail drawings and superintend Capitol according to Thornton's drawings and directions.
	Geo. Hadfield	1795–98	1400	
	James Hoban......	1793–94 / 1794–95 / 1798–1802	....	
Clerks of works	John Lenthal	1803–08	$4.00 per day	"Sole judge of merits of workmen; sole judge in the Architect's absence of the fidelity with which contracts are fulfilled; money paid on their certificate." They also judged material and made working drawings.
	Shadrack Davis	1815–1817	4.00 "	
	Peter Lenox	1817–29	1500 per annum	
Draftsmen	Robert Mills	1803–11	pd by Latrobe	Draftsmen for Latrobe
	Wm. Strickland	1803–11	pd by Latrobe	

		1793–1826	1500 per annum	
Superintendent of stonework and quarries	Geo. Blagden	1793–1826		In charge of stone, stonework, and quarries.
Sculptors	Giovanni Andrei	1806–25	1500	
	Guiseppe Franzoni	1806–16	1500	In charge of ornamental plaster and stone work and sculpture.
	Francisco Iardella	1816–29	{1187.50 / 1250.00}	
	Carlo Franzoni	1816	....	
	Enrico Causici	1823	(3)	
	Nicholas Gevelot	1823	(3)	
	Antonio Capellano	1823	(3)	Bas reliefs and figures.
	Valaperti	1823	(3)	
	Luigi Persico	1826–1836	(3)	
	Hobentein Greniv	1832	(3)	

3 Work done by contract for each piece, usually.

[P. 100, Glenn Brown, HISTORY OF THE UNITED STATES CAPITOL, Vol. I.]

522

SURVEYING DEPARTMENT — List of men employed from the beginning. Taken from a manuscript list prepared by Capt. John Stewart, for many years in charge of the city records in the office of the commr. of public bldgs and grounds:

Andrew Ellicott, Feb. 4, 1791–July 19, 1793.
Peter Charles L'Enfant, March 7, 1791–March 6, 1792.
Benjamin Ellicott, Apr 4, 1791–Jan. 28, 1794.
Ignatius Fenwick, Oct. 21, 1791–Jan. 10, 1792.
Richard Johns, Oct. 21, 1791–July 4, 1792.
Thomas Ormes, —— to Feb. 16, 1792.
Jas. R. Dermott, Mar 4, 1792–Jan 3, 1793.
Bennett Fenwick, Dec. —— to Sept 20, 1793.
Isaac Briggs, June 6, 1792–Oct 22, 1793.
Thomas Curtis, June 6, 1792–Oct 21, 1793.
George Fenwick, Aug 3, 1792–Nov 30, 1793.
Joseph Ellicott, Jan 1, 1792–Jan 25, 1794.
Alexander Ralston, June 17, 1793–Oct 15, 1796.
Thomas Freeman, Mar 25, 1794–July 7, 1796.
Washington Boyd, Apr 15, 1794–May 1, 1798.
James Blois, June 1, 1794–Jan 2, 1795.
Nicholas King, Sept 24, 1796–Sept 12, 1797.
Robert King, Sr., Sept 12, 1797 to Aug 13, 1802.
Robert King, Jr., Aug 21, 1800–Aug 13, 1801.

The office of surveyor of the city was created by the law of Mar 3, 1803 and the duties were defined by the law of Jan 12, 1809. The list of surveyors appointed by the supt. of the city is as follows:

Nicholas King, June 1, 1803–May 1812.
Robert King, Jr., May 21, 1813–Mar 14, 1815.
Benjamin H. Latrobe and Robert King, Sept. 5, 1815.

[Wilhelms B. Bryan, *A History of the National Capital* (2 vols., The Macmillan Co., New York, 1914) I, 300, reprinted through the courtesy of the Macmillan Co.]

☆ U. S. GOVERNMENT PRINTING OFFICE: 1946—593650

Date Due